A Legacy of Exploitation

A Legacy of Exploitation
Early Capitalism in the Red River Colony, 1763–1821

Susan Dianne Brophy

© Susan Dianne Brophy 2022

All rights reserved. No part of this publication may be reproduced, stored in a retrieval system, or transmitted, in any form or by any means, without prior written permission of the publisher, or, in Canada, in the case of photocopying or other reprographic copying, a licence from Access Copyright, www.accesscopyright.ca.

31 30 29 28 27 26 25 24 23 22   5 4 3 2 1

Printed in Canada on FSC-certified ancient-forest-free paper (100% post-consumer recycled) that is processed chlorine- and acid-free.

Library and Archives Canada Cataloguing in Publication

Title: A legacy of exploitation : early capitalism in the Red River Colony, 1763–1821 / Susan Dianne Brophy.
Names: Brophy, Susan Dianne, author.
Description: Includes bibliographical references and index.
Identifiers: Canadiana (print) 20220153949 | Canadiana (ebook) 20220154023 | ISBN 9780774866354 (hardcover) | ISBN 9780774866361 (softcover) | ISBN 9780774866378 (PDF) | ISBN 9780774866385 (EPUB)
Subjects: LCSH: Settler colonialism – Red River Settlement. | LCSH: Indigenous peoples – Colonization – Red River Settlement. | LCSH: Indigenous peoples – Red River Settlement – Economic conditions. | LCSH: Red River Settlement – Economic conditions. | LCSH: Manitoba – Colonization.
Classification: LCC FC3372 .B76 2022 | DDC 971.27/01—dc23

Canadä

UBC Press gratefully acknowledges the financial support for our publishing program of the Government of Canada (through the Canada Book Fund), the Canada Council for the Arts, and the British Columbia Arts Council.

This book has been published with the help of a grant from the Canadian Federation for the Humanities and Social Sciences, through the Awards to Scholarly Publications Program, using funds provided by the Social Sciences and Humanities Research Council of Canada.

UBC Press
The University of British Columbia
2029 West Mall
Vancouver, BC V6T 1Z2
www.ubcpress.ca

To

Ma, Bean, Equinoxes, and Dew

Contents

List of Illustrations / viii

Acknowledgments / ix

Introduction: Exploitation and Autonomy / 3

1 Reciprocity and Dispossession: Processes of Transformation / 19

2 Monopoly and Competition: Contests over Indigenous Peoples' Labour and Land / 53

3 Honour and Duplicity: Debts of Rivals, Dreams of an Aristocrat / 73

4 Servitude and Independence: The Settler Colonial "Experiment" Begins / 103

5 Menace and Ally: Proclamation as Provocation / 130

6 Consciousness and Ignorance: New Nation, Old Grievances / 150

Conclusion: Continuity and Change / 179

Notes / 188

Bibliography / 253

Index / 274

Illustrations

I.1   Map of North America, 1779 (detail) / 2

1.1   Chief Peguis Monument, Kildonan Park, Winnipeg / 21

2.1   Map of key fur trade sites from Montreal to the Great Lakes, Hudson Bay, and the Saskatchewan River / 55

2.2   "A map of America ... exhibiting Mackenzie's track from Montreal to Fort Chipewyan and from thence to the North Sea in 1789 and to the West Pacific Ocean in 1793" (detail) / 63

3.1   Thomas Douglas, Fifth Earl of Selkirk (1771–1820) / 89

4.1   Map of the District of Assiniboia, 1811 / 116

5.1   Fort William, an establishment of the North West Company, on Lake Superior, 1811 / 137

6.1   Map from the Treaty of 1817 / 174

6.2   Text from the Treaty of 1817 / 175

C.1   "Winter fishing on ice of [Assiniboine] and Red River," 1821 / 183

Acknowledgments

I wish to express my appreciation for the generosity of scholars working in the overlapping areas of prairie history, Indigenous studies, and fur trade studies, particularily those who shared their enthusiasm, experiences, and ideas. This reception helped cultivate my curiosity about prairie history that has abided since childhood. I am also grateful for the work of those who make archival documents widely available through digitization, especially students at public institutions. Due to how and when this book evolved, these digitized records proved invaluable. In addition, I benefited greatly from the range of skills deployed by the team that I worked with at UBC Press, the anonymous reviewers, as well as various family, friends, and colleagues. From proposal through to production, I was given shrewd guidance, steadfast support, and expert counsel.

Most importantly, I want to acknowlede the labours of Indigenous peoples on the frontlines of movements across this country and around the world. Exploitation in its many iterations stems from a destructive mode of being, and their labours make it clear that there are better ways of being in this world.

A Legacy of Exploitation

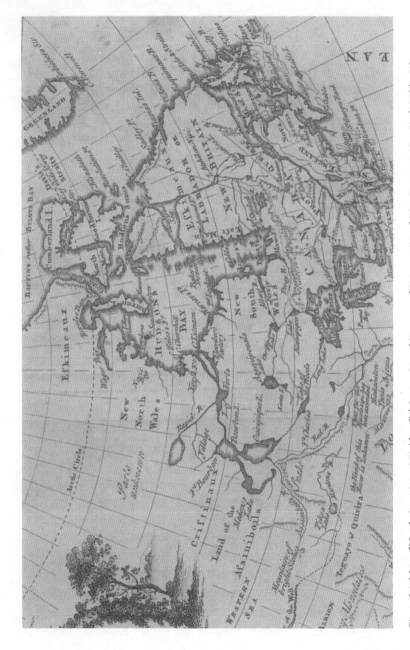

Figure I.1 Map of North America, 1779 (detail) | *Source*: Lionel Pincus and Princess Firyal Map Division, New York Public Library Digital Collections

Introduction

Exploitation and Autonomy

> *You cannot dominate without seeking to possess the dominated.*
> – AILEEN MORETON-ROBINSON[1]

THIS QUOTATION FROM Aileen Moreton-Robinson resonates in two events of varying magnitudes.

First, the Hudson's Bay Company (HBC) History Foundation released promotional videos in 2015. These slickly produced vignettes depict grimacing white men overpowering the forces of nature.[2] Each centres on one of two explorers who worked to expand the commercial fur trade networks of the company between the 1780s and the 1850s, men who had in common a steely endurance and a desire to conquer the terrain. Their perseverance made Canada, it is implied, punctuated by the voiceover declaring that "we are a country of adventurers."[3]

Second, in an investigative report titled "After Tina Fontaine: Exploitation in a Prairie City," Martha Troian writes that "her death shook the nation,"[4] referring to the killing in August 2014 of a fifteen-year-old Indigenous girl in Winnipeg, Manitoba. After the trial of the accused killer ended with an acquittal, Nahanni Fontaine, a provincial politician representing the jurisdiction that includes the Red River Colony site established in 1812 (in the area of what is now Winnipeg's North End), wondered "if this was a non-Indigenous girl murdered, and the accused was an Indigenous man, I ask and I pose the question: what would be the response?" She added that "it is an uncomfortable question and an uncomfortable experience that we as Canadians have to explore."[5] A national public inquiry was announced in 2015 after Tina Fontaine's killing drew attention to a problem long ignored,[6] namely the habitual negligence at different levels of law enforcement when it came to investigating cases involving missing or murdered Indigenous women and girls. By 2018, however, Troian wanted to assess what had changed when it came to addressing sexual exploitation in Winnipeg, especially among those in the "racially coded ... 'at-risk'" category.[7] One woman whom she interviewed was drawn into exploitation at twelve years of age. In reflecting on what led to this, Troian comments that "I can't help but look at the city differently. I am left wondering who is being exploited and for whose gain."[8]

These two facets of the legacy of exploitation of Indigenous peoples define Canada as a settler colonial state. In what follows, I contest the claims of the HBC vignettes by exploring the "uncomfortable" roots of exploitation, offering a longer view of dispossession that rejects the parochialism lurking in studies of Canada's settler colonial history.[9] By accounting for the processes of dispossession intrinsic to the colonial settlement at Red River, I target a bias that, to this day, celebrates the "adventurers" and ignores the exploitation.

As the first planned settlement initiated by the Hudson's Bay Company, the Red River Colony is an apt case study for the purpose of analyzing exploitation, particularly at the crossroads of the transition to capitalism in the Canadian context. The letters and journals written between 1763 and 1821 by HBC men, especially those championing the settlement, provide evidence in this regard. Flushed with disdain, they often described nearby Indigenous populations – principally the Maškēkowak, Nēhiyawok, Saulteaux, Assiniboine, and Métis – as "troublesome."[10] These records reveal how the enduring autonomy of Indigenous producers – exercised in various ways, including customs, consumption, and productivity – frustrated the officers' appetite for control,[11] and they emphasize that, although exploitation was a conspicuous feature of the commercial fur trade leading up to and including the Red River Colony, the processes of dispossession that such exploitation entailed were complicated and contradictory.

However much the fortunes of the fur trade companies were tied to Indigenous peoples' productivity, and by extension however much Indigenous peoples' labour fuelled capitalist accumulation, theirs was a labour that perplexed capitalist minds: "The Indian quite lacked any sense of the need to work for the morrow or to grow in riches."[12] Such depictions can suffer from a two-pronged, racist essentialism.[13] Either Indigenous peoples were inherently "ungovernable," exhibiting a slavish submission to base impulses[14] in a manner irreconcilable with European values,[15] or they were economic actors in the embryonic stages of their education in capitalist relations and as such could be forgiven if not all of their decisions seemed to be rational.[16]

The former was a more widely held opinion in the decades up to and after settlement of the Red River Colony in 1812, a judgment that made it easier to overcome ethical obstacles to the exploitation of Indigenous peoples. Their perceived subhumanity incited campaigns to "civilize" them, even lending a thin veneer of benevolence to dispossession. The latter take is more recent, owing its popularity to the re-emergence of neoclassical economics. Although it recognizes the economic agency of Indigenous peoples – a basic consideration uncommon well into the 1960s and 1970s[17] – it still assigns to them a foundational immaturity using the rational actor "model" of *homo economicus* as the standard.[18] Both perspectives reappear under different guises throughout this book.

Each time advocates of both perspectives fail to grasp that reactions to the relative autonomy of Indigenous producers were a key driver of events within and surrounding the Red River Colony. Standard narratives have this misapprehension in common, relying instead on an amalgam of economic exigencies and aristocratic altruism to explain what propelled the transformations at the colony.[19] Because I foreground the relative autonomy of Indigenous producers in this critical re-evaluation, I can offer a historical study that challenges conventional accounts of this settlement.

I demonstrate how the relative autonomy of Indigenous producers in part drove historical transformations, and I explore the "transformative potential of Indigenous knowledge."[20] This principle informs specific modifications that I undertake to devise a Marxist framework more appropriate for the study of settler colonialism,[21] the objective being an incisive commentary on the particulars of the transition to capitalism in the context and era in question.

Modified Marxism

When it comes to historical studies of colonialism, Linda Tuhiwai Smith explains that "*coming to know the past* has been part of the critical pedagogy of decolonization. To hold alternative histories is to hold alternative knowledges. The pedagogical implication of this access to alternative knowledges is that they can form the basis of alternative ways of doing things."[22] I take this to heart in how I approach the material.

The search for easily digestible narratives can lead to flawed framing; exemplary in this regard is the idea that human progress is linear and develops in stages. The opposite of this is a "necessarily unstable position,"[23] one that emphasizes the uneven and combined dimensions of change with an eye on the contradictory forces that propel transformation. Dialectical materialism lends itself well to the study of history as constant motion,[24] although Indigenous histories, knowledges, and practices oblige amendments to the framework.

The dynamic quality of dialectical methodology stems from thinking oppositionally and fluidly. To explain this, Friedrich Engels writes about rest as both the opposite of motion and an expression of motion in a relative state: since rest contains the possibility of motion, they are conditional on each other and can only be understood relationally rather than as absolutes. Dialectically speaking, rest contains the possibility of its anithesis, and the same is true for motion.[25] That there is no such thing as "absolute rest" is more than an illustrative device that he uses to explain dialectical thought; it is also the substantive starting point for how Engels understands materialism and, by extension, history. He famously states that "matter without motion is just as inconceivable as motion without matter,"[26] implying that change is incessant and a condition of matter.

To study "historical science," therefore, is to examine material that is "constantly changing."[27] The aim of such an analysis is not to begin with a concept and then contort historical material to conform to that concept; it is to begin with "objective reality which is given us in sensation,"[28] and to grow knowledge through dialectical analysis, moving between the abstract and the concrete.[29]

When applied, dialectical materialism allows change and continuity to bear shared explanatory weight by emphasizing the metamorphic relation between ideas and practices.[30] Idealism takes the mind as its source of knowledge, whereas materialism takes the material world as its source of knowledge;[31] dialectical materialism takes the material world that is always changing as its source, meaning that the knowledge that corresponds to the source is always partial and qualified.[32] To comprehend the interrelation among the material world, our knowledge of it, and our knowledge of our place within it is to grasp the history of social change, and this is the "highest task of humanity," to which dialectical materialist analysis aspires.[33] Attentiveness to change, as a methodology, involves identifying instances of unification, fragmentation, and rupture,[34] as well as patterns or continuities across different times and spaces.[35] No "rigid" formulas exist that dictate the scope, pace, or nature of social transformation – nothing can replace dialectical materialist–informed, historically specific analysis in the quest to understand the social.[36]

This approach is fitting when trying to make sense of the social relations integral to settler colonial histories of dispossession, but it is not enough on its own. Especially cognizant of the pitfalls of past attempts to bring a Marxist-informed framework to the study of settler colonialism,[37] I strive to stretch my dialectical materialist approach and to rethink prominent Marxist tenets with the help of what Vanessa Watts terms "Place-Thought": "It is not that Indigenous peoples do not theorize, but that these complex theories are not distinct from place."[38] At the core of Place-Thought and dialectical materialism is a shared drive to make sense of how human beings act on and think about the world, which in both approaches compels the interrogation of the relation between the abstract and the concrete. This drive and this mode of interrogation are evident in what follows. As I plot the conceptual nodes of this book – dispossession and social relations; violence, labour, and land; and finally law, economy, and geopolitics – I show how and why I modify aspects of my approach.

Dispossession and Social Relations

Dispossession is made up of an array of dynamic ideas and practices specific to different times and places; it is incomplete and ongoing, as well as combined and contradictory. An approach that reveals the extent to which fluidity existed alongside rupture is therefore exceptionally useful when it comes to assessing the capitalist exploitation of non-capitalist realms.[39] Rosa Luxemburg's *The Accumulation of Capital* touches on the dialectical dimensions of the drive to accumulate and the social effects of dispossession: "The accumulation of capital is a kind of metabolism between capitalist economy and those pre-capitalist methods of production without which it cannot go on and which, in this light, it corrodes and assimilates."[40] With the expansion of capitalism, antecedent social relations are not eradicated and replaced, but "a kind of metabolism" occurs when two modes of production enter into a fragile synthesis.

Luxemburg here is positioning herself in response to Marx on the topic of the origins of capitalism, which he discusses at the end of the first volume of *Capital*. Original accumulation, controversially translated as "primitive accumulation,"[41] implies that there is a moment in the midst of the emergence of capitalism when something akin to primary capital – be it usury or commercial in origin – was reinvested into the productive process and fuelled the insatiable appetite for profit through plunder. Marx contends that this is the "prehistory of capital," a violent stage of original accumulation that was the springboard for the growth of capitalism.[42] Colonial dispossession was a means of achieving this precipitous original capital, which in turn served as one of the conditions that led to the emergence of the "manufacturing period"[43] in Europe – the prelude to full-scale industrial production.[44]

Debates about original accumulation continue today,[45] with many still trying to square the general idea with specific historical practices.[46] Although the idea of original accumulation as a violent moment might be a logical touchstone for a study of settler colonialism, I see it as misleading. Instead of understanding colonies solely as peripheral sites wrought by extraction for accumulation, a dialectical materialist approach underscores the value of analyzing the discrete histories of colonial sites themselves. In this sense, the history of the Red River Colony is not simply dictated by its status as a source for British capital; it is a site with its own complex social relations undergoing its own transition to capitalism. By focusing on the transformations within and surrounding the settler colony itself, I show how its own transition to capitalism intersects with multiple transitions to capitalism on a global scale.

For this purpose, I turn to other aspects of Marx's works, such as his views on labour compulsion in the transition to capitalism, in order to assess the settler colony as a transitional site in its own right. Marx explains that, in the transition to capitalism, "direct extra-economic force" as a standard means of compulsion fades away with the rise of the "silent compulsion of economic relations" and the proletarianization of workers, after which such force reappears "only in exceptional cases."[47] In the highly debated context of English feudalism,[48] for example, extra-economic means of exploitation included rent imposed by landlords on tenant farmers[49] or, more aptly, the "personal labour relationships" in the form of paternalistic contracts binding servants to the Hudson's Bay Company.[50] To illustrate this divide further, Marx compares the enchained slaves of ancient Rome in the pre-capitalist context to the "invisible threads" of the wage labourer in the capitalist context.[51] The premise underlying this distinction offers a vital statement on the transition to capitalism. In the capitalist mode of production, the extra-economic force of pre-capitalism slides into the background to become an instrument of conflict resolution or more generally a formal system of order, while market dependence becomes that which disciplines "free" wage labourers in day-to-day life.[52]

The essential takeaway is that the "form of compulsion" matters: how labour compulsion or (inversely) autonomy is understood is crucial to differentiating the capitalist mode of production from other modes and clarifying how capitalism itself advances.[53] I take this as a guiding principle in my assessment of the Red River Colony – but not without some adjustments.

Between change and continuity is the mediating principle of reciprocity. As a principle common to a host of customary practices, reciprocity was both a target for the purposes of exploitation and an abiding source of autonomy. As I detail in the first chapter, the terms of exchange between Indigenous producers and company traders appeared to synthesize in a manner that upheld the social relations that centred the principle of reciprocity; however, because the exchanges were skewed in the company's favour and attendant social obligations were routinely negated by the company, the principle was distorted in a way that obscured the manifestly exploitative facets of the exchanges. Kahente Horn-Miller contends that such processes of distortion are intrinsic to colonialism.[54] This is reminiscent of mystification in the Marxist sense, which suggests that the actual social relation between the worker and the capitalist is mystified by "the relation of exchange": "The relation of exchange between capitalist and worker ... is alien to the content of the transaction itself, and merely mystifies it."[55] Both mystification and distortion underscore the importance of interrogating the relation between form and content, which on this occasion reveals a contradiction between the social relations that centre reciprocity and the practices of exploitation. By using the term "distortion" rather than "mystification" throughout, I modify the Marxist lens to better grasp the particulars of these colonial realities.

Transformation associated with these relations of exchange also entailed the "social differentiation" of Indigenous producers.[56] This was manifest in various ways: certain Indigenous individuals (e.g., trade captains) or groups (e.g., military allies) were given special standing in the trade with company officers, which likely introduced a distinct means of differentiation within and between

Indigenous societies. Howard Adams speaks to another aspect of this process: "As long as Indians were isolated as a special group, they were easily exploited as trappers; isolation or segregation of native people was therefore essential for the fur industry."[57] Meanwhile, Indigenous individuals in general were rarely hired as labourers on contract, which led to the racial divide between their legal and economic standing and the status of company servants, free Canadians, and eventually settlers.[58] Sites of exchange were much more than formal occasions for commercial activity; they were sites of contest, where distortion and differentiation were manufactured with the relative autonomy of Indigenous producers as the linchpin. Even as some adapted with new practices, many Indigenous peoples resisted the destruction of their societies and support systems. These transformations occurred in the face of a gradual, multifaceted settler colonial imposition rooted neither in some developmental destiny nor in an ingrained psychological yearning among the colonized.

Violence, Labour, and Land

The validity of the stagist orthodoxy of the transition to capitalism necessitates the over-identification of pre-capitalism with the extra-economic, which in turn highlights four misleading assumptions. The first reflects biases related to economic rationality and advances the racist and presentist insinuation that Indigenous peoples did not have an economically attuned mindset prior to the commercial incursion of the fur trade. The second arises from the first and maintains that, in the shift from pre-capitalism to capitalism, land was stripped of its social or extra-economic qualities and became "absolute private property" in a purely economic sense.[59] The third is that the framework of the transition to capitalism remains valid as long as one centres the changes that underpin the proletarianization of settlers, which supports ignoring the particular transformations that occur with respect to Indigenous peoples' labour. And the fourth is that the over-identification implicitly alloys pre-capitalism with violence and capitalism with the retreat of violence.

The lure of "normative developmentalism"[60] is overwhelming, and the narrative is simplified: pre-capitalism is driven by violent extra-economic force up to the dominance of the capitalist mode of production, at which point economic forces of production have their own disciplinary power and extra-economic force is an option of last resort. However, when accounting for actual social relations in specific historical contexts, this vulgarization raises a new line of inquiry, particularly around what is meant by and what becomes of "force."

My emphasis on Indigenous peoples' labour purposefully upsets the assumed symbiosis between pre-capitalism and violence and lays the groundwork to challenge the other three assumptions. I start by questioning the dichotomy that follows when pre-capitalist relations are couched in terms of extra-economic force, preferring instead Mahmood Mamdani's observation that "the distinction between market relations and direct compulsion is not quite that between force and its absence."[61] As is the case for Mamdani in his study of Uganda and South Africa, my inquiry strains the accuracy of this dichotomy. My findings suggest that direct, violent extra-economic force was not the primary means of labour compulsion; rather, the exploitative relations that constituted the fur trade and the founding of the Red River Colony were awash with customary practices and social obligations intrinsic to production. To be sure, it was a violent, vengeful era, replete with beating, murder, arson, kidnapping, and confinement. However, given the reality of Indigenous producers' relative autonomy, it is not possible to conclude that the day-to-day relations of exchange and the conditions of production endemic to the fur trade at that time and place relied on direct, violent extra-economic force as a norm. Early relations of exchange were exploitative yet were precursory to the increasingly direct violence that became the norm later, hinting that extra-economic force does not fade into the background in the manner implied by the standard thesis on the transition to capitalism.[62]

My objective in this book is to contest two rival ideas: that the transition to capitalism and settler colonialism alike necessarily entailed a shift from violent chaos to peaceful order, and that the relative lack of violence as the direct, primary means of compulsion in exchanges with Indigenous producers implied equanimity or complicity. To challenge both ideas, I focus on specific practices to see what, why, and how transformations were really occurring. At the centre of these transformations I find a tension between exploitation and autonomy. Violent coercion targeting this autonomy was not predominant for many reasons, including Indigenous peoples' resistance, the nature of fur trade production, and the strategic alliances that emerged in times of jurisdictional conflict. Consequently, measures of relatively "gentle compulsion" were essential to these exploitative practices and at the core of "the most peculiar combinations" of modes of production in the settler colonial context.[63]

To grasp these peculiarities, I avoid conceptions of land or property that privilege "white possessive logics"[64] and focus on processes of dispossession "rooted in the nation's prehistory."[65] Efforts to make sense of such changes without this focus on Indigenous peoples' labour grant explanatory preponderance to the white possessive form, which can have the unintended effect of lionizing "settler nation-building myths" and restricting our ability to see the inner workings of dispossession.[66] My approach therefore challenges the perpetuation of the idea that dispossession began with the takeover of Indigenous peoples' lands.[67] Such a view treads too closely to an ahistorical assessment of settler colonial relations by inadvertently, if only partially, supporting the simplistic version of Marx's "primitive accumulation thesis,"[68] which elevates the takeover of lands as the precipitously violent moment of the birth of capitalism. This abets the erasure of Indigenous peoples from the longer history of the transition to capitalism. Stripped of agency and their labour rendered invisible, Indigenous peoples become "if unwittingly ... a *thing* to be profitably surmounted"[69] – like land, humans become objectified collateral in the march toward industrialization.[70] Such an analysis violates the Place-Thought framework by ignoring social relations and upholding the Eurocentrism implied in the notion of original accumulation.[71]

With a focus on the means of labour compulsion in the context of a specific time and place during the commercial fur trade, I show that because Indigenous peoples' labour remained beyond the direct control of the companies, transformations associated with the settlement at Red River were informed largely by reactions to Indigenous producers' relative autonomy. This also demonstrates that passivity is not a condition of exploitation. Indigenous producers exercised agency in the course of exploitative practices;[72] adaptation and autonomy assume agency, but these acts do nothing to "absolve" the colonizer.[73] To resist the "insidious tendency to turn Native agency into colonialist alibi,"[74] I keep the power disparity of the settler colonial relationship in mind when speaking to the relative autonomy of Indigenous producers. That this differential is not immediately evident in many histories of the Red River Colony is indicative of the value of my approach. The goal is not to "explain away" this differentiation by fetishizing the "imperatives of accumulation and competition" but to excavate its social, political, and legal dimensions to better comprehend its legacy in the present day.[75]

All of this compels another modification to how I approach this instance of the transition to capitalism: I do not adhere to a notion of land as private property, adopting instead a notion of the social relations of land. By "the social relations of land," I have in mind specific practices related to land that are the constitutive bases for predominant social relations among certain Indigenous societies, which I detail in the first chapter. Conceptually, this approach to land represents a loose reworking of Robert Brenner's notion of "social relations of property and force," which he sees as the foundation of "the structure of exploitation."[76] Brenner contends that relations of property are not determined by the exploitative drives of the capitalist class, arguing instead that it is necessary to dissect the political dimensions at the core of class conflict to comprehend economic transformation.[77] I agree with this intuition, with two caveats. First, when Brenner discusses "social relations," he reverts to economic explanations in a way that undermines his thesis. Second, "extra-economic controls" and the like appear to be designated as relics of non-capitalist societies,[78] which risks reinforcing the over-identification of the pre-capitalist era with the extra-economic and endorsing the four misleading assumptions already discussed.

When capitalism is typified by the shift from extra-economic force to "purely 'economic' coercion"[79] and by the emergence of "absolute private property"[80] in general, this suggests a "temporal and conceptual cleavage" between the violence and chaos of pre-capitalism and the totalizing but muted compulsion of capitalism as such.[81] Analysis of the social relations of land compels a reckoning with what is at stake when one assumes the emergence of "absolute private property" and the predominance of "purely 'economic' coercion," which stimulates a serious rethink of the configuration of capitalism as a mode of production in the settler colonial context.

How certain Indigenous producers' autonomy was variably exercised or circumscribed in the course of commercial exchanges is key to understanding the evolution of "free" labour in the region and era.[82] I assert that the emergence of the "free and equal"[83] settler as an independent producer evolves in conjunction with changes to certain social relations of land practised by Indigenous peoples, and as such an account of Indigenous peoples' labour is central to comprehending early capitalism at Red River.[84] On the one hand, the misapprehension of these early relations of exploitation as equal and equanimous has a veiling effect, which is how "we" can come to be celebrated as "a country of adventurers"; on the other hand, by ignoring the particulars of Indigenous peoples' labour and the exploitation thereof, it becomes difficult to see how these relations set the groundwork for more regularized, overtly violent, and genocidal facets of this settler colonial relation that arose after the formal establishment of the Canadian settler state.[85] Proper verification of this hypothesis requires extending this analysis well past 1821; since doing so is beyond the scope of this work, all that I offer here are potential entry points to build upon later. The immediate objective is to foreground social relations of land and, in doing so, to show how the transition to capitalism at the Red River Colony challenges the over-identification of pre-capitalism with direct violence as the primary means of compulsion. By examining the economic and legal terms of labour compulsion related to Indigenous producers, I can support this objective.

Legal and Economic Transformation in a Geopolitical Context
Fidelity to the sources consulted prevents me from providing a simple account of the Red River Colony. This more exacting approach arises from an attempt to keep two historical realities in view: hugely disruptive forces of dispossession are intrinsic to settler colonialism,[86] yet "most of the time ... Aboriginal people

lived their own lives and were not always responding and reacting to external (and negative) forces."[87] My focus on the particulars of this tension germane to the Red River Colony brings to light three important findings: first, relative autonomy was intimately connected to Indigenous peoples' social relations of land; second, changes to these social relations of land had legal, economic, and geopolitical dimensions; and third, these transformations occurred in an uneven and combined manner.

In pre-capitalism, a slave was a specific legal subjectivity upon whom a proprietor exacted extreme measures of force in the course of labour compulsion; other gradations of subjectivity underpinned the legal status of serfs, servants, and soldiers, as well as women and children. It is therefore evident that legal relations are integral to labour compulsion, and as such law is part of the panoply of force in the extra-economic context. However, by alloying labour compulsion and force in pre-capitalism, the capitalist mode of production appears to be relatively free from forceful means of compulsion. The legal relations that constitute labour compulsion as force are seemingly defused, rendered extra in relation to economic factors and treated as relics of the pre-capitalist era.[88] These two consequences reflect the tradition of confusion in Marxist-informed thought about law's relation to the economic realm, commonly evoked by notions of law as "artificial means," "superstructural,"[89] or a "fetter"[90] or "limitation"[91] on economic production. A corresponding relegation of law is assumed by the transition to capitalism thesis in which labour compulsion shifts from the extra-economic to market discipline. Intrinsic to this economic stagism is legal stagism: namely, a presumed transition from lawless violence to lawful non-violence. Two intriguing questions arise from this intersection of narratives: How is it that pre-capitalism can be presented as lawless yet defined by extra-economic force? And precisely how do legal relations factor into the transition to capitalism?

Here I follow a pathway of critique cleared by Luxemburg a century ago. She not only insisted that "political power and economic factors go hand in hand" but also understood that the process involved in the expansion of the capitalist mode of production "belongs to the spheres of political power and criminal law no less than with economics."[92] Legal considerations are key to how Luxemburg made sense of the historical changes that accompanied capitalist accumulation, which makes one question the validity of treating legal relations as extrinsic to economic change. I address aspects of this in other works, penning the basis for "an uneven and combined development theory of law,"[93] which grew out of prior efforts to comprehend the flexibility of law in the settler colonial context.[94] The main continuity extending to this book is the shared objective to retrieve law from its banishment to the periphery of Marxist-informed thought and to do so in a way that resists simply shifting to a position of legal primacy by assigning law a singular role, form, or function in relation to economic change.

It is an over-simplification of the history of capitalism to deem legal relations as exercising a fettering effect on the commercial exchange,[95] nor are legal relations a type of extra-economic force in the sense that it has an overtly coercive function or emanates principally from a non-economic realm.[96] Neither "fetter" nor "extra-economic force" suffices because, although the former is a hindrance and the latter is a catalyst in relation to the economic conditions, both terms connote something that is an extrinsic reactant – an accessory to the machinations of history. Once placed in an intrinsic relation to the economic realm, the legal facets can begin to be seen as transforming in a similarly uneven and combined fashion – sometimes as catalyst, sometimes as fetter. Practices intrinsic to social relations of land illustrate this most clearly: customary, as well as economic, such practices were at once sources of autonomy and bases for exploitation. It is this variability that underpins why the processes of dispossession are fragmented yet unified, as well as inconspicuous and enduring.

This perspective, by extension, does not comply with a notion of state law in the formal sense. My stance is like that held by advocates of legal pluralism such as Lauren Benton and Richard Ross, who include codes and customs within the purview of legality in a manner that resists the over-identification of law with the nation-state.[97] Although controversial insofar as it tests the conventions of what one typically understands to be "law,"[98] this adjustment is necessary since it pertains to the pre-1821 era and the contested jurisdictions in question. Plainly, adhering to a rigid notion of "state law" when discussing the range of legal relations at play would be erroneous, mainly because it risks excluding customary law and elevating a type of law not predominant at that time or place.

Studies abound that detail the canonically derived customs that for some made dispossession intellectually agreeable and morally conscionable.[99] In critical legal history and international law, these studies include compulsory references to *ius gentium, ius naturale,* and *terra nullius,* each derived from (or, in the last case, misattributed to)[100] ancient Roman customs. Over the centuries, depending on the source and objective of the imperial campaigns of the age, these customary concepts were wielded with varying degrees of fidelity to theology; this was done to naturalize the fusion between Christianity and civilization[101] and to mitigate the dissonance between divinely inspired right and commercial imperative.[102] The salience of customary law in the international sphere dispels upfront the notion of "custom as a mordant stasis" and supports the late Peter Fitzpatrick's point about custom as a "formative force."[103] I take this a step further by deploying the terms "law" and "legal" in a manner akin to Val Napoleon's usages: "Customary law is not an easily codified set of rules for what to do and not do ... Rather, customary law inheres in each Aboriginal cultural system as a whole, forming legal orders that enable large groups of people to live together and to manage themselves accordingly."[104] This supple notion of legality includes the many customary social and political rules engendered by a range of societies and facilitates an understanding of legal relations as simultaneously formative and destructive, central and peripheral, formal and informal, fettering and catalyzing.

Accordingly, various spheres of law are discussed that span the imperfect and often misleading categories of public and private law: criminal, constitutional, international, and commercial, to name the most prevalent. Civil disputes, common law principles, natural law doctrine, and positivist tenets are all given consideration at various points, with narratives (i.e., stories and ballads), agreements, customs, statutes, royal charters, proclamations, treaties, and case law all having their time at centre stage. What for some might be a frustrating medley of legal practices, sources, and concepts is, for the purposes of this study, the best means of capturing the multitude of practices related to social relations of land and in turn demonstrating the pervasiveness and complexity of legal considerations as they relate to early capitalism in this settler colonial context.

A corollary of this undertaking involves challenging the abiding notions of stagist developmentalism that likewise reign in the field of legal history, variations of which thematize the seemingly fated movement out of arbitrariness and chaos and into formalism and order.[105] By holding the abstract and the concrete in tension, the contradictions and continuities that shape the processes of dispossession become evident. In an essay from 1985, the late Alan Hunt explains the value of such an approach, warning against simply taking legal concepts and testing them against "reality," a practice that reifies ideas by overlooking their generative connections to specific times and places.[106] Instead, Hunt insists "that the ideological analysis of law must be understood as operating at a number of different levels, and that these different levels are both conceptual and empirical."[107] This approach is on display throughout this book in the connections that I draw between local practices and geopolitical events and in the balanced assessment of abstract principles and concrete practices.[108]

Although I do not dwell on the philosophical particulars of this framing beyond this introduction, it resonates explicitly in the title of each chapter. I bookend the time frame roughly from the end of the Seven Years' War in 1763 to the merger of the Hudson's Bay Company and the North West Company in 1821, although the bulk of the book focuses on the years 1810 to 1816. These years were marked by rapid and significant transformations, and in tending closely to these years I can focus on what Lisa Ford refers to as the "everyday" or "daily struggles."[109] Such attentiveness reveals that, within a wider view, sites of legal pluralism might appear to be fraught and contentious, but everyday practices prove the flexibility and durability of social norms and expectations.[110]

Overview

Throughout the era in question, legal matters were intrinsic to economic change insofar as the variability of legal relations underpinned the fragmented but unified facets of dispossession. In staking such a claim, I situate this work amid ongoing and overlapping debates in prairie history, Indigenous studies, fur trade studies, critical legal history, capitalism studies, and settler colonial studies. In terms of the overall framework, I devote the bulk of the book to the historical agents and their practices, and in the course of those discussions I examine the relation to thinkers and their ideas.[111] Ultimately, as I tend to the particulars of dispossession-related commercial rivalry and colonial settlement (namely, exploitation, distortion, and differentiation), I show how it all connects to the relative autonomy of Indigenous producers. The title of each chapter evokes the transformative tensions that animate this historical study and keeps in check the tendency to provide a stagist account of dispossession and the Red River Colony.

In Chapter 1, "Reciprocity and Dispossession: Processes of Transformation," while explaining what I mean by "social relations of land," I introduce specific Indigenous societies whose histories are most entwined with the Red River Colony – the Nēhiyawok, Saulteaux, and Métis – and include a discussion of the principle of reciprocity and the practice of gift-giving. I then provide an account of the truck economy, which proved to be a useful conduit for mercantile expropriation and control deployed across the British colonies and no less in what became Canada. A brief legal, economic, and geopolitical history of the Hudson's Bay Company shows the relevance of the truck economy as the company's primary tactic for exploitation in the quest for profits. I end the chapter with an account of how the principle of reciprocity combined with the practices of dispossession associated with trucking, and I show the important role that the relative autonomy of Indigenous producers played leading up to the juncture between the eighteenth and nineteenth centuries.

As I note in Chapter 2, "Monopoly and Competition: Contests over Indigenous Peoples' Labour and Land," a decade after the end of the Seven Years' War in 1763 there was a new wave of competition that threatened the exclusive privileges of the Hudson's Bay Company. Rival Montreal-based fur traders from the North West Company (NWC) benefited from transportation and trade links to the south, an arrangement that became less dependable in the era following the US Revolutionary War. In response, the company made a move into the northwest and fortified its claim, while the HBC directors championed a shift of business inland, away from the bayside. I show that the relative autonomy of Indigenous producers was at the heart of the legal, economic, and geopolitical disputes in this era. New trade restrictions, commercial consolidations, and international borders amounted to a contest over Indigenous peoples' labour and land as profit margins narrowed.

In Chapter 3, "Honour and Duplicity: Debts of Rivals, Dreams of an Aristocrat," I show how debt collection became critical as the rival companies incurred losses, which placed Indigenous traders and producers in the crosshairs by the end of the eighteenth century. In the early 1800s, meanwhile, Lord Selkirk became a majority shareholder of the Hudson's Bay Company and was awarded a sizable grant of land from the company to establish a settler colony at Red River. I posit that, if understood as an economic decision alone, we risk treating the company's turn to settler colonialism as an inevitable by-product of increased competition and as a break from its past practices. Rather, this settler colonial initiative reflected the geopolitics of the era and built upon past exploitative measures. What becomes entrenched is the duplicity at the core of the established practices of distortion; as lofty principles clashed with the realities of colonial dispossession, attempts to extend the reach of formal law into "Indian Territories" chafed against the relative autonomy of Indigenous producers, setting in place the basis for legal and economic segregation.

In Chapter 4, "Servitude and Independence: The Settler Colonial 'Experiment' Begins," I indicate that, with HBC officials attempting to exercise their monopoly charter privileges through a settler colonial endeavour, processes of dispossession became selectively alloyed with more formally legalistic claims. After all, for the company's servants to become settlers proper, they needed to be in possession of land, which assumed the successful dispossession of Indigenous peoples; the relative autonomy of these two groups therefore moved in opposite directions. Yet attempts to formalize legal administration could not hide the reality that the system relied on pecuniary and sometimes corporal punishment, nor could it be reconciled with the fact that the North West Company refused to submit to the settler colony's jurisdictional authority. I claim that, from the official granting of the land (1811) to the second winter of the settlement (1813), the destitution of the servant-settlers and the lack of effective authority led to increased dependence on Indigenous peoples' labour. This situation contrasted with the original purpose of the settler colony itself: that is, to control the territory and its people and to become self-sufficient producers of food and goods for the Hudson's Bay Company. For an "experiment" meant to bolster the company's position, the setbacks were severe, opening the door for even more drastic measures meant to curtail the relative autonomy of Indigenous producers.

By 1814, as I indicate in Chapter 5, "Menace and Ally: Proclamation as Provocation," the procurement of provisions (especially the local staple, pemmican) became the spark for a series of clashes, culminating with the Pemmican Proclamation issued by Governor of the Red River Colony Miles Macdonell. I detail how extra-economic coercion was both the result of and resulted in a host of transformations to social relations wrought by the established pattern of dispossession. It was in response to some of these changes that the partners of the North West Company proceeded to exert their own legal prerogative, demonstrating the extent to which legal matters and economic interests were inextricably entwined. Yet, while both sides acted to execute arrest warrants and detain prisoners, each claiming to have royal prerogative on its side, the relative autonomy of the Métis was at the centre of this new series of disputes.

In Chapter 6, "Consciousness and Ignorance: New Nation, Old Grievances," I show how struggles for control ramped up, with each side making military appointments and attempting to secure allies among members of local Indigenous societies. After two years of this posturing, a violent clash occurred in 1816 that resulted in the deaths of twenty-one men on the HBC side. I assess how measures of social differentiation – especially those that attempted to undermine the relative autonomy of the Métis – were intrinsic to the transformations that shaped this conflict and how practices of distortion were extended in the aftermath with the signing of a land use agreement in 1817 between local Indigenous leaders and Selkirk.

Finally, in the Conclusion, "Continuity and Change," I bring the dominant themes and theories together as I examine the events that occurred from 1818 to the merger of the two companies in 1821. I end the book by revisiting the anecdotes raised at the beginning and speaking to the troublesome legacy that resulted from these continuities and changes. This recap helps to explain the value of such a historical perspective and allows me to emphasize the primary ways that this book advances interdisciplinary scholarship in a range of fields.

The thread that connects each chapter in this account of the Red River Colony is the relative autonomy of Indigenous producers, at every turn a driver of economic activity and legal transformation alike. It is this reality that challenges staid concepts and narratives, compelling a different way of understanding early capitalism in general and the Canadian settler colonial context in particular.

1
Reciprocity and Dispossession
Processes of Transformation

THE LAND SEIZURE at the Red River Colony occurred with the physical occupation of the site by Miles Macdonell and his servant-settlers in 1812; however, from a longer historical view, it was one aspect of the processes of dispossession – exploitation, distortion, and differentiation – practised in the preceding decades. This longer view moves us past an understanding of the dispossession of land as a singular event and goes beyond the private property paradigm when discussing the ideas and practices associated with land. The importance of this shift becomes evident as I explain how customary practices mixed with commercial objectives of the Hudson's Bay Company to give rise to a range of transformative effects. Finally, as I detail the specifics of social relations of land and commercial exchange in the context of the British North American fur trade, I begin to refine the connection between exploitation and autonomy.

Below I trace the intersecting legal, economic, and geopolitical dimensions that informed the commercial fur trade. I start with an account of the main Indigenous societies central to the history of the Red River Colony, focusing on establishing a basic understanding of their discrete histories, social relations of land, and practices of customary reciprocity. I then introduce the Hudson's Bay Company and explain its internal structure, the scope of its chartered monopoly, and the truck system that it relied on as a means of exploitation. From there, I show how the adoption of customary practices centred on gift-giving and reciprocity was a necessary condition of the HBC strategy for profit realization. Although distorted practices of reciprocity-based exchanges became the exploitative conduits of dispossession, trade captains were singled out in a way that differentiated Indigenous producers from each other, which had important implications for their social relations of land in the decades ahead. This discussion sets the groundwork for the rest of the book by demonstrating that exploitation, distortion, and differentiation were the means and outcomes of the processes of dispossession but that reactions to the relative autonomy of Indigenous producers helped drive these transformations.

Social Relations of Land
In the settler colonial context, dispossession is most heavily associated with an "eliminatory logic"[1] that informs the theft of land from Indigenous peoples.[2] Cast too narrowly, however, this view risks privileging a certain idea of land as

private property,[3] which precludes a richer outlook on what these processes entail. To breach the colonizing mindset, it is necessary to forge a more apt perspective on land, one that makes it possible for the very concept of land as it is often discussed in settler colonial studies "to be reconfigured by Indigenous knowledge."[4] As a non-Indigenous scholar, I take this challenge seriously, and it is for this reason that I open this book with a foundational rethink of dispossession that steers it away from an understanding of land as private property.[5] But I do not pretend that this intellectual manoeuvre absolves or shields me or this text from criticism. Good intentions are empty without right actions, and, as much as I endeavour to do justice to Indigenous knowledges referenced herein, I also know that it is not my place to judge whether or not I have succeeded.[6]

This is why it is imprudent to begin with idealist preconceptions of land as an archetypal form. Instead, I take as the starting point for such an assessment of land a position that avoids "reifying statist notions of bounded space"[7] and that does so with an account of social relations that speaks to a host of intertwined labour and customary practices. Admittedly, some baseline is useful if for no other reason than to be able to gauge the scope of change to social relations of land with respect to Indigenous societies involved in the fur trade; however, in the quest for a working notion of "pre-contact social configurations,"[8] *caution* is the watchword. It is important to buck the tendency to see Indigenous peoples and their cultures as static "objects to be studied" or as "disappearing,"[9] "*natural* and *innate*,"[10] "pristine,"[11] or "uniform" (and by extension "constraining").[12] At root, there are no generalizable notions of land that might bear transhistorical or supracultural currency since different societies developed their own customary practices in different regions and eras. A multifaceted understanding of land involves recognizing it as simultaneously necessary for subsistence, constitutive of identity, definitive of social relations, delineative of labour productivity, and the basis of a conception of justice as "a debt to the future."[13] This perspective does not reduce Indigenous peoples to a primordial state by essentializing supposedly naturalistic facets of identity but acts as a vital check on the racist practice of objectification[14] by stressing the complexity of the relation between life and land.

For millennia prior to settler colonialism, Indigenous peoples were migrating, some overtaking others, forging and then flouting peace agreements, intermingling and breaking apart, all the while adapting to changing climate, new techniques, and different terrain.[15] The commercial fur trade did not start until the sixteenth century on the eastern side of the continent along the Gulf of St. Lawrence,[16] and then it moved to the Great Lakes region courtesy of established trading networks among Indigenous societies from the Atlantic Ocean to the

Great Lakes.[17] I mention various groups throughout this book, but for the specific history of the Red River Colony the three most discussed are Anishinaabe (known as Ojibwe, with a focus on the Saulteaux or Plains Ojibwe),[18] Cree (namely, the Nēhiyawok, Maškēkowak or Omushkegowak, and Eeyou), and Métis (Métis Nation at Red River).[19] These societies have discrete yet overlapping histories, and, although I do not go into as much depth as each warrants in this preliminary assessment, I challenge the dependency thesis that shaped much of fur trade studies and promote a working understanding of the various ways that these societies related to land.

For centuries, the hub of Anishinaabe activity – hunting, fishing, trapping, trading, and congressing – was at the juncture of Lakes Superior, Huron, and

Figure 1.1 Chief Peguis Monument, Kildonan Park, Winnipeg, October 2021 | *Photo*: Delores Antonation

Michigan, around the site that is present-day Sault Ste. Marie. So named by Jesuits in the 1660s when they founded a mission there, Anishinaabeg from this region came to be known as Saulteaux (or Saulteurs).[20] With their easterly origins,[21] the Saulteaux initially interacted more with French Canadian traders (known as *engagés*, eventually also as *voyageurs*) throughout the seventeenth and eighteenth centuries.[22] A prominent Saulteaux leader in the history of the Red River Colony was a man, Peguis, who moved from the Sault Ste. Marie area to the plains.[23] In 1815, he delivered a speech to the settlers at Red River that referenced the lands in question, commenting that "these are not my Lands – they belong to our Great Father – for it is he only that gives us the means of existence, for what would become of us if he left us to ourselves. We should wither like the grass in the Plains, was the Sun to withdraw his animating beams."[24] Of note is the life-giving dimension of land wherein the Great Father is likened to the sun and the people to the grass; land here is claimed not as personal property but as a "means of existence" in both a biological and a spiritual sense.

"Our truth," writes Vanessa Watts, "not only Anishinaabe and Haudenosaunee people but in a majority of Indigenous societies, conceives that we (humans) are made from the land; our flesh is literally an extension of soil." She explains further that, "if we begin from the premise that we are in fact made of soil, then our principles of governance are reflected in nature."[25] In addition to the biological and spiritual facets of the relation between life and land that Peguis mentions, Watts's reference to "principles of governance" underscores how this approach to land is reflected in broader social norms. "Balanced and reciprocal relationships are what sustain the Anishinaabe," explains Jill Doerfler.[26] For more details, Heidi Kiiwetinepinesiik Stark's writings about Indigenous perspectives and practices of sovereignty are instructive, particularly as a bridge between the principles of governance that Watts speaks to and the spiritual dimension that Peguis mentions.

Stark notes that Anishinaabe leaders regularly privileged the language of accountability to the Creator when negotiating treaties with officials from the United States, which was done in public and served as the basis for shared meaning while also reinforcing mutual responsibilities.[27] She adds that, through creation stories and treaty-making, "Anishinaabe uttered the place names that delineated their relationship to their land" and that these transformative practices of sovereignty "necessitated the recognition of our interdependence, our connection to one another and creation, and our relationships."[28] The sovereign act was an acknowledgment of inheritance from the Creator, and subsequent negotiations were not an abdication or renouncement of this responsibility but an affirmation and extension of it, requiring others to recognize the sacredness of this original inheritance and the expectations of accountability attached. This connection between sacredness and sovereignty underscores the deficiencies of a private property paradigm when it comes to understanding the dispossession of Indigenous peoples by settler colonial agents. At best, an emphasis on land as alienable property abides the notion of treaty-making as a contractual relation in which an unequal exchange of assets delineates the scope of the agreement; it also ignores the dynamic social relations of land and the core truth that, though the sovereign act is transformative, the sovereign claim remains unextinguished and inextinguishable. Evidence of both the transformative and the enduring dimensions with respect to social relations of land can be seen in the history between the Saulteaux and Nēhiyawok.

Sara Mainville explains that "the Anishinaabeg believe we have been in [the Rainy Lake of northern Ontario] area since time immemorial."[29] To explain the westward movement to the plains, Elder Danny Musqua points to outbreaks of disease and the US Revolutionary War, which led to a mixing among Ojibwe and Cree peoples:

> In some places we are called the Oji-Cree, but we just call ourselves Saulteaux. We intermarried with the Crees for five hundred years, maybe more. This occurred much more-so when we came to these prairies because the Crees were already here. So being a brother tribe we allied with them and we protected one another. They were protective toward us. We lived in close proximity.[30]

This point is echoed by Carolyn Podruchny, who – in relaying a comment from Blanche Cowley-Head of Opaskwayak Cree Nation – states that "her ancestors did not ask whether they were Ojibwe, Cree, Oji-Cree, French, or Métis; rather, they cared that they lived and flourished in the area around The Pas in northern Manitoba and that they were proud that their families and community grew and supported one another over time."[31] Although it is possible, therefore, that in the fur trade literature those identified as Saulteaux did not necessarily have their origins in the migration from the Great Lakes region,[32] the prevalence of cultural affinities across groups appears to have stemmed from the transformative dimensions of the social relations of land discussed above, which emphasized mutual responsibility and shared meanings.

Among the Saulteaux who did migrate to the prairies, they brought with them extensive experience growing wild rice and fishing, introducing these skills to an area where the buffalo hunt reigned,[33] as Laura Peers explains: "The Saulteaux had a much broader, more flexible subsistence base better able to cope with ecological fluctuations."[34] It was on the plains that they encountered Nēhiyaw peoples, whose own history continues to be a source of controversy in fur trade studies among writers who dispute the scope, timing, and causes of migrations that occurred. Relevant to the origins of the Nēhiyawok, David Mandelbaum comments that they dwell in the "transitional area between the forests and plains" and have done so "only since the beginning of the nineteenth century."[35] Per his study in 1940, Cree integration into the commercial fur trade was swift and deep: "The first English supply ship came into Hudson Bay in 1668. Two years later posts were established at the mouth of the Nelson, Moose, and Albany rivers, and the Cree flocked in to trade."[36] John Milloy builds upon Mandelbaum's thesis[37] and contends that they were originally Woodland Cree from as far as Eastern James Bay but that they migrated deeper onto the prairies concurrent with the shifting commercial fur trade.[38]

Others rebuke this theory of migration, along with the thesis that the Indigenous populations in question were dependent on the foreign companies, and they argue instead that the westernmost extension of Cree peoples predates the commercial fur trade. James Smith, for one, contends that "the region was already occupied by Cree."[39] Likewise, Dale Russell challenges the view that the depth of Cree integration into the commercial fur trade provided the means (i.e., the arms necessary to vanquish other Indigenous societies) and motivation (i.e., a desire for more beaver pelts) for the purported migration.[40] He also notes that the records of foreign explorers themselves – namely, David Thompson and Alexander Mackenzie – provided contestable first-hand accounts of the migration of certain peoples.[41] Smith comments that, "whenever the fur traders arrived in the area between Lake Winnipeg and the Peace River, the Cree were always there before them," also suggesting that the evidence to support the notion of Nēhiyaw peoples as relative newcomers is unconvincingly thin.[42] Archaeological findings by David Meyer likewise show that Cree peoples were very early inhabitants along the Saskatchewan River,[43] a waterway that feeds Lake Winnipeg and where the HBC post of Cumberland House was established in 1774 – what became a critical inland trading site for the company.[44]

In addition to the plains, Cree peoples involved in the commercial fur trade occupied a range of geographical areas: along the western and eastern shores of Hudson Bay, in the woodlands, and in the parklands. Eeyou Istchee are the lands along the eastern bayside in what is now the province of Quebec and home to societies regionally divided between those along the coast (Wiinibeyk Iiyuu) and those inland (Nuuchcimiihc Iiyuu).[45] Philip Awashish explains that for his people the land "is the foundation of our identity, governance, history, heritage, culture and way of life, spirituality and Eeyou *Eedouwin* (Eeyou way of doing things)," upheld "through the teachings of Eeyou elders, customs, traditions and practices."[46] The more inland Eeyou of these territories tended to focus on hunting for provisions as opposed to trapping for furs,[47] though survival also required moving with the seasons and across landscapes – from shorelines to valleys to forests.[48] Among the Mistissini, territorial claims were upheld by leaders of hunting groups and forged on the basis of the spiritual relation to the animal, not through a boundaried claim on land as such.[49] Although they were on the frontlines of the HBC transportation route to and from Europe, the Eeyou were neither uniformly nor completely absorbed into the commercial trade thanks to practices and "legal traditions [that were] ... strong and dynamic."[50] This fortitude is evident in the research of Hans Carlson, who finds that the foreign techniques were not taken up and that the company's dependence on Indigenous peoples' practices persisted.[51]

On the western side of Hudson Bay, among the Lowland Cree (Maškēkowak; Muskekowuck, Mushkego, Omushkego, Swampy Cree, or Homeguard Cree), there is a distinction (comparable to that on the eastern side) between coastal (Winipeg-athinuwick) and inland (Muskekowuck-athinuwick) populations,[52] though this regional divide is more fluid perhaps because the boggy lowlands of the western side extend farther inland compared with the eastern side.[53] Eminent Omushkego storyteller and historian Louis Bird refers to "sacred ground" as a site of communion with the natural and spiritual worlds alike[54] and recounts how, prior to the incursion of commercial fur traders, his people "always moved with the seasons."[55] Some interpret the societies of this area, which includes the site of York Factory, as having become rapidly enmeshed in the commercial fur trade and by extension "quickly dependent" on foreign goods.[56] Victor Lytwyn's extensive analysis of the HBC Archives questions this dependency thesis and supports Bird's account that Indigenous societies were drawn to the bayside on a seasonal basis prior to the encroachment of foreign traders.[57]

With the arrival of Europeans and the smallpox outbreak in the early 1780s, the pattern of movement was altered: the Maškēkowak avoided the trading posts and were less involved in the commercial trade, which Lytwyn interprets as evidence of the relative autonomy of this population.[58] Instead, in continuing to exercise and transform their social relations of land, they retained the capacity for self-sufficiency and did not become dependent on foreign traders and their goods. Lytwyn comments on how HBC officers marvelled at the lack of any notion of "'propriety of exclusive right'" among certain Maškēkowak groups. However, in one journal entry in particular, James Swain at Severn House observed in 1815 that there was "'a kind of Custom of reckoning their own Ground.'"[59] This speaks to a notion of territoriality comparable to that found among the Eeyou; different from exclusive title to land as private property, there were nevertheless established, recognized, and ongoing – albeit shifting – territorial claims.

Farther inland from the bay, the Métis emerged as a new presence.[60] Although some established Métis families moved toward the plains in response to the employment barriers that they faced after 1763,[61] and others in response to the scarcity of animals at earlier establishments along the Great Lakes,[62] still other prominent Métis families have their origins in the Red River area of present-day Manitoba.[63] It is the mobility among Métis that scholars identify as one of their distinctive qualities; as Carolyn Podruchny and Nicole St-Onge remark, "webs of kin were not rooted to a tangible place," explaining that "Metis people moved west to find new land to cultivate, to follow the fur trade posts to continue selling country produce, and to follow the buffalo herds as they shrank and moved farther away."[64] Economically motivated considerations, culture, and kinship ties pervade recountings of Métis history,[65] which hint at important transformations under way with respect to social relations of land in the area. Podruchny and St-Onge refer to a "mercantile network" that extended from Montreal in the east to the west along the Saskatchewan River, a main source of labour for the emergent Métis kinships that revolved around common language and religion.[66] With antecedents in various Indigenous, French, and Scottish customs, the amalgam of cultural influences furnished the basis for substantive social and economic linkages across this expanse; consisting of mobile and adaptive familial groupings, the Métis both responded to and influenced changes to the prevailing productive processes that constituted the fur trade industry.[67] However, as already shown with respect to the Saulteaux, Nēhiyawok, Maškēkowak or Omushkegowak, and Eeyou, mobility is not unique to Métis history, nor are "mixedness and hybridity" exclusively Métis identifiers.[68] These clarifications must be made explicit in order to reject the racist colonial practice of denying the Métis as Indigenous peoples.[69] This insistence trades on a distorted biological conception of race, which in turn facilitates ongoing relations of dispossession by barring the legitimacy of Métis land claims.[70]

A valuable takeaway from these brief introductions is a critical understanding of the dependency thesis, which sees Indigenous societies moving across lands as though motivated primarily by commodity exchange.[71] This commodity-dependence lens serves the implied stagism of a standard narrative of the transition to capitalism, and it does so in two related ways: first, by downplaying the ongoing autonomy of Indigenous producers in the face of the commodity, which entails ignoring the social relations of land that ensconced that autonomy; second, by banishing the activities of pre-commercial trading societies to the extra-economic realm, which feeds the assumption that, prior to the commercial fur trade, Indigenous societies interacted absent an economic mindset. That alienable land was not the defining quality of Indigenous social relations served the twinned myths of civilizational superiority and *terra nullius*,[72] but it is counterfactual to equate the lack of a European notion of private property with the absence of an economic facet of their social relations of land. In core respects, these perspectives underscore what Aileen Moreton-Robinson describes as an "ontological relationship to land"[73] in that prevailing ideas about "land" reflect and are reflected in the quotidian practices that underpin the social relations of a given society.[74] Because these relations are "*practiced* daily," it is necessary to focus on "actual Aboriginal customs and social institutions"[75] and to resist privileging the abstract form – that is, land as alienated property, legal title, or economic commodity – as the cipher for understanding social relations.

The daily practices that reflected particular social relations of land were not the exclusive activities of male hunters or leaders; paramount in this respect was the role of Indigenous women in the fur trade as agents of social reproduction. It included the biological facets of actual life-giving labour, as well as the day-to-day production of labour power as such, ranging from sustaining social connections to preparing meals and making clothing.[76] Matrilocality forged social obligations and established kinship relations across generational and cultural lines.[77] Prior to the incursions by foreign commercial ventures, women were central to trade relations with other Indigenous societies,[78] such as among the Maškēkowak, Nēhiyawok, and Saulteaux, and it was women's labour that produced the more fungible items such as clothing and preserved meats.[79] Among the latter peoples, women fished, harvested turnips and maple sugar, trapped small game, and cultivated wild rice – all of which was integral to subsistence and trade though often underacknowledged because of a tendency to "present a vivid image of the Saulteaux as being dominated by men and men's economic activities."[80] Noted storyteller and teacher Basil Johnston offers a glimpse of how male hunters are revered in Anishinaabe culture, though in discussing the labour of providing for one's family he also states that "the men and women so engaged satisfied man's basic and constant need," noting women's labour and the social reproductive dimensions of these practices.[81]

With the arrival of European fur traders, the scope, focus, and terms of exchange shifted in new ways,[82] as did gender-based social differentiation.[83] In addition to other indispensable contributions,[84] women gathered the spruce gum and roots necessary for canoe making, and when there were labour shortages they were called on by the Hudson's Bay Company to steer their canoes.[85] Among some Maškēkowak, if hunters or trappers ended up with smaller catches, the items would go to the women, who sometimes bartered on their own behalf for smaller luxury imports, such as bracelets.[86] Some Saulteaux women could influence the direction and capacity of trade on a larger scale, especially by entering into strategic marriages with the foreign traders. Such marriages forged social bonds that in turn helped to establish both "access" to and "favourable terms" of trade.[87] Sylvia Van Kirk focuses on the prevalence of intermarriage between high-ranking officers and Indigenous women from groups involved in the fur trade in the Red River area,[88] noting that early on these unions were sought as a strategy to ensure reciprocity: "In return for giving the traders sexual and domestic rights to their women, the Indians expected reciprocal privileges such as free access to the posts and provisions."[89] By initially banning intimate relations with Indigenous women, the Hudson's Bay Company was not as willing as the early French traders to encourage intermarriage, but the lack of white women and the trading advantages that these unions presented made it difficult to forestall. The women were neither solely "acted upon" nor "compliant playthings,"[90] and their wishes and consent were sometimes considered; although some appeared to seek intermarriage,[91] it is important to keep the overarching racialized and gendered power differential in mind.

The term "social relations of land" is meant to encompass this panoply of practices. It is not about private property and fabricated borders; rather, it is about the capacity to execute and transform those practices – economic, political, or legal – crucial to sustenance and survival. Consider that seasonal movement and access were not dictated by contracts but through ongoing reciprocal agreements among societies, the terms of which were reflected in practices that upheld relations of accountability to land, animals, the Creator, and each other. Because of the dynamism of social relations of land, the profit-motivated commercial outfits could not simply introduce commodities and create dependencies; instead, Indigenous peoples retained a relative degree of autonomy over their means of production and social reproduction alike. This vital consideration is lost when focusing on dispossession, beginning with the theft of land, narrowly conceived. Instead, the chapters ahead reveal the alienation of land as the contested and partial alienation of social relations of land through exploitation, distortion, and differentiation.

To comprehend dispossession as a process that precedes the alienation of land, therefore, it is necessary to break the assumed connection between dispossession and property (strictly speaking) and instead to consider dispossession as occurring on several fronts simultaneously and to different degrees. By focusing on the processes of "gradual dispossession"[92] inherent in the transformations to social relations of land, it becomes clear that efforts to dispossess Indigenous peoples of their mobility, customs, time, skills, beliefs, wealth, community, health, and sovereignty (or, in short, their autonomy) are intrinsic to the eventual dispossession of land. Key drivers of such change are the partiality and contestation of exploitation – in other words, the abiding autonomy of Indigenous producers and reactions to that autonomy. A closer look at the practices and principles associated with the social relations of land elucidates this point.

Reciprocity and the Gift

Historically, some Métis, along with some among the Nēhiyawok, Saulteaux, and Assiniboine, comprised the Nehiyaw Pwat or Iron Alliance.[93] In his history of the alliance, Robert Alexander Innes emphasizes similarities among the four societies; on the fluidity of membership and the salience of reciprocity, he remarks that "generosity was highly valued, and as a result chiefs had to accumulate wealth, then give it away. A person who demonstrated skills as a good hunter and/or warrior was usually able to accumulate wealth, and could count on support from his relatives as his core members."[94] Among the practices common to the histories of these various societies was redistribution. "There was no selfishness. It is an Indian custom to share with others. That has always been so; the strong take care of the poor; there is usually enough for all," explains Edward Ahenakew on the history of Nēhiyaw governance.[95]

Members from each of the four societies inhabited overlapping lands, with lodges located across present-day Saskatchewan, Manitoba, and North Dakota, from the Interlake to the Forks in the Red River Valley and along the North and South Saskatchewan Rivers.[96] Together they fought against the Sioux and Blackfoot, with the Iron Alliance remaining intact until 1870.[97] Over time, these networks grew and shrank, converged and dispersed, for a range of social, political, and economic reasons.[98] Still, the principles of kinship and reciprocity remained paramount.[99] Innes explains that the values that informed kinship-related practices were shared through stories. In many stories, kinship terms were used to refer not just to people but also to non-humans, and from this the listeners gained an understanding of social obligations; as Innes comments, "for most Indigenous groups ... cultural protocol required that a kinship relationship be established between strangers for any sort of social, economic, or political dealing to occur."[100] He further notes that, in trickster stories, expressions of kinship are sometimes used as a deceptive ploy.[101]

One exemplary figure is "Elder Brother," whom Innes describes as "more than just a trickster, he is really the Cree/Ojibwe cultural hero,"[102] and in communicating customary practices his "stories conveyed Cowessess traditional law to the people."[103] Innes includes two stories about Elder Brother, one that demonstrates positive norms of kinship when Elder Brother is taken in by wolves and in turn becomes responsible for a younger wolf as his nephew, another that reinforces kinship norms when Elder Brother develops an elaborate deception so that he can marry his own daughter, which ends with his banishment because of his self-gratifying impulses and "extreme violation of social norms."[104] John

Borrows underscores that "the Trickster helps the listeners conceive of the limited viewpoint they possess," revealing "the partiality of perspective"[105] in a manner that reinforces or reinterprets social norms.[106] Known variably as Nanbush and Nänibozhu among some Anishinaabeg or as Wîsahkêcâhk among western Cree, the figure whom Innes refers to as Elder Brother appears in the traditions of both peoples.[107] The prairie history of the two societies is also evident in an origin story compiled and told by four Nēhiyaw elders; it begins with "our relations to the east, the Ojibwa – like our own Cree people," and ends with a recognition of the similarities in language between the two peoples.[108] Shared prairie history was the focal point of land use negotiations undertaken by Peguis in 1817, but it also underpinned transformations of their respective social relations of land throughout the eighteenth and early nineteenth centuries.

Alongside storytelling, the practice of gift-giving was a means of extending kinship in the building and maintenance of political allegiances and established "obligations of care" within a family and beyond it.[109] This practice predated the commercial fur trade and did not arise as an adaptive reaction to the incursions of the European traders. John Milloy, writing about evolving Nēhiyaw rituals in the late nineteenth century, speaks to the intersection of gift, spirituality, and social obligation. He explores the sacred roots of the plains buffalo, seen not only "as a gift from the Creator" that "belong[s] to an 'us' exclusive of others not of our community" but also as the basis of the Nēhiyawok claim to the land's resources as the primary beneficiaries.[110] This claim was not a form of entitlement but a reciprocity-based agreement that reinforced a "sacred right" and reflected specific social relations of land.[111] Such customary exchanges were forged by relations of interdependence among various Nēhiyaw societies[112] and integral to their social reproduction.

Sometimes the redistributive principle was an intrinsic dimension of one's status within a given Indigenous society. For example, in a transcribed oral history from 1934, Nēhiyaw leader Kamiokisihkwew (Fine Day) explained to D.G. Mandelbaum that it was common for the chief's wife to leave the "fattest meat" for a widow, and worthy men were required to "look after all the people," recalling one occasion when his wife gave her own clothes to a widow and combed her hair to relieve the stranger of lice.[113] Leaders therefore incurred additional obligations,[114] and they offered presents such as meat or cloth in order to satisfy the expectations of redistribution and protection. These in-group obligations also existed alongside a broader network of customary reciprocity. Among Anishinaabe peoples who inhabited the areas west and south of Lake Superior, customary reciprocity helped to offset the difficulties that arose "due to the vagaries of the natural world," where food shortages were a constant threat;[115] the exchange was not between commensurable values abstractly conceived but between "object[s] of utility"[116] in response to the *unevenness of production.*"[117] When gifts from the land were not abundant and certain societies suffered more in times of scarcity, this intersocial network of reciprocity could operate as a backstop against extreme privation and later against complete dependence on commercial traders.

Cooperation was a guiding principle in the exchange relations within and beyond varied kinship-based Indigenous societies, with the incumbent obligations operating as a condition for allegiance. This was demonstrated with respect to hunting among the Maškēkowak; for instance, when a beaver was trapped, its meat was divided among the participants, but the fur belonged to the person who made the initial discovery,[118] a practice also common among the Innu east of Hudson Bay.[119] The term "trapper" is employed in the individual sense but not meant to suggest an individuated process overall given that "production, distribution, exchange, and consumption" were organized in a way that fostered kinship-based interdependencies among families.[120] Consequently, reciprocity and sharing are often held up as norms common to many Indigenous societies, although they varied according to band or group,[121] time, and place.

Prominent fur trade historian Arthur J. Ray remarks that, "according to the rules of general reciprocity, one did not expect an immediate return for aid rendered nor was any economic value placed on the obligation. The reciprocal obligation that accrued was generalized."[122] The beneficiary of aid did not become a debtor in either a quantifiable or a contractual sense but bore a general obligation to distribute whatever was held as a surplus in the future. This system of assurances was buttressed by the social advantages that accompanied redistribution as opposed to the compulsion to accumulate for individual profit – as Ray explains, "generosity was a virtue," and "individuals derived prestige from wealth by giving it away."[123] This view is reinforced by Janna Promislow's observation that among the Maškēkowak "wealth was valued only as something that would be shared rather than accumulated."[124] Importantly, for the purpose of understanding the transition to capitalism in the settler colonial context, just because wealth was shared and not accumulated did not make it any less an economic relation.

It is inaccurate to comprehend the customs of trade among Indigenous societies as though there was no economy before the Europeans arrived;[125] there were definitive and discrete norms related to the distribution of goods, exchange, production, and consumption.[126] At the same time, it is unwise to assume that these customary norms were coercive fetters that withered away in concert with increasing incursions by Europeans. Both of these assumptions can be inferred from Arthur J. Ray and Donald Freeman's thesis that the "political aspects" of

Indigenous peoples' trading "diminished in importance at an early point in the development of exchange," which reflected the "increasing dominance of economic considerations" in their decision making.[127] Although Europeans introduced foreign-manufactured commodities into the exchange, one cannot conclude *tout court* that the direct consequence was "instant dependence" on either the goods or the Europeans' commercial trade network.[128] Manifestly, economic motivations were not new,[129] and political considerations did not lessen, although the productive capacities and political consequences changed in specific ways. It is more accurate to consider this as a convergence among multiple modes of production, recognizing that each mode consisted of particular social relations of land.

Some scholars today propose a return to "the gift paradigm" as a means of promoting Indigenous peoples' autonomy and resisting the perils of capitalism.[130] From a historical perspective, there is good reason for such an appeal: on some occasions for certain Indigenous peoples, this customary practice was the basis of resistance to the encroachment of commercial capital. But the historical circumstances in which these particular relations of reciprocity were exercised were exploitative, which suggests that a return to gift-giving is not in itself a bulwark against mistreatment. Arguably, one way that the network of social obligation expanded and commercial capital continued to make inroads was through the "strategic 'domestication'" of the practices of customary reciprocity by the fur trade companies.[131] Others have termed comparable relations "strategic congruities,"[132] "strategic accommodations,"[133] "persistent pluralisms,"[134] and "commercialization ... of daily life,"[135] but it is Mamdani's observation with regard to Britain's colonial practices that is the most evocative: "Britain creatively sculpted tradition and custom as and when the need arose."[136] This perspective underscores the need for a flexible yet exacting method of analyzing the convergence among different modes of production.

With the proliferation of commercial trading, principled reciprocity underwent a distortion, a process that Kahente Horn-Miller describes as "the tendency of people to fall out of balance with themselves and the world" during colonization.[137] Reciprocity as a principled practice that expressed and reinforced specific social relations of land did not fade among Indigenous societies, but it was distorted in certain instances and to different degrees under the weight of a growing scope of obligation that emerged through exploitative exchanges with European fur traders.[138] Commercial incursions did not portend the end of a "reciprocal period";[139] customary practices based upon the principle of reciprocity were stretched alongside a growing scope of obligations, except that these obligations entailed increasingly exploitative exchanges with European fur traders, rendering them reciprocal in form but decreasingly so in substance.[140]

At stake in the processes of dispossession germane to this settler colonial context, therefore, are the ideas and practices that constitute the prevailing social relations of land.

The social relations of land among Indigenous communities involved in the fur trade reflect and are reflected by processes of production, exchange, consumption, and social reproduction – in this sense, ideas and practices related to land are bound up with ideas and practices related to labour. Patricia McCormack elaborates on this point, writing that "Indian knowledge of the resource base" and "the sovereignty they exercised over their lands" is central to their economic and political autonomy alike.[141] All matters pertinent to production and exchange implicate social relations of land or, more precisely, the customary practices thereof. As such, customary practices related to the principle of reciprocity (e.g., gift-giving, kinship, and cooperative social obligations) were targets of dispossession prior to the settlement at Red River, while exploitation, distortion, and differentiation prevailed as both means and outcomes. By advancing this thesis, I erode three general stereotypes that skew in different directions: first, that the history of settler colonialism entails a conspicuous shift from violent dispossession to administrative containment;[142] second, that extra-economic labour compulsion was the reigning standard prior to the commercial trade, which backslides too quickly into the assumption that Indigenous peoples lacked an economic outlook; and third, that the fur trade was awash with voluntariness and benevolence, evinced by relations of reciprocal exchange between Indigenous peoples and company traders.

To build upon Marx's famous observation that "the expropriation and partial eviction of the rural population" helped to "hasten, as in a hothouse," the transition from feudalism to capitalism in England,[143] it would be accurate to say that "the First Nations of western Canada forged their relations with Europeans in the crucible of the fur trade."[144] From the founding of the Hudson's Bay Company by charter in 1670, the primary source of its profits came from Indigenous peoples, who (among many other tasks) hunted, trapped, and transported the items themselves to the posts in exchange for manufactured wares and consumables.[145] Plainly, Indigenous peoples were the company's "principal source of labour,"[146] and, though it is evident that the commercial fur trade was inconceivable without their labour, it is less straightforward how this was connected to the dispossession of land that came to define the Red River Colony. In the following section, I provide a broader geopolitical context for the surge of merchant credit, which – when extended to Indigenous producers – fuelled the commercial fur trade and the attendant processes of exploitation, distortion, and differentiation.

The Truck System

In the time leading up to and including the establishment of the infamous East India Company by royal charter under Elizabeth I in 1600, the emphasis was on imports of luxury goods, such as spices and silks.[147] Merchants competed for the shortest routes with the fewest hazards; these transport advantages in combination with increased demand led to the import trade overtaking the export cloth trade that dominated British mercantilism until the middle of the seventeenth century.[148] Within decades, it was the lure of a still shorter trade route that eventually led British merchants across the North Atlantic. Grand aspirations became realizable by pooling capital and credit, or such ambitions became feasible once the merchant capitalist was poised to "[risk] other people's capital instead of his own."[149] The roots of capitalism, therefore, are wedded to the international movement of goods and the availability of merchant credit, with discrete effects across the globe.[150]

As an outgrowth of the merchant credit flowing from at least the sixteenth century (in the European case),[151] by the seventeenth century it was not unusual for British workers to receive goods or services in exchange for their labour. Marx and Engels go so far as to claim that the practice of payment in company goods, known as the "truck system," was "universal in England" at that time.[152] To a degree, the truck system is recognized as a catalyst in the emergence of social relations more suited to the growth of capital. Merchants did operate in some instances as "'agents' in the transition to capitalism,"[153] but such a fate was not guaranteed. Rosemary Ommer observes that "merchant capital was dynamic, not merely parasitic and static with no transforming effect on labour"; in certain contexts, it was "a dynamic part of economic development," and in others it "contributed to the failure of a region to develop."[154] I reject the idea that there was a developmental "failure" in areas where capitalism did not flourish, but I agree with Ommer's main contention regarding the concurrence between the global reach of merchant capital and the variability of economic change at the local level.

Although there was no archetypal arrangement, the truck economy tended to involve connecting consumption to compensation, often permitting companies to retain control over labour by refusing to pay entire wages in a more transferable form of currency.[155] In some cases, individuals were extended credit for company goods in a manner that kept both production and consumption in house, or at least within the profitable purview of the company through collusion with commercial partners.[156] Such was the arrangement in the mid-nineteenth-century British nail-making industry, in which it was expected that the nailers would sell their products to the truck shop, usually adjacent to the warehouse where they received the iron, and that some of the cash received in the exchange would be spent at the shop – if not, then the nailers "ran the risk of early discharge in slack periods."[157] Shops stocked common grocery items and staples of labourers' quotidian subsistence, and prices fluctuated dramatically.[158] Two profit-making benefits were associated with this system: companies overpriced the goods, meaning that they effectively underpaid for labour, and companies did not have to keep stocks of cash on hand, scarce as it was in some locales and periods.[159]

Social and economic historian George Hilton observes that the truck system evolved differently across industries, jurisdictions, and eras.[160] One advantage for workers was the increased flexibility in payment schedules – their willingness to accept goods or company credit instead of cash sometimes meant earlier remuneration outside a standardized wage schedule.[161] The drawbacks, meanwhile, were considerable. By accepting consumer items in lieu of (or as a complement to) cash, the company could better ensure that money was not being spent on alcohol, which would sometimes cost them lost productivity because of payday revelry.[162] It was this disciplinary facet of the truck system that Hilton finds perplexing. As onerous as it was despised, in some industries and periods it was the preferred means of exercising control over the sumptuary practices of workers;[163] however, the prospect of disciplining workers through truck shop debt was not demonstrably more effective since workers themselves preferred cash, and a "cash advance would have established the debt" more directly.[164]

Statutory bans on trucking were in place in England as early as 1465, but it was not until the height of English industrialization that there was a proliferation of both the truck system and laws against it, notably the Truck Act of 1831[165] – a statute "enforced only here and there."[166] Hilton's analysis therefore raises a pertinent question that Marx and Engels were aware of nearly a century earlier: Given the relative inefficiency of the truck system alongside feeble attempts to curtail or prohibit it, why did the system endure in some industries and eras? I propose an explanation specific to British North America.

Extant systems of labour compulsion clashed with changing realities. The medieval guild system had a network of established regulatory frameworks that stipulated, *inter alia*, the conditions of membership,[167] whereas British feudal society was characteristically divided by assorted rules that likewise dictated the terms of labour.[168] Although the legal rights and obligations of subjects were once rather strictly allocated in accordance with the kind of labour that they performed, this loosened as the types of jobs proliferated beyond the confines of established labour classifications,[169] most perceptibly so in areas far removed from the legal order of the metropole. In British North America, the truck system both necessitated and accommodated new social obligations, as seen in fisheries in Newfoundland where "store credit was tied to production."[170] Prior to 1850, requisite fishing supplies were advanced from the merchant to the "planter" on the condition that the fish caught be sold back to the supplier at a price set by the latter.[171] From this credit advance arose a duty in the form of a "custom,"[172] in which the supplier covered the wages for the crew as the first debit on the profits from the haul, and the planter would end up returning to the same supplier for credit in the future. As Jerry Bannister remarks, "because merchants influenced both the costs of provisions and the price paid for codfish, planters often found themselves in debt when their accounts were settled in the autumn," which he observes led to a "cycle of debt and dependence."[173] In this type of arrangement, productivity was closely aligned with personal consumption, not of luxury goods alone, but also of items necessary for production and reproduction alike.

This sheds light on two of the advantages of the truck system in British North America: namely, its adaptability and its disciplinary function. This credit-backed disciplinary enterprise was easily adapted to the farthest reaches of the colonies as a type of "decentralized administration,"[174] in which social obligations stemming from customary practices could be tailored to debt-based obligations. Although British merchants and creditors might have been accustomed to the social hierarchies of their homelands, trucking was a relatively expedient way to insert themselves into networks of social obligation and establish relations of exchange in their favour. The truck economy offered an added disciplinary element when the consumption of goods for the purposes of production became bound up with consumption in general – at that juncture, the sumptuary practices of consumers influenced whether or not they could acquire the goods necessary for both commercial production and social reproduction. This was of particular concern regarding Indigenous producers involved in the fur trade. Indigenous networks of social obligation and gift-based reciprocity became entwined with the disciplinary facets of the truck economy through relations of debt; this manner of influencing both production and consumption became regularly deployed by HBC officers.

The Hudson's Bay Company

Compared with the East India Company, the Hudson's Bay Company pales in significance in terms of profits from international trade. But one of the most remarkable outcomes of the latter company's monopoly charter was evident in 1870 when the Hudson's Bay Company sold the interest in the land to the Dominion of Canada under the terms of the Deed of Surrender. In this transaction, the company received from Canada £300,000, the right to keep all of its trading posts and associated lands up to 50,000 acres, plus the right to claim and sell up to one-twentieth of the prairie lands.[175] The import of this transaction was not lost on Rosa Luxemburg, who refers to Canadian economic history as being "dominated to an even greater extent by big capital than elsewhere," referencing specifically the far-reaching HBC hold on fertile lands as evidence of the extent to which "the Canadian farmer was practically everywhere ensnared by capital and capitalist speculation."[176] Epochal as it was, this domination arose from gradual and irregular processes of dispossession that prevailed in the first two centuries of the company's history, sowed first by its founding charter.

Established under Charles II by charter in 1670, the Hudson's Bay Company was granted a monopoly on trade in the territories surrounding Hudson Bay, precisely yet prodigiously defined as all waterways that fed into the bay and those lands alongside and in between that had not already been claimed by "any other Christian Prince or State."[177] "Vast," as it is often described, can scarcely conjure up an intelligible sense of the scale of the millions of square kilometres of terrain in question.[178] The land was then named "Rupert's Land" after Prince Rupert, the king's cousin and the first governor of the Hudson's Bay Company,[179] and the explicitly possessive moniker leaves little ambiguity regarding colonial intent, variably described as intent that "waxed and waned"[180] or as "low-key imperialism."[181] The text of the royal charter of 1670 makes this possessiveness explicit – "the said Land be from henceforth reckoned and reputed as one of our Plantations or Colonies in America" – further declaring that the charter accords to the "true and absolute Lords and Proprietors" the authority "to have, hold, possess and enjoy the said Territory, Limits and Places."[182] These authoritative powers were exercised by the directors at the headquarters in London, which consisted of the seven-member committee (elected by shareholders) with the governor as the head. A class identified as "officers" populated the upper- and middle-management faction, whose responsibilities included trading furs and supervising workers.[183] Workers were classed using the formal feudalist legal designation "servants," a label that identified them as "dependents within a household"[184] who laboured in the territories to facilitate the trade.[185]

From the earliest days, the servants' principal intent was not to settle in the area but to repatriate to their homelands – usually the Orkney Islands of Scotland – after their contracts expired.[186] Although the Hudson's Bay Company was not a settler colonial initiative from the outset, its durable outposts and encroaching infrastructure – bolstered by its "figurative" but staunchly defended legal prerogative – positioned the company and its governor in a distinctly colonial relation to the Indigenous producers of so-called Rupert's Land. The original charter inaugurated a type of "figurative possession" in which the formal nature of the sovereignly inscribed dictate lent a lustre of legitimacy to the expansionary impulses of merchants, aristocrats, and royals.[187] Yet despite – or because of – the emanation of the company from royal decree, the legitimacy of the charter of 1670 was not absolute. One pressing consideration had to do with the legality of the monopoly: following the "Glorious Revolution" of 1688, conferrals of commercial activity had to receive assent from the British Parliament, which suggests that the Hudson's Bay Company's claim to a monopoly was prima facie false because of the absence of parliamentary assent.[188] The company won a brief reprieve in 1690 when its authority was buttressed by a statute entitled An Act for Confirming to the Governor and Company, Trading to Hudson's Bay, Their Privileges and Trade. The act stipulated "that such a company should have sufficient and undoubted powers, and authorities, privileges and liberties, to manage, order, and carry on the said trade,"[189] which confirmed the company's power to execute orders that promoted trade, including the right to punish transgressors.[190] But this endorsement had a terminal date attached. The act formally expired after seven years, a clause that might have reflected opinions raised in two petitions to the House of Commons by the felters of London, as well as British merchants involved in trade with New York and England, both anxious about how the continued monopoly might undermine their interests.[191]

This conflict between royal and parliamentary authority in Britain also caused confusion in the colonies. It was on the basis of royal command that lands were claimed, but the charter that operated as the vehicle of domination stipulated that administrative systems were a matter of prerogative and not compulsory. When governance structures were established in British North America, shifting jurisdictions and growing settler colonial administrations strained the might of royal sovereignty.[192] At the same time, the limits of the British Parliament were evident in how HBC directors exercised their prerogative. That the extension of privileges in 1690 ceased to carry formal weight had little bearing on the actual claims to authority, and the specific terms of the charter itself were never revisited by the British Parliament except to be selectively confirmed by individual pieces of legislation whenever doing so advanced a certain interest. For example, after an initial attempt by the Hudson's Bay Company in 1719 to locate the famed Northwest Passage, the British Parliament intervened in 1745 with a statute that offered a £20,000 reward for the discovery of a navigable northern waterway.[193] The parameters of this act contained notable provisions: namely, it did not "extend," nor was it a "prejudice" against, the Hudson's Bay Company's "estate, rights, or privileges," leaving intact the broad reach of the original charter.[194]

As expansive as it was, the language of the charter of 1670 did not guarantee the right to expropriate all lands, only those lands not previously claimed by "any other Christian Prince or State." This was a significant qualifier because, until the end of the Seven Years' War in 1763, rival Montreal-based fur traders operated relatively freely inland from Hudson Bay, and in doing so they made use of the varied skills of Indigenous producers and settlers in New France.[195] When the war ended, perhaps understandably France ceded its North American territories to Great Britain and kept the "jewels of the Atlantic economy,"[196] the more lucrative sugar-producing islands of the Caribbean.[197] Had the British desired immediate gains, the slave economy of the islands would have been ideal, though it was the continental land mass that offered the greatest potential for colonial expansion.[198] This land claim was contested, however, when a group of Montreal merchants argued that the North West Company had the first rights to the prairie territories. For decades, this inconvenient history of the early eighteenth century was difficult for the directors of the monopolistic Hudson's Bay Company to accept,[199] and the period after the Seven Years' War was most rivalrous as a result. To reduce costs during this phase of competition, the HBC committee adopted a retrenchment plan in 1810–11 that not only introduced piecework but also provided the backdrop for the company's first settler colonial initiative in the west, the Red River Colony. The actual settling of the territory did not occur until 1812, nearly 150 years after the company's founding charter. Although it was an expression of the company's colonial prerogative, more than anything else the Red River Colony proved that the scope and effects of its commands were far from guaranteed.

Up to the point of the retrenchment plan, the company deployed "paternalistic techniques in building its labour force," what others have identified as "pre-capitalist"[200] or "pre-industrial"[201] in nature. As Podruchny observes regarding the servant class, "the labor system of the fur trade was built largely on indentured servitude."[202] The Hudson's Bay Company preferred long-term servant contracts as pillars of its hierarchical paternalism, a structure thought to address the chronic problem of labour scarcity and bolster loyalty among servants to the company.[203] Servants signed "oaths" or "covenants," which blended aspects of the ancient expectations of fealty with traces of the transactional mindset more common in present-day employer-employee contracts.[204] To cultivate this balance, the Hudson's Bay Company hired men mostly from the "isolated, poor, and underdeveloped" Orkney Islands in northern Scotland, men thought to be accustomed to harsh labour conditions and hierarchical structures and, on that basis, more likely to acquiesce to meagre pay.[205] For the first century, when trade activity was consigned to posts along the bay, it is debatable whether labour compulsion was enacted more through debt and punishment or whether the paternalistic structure bred military-like loyalty.[206]

Records show that some Indigenous workers were also hired on a seasonal basis by the Hudson's Bay Company, specifically as canoemen and general labourers stationed at various posts.[207] This was more common in the period immediately after 1763, when the company briefly benefited from the temporary withdrawal of the French from the fur trade.[208] Around that time, Indigenous workers were hired as guides and interpreters, and sometimes they toiled alongside servants building and repairing canoes before leaving again to trap in the winter.[209] Unlike servants, however, Indigenous workers were not engaged for multi-year contracts but hired as needed, especially when labour was scarce or on the rare occasion when servants attempted to agitate for better terms.[210] On one such occasion in 1805, "servants, former servants, their friends, and their relatives" joined together to pressure HBC officers and the committee for higher wages,[211] and Indigenous workers were hired to force an end to the agitation.[212]

During the era in question, the truck system operated as a scheme of compensation and discipline. Alongside the legally sanctioned fealty to officers, servants incurred debts, were often paid in kind (e.g., with alcohol),[213] and subsisted exclusively on company goods either imported or procured through exchanges with Indigenous traders.[214] Since Indigenous peoples were not associated with the company through contractual servitude, the merchant-backed credit system was the paramount means of labour compulsion as it pertained to their fur trade–related productivity. As historical evidence of the HBC committee's early intention to use the truck economy to secure favourable standards of exchange with Indigenous producers, Ray quotes a dispatch from London to York Factory in 1689 in which the instructions to HBC officers were to "'allow more beaver in Truck for our goods then [sic] heretofore.'"[215] Toby Morantz, prolific historian of the fur trade in Eeyou Istchee, describes this relation in more detail: "As applied to the fur trade, the practice of extending credit involved an advance of merchandise to the hunter by the trader in the late summer or early fall, to be repaid by the hunter in fur pelts the following June."[216] The truck system was not a short-term strategy but was intrinsic to HBC labour compulsion practices over two centuries.

In a calculated speech to HBC shareholders, James Dodds addressed the future of the company at a pivotal time in 1866. The company was at a crossroads. With the founding of the Dominion of Canada imminent, at stake was the company's exclusive right to the continued expropriation of Rupert's Land. Dodds sensed that the HBC committee was withholding information that he thought vital to a sound business decision, leaving its owners ignorant of the prospects of the company should it have to relinquish its monopoly. He appears to have taken it as his duty to inform shareholders of the state of affairs, and in this capacity, he divulged a frank history of the Hudson's Bay Company as context for the predicament that it was facing. Dodds announced that the trade in goods was always secondary to the trade in furs, stating that the "goods-trade hitherto has only been a pendant of the Fur-trade, meant to do little more than supply the outfit; and its profits again have been kept up and swelled by the actual monopoly, long supposed legal."[217] Although his primary concern was the loss of what defined the company, namely the "long supposed legal" monopoly, this hierarchical classification of the company's spheres of trade provides two more insights into the structure and sustainability of its business model.

First, Dodds explains that "our Goods-trade was entirely barter – an enormous truck system; and formerly, from the ignorance of the Indians, we disposed of our goods at twenty times their real value."[218] Here he offers an unequivocal description of the exploitation behind the profit extraction strategy of the Hudson's Bay Company: trucking under preposterously skewed conditions. That "the ignorance of the Indians" was the basis of this exploitation is a gross misrepresentation, obviously, but even this open racism offers a glimpse of the mindset of capitalist speculators. Dodds admits that the profits were derived from truck system cheats and implies that the capitalist's cunning was at play in the exploitative exchanges – this idea of the crafty capitalist manipulating the levers of production is a supposition that I challenge throughout the chapters ahead.

Second, the success of the truck system was bound together with the Hudson's Bay Company's monopoly, as Dodds elucidates: "Now that this charm of our exclusive right has been dispelled, traders come up from the States and traverse the country ... So closely is competition grazing our heels, and stamping out the excessive profits which alone rendered our Goods-trade possible."[219] By inference, the royal charter did not yoke the company to a specific order and stifle its profitability; rather, because of the "charm" of its privilege, the company could sustain the profitable margins insofar as the truck system was buoyed by its exclusive right (and vice versa). With the transportation advantage that it held by not relinquishing its authority over the Hudson Bay basin, the company could transport and distribute larger quantities of foreign goods with relative ease, flooding the trade with items from its own ships and exercising discretion in terms of the quality and quantity of commodities in order to ensure profitable exchanges. By shoring up profitability through unequal exchange, the company retained its capacity to defend – if not expand – the scope of its monopoly, and it remained a primary importer of transatlantic goods. Dodds therefore reveals the significance of the truck system, specifically the degree to which it both blossomed from and reinforced the HBC's monopoly, as well as acknowledges that its success turned on the exploitation of Indigenous producers.

Exploitation
"When the fur trade people come in and understand the character of the Omushkegos, they take advantage of that nature. They encourage the hunters

to compete with each other, to bring more fur than the next guy, so [they] create some kind of hatred, and they resent each other," explains Louis Bird. "It changes the habit of the people."[220] The truck system was not a hegemonic imposition that corroded existing social relations of land in a swift and totalizing way; instead, it joined with customary practices to create an amalgam that, in combination with its monopoly, served the Hudson's Bay Company well for a considerable time. But built into the truck system was a tension born from divergent expectations: company men had mainly exploitative aims, leading them to engage in relations of customary reciprocity, whereas Indigenous producers often expected due regard from the company's representatives, as was the case with the "practice of providing provisions and relief" common to kinship relations among the Maškēkowak.[221]

The norms attendant to customary reciprocity discussed earlier are assessed here based upon how they intersected with commercial forces to produce relations of exploitation, specifically in the pre-1774 phase of the British North American fur trade. My objective in the latter half of this chapter is to show how exploitation, distortion, and differentiation are intrinsic to the processes of dispossession leading up to the formal settlement at Red River, as was the abiding albeit varying autonomy of Indigenous producers.

Until 1774, most of the Hudson's Bay Company's commercial activity occurred along the Hudson Bay coast. The company's infrastructure was concentrated on the export side of the process and not on inland production, a point evinced geographically by the peripheral placement of trading posts along the shoreline.[222] Logistically speaking, the docking of an HBC ship from London would be an almost annual event,[223] and the vessel would be laden with the objects exchanged for furs or food, offered as gifts, given as compensation to servants, or consumed for the purposes of the company's own utility, including the subsistence of its employees. York Factory on the western bayside was a common destination, where items received in 1770, for instance, fell into four categories: "producer goods," which included items such as twine, guns, and powder; "household goods" such as blankets and kettles; "tobacco and alcohol" by the pound and the gallon; and "other luxuries," which counted cloth, shirts, and buttons among the items.[224] Shipped goods not channelled into the truck system were otherwise necessary for the building and maintenance of company infrastructure, including shelters and canoes.

Indigenous peoples' principles of reciprocal exchange emphasized gift-giving, a practice that had both economic and customary dimensions associated with social relations of land.[225] With the infiltration of merchant credit and manufactured commodities, the Hudson's Bay Company had to advance a gift in a ceremony that preceded the exchange in order to acquire the coveted furs,[226] as

Ray elucidates: "The reciprocal gift-giving ceremony was an Indian institution which served to affirm friendship. Had the company refused to participate, no trade would have taken place."[227] The company budgeted for such gift-giving, as indicated in the tabulated records from York Factory in the mid to late eighteenth century that list expense lines for gifts, including everything from guns to lace.[228] Accounts from York Factory also depict the ceremonial dimensions of exchange with Indigenous populations (principally Maškēkowak), beginning at the trading post, where HBC officers presented gifts, then a procession to Indigenous peoples' living quarters, where a welcome ceremony took place and gifts were granted in return.[229] At least another day would pass before the actual fur trade took place, with the intermediary time spent performing songs and dances, smoking pipes, and making speeches.[230] Symbolically, the exchange was balanced, with each side offering presentations and listening to each other's speeches, lending an air of mutual recognition as opposed to coercive expropriation.[231] Strategically, this measure of deference to Indigenous peoples' customs was a minimum requirement in order to gain access to the objects of their labour, as Promislow explains: "In Cree and Anishnabek territories, for example, pipe ceremonies established and renewed brotherhood, a status necessary to trading relationships and that potentially entailed other obligations as well."[232] Promislow indicates that, beyond securing access to furs, commitments of support in times of conflict were also established, blending military strategy with legal and economic considerations.

Once the exchanges were regularized through the customary practices of gift-giving, reciprocal social obligations were meant to bind both parties to continued trade. Gifts offered and received took on multiple functions not only in terms of establishing the cooperative relationship and strategic alliances[233] but also by way of remuneration. This hints at the complexity of labour compulsion pertinent to Indigenous producers involved in the commercial exchange. Some refer to the prevailing arrangement as a type of "moditional"[234] or "mixed" economy. Ray classifies the system of exchange that dominated the fur trade up to 1867 as a kind of "credit/barter" arrangement in which credit was advanced to Indigenous traders and producers in amounts roughly indicative of the quantity and value of goods that the company expected to receive the next season.[235] Elsewhere, however, Ray and Freeman state that this "trading system is impossible to label neatly."[236] To explain this apparent vexation, Cary Miller offers a rough breakdown between "market exchange" and "gift exchange" economies: the former involves "the exchange of commodities that establishes a relationship between the objects exchanged"; the latter "establishes a relationship between the partners engaged" in which "social relationships were affirmed by the gifts rather than the gifts themselves representing the true value of the exchange."[237] These relationships were essential in terms of regularized access (for Indigenous producers) to items that facilitated the labour of trapping in order to supply the commercial fur trade and (for HBC officers) to the furs themselves – a type of "down payment for future services."[238] On this point, C.A. Gregory explains that commercial exchange "establishes a relationship between the objects," whereas gift-giving "establishes a relationship between the subjects,"[239] which reflects the commercial and customary dimensions of gift exchange. In actual practices of exchange, the demarcation between the economic and the social is not so clear-cut.

The exchange for furs in this era involved a company-appointed Indigenous "middleman" or "trade captain,"[240] a specialized agent who travelled with his entourage and the furs to a trading post along the shores of Hudson Bay.[241] Although much remains unknown about their specific activities, it appears that trade captains assumed a significant amount of risk as transporters of the furs to the posts and that their skills as negotiators had effects on the outcomes of bartering. As traders, they were not the primary producers of the commodities themselves but laboured as transporters who exchanged furs for tools and assorted provisions that, in turn, facilitated trappers' labour – hence their other alias of middlemen. The commensurability of items exchanged was variable and relative, though the process itself was rather standardized,[242] with a preliminary gift exchange, followed by gifts from the Hudson's Bay Company to the Indigenous trade captain, which were then redistributed among his entourage.[243] Trade captains bartered on at least two separate occasions: at the one end using the commodities received from the company and at the other using the goods received from the trappers, who often lacked direct trading contact with the heads of HBC trading posts, known as "factors" or "masters."[244] The commodities acquired by trade captains in the exchange with Indigenous trappers became the gifts and commodities exchanged with bayside factors.

In some instances, trade captains among the Maškēkowak were gifted a military-style coat of a distinctive red or blue, differentiating them within their group and broadcasting their allegiance to a given company.[245] Although this was a way of transacting with Indigenous societies farther inland, on occasion foreign traders less familiar with the cultural particularities of the varied Indigenous peoples misidentified men as leaders.[246] In her assessment of the Maškēkowak at York Factory in the late seventeenth century, Promislow observes that, despite the occasional misidentification by HBC officers, these appointments did not cause lasting ruptures to their cultural fabric, and she suggests that these designations be understood as instances of "cultural recognition."[247] Although it might be possible to discern a degree of respectability behind the "strategic 'domestication'" or "accommodation" of Indigenous peoples' customs by the foreign traders, these appointments also mark the infiltration of "mercantile spheres of influence" into Indigenous societies.[248] Trade ceremonies represented a symbolic rapprochement, but there was no actual "exchange of equivalents."[249] In mistaking estrangement for recognition, there is a risk of complicity with the illusion of equivalent exchange, a complicity that can corrupt efforts to distill the processes of "gradual dispossession."[250]

Inducements for greater productivity were made to these trade captains and not directly to the Indigenous trappers, with factors offering additional gifts on the condition of abundant returns the next season.[251] As officers of the Hudson's Bay Company, factors received remuneration mostly in monetary form and did not consume the key objects received in the trade, namely furs. Homogeneous in terms of class background, they were supposedly of honourable stock and ignorant of privation. They operated in conditions of "isolation or semi-autonomy,"[252] and they were given incentives to remain honest and faced reprimands and demotions if they were found cheating.[253] Ann Carlos interprets this as the company's attempt to control "opportunistic behavior" that stemmed from the factors' discretionary power in the trade.[254] This latitude might have allowed independent factors to exercise a type of "decentralized administration," a template for colonial governance that became indispensable for the establishment and administration of the Red River Colony.[255]

Factors were expected to recover the expenses of the gift-giving ceremony and make extra or "overplus" on the trade.[256] "Overplus" is a term that appears in the HBC records; it "represented the gains traders made by shortchanging their Native customers" and was "a form of profit that company traders returned to London every year as part of the value of their fur returns."[257] Still more precisely, overplus comprised the profits gained in the course of trucking: HBC profits were extracted through "cheats"[258] – undervaluing the labour of Indigenous peoples and the products of that labour, having them incur debts in the process of acquiring tools, and shorting them by offering less than the stipulated amounts of "cloth, shot, and powder."[259] It was in this indirect manner that trappers in particular were subjected to a "basic form of surplus extraction,"[260] although the nature of the production of furs did not lend itself to straightforward means of labour compulsion. Attempts to extract the most profit from the truck system regularly collided with Indigenous peoples' agency exercised on the ground.

Demand and Profit

Labour supply was elastic in the sense that there was no fixed output or time,[261] evidence of a relation of "nonalienated labor" in which the labour of the Indigenous producer was not a commodity bought and consumed by the

Hudson's Bay Company.[262] Also, it seemed that Indigenous trappers offered for trade only as many furs as they needed to in order to obtain the goods that they required for subsistence, which could indicate that theirs was a type of "inelastic demand."[263] Both claims – elastic productivity and inelastic demand – point to Indigenous trappers as relatively autonomous producers, but they diverge when it is a matter of surmising what motivated demand. To shed light on the particulars of the profit-making strategy of the Hudson's Bay Company, I explore the controversies associated with the question of consumer demand.

On the one hand, that Indigenous producers involved in the commercial fur trade did not flood the posts with furs suggests that the societies in question lacked any conception of either private property or profit,[264] and absent a drive for private accumulation they were exiled to the realm of strictly extra-economic compulsion. On the other hand, it was not cultural factors that dictated demand but economic factors: namely, the increase in "the price of furs" also informed economic behaviour.[265] However, either view, if taken too far, twists the question of demand by adhering to misleading notions of *homo economicus* as the benchmark of rationality. The first explanation does so by exclusion and veers close to the racist practice of objectification flagged earlier; the second explanation does so by inclusion and validates a fatalism of capitalist rationality that looks to consumer choice as a gauge of relative autonomy. The former is more common in early- to mid-twentieth-century writings on the subject, whereas the latter appears in late-twentieth-century and early-twenty-first-century works.

In their assessment of the records kept at York Factory, Carlos and Lewis find that, "in terms of their consumption choices, Natives were responding to price much as do modern consumers," suggesting that, as the prices for furs increased, so did the output of Indigenous producers.[266] This appears to contradict the commonly held view that Indigenous producers trapped only as many furs as could procure the goods that they required in exchange, behaviour that the authors see as similar to "peasant behavior in the face of rising wages."[267] Carlos and Lewis categorize this as "unindustrious," whereas in an "industrious society" there is an increase in consumption matched by an increase in productivity.[268] In making the case that Indigenous producers' demands were symptomatically industrious, they note a rise in the consumption of tobacco, alcohol, and luxury items (e.g., cloth and beads) and a decline in the consumption of producer and household goods between 1740 and 1770.[269] This was measured using a series of economic formulas, accounting for subsistence, utility, labour time, output, and prices of furs, all of which form the basis of their conclusion that "Native groups were taking part in the consumer revolution of the eighteenth century."[270] I agree that these groups were implicated in the "consumer revolution" as a way of questioning the assumption that strictly extra-economic compulsion dictated relations, but I am less inclined to classify Indigenous peoples' consumer demand at any level of implied commensurability with that of peasants – a commensurability that veils more than it uncovers.

"Motives must always remain, in some part, obscure,"[271] warns E.P. Thompson. If the "process of accumulation" itself is "elastic and spasmodic,"[272] then there is reason to question why individual motives in production and consumption should be any different. But debate regarding the motives of Indigenous peoples has suffered from precisely such an expectation, shaped by "market-oriented, neo-classical" expectations of "economic motivation"[273] and disclosed by the dependency thesis already discussed. More attention needs to be paid to the productive processes of the fur trade in general and the nature of Indigenous peoples' agency in particular.

Rather than focus on exploitative relations from a production angle, Carlos and Lewis focus on the inward flow of goods from a consumption angle: that is, they focus on increasing commodity possession instead of growing dispossession. What gets lost is the division of labour between trapper and trade captain, a division that arguably became more pronounced as the latter "acquired status by redistributing wealth."[274] It is difficult to assume that the trapper and the trade captain had the same motives given their variable placement in the process – to assume that is to flatten the analysis. Also, the spheres of influence diverged in another way: HBC officers could establish more direct relations with Indigenous producers designated as the "homeguard," those who remained near the coastline and supplied provisions and labour to the bayside posts. Since they did not venture inland with the same frequency, they developed a closer relationship with the Europeans and became more regular consumers of manufactured goods.[275] Such variability underscores the need to be careful when differentiating between the Indigenous producer and the Indigenous consumer, two subjectivities that become collapsed in a truck economy that entails the "exchange of labour for goods."[276] Given the complex nature of the social relations of land, it is not as straightforward as it might appear to be to distinguish the two, especially given the overlap between compensation arising from the exchange of goods and any discernible pattern of "Native expenditure" or consumer demand.[277]

In a conventional capitalist wage labour arrangement,[278] an individual receives money in exchange for labour, which the capitalist consumes in the production of a commodity. In this region and era of the fur trade, the commodity was produced by labour, but the labour was inalienable; instead, what was "paid" for (by an advance of credit – or more aptly, by the extension of debt – in a gift exchange) was the product itself and not the labour as such. Arguably, the transactional moment of the individual trade is two moments collapsed into

48   *A Legacy of Exploitation*

one. It is the moment when the productive labour is compensated; however, because there is a degree of choice in terms of the form of compensation, it is also a moment of consumption exercised as consumer demand. Money as a universal bearer of value does not enter the exchange as remuneration for Indigenous peoples' labour. From the perspective of HBC officers, the act of compensation for the labour of Indigenous traders and trappers was simultaneously an act of consumption by those traders and trappers.

For company officers, compensation and consumption not only remained separate moments in the formal exchange but also had an extra transaction that allowed for the realization of a profit. The furs received by the company in the exchange went into additional trade circuits: that is, the realization of profit through sale. When the furs were exchanged for money on the European market,[279] the Hudson's Bay Company realized the profit not because of the sale price as such but because "the furs received were of greater value than the goods that had been traded for them" according to the company's adopted measures of value.[280] Despite the lack of money as a universal equivalent as a regular means of remuneration for Indigenous peoples' labour, the company used a standard to calculate relative value: made beaver (MB). As the official unit of measure, MB "was the price of a prime beaver skin, either parchment or coat,"[281] and the value of the objects imported from Europe was calculated in MB. For example, in the mid-1700s at York Factory, the official price for one gallon of brandy was 4MB, and the official price for a blanket was 7MB.[282] As the "official standard,"[283] MB represented a baseline to express the value of items exchanged, in particular the value in MB of manufactured goods. The items received in the exchange, such as the furs themselves, were measured according to the "comparative standard."[284] There was also a relative equivalency measure that in practice functioned to ensure inequality: the *factor's* or *double standard*. This measure allowed the factor to exercise his discretion by calculating the least risky way (to avoid insulting Indigenous trade captains) of securing either more fur in relation to the official standard or the same amount of fur for less than the official standard.

For instance, records from York Factory in 1730 show that the official value of goods expended by the company in that year's trade was the equivalent of 31,834MB, plus 1,900MB for gifts (for a total of 33,734MB). Meanwhile, the value of furs received was 47,656MB, amounting to an overplus equivalent to 13,922MB.[285] This was the essence of the truck system: "The value of the goods traded was always less than that of the furs due to the application of the double standard."[286] Once the gift instalments and the sales of the furs on the European markets are accounted for, two transactional moments of profit become apparent: one is the direct commodity-for-commodity exchange, in which furs were acquired according to the double standard, and the other is the commodity-for-money exchange, in which the monetary value of the furs was realized at the point of sale.

There were differentiated experiences associated with the practices of consumption and compensation – relations standardized by the company to safeguard profitability and, by extension, exploitation. As Alexander Anievas and Kerem Nişancıoğlu deftly observe, "differentials in the rates and forms of exploitation generated by uneven but combined labour processes can serve to facilitate capitalist accumulation in new and unprecedented ways."[287] Given that these experiences were differentiated, the evidence is mounting about why the term "relative" is a necessary qualifier when discussing the autonomy of Indigenous producers.

Relative Autonomy

In the global expansion of capitalist accumulation, it was standard practice that the "commodity economy" was established on the back of the extant mode of production, which appears to have been the case with the British North American fur trade.[288] By introducing commodities, shifting productive energies, and courting adaptable relations of exchange, the producer's autonomy became strained in accordance with changes to the social relations of land that spanned the network of interdependencies across allied Indigenous societies.[289] The appointment of trade captains was one overt measure of inserting company interests into Indigenous societies. These men, as the bearers of commodities tasked with ensuring the fluidity of circulation, were beachheads in the expansion of capitalism, manifested as an amalgam of sorts among customary practice, commodity production, and colonial dispossession. This is akin to how Richard White explains aspects of his notion of "the middle ground": "I presume the persistence of many aspects of the old alongside the creation of the new."[290] A still more revelatory take comes from Mamdani, who observes that these adapted customs necessarily borrowed from tradition but became increasingly "free of traditional restraint,"[291] which suggests that customary practices can be conduits of accumulation and not mere extra-economic fetters.

Because of the factor's standard, the relative value of goods traded in exchange for furs remained favourable to the Hudson's Bay Company regardless of the variable prices that the furs eventually fetched at auction. Often without direct contact with the fur producers themselves, one strategy that the factors used to entice greater productivity was to promise more and/or higher-quality gifts as credit to the trade captains on the condition of still greater returns the following season.[292] Consequently, gift-giving – a hallmark of customary reciprocity – was targeted not only as a point of entry into existing social relations of land but also as a means of accelerating dispossession. This involved distortion by means of incentivized demand that abetted the proliferation of merchant credit–backed "unequal exchange."[293] In practice, gift-giving combined with the truck system in a manner that had a hand in both obscuring and normalizing unequal exchange, and the customs that constituted the new norms of exchange were "neither just arbitrarily invented ... nor faithfully reproduced" but "crafted out of raw material on the ground and in contention with it,"[294] a strategy of commercial profit that involved both continuity and change.

At the time, the Hudson's Bay Company was becoming integrated into "capitalist commodity production,"[295] as it was shifting from a feudalist structure with a mercantilist imperative to a capitalist enterprise competing for market share. Through this truck system, some Indigenous producers were likewise becoming integrated into the circuits of capital to a certain extent, as producers of raw materials and consumers of foreign goods, but they did not undergo a fatalistic metamorphosis into a wage-labouring proletariat. Marx contends that this is what tends to occur when production is drawn into the capitalist process of circulation, yet in this instance the integration into commodity circulation and the normalization of "commodity-dealing" were not sufficient conditions for such a transformation.[296] That the furs were appropriated through unequal exchange and sent into the global commodity market does not mean that the means of appropriation were capitalist as such; rather, it was a gradual and irregular transformation that occasioned different types of social stratification. Crucial in this regard was the proletarianization of the servant class itself. Plainly, their proletarianization was closely connected to the exploitation of Indigenous producers.

Exploitation defined the sites of exchange, yet the particulars of production left intact – in a disparate and relative manner – the autonomy of Indigenous producers. Consider, for instance, that it was not possible to intensify fur trade production, as one would in a manufacturing setting, by housing it under one roof and extending the working day. For fur trading outfits, this entailed a frustrating lack of permanent or reliably increasing demand for foreign goods: incentives for more furs by plying trade captains with more gifts were a "gentle compulsion" aimed at influencing production, but once the producer's needs were met they might have been disinclined to request more goods from HBC factors through the trade captains.[297] Not surprisingly, HBC officers thought little of the truck system, and as early as 1739 they wanted to "'end the practice of allowing debts,'" tersely described by the London committee as "'so evil a practice.'"[298] This antipathy toward the merchant credit-backed truck system was an expression of the lack of direct control over production, although its abolishment was unlikely because it was the principal means of labour compulsion. As such, the social relations of land that assured Indigenous producers some measure of autonomy persisted to varying degrees alongside measures of exploitation through unequal exchange, distortion of the principles of reciprocity, and differentiation within Indigenous societies and later in relation to settlers.

In oversimplified terms exemplified by Dodds, one party exercised discretionary power, and the other reacted passively with a stubbornness born from a lack of clarity regarding the formulas behind these standards. But geopolitical intrigues and fluctuations in the global market for furs influenced the factor's standard, and so did the Indigenous producers themselves. Ray explains that Indigenous trade captains did not "tolerate radical departures from accepted norms," suggesting that, although they had "relatively inflexible attitudes," they sometimes accepted modest variations of the standards.[299] He also highlights the agency of the trade captain, who negotiated with the HBC factor when he recognized that he was receiving less powder for one pelt compared with previous trades. Even with these formalized standards of measurement, trade captains retained some leverage and were able to influence the outcomes of exchange.[300]

On this point, Roxanne Dunbar-Ortiz explains that "precolonial Indigenous societies were dynamic social systems with adaptation built into them. Fighting for survival did not require cultural abandonment. On the contrary, the cultures used already-existing strengths, such as diplomacy and mobility, to develop new mechanisms required to live in nearly constant crisis."[301] That the legacy of the fur trade is one of dispossession does not mean that there was no agency among Indigenous peoples – accord often existed alongside discord,[302] and capacities for adaptation predate commercial influence. It is important to keep in check the erroneous tendency to view the expansion of the commercial fur trade as an undifferentiated and undifferentiating process, a historical erasure that ignores the agency of Indigenous peoples involved in the commercial fur trade and paints an all-around misleading version of the distinct colonial forces at play. Yet, in rebuffing the dependency thesis, a void is created in the standard accounts of the commercial fur trade that is in danger of being filled with flawed notions of equal exchange, benevolent capitalism, and voluntary dispossession. One way to avoid this is to keep in sight the transformations of Indigenous peoples' autonomy and the wider geopolitical context within which these changes occurred.

Mamdani offers two warnings worth keeping in mind when it comes to the analysis of colonial relations. First, he contends that "there was nothing voluntary about custom in the colonial period,"[303] stating in plain language that, although customary practices continued, they were not "as they always had been": that is, conducted on the terms of Indigenous societies alone. Second, he explains that it is "important not to see in the specificity of experience nothing but its idiosyncrasy";[304] treating the specific constellation of interests and forces as intrinsic to that moment and locality severs its connections to the broader context and, as a consequence, limits our capacity to comprehend how the particular practices associated with the fur trade were part of transformations occurring on a global scale.

As revolutionary fervour and reactionary fear were in the air, and with the commercial fur trade entering a new expansionary phase across the continent,[305] the Royal Proclamation of 1763 showed that the British placed a premium on the pacification of Indigenous populations.[306] Colonizers were drawing borders across Indigenous peoples' lands – hostile acts that continue to be resisted today.[307] Among lawmakers and company officials alike, the related matters of access and jurisdiction increasingly collided with Indigenous peoples' autonomy, both as it was practised and as it was "tacitly" acknowledged in the preamble to the proclamation.[308] Despite this, the HBC committee never relinquished its monopolistic claim to Indigenous peoples' lands, resources, and labour. In response to challenges from rivals to their exclusive privileges, HBC directors and officers sought new avenues to fortify this claim as the fur trade entered a period of pitched competition.

2

Monopoly and Competition

Contests over Indigenous Peoples' Labour and Land

WITH NEW COUNTRIES and companies on the horizon in the post-1774 era, it is impossible to forgo an account of the broader political climate within which the Red River Colony was conceived, but this account must include an awareness of the acute perils of settler colonial historiography. Jodi Byrd explains that "the United States deploys a paradigmatic Indianness to facilitate its imperial desires,"[1] a paradigm in which Indigenous peoples are the cipher of a fatalistic notion of colonialism, which in turn implies that "conquest" was a singular and absolute event. Audra Simpson, writing about Kahnawake Mohawks, clarifies that "they continue to live under the conditions of this occupation, its disavowal, and its ongoing life, which has required and still requires that they give up their lands and give up themselves."[2] Once Indigenous peoples are instrumentalized in the process of historical whitewashing, the consequence is a denial of what Emma LaRocque refers to as "the presentness of their colonization,"[3] akin to what Jill Doerfler refers to as "terminal histories of the dominant society."[4] These implicit tendencies appear in writings about the fur trade spanning at least two centuries.[5] One means of resisting the singular-absolutist notion of conquest is to examine the processes of dispossession more closely and to make explicit the ways that Indigenous peoples variably adapted to and resisted them.

The truck system was exploitative, yet Indigenous peoples exercised autonomy because they were neither wholly disciplined by, nor dependent on, the emergent commodity economy thanks to the nature of fur trade production in general and their social relations of land in particular. This autonomy became both more pronounced and more contested in the mounting competition of the late eighteenth century, a time when an array of geopolitical changes was taking place and when the monopoly of the Hudson's Bay Company was being targeted. Merchants from Montreal financed fur trading expeditions to offset the loss of access to the United States after the Revolutionary War, which fuelled competition in the northwest and brought additional Indigenous societies more directly into the commercial trade. This competition also strained existing relations between the companies and the Indigenous producers; disease and scarcity meant that furs were at a premium, which fuelled a host of transformations leading up to the settlement at Red River. Commercial values increased,[6] which meant more leverage among Indigenous producers but at a cost to existing social relations of land.

54 *A Legacy of Exploitation*

In this chapter, I trace the intersecting legal, economic, and geopolitical facets of the intensification of competition between rival companies in an era when each side sought to exert control over lands, resources, and peoples. Relevant historical materials divulge the extent to which the processes of dispossession were exercised to varying degrees across different locales, and – though the consequences of these efforts were mixed – never far from the directing minds of the companies was a wariness of the relative autonomy of Indigenous producers.

Border Making

Prior to the concession of New France to the British, assorted jurisdictional authorities were attached to a range of inland trading posts. As adumbrated by Wayne Stevens a century ago, first were "free posts," such as at Michilimackinac (a narrow strait separating Lakes Michigan and Huron), where a licence to conduct trade was required;[7] second were the "king's posts," such as at Niagara, where "the trade was carried on in behalf of the king, from whose magazines the merchandise used was supplied"; and third were the "leased" posts, where exclusive privileges to trade were granted to individuals in exchange for rent, such as at Sault Ste. Marie.[8] French traders operated in accordance with the jurisdictional authority of the post, but since they lacked the exclusive privileges of a monopoly most of their activity occurred at the free posts. After 1763, the leasing system was abolished in favour of a licence to trade extended to "all of his majesty's subjects."[9] On these terms, the loyalist merchants moving north to Montreal displaced the French monied class but used to their advantage the skills and knowledge of the voyageurs[10] – a class of workmen from New France who had long been active in the fur trade. Thereafter, the king's posts were available for rent. For example, at the cost of a thousand louis,[11] the rights to posts along the St. Lawrence River were secured by one Montreal outfit for twenty-one years.[12]

As the reach of the British crown swelled with the defeat of the French and shrank with the loss to the United States, the quest for guaranteed returns on investments informed reactions to evolving jurisdictional boundaries. The relative weight that commercial fur trade interests carried in the prelude to the Revolutionary War is debatable,[13] though it is certain that the outcome of the war had a significant effect on the future of the trade. One consequence was the contentious boundary erected to restrict the trade activity that Quebec merchants were permitted to undertake in newly claimed US territories.[14] Prior to the Revolutionary War, there was an active transit route between Albany and Montreal,[15] but then divided loyalties and shifting allegiances led to new rules on the transportation of goods, interrupting the waterway passages between

Monopoly and Competition 55

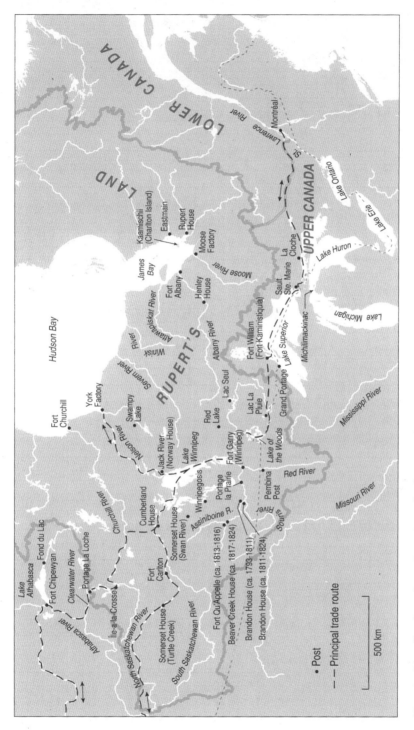

Figure 2.1 Map of key fur trade sites from Montreal to the Great Lakes, Hudson Bay, and the Saskatchewan River | Cartographer: Eric Leinberger

New York City and the Great Lakes.[16] War precipitated a series of restrictions on the movement of goods as a way for the fledgling republic to limit the commercial traffic that might benefit its enemies.[17] This spoke to its apprehension that the beneficiaries of this north-south traffic were the colonies of loyalists whose allegiances led them to migrate north, as well as the Indigenous societies that fought against US interests during the conflict.

The end of the Revolutionary War meant new regulations on the transportation of goods in 1780, with a formal ban on private vessels on the Great Lakes and an overall limit on the number of passes that a given merchant could make.[18] This served the British interests well since the interior trade routes became lined with strategic military bases. Control of the fur trade was amplified when the British Parliament enacted trade barriers between the United States and the British colonies, stipulating that "all furs must first be sent to London before reexport to the United States."[19] Such legislation was advantageous to the Hudson's Bay Company, although the Montreal merchants were not inclined to acquiesce. By the mid-1780s, the Montrealers expressed dissatisfaction regarding their diminished capacity to transport as much and as frequently as they once could.[20] Letters of protest multiplied over the subsequent years, awash with claims that these rules made the illicit shipment of goods more likely and allowed US interests in the fur trade to supplant those of the Montreal merchants.[21] Although some leeway within the terms of the regulations was granted, the trend tilted toward limiting access. Once admittance via Grand Portage – at the west end of Lake Superior (on the US side, just south of present-day Thunder Bay) – became restricted by the increasing formalization of the border with the United States, a new interior route was established via Kaministiquia, initially a French fort that became Fort William, now part of Thunder Bay.[22]

The Treaty of Paris of 1783 signalled the formal end of hostilities between the United States and Britain, though in reality these negotiations continued for some time because the execution of the clauses remained under dispute. One source of contention was the reluctance to abandon posts situated along the nascent boundary, a matter aggravated by the lack of a definite timeline that would have stipulated an end date for British withdrawal.[23] An uneasy détente followed, with both sides keen to avoid provoking hostilities. On the northern side, the newly installed governor general of the Canadas, Lord Dorchester (Guy Carleton prior to being elevated in 1786), maintained the status quo through 1787 "to bolster the defense of the occupied posts by an Indian buffer hostile to the advance of the Americans."[24] By the late 1780s, however, the new republic was straining under the pressure wrought by the appetite for sovereignty among individual state legislatures.[25]

Although borderlines shifted in the intervening period between 1783 and 1795, the Indigenous peoples living along the boundaries were mostly disinclined to accept an imposition by either the British or the Americans.[26] In her writing on this era, Roxanne Dunbar-Ortiz explains that "Britain's withdrawal in 1783 did not end military actions against Indigenous peoples but rather was a prelude to unrestrained violent colonization on the continent," noting that this was when "a culture of resistance" was born.[27] Concessions on any side – Indigenous societies included – were few and tenuous. One possible pathway proposed by the British was the founding of "a neutral Indian barrier state," which would operate as a buffer zone between the United States and British holdings to the north.[28] This was not agreed to, and as the prospect of war loomed[29] George Washington made use of violent tactics to clear the land so that it could be alienated and sold, with the profits going into the public purse in the hopes of building a standing army.[30] Notably, Washington pursued this tack after the decisive victory in 1791 of allied Indigenous groups – representatives of the Ojibwe, Ottawa, Potawatomi, Lenape, Miami, and Shawnee – over US General Arthur St. Clair and his complement of soldiers, which occurred on the western border of the present-day state of Ohio.[31]

Farther north, meanwhile, the powers of the provinces of Canada were divided by the Constitutional Act of 1791.[32] Increasingly, following that act, treaties were used by administrators in Upper Canada as a means of dispossessing Indigenous peoples of "millions of acres for colonial occupation by British emigrants," whereas until then treaties were used in part as a means of building alliances. Some historians suggest that this reflected a shift from a relatively diplomatic approach toward Indigenous societies – characterized by the espousal of a nation-to-nation framework – to an agenda to "civilize" Indigenous peoples according to British and Christian standards.[33]

In the United States, the dividing lines were already set: Democrats, believing that the health of the economy relied on good British relations, wanted to maintain favourable terms; Republicans abhorred the British monopoly and its powers over the independent United States;[34] and Indigenous peoples actively resisted murderous territorial incursions by US militias.[35] An attempt to close the gaps of the Treaty of Paris of 1783 led to the Treaty of Amity, Commerce and Navigation (commonly known as the Jay Treaty), the negotiations for which were headed by Chief Justice John Jay for the Americans and Foreign Secretary Lord Grenville for the British. It passed in the Senate with a comfortable majority in 1795 but met greater opposition in the House of Representatives, where some found it "highly injurious to the interests of the United States."[36] The Jay Treaty has been praised by many historians as the fruit of the first attempt at diplomacy by the United States as an independent state; more salient is that it seemed to "pave the way for Indian removal and white settlement ... by securing the withdrawal of the British garrisons from the western posts south of the Great Lakes."[37] These were important concerns for the commercial interests of the HBC committee but of growing existential relevance for Indigenous peoples across the continent.

On the surface, this agreement risked stripping the Hudson's Bay Company of the British state-sponsored girders established in part to protect its monopoly; however, with respect to the fur trade in more general terms, the third article of the treaty nominally permitted the status quo. In fact, the company won an exemption: British subjects, US citizens, and Indigenous peoples were allowed "freely to pass and repass by land or inland navigation, into the respective territories and countries ... (the country within the limits of the Hudson's bay [sic] Company only excepted)."[38] Caveats of this sort that secured ongoing trade with Britain irked Republicans. Although the Jay Treaty restricted the movement of British ships in the northeastern United States, there was a sense that the "porous border" that remained did not go far enough to offset the advantages of British commerce and boost American interests.[39] For the Canadas, initially at least, there was little advantage lost with the advent of the treaty.[40]

The North West Company

The interlude after the Proclamation of 1763 and prior to the Revolutionary War was filled with uncertainty for the Montreal merchants, an era that made for fast friends and even faster enemies. Without the backing of royal prerogative, the North West Company was established through mergers and takeovers headed by Scottish merchants operating out of Montreal who incurred debts to finance the various iterations of the company.[41] It was more than geopolitics, however, that informed the NWC challenge to the HBC monopoly. To understand the many social, political, economic, and legal considerations that fuelled the rivalry is also to comprehend the HBC turn toward settler colonialism as an effort to domesticate production and curb the relative autonomy of Indigenous producers.

The Hudson's Bay Company's shift inland gradually transformed the past century of reliance on Indigenous trade captains, who had defined the company's business model.[42] This dependence was one of the elements that helped the Indigenous societies around the Hudson Bay area to maintain ownership of their means of production and some discernible control over their well-being, for they retained the exclusive advantage in terms of skill that the company benefited from without "mastering" it in their own right.[43] But Samuel Hearne's founding of Cumberland House on the Saskatchewan River in 1774 was the beginning of the end of this practice.[44] In subsequent decades, HBC traders erected posts close to the activities of the North West Company, eventually installing themselves at the northernmost point of the Assiniboine River (in present-day Saskatchewan) in 1790.[45] The Hudson's Bay Company's shift inland was met with waves of activity in Montreal, a veritable "trend toward consolidation," as described by historian Jennifer Brown.[46] She explains that changes were taking place in the upper echelons of the Montreal fur trade companies as British businessmen started taking over companies once helmed by French Canadians. Although the mainly Scottish partnerships that formed most of the iterations of the North West Company did not have the benefits of a charter like the Hudson's Bay Company, they did have the advantage of kinship-based allegiances, which congealed especially among the segment of loyalist migrants to what was then the province of Quebec in the wake of the Revolutionary War.[47]

Some historians consider the formal nativity of the North West Company to have occurred in 1787 when there was an injection of funds on behalf of the credit-backed Montreal merchants.[48] Later, after retirements and more investments, the XY Company (XYC, the "new" North West Company) was founded in 1798.[49] Headed by famed explorer Alexander Mackenzie, this outfit became Simon McTavish's and the "old" North West Company's chief rival until the merger of the new and old companies in 1804, which occurred only after McTavish's death. The timing of these consolidations and financial influxes up to 1804 are significant. Expenses associated with transportation from Montreal to Kaministiquia, then onward to the plains and finally to the northern climes of Lake Athabasca were exorbitant compared with the costs of the same journey via Hudson Bay.[50] The more the North West Company moved into the northwest, the more dependent it became on Indigenous peoples' labour for subsistence. Because canoes were not viable cargo vessels, a network of stations also needed to be erected along the Assiniboine River, where posts would offer opportunities not only to trade for provisions but also to store supplies.[51] From the time the goods were requested to the time they arrived at the post, almost two years elapsed.[52] Consequently, interest on the merchants' debts increased since the partners still had to hire the labourers, front the costs of goods exchanged with the Indigenous traders, and pay for the canoes – meanwhile the commodities themselves took longer to realize as capital on foreign markets.[53]

Nevertheless, "the progress of capitalist production ... lays open, in the form of speculation and the credit system, a thousand sources of sudden enrichment."[54] The North West Company's profits eventually realized were worth the outlay: among the "sources of sudden enrichment" were the unequal exchanges with Indigenous traders, as well as the exploitation of the more than one thousand men employed by the company by 1805.[55] With management ranks increasingly occupied by men from the British Isles, labourers were mostly French – young men often on three-year terms – as well as those with mixed backgrounds.[56] The French voyageurs had been involved in the inland trade for much longer than the English,[57] acquiring during that time intimate knowledge of the terrain and techniques that W.L. Morton suggests led them to become more "Indian-ized" than the British coastal traders.[58] This might explain in part the "ethnicity reinforced class divisions" of the North West Company,[59] which prevented the upward mobility of the labourers and allowed the primarily Highland Scots to aspire to the rank of "wintering partner" of the company.[60] So named because they wintered inland, these partners could claim a more comprehensive understanding of the inland fur trade compared with the highest-ranking HBC men,[61] whose business stayed bayside until the late eighteenth century while they remained headquartered in London until 1970.[62] As a conspicuous testament to how steadfastly the HBC brass guarded their royal entitlements – the main point of contention with the North West Company – it was not until the 300th anniversary of the company that Queen Elizabeth II signed supplements to the charter that rescinded the monopoly and moved the headquarters to Winnipeg.[63]

Like the Hudson's Bay Company, the Montreal merchants of the North West Company adopted an officer-servant hierarchical structure. Contracts, offered in Montreal and Grand Portage, were standard in form with variations in length and earning – more for "skilled canoemen" and less for guides on the Red River compared with Athabasca-bound guides.[64] The disciplinary terms generally required that the servants remain "obedient and loyal to their master in exchange for food, shelter, and wages,"[65] but the contractual language alone does not explain why this "primarily nonliterate"[66] servant class "put up with their tough lot without overt revolt."[67] In her study of the terms of labour compulsion, Carolyn Podruchny observes that the contracts were not formalized until 1796 by the government of Lower Canada.[68] After that year, some cases were brought to Montreal, echoing what Edith Burley observes with respect to the Hudson's Bay Company: "Contracts were legal documents and, in the hands of many masters, also legal weapons."[69] NWC servants enjoyed a degree of autonomy up to 1796,[70] and the formal legal threat was not enough to prevent the voyageurs "from continuing to desert, cheat contract terms, and steal from their employers."[71] Beyond legal redress, Montreal merchants exercised disciplinary mechanisms such as collusion with competitors to bar some deserters,[72] encouragement of alcohol addiction (using rum as compensation "at inflated prices"), and limitless debt.[73] Together these practices suggest a tendency to adopt informal sanctions and economic incentives as means of labour compulsion, again pointing to the complicated relation between consumption and compensation experienced by those who operated at the lower rungs of the truck economy.

For a short period, the Montreal merchants retained control over the St. Lawrence, as trade traffic via US posts increased through 1796, because of their privileges with respect to the French territories along the Mississippi River. By the time of the Louisiana Purchase in 1803, the Montrealers were relegated to bystander status,[74] although border disputes and seizures[75] did not immediately cause the Montreal merchants to withdraw and forget the potential economic windfalls in the United States. After consolidation with the XY Company, the NWC partners undertook a series of new commercial ventures to trade along the Missouri River, one in 1804, another in 1805, and a third in 1806.[76] But the latter two expeditions were failures, at least from the perspective of the company's commercial interests in the American west. In his work from 1918, Gordon Davidson recounts the Missouri expedition as "none too successful in a trading way," attributing the difficulties to the autonomy of the Mandan, who had no economic reason "to hunt beaver for the advantage of the whites."[77] From a different perspective, however, this final expedition was a triumph in terms of solidarity building between the voyageurs and the Mandan (in present-day North Dakota). When four of the company's servants deserted, they "traded away all of their property to Native people"; when expedition leader Charles McKenzie learned of this event from Mandan leader Black Cat, McKenzie "declared he would punish his men."[78] Black Cat intervened and told McKenzie that his people would stand with the voyageurs. Despite pressure from McKenzie, the servants were eventually successful in their efforts to break away from the North West Company and abandoned it in Missouri,[79] having been obvious beneficiaries of the Indigenous peoples' culture of resistance.

Two years later lauded explorers Meriwether Lewis and William Clark reached the Pacific Ocean after departing from St. Louis in 1804,[80] a journey that established the route that later became known as the Oregon Trail and led to the influx of colonial settlers in the west and the mass displacement and dispossession of Indigenous peoples. HBC directors and NWC partners were distressed by what this meant for their respective bottom lines, since permanent settlements on the southern border risked leeching from their trade routes and encroaching on their territorial claims. Increasingly, therefore, the rivalry entailed not only competition for an inland advantage but also the upper hand in exploiting the peoples and lands of the northwest.

Profitable Expansion

Although its market share was shrinking in the United States, the North West Company enjoyed an increasing advantage, along with the associated costs, in the northwestern territories. Efficient transportation was a paramount concern for the company, and the Grand Portage post – the gateway to the north – was a significant station along this route until at least 1803.[81] Grand Portage was the NWC answer to the westernmost HBC post at Cumberland House and was put to heavy use from 1777 on; it afforded access to the important Saskatchewan River and, by extension, made it possible to intercept Indigenous traders at the intermediate posts that served Hudson Bay.[82] This underscores the strategy behind the placement of posts: informed by the seasonal labour practices of Indigenous societies, each company would situate posts along the transit routes of Indigenous producers to ensure that it was the first to transact with them. Increases in the number of trading posts can be linked to this gamesmanship, especially in the 1770s to the 1790s along the Saskatchewan River and its tributaries.[83] In the expansionary phase to the northwest that occurred between 1790 and 1804, for example, the Montrealers built 194 trading posts, compared with 129 by the Hudson's Bay Company.[84]

Mackenzie headed the campaigns that led to the establishment of posts in the northwest throughout the 1790s,[85] forcing the boundaries of trade to new ends while extending the reach and clout of the North West Company. Because of these expeditions, he was able to impress himself on his contemporaries, as well as future generations, by recounting his adventures in *Voyages from Montreal through the Continent of North America*. This cemented his glory, as George Bryce exclaimed over a century ago with hagiographic flair: "Running rapids, breaking canoes, re-ascending streams, quieting discontent, building new canoes, disturbing tribes of surprised Indians, and urging on his discouraged band, Mackenzie persistently kept on his way."[86] This inclination to exalt the bravery of the singular explorer proves to be difficult to shake, as alluded to in the opening pages of this book regarding the HBC History Foundation vignettes.[87] With each rapturous account, Indigenous peoples' labour – the primary engine of the companies' profits – is lucky to find a fleeting reference[88] beyond being rendered as a catalyst for the greatness of the adventurer and the fulfillment of a perceived "imperial destiny."

Where there is mention of Indigenous peoples, such as in Gordon Davidson's work from 1918, assessments of their character accord with their perceived amenability. On the one hand, they were depicted as passive, effortlessly won over by gifts, and willing to offer advice and guidance to Mackenzie,[89] with the added benefit of being easily "paid-off" when they no longer served a purpose.[90] On the other hand, they were obstacles that Mackenzie had to conquer, lending credence to his stature. Davidson notes that, during one of Mackenzie's expeditions, "trouble was started by an Indian," and "there was more trouble with the Indians in the village at the mouth of the Bella Coola River, but it was over come by a bold front."[91] We are deprived of any

Figure 2.2 "A map of America ... exhibiting Mackenzie's track from Montreal to Fort Chipewyan and from thence to the North Sea in 1789 and to the West Pacific Ocean in 1793" (detail) | *Source:* Bibliothèque et archives nationales du Québec, https://collections.banq.qc.ca/ark:/52327/2244575

comprehensive account of why these clashes took place, and their placement at the edges of official accounts is useful to the narrators since it leaves that much more space for the glorification of the company men. The offshoot is the nihilistic naturalization of a specific historical trajectory: a colonial imperative that no obstacle could withstand.

After Mackenzie's exploits, posts were established in what are today the Northwest Territories and northern Alberta, and new Indigenous societies were brought into the commercial fur trade in a more direct manner. This had cascading effects on their social relations of land, as evident from the increased presence of manufactured items and the proliferation of unequal exchanges along a roughly similar pattern already discussed.[92] Notable on this point is Harold Innis's comment regarding the commercial benefits of these new associations, particularly the opportunities presented by intergroup warfare: "Under these circumstances trade with the remote Indians proved extremely profitable through the demand for European goods, especially guns with which they could defend themselves, and which they had previously obtained at very high rates and with great difficulty."[93] The Dene peoples – specifically the Dane-zaa (Beaver Indians) and the Denesuline (Chipewyan) – were central in this expansionary vision.[94] By the early 1800s, it was Alexander McKenzie – nephew of the elder Mackenzie – who was building trade networks with the Dene on behalf of the North West Company.[95]

In early- to mid-twentieth-century scholarship, there is a prevailing sense that the practices intrinsic to Indigenous peoples' social relations of land (e.g., cultivation, transportation, food and clothing preparation, as well as trading, trapping, and hunting) were made economically meaningful by the proficient management of the partners. Bryce, in his reverence for the "lords of the fur trade," lent support to such ideas by touting the company men's "management of the Indians."[96] This is also apparent in W.L. Morton's essay on the North West Company, in which the "primitive economy" of the Indigenous population provided the means of production, but by his account it was "demand and capital" that made the fur trade "a functioning system"[97] – a truck system twist on the Lockean notion of "improvement."[98] For Morton, it was a credit to the deftness of NWC merchants that they achieved the success that they did: "It was this ability of the North West Company to use the manpower and the skills of primitive culture that made it at its height the greatest of all Canadian – perhaps of all – fur trading companies."[99] In commending the NWC men, Morton reduces commercial success to a cunning capacity to exploit these social relations of land.

W.L. Morton's laudatory attribution of "ability" to capitalists is the "secret of the self-valorization of capital" that Marx exposes,[100] yet the realities of dispossession remain "secret" when it comes to the fur trade. It is this delusion that inspired the aforementioned HBC History Foundation commercials, which boast that "we are a country of adventurers" as an ill-advised coda.[101] This fabled depiction has a precedent in the portrayals of Mackenzie's heroics, which serve audiences triumphant tales of "the first crossing by white men" of a northwestern portage.[102] In both instances, Indigenous peoples are dispossessed of their agency: feats accomplished on their terms became historically noteworthy only once executed by "adventurers" and gained legendary status because of the wealth that flowed from the ignored labours of Indigenous peoples.

These confused remembrances paper over the realities and falsify what were considered at the time self-defeating economic decisions. Recall the desertions and the failed southward expansion, not to mention the fact that between 1804 and 1812 the value of NWC shares post-amalgamation slid by 56 percent.[103] Stock devaluation is enough reason to believe that the Montreal merchants were not wily beacons of economic proficiency but floundered in the face of a rapidly changing political, legal, and economic climate.[104] Redundancies that arose from the merger between the XY Company and North West Company left the newly consolidated company with a surplus labour reserve and the personnel needed to extend operations to the Pacific Ocean using skills once exclusive to Indigenous societies.[105] As proof of the dubious decision to pursue trade in that region, NWC partner Duncan McGillivray wrote in 1808 that "'the trade as it is carried on at present beyond the mountains, instead of getting any profit, is a very considerable loss to the Company; as the Furs did not pay the transport to Montreal where they were shipped.'"[106] Shed the presentism that colours early-twentieth-century economic assessments, and it is clear that the directors of the rival companies were not quite as savvy as some writers have suggested and that the labour of Indigenous peoples was the secret source of commercial profit.

Select economic studies present the decisions of elites as logical outcomes of a rational thought process rather than the actions of those "fanatically intent on the valorization of value."[107] This framing appears in Elizabeth Mancke's 1988 essay, which focuses on changes to HBC managerial strategies from 1670 to 1730. Mancke refers to "price fixing" through company standards as a form of knowledge production necessitated by a dearth of "market information," and she points to supply-side market share controls as evidence of clever management.[108] New dealings with "Indians unaccustomed to the trade,"[109] meanwhile, meant a more resilient monopoly on market information and entrenched exchange imbalances or, as Mancke explains, "created information, reduced uncertainty, and increased market transparency."[110] In a more recent study of the early 1800s and the race for the upper hand in the northwest, Ann Carlos and Elizabeth Hoffman explore "why the two companies took seventeen years to arrive at a profit-maximizing agreement."[111] They note the hazards of bargaining under "incomplete information," in which neither party has all of the information that would assist decision making for the well-being of the company, and in some instances one or both might employ deception as a means of strategic misinformation.[112] Both scholarly attempts to explain decision making are the apogee of capitalist rationalization, which Marx undertook to expose as fallacious from premise to conclusion.

Capitalists, like capital itself, were seemingly born with and of the impulse to accumulate; profits were taken as proof of this destiny and their shrewdness alike. "Only as a personification of capital is the capitalist respectable," writes Marx, lending insight into the type of character and cunning elevated in lore.[113] The notion among merchants that their interests emanated from "honorable intentions" helped to assuage creditors' worries,[114] but an overemphasis on the principles and prowess of the monied class sustained an "upside-down" view of the actual processes of dispossession.[115] Investor confidence, essential in terms of financing the expansion into the northwest, was a symptom of the efficacy of said processes that drove the truck system – namely, exploitation, distortion, and differentiation – rather than a testament to acumen or honour.[116] Confidence implied low risk from an investor's perspective, which meant that the weight of associated risks was borne by other parties at various points in the circuits of capital: by Indigenous traders especially at the point of unequal exchange; by servants subject to the conventional hierarchies that enshrined paternalism; by Indigenous producers disciplined by the merchant credit–backed truck system; and by the French and Métis who suffered from the prejudicial policies of the North West Company, which kept them from rising above a certain station.

In short, investor confidence was the result of well-established relations of intensive and extensive exploitation. With a complex network of disproportionate economic advantage interspersed with a patchwork of legal privilege, it was the material conditions of profitable commercial activity that provided the basis for vaunted expectations. Despite destructive competition, expanding (or defending) these confidence-boosting advantages and privileges appeared to outweigh the potential benefits of commercial cooperation. Investor faith in the system, therefore, was not an expression of abiding conviction in an idealist sense but the by-product of the actual realization of returns stemming from extant relations of exploitation bound up with the ability to exercise both formal and informal controls. Legal and economic relations were confluent, and the northwest movement of the fur trade served to extend this network of influence and control. The circumstances of the protracted rivalry, which appears to have been needlessly dear for both sides, suggest that conceit and short-sighted self-interest played important roles in the business decisions at the time. That the HBC-NWC merger occurred in 1821, after the loss of profits and lives alike (e.g., at Seven Oaks in 1816 and the decade prior), is perhaps the greatest testament to the dearth of guile.

Autonomy Conundrum

The lands and waterways between Grand Portage and Hudson Bay became battlegrounds for the rivalry, as did the posts along the Saskatchewan River and northwest from there along the Mackenzie River, all of which made the Red River area an increasingly significant site in the supply chain. Given the North West Company's lack of permanent posts in the Hudson Bay area to facilitate the movement of goods, the company required these well-situated locales where provisions could be stored and moved.[117] This applied to food, none more important than pemmican – dried buffalo meat preserved in melted fat.[118] NWC men and local Indigenous peoples depended on pemmican during their arduous treks, and the buffalo ranges in the area were prime hunting grounds. Notably, meat, not fur, was the "principal item of exchange along the Saskatchewan River" – proof of the changes under way to social relations of land and to the ongoing importance of Indigenous producers.[119]

As competition for furs in the interior and northwest intensified in the late eighteenth century, the stock of furs grew alongside the competition for the best trappers,[120] with various Indigenous groups inclined to switch allegiances if more favourable exchanges and greater gifts were offered.[121] The advance of credit played a role as a means of incentivized demand, a point that Ray acknowledges when he writes about "the increased importance of gift-giving and the extensive use of credit as an allurement to trade."[122] The framework of social obligation that underpinned customary reciprocity stretched with the incursions of the commodity economy, providing the indirect means by which company agents could compel some Indigenous trappers or hunters to produce more. Plainly, however, the companies still did not have any direct control over the means of production. They supplied the tools that facilitated hunting and trapping, but once traded the productive tools were no longer owned by the companies themselves. Without direct ownership of the means of production, the principal avenue of labour compulsion at the companies' disposal involved offering better and/or more goods at the point of exchange to encourage competition among the Indigenous producers themselves. This was the tack that the outfits chose at the end of the eighteenth century and the beginning of the nineteenth century.

Alongside and intersecting with debt-based obligations, incentivized demand was a key means of corroding the social relations of land that allowed producers to maintain a degree of autonomy.[123] These commercial interests narrowed the "generative quality"[124] that underpinned the social relations of land, rendering Indigenous peoples' paradigms and practices of sovereignty vulnerable to distortions. This is an integral component of broader processes of dispossession because it divorces company agents from the expectation of accountability that was a condition of exchange. From the companies' perspectives, the goal was to secure the loyalty of Indigenous producers to ensure that they would bring the products of the hunt or trap back to the posts in the future. But when HBC men could not exercise their monopoly to its fullest extent, ostensibly because of the exigencies of competition, the system provided opportunities for some Indigenous producers to exercise their agency by withholding the products of their labour and refusing to take on debts.[125] One repercussion was that the overextension of credit risked the curtailment of debt-based obligation itself: offering more goods reduced the demand among Indigenous producers as well as the need to trade for items used in production.[126] This could give, in turn,

Indigenous producers greater control over the means of production since they did not depend on company credit to advance the necessary supplies.

As Morantz notes, with a focus on the Cree of Eeyou Istchee, if there was a better-located company that offered more favourable trades, then there was no overriding reason why the Hudson's Bay Company should expect to be the commercial outfit of choice.[127] The fact that it could not dismantle the credit system suggests that the Eeyou were able to use it as leverage, "turning competition to their advantage by patronizing, or threatening to patronize, the rival company's posts."[128] She argues that, in the period of increasing competition between 1775 and 1805, this threat was the most effective as rival companies flooded the fur trade with gifts. For some Eeyou, the merchant credit relation led to a degree of flexibility with respect to the relative productivity of their labour, to which Morantz immediately adds that "as a system of obligation it also conformed perfectly with the Cree expectations of sharing and looking out for one another."[129] This passing statement echoes Ray's point about credit and gift-giving as incentivizing measures and lays bare a crucial point: the customary reciprocity common to various Indigenous societies combined with the debt-based legal obligations that arose from the merchant credit–backed truck economy. Morantz insists that her data show that the Eeyou in question maintained a meaningful degree of agency in terms of their labour,[130] even though it was a truck economy that exploited them through relations of debt and regular manipulation of the standards of exchange.

Although Morantz insists that these findings pertain only to that specific group in that particular era and should not be generalized, Ray likewise suggests that the system of merchant credit in this era of the fur trade was able not only to tolerate but also to facilitate a degree of autonomy among Indigenous producers.[131] Journal entries by Donald McKay show that this was the case in 1793–94 on a high-traffic trade route along the Assiniboine River.[132] Then master of the HBC's Brandon House post, which was frequented by Assiniboine traders, McKay at first refused to trade for low value items at higher cost,[133] only to realize that "no Indians will come to us if we do not take everything the Canadians take from them."[134] A similar perspective is evident in the work of Peers, who recounts that, at times of peak competition, some Saulteaux chose not to repay debts and would evade HBC officers' attempts to collect them, and others simply sought less credit.[135] On the interconnectedness of debt, subsistence, and fur production, Peers explains that some Saulteaux might have suffered a loss of "income" in instances when hunting for food took precedence over hunting for furs, which led to "the decrease in the quantity and significance of presents."[136] Together these findings point to the fragmented nature of dispossession; by "fragmented," I mean that processes of dispossession were not evenly spread in terms of depth, scope, and effect, exemplified by the relative degree of autonomy that some societies were able to practise despite the burdens of debt and the networks of obligation.

This distinctive lack of linearity in the processes of dispossession not only underscores their fragmentary facets but also hints at why exploitation becomes inconspicuous in narratives recounting the founding of the nation-state and the early capitalism of British North America. On this basis, the historical evidence makes it possible to eschew the simple developmental stagism that some read into Marx's account of "primitive accumulation," seeing it as a "moment" in pre-capitalism when violent exploitation fuelled the transition to capitalism.[137] Although violence occurred everywhere in the fur trade – be it murder, kidnapping, brawling, privation, robbery, or corporal punishment – the primary means of exploitation in the day-to-day life of the fur trade did not rely on direct coercive force. The reality of dispossession is more complicated, but it is equally important not to read these historical events from the opposite perspective. That the debt-based obligations of the fur trade "conformed perfectly" risks recasting relations of exploitation as mutually beneficial, voluntary, pacific, and natural, making it possible to misapprehend instances of relative autonomy among select Indigenous societies as absolute independence and to create a false equivalence regarding the scope of influence between the commercial outfits and the Indigenous societies being dispossessed. When that is done, the realities of exploitation, differentiation, and distortion are ignored.

Neither "defenceless" nor "servile" in the face of commercial encroachment, some Indigenous societies benefited from a strong system of "social organization" that defies any notion of economic dependence.[138] However, with the encroaching commercial fur trade, aspects of these social relations of land became gradually – not in a fatalistic, uniform, or absolute way – distorted by the companies in their interests. Trapping, hunting, and cultivating (for the subsistence of company employees) continued as before but on a larger, more competitive scale. With the North West Company and its antecedents rivalling the Hudson's Bay Company, more Indigenous peoples' labour power was redirected toward commercial exchange,[139] accompanied by an incentivized demand for European goods that facilitated commercial production, such as firearms and fishhooks.[140] Such was the circularity of debt-based obligation, making it difficult to dispose of the truck system – it was both difficult to control (because of the lack of ownership of the means of production) and a profitable arrangement for the companies. This debt-based disciplinary enterprise was also easily adapted to the contested reaches of the northwest as a type of decentralized exercise of authority, introducing new norms in which supposedly delinquent debtors were chastened as though they were wards of the honourable creditor.[141]

In general, the debt relation was integral to the fur trade, and one reason for the preponderance of debt was the irregularity of the commercial trade itself. Possible scarcity as well as natural weather events intervened and disrupted trapping or transportation, making it difficult to predict when capital would be realized.[142] Given such circumstances, increased reliance on credit offered a bridge between the outlay of capital that facilitated production and the realization of profit upon the sale of furs abroad. With this advance, certain Indigenous producers could acquire the tools necessary for their labour, and the debt relation placed an obligation on producers to return with the furs the following season as a means of repayment.[143] In terms of reputation, those who obliged were judged "steady" and "reliable," and those who did not return were "either insolent, lazy, unreliable, unsettled, or useless."[144] Honour among merchants was a type of risk assessment tool and a measure of one's reputation,[145] which explains in part why character attacks and moralistic judgments prevailed when company officers believed that they were not given their due by Indigenous individuals whom they considered debtors. With greater outlays as inducements came a greater sense of entitlement to Indigenous peoples' labour and less patience as a result.

These exploitative strategies were neither strictly extra-economic nor were they direct, violent means of labour compulsion, but when the HBC committee undertook a pivot in the main business structure and relegated many of the posts along the bay, these strategies intensified.[146] After attention shifted to the interior, certain Indigenous societies were less well positioned to exercise their leverage as trade captains,[147] such as the Maškēkowak around Cumberland House, some of whom refused to offer their knowledge and skills to HBC men, "set fires that drove game away," and "harass[ed] their former partners."[148] The agency of the Indigenous producer in question therefore played a central role in the uneven and combined nature of legal and economic transformation. For instance, despite enticements for some Nēhiyawok to engage in the beaver pelt trade in 1795, they focused on hunting buffalo,[149] their access to which for clothes and food meant that they could determine their own placement in the commercial networks.[150] Eventually, some of these producers found new roles as providers of meat for the interior posts,[151] exacerbating the problem of scarcity by increasing the number of hunters.

Because HBC factors began to rely less on intermediary trade captains and several groups turned to hunting and agriculture, it was possible to establish different debt relations with the producers themselves – different in terms of quantity (i.e., more) and quality (i.e., direct). Indigenous producers were advanced the means of production from company officers,[152] creating an expectation that they would return with the commodities while expanding the network of debt-based obligations beyond designated trade captains. This is plain in McKay's March 1794 journal entry from Brandon House, where he described himself chasing two Indigenous debtors to stop them from trading with the rival outfits.[153] Later, when he wrote that "some Method must be contrived to make those Indians kill furrs [sic], or otherwise trade is totally destroyed,"[154] his frustration at the lack of direct control over Indigenous producers is clear.

Although debt-based obligations provided disincentives to abandon the trade, sumptuary habits proved to be a more controversial lever of compulsion. Some traders sought to limit alcohol consumption and refused to trade in spirits,[155] but the overall quantity of alcohol in gallons more than doubled between 1790 and 1803 in the interior. David Smyth recounts that "vast quantities of rum" were distributed by some company officials at the height of the smallpox outbreak in the 1780s, apparently aiming "to exacerbate the condition of First Nations people even further."[156] In records describing trade activity along the Assiniboine River in February 1794, McKay observed that "the Canadians is [sic] all now in the plains and will gather all the furrs [sic] … for they have Oceans of Brandy with them,"[157] and when visited by two Indigenous traders later that month, he complained of "the Canadians pouring Rum to them like water."[158] While in 1805, prominent NWC trader Alexander Henry (the Younger) boasted about being in a position to deny local Saulteaux rum and to "'oblig[e] them to pay their debts,'" these varied accounts suggest that the competition between the newly consolidated North West Company and the Hudson's Bay Company did little to stem the flow of alcohol into the region.[159]

Following the shift inland in the latter decades of the eighteenth century, the spread of disease coincided with the increased opportunities for direct contact,[160] and this in combination with scarce resources led to new heights of privation.[161] Relocation was one option and involved reconstituted networks of social obligation and fresh feuds as Indigenous groups confronted each other under these dire conditions. Displacement, therefore, had cumulative effects. The turmoil occurring among various societies in the first decade of the nineteenth century was rife with "the frenzy of competition and violence."[162] Some Denesuline in the Athabasca region – compelled to enter the fur trade by free Canadians who kidnapped and sold Denesuline women – were plagued by disease and starvation, and they ended up migrating to territories occupied by another group likewise weakened by illness, the Dane-zaa.[163] Research on the effects of disease on Nēhiyawok and Saulteaux, meanwhile, has hinted at displacements among both at the southern end of Lake Winnipeg, as well as a possible shift among the more northern Missinipe Cree and their Denesuline neighbours.[164]

At the same time, a campaign of paternalism began to take shape as the British government increasingly answered a moral call to "civilize" Indigenous peoples.[165] The timing and context for this are striking. Abetted by decades of exploitation, distortion, and differentiation, combined with waves of disease and increased displacement, the decision to undertake permanent settlements was a lethal mix of opportunism, conceit, and entitlement. With the move to the northwest, therefore, more concerted strategies of labour compulsion were in store since the push was on to dispossess Indigenous peoples of their means of production (i.e., their skills as hunters and trappers) and eventually their object of labour (i.e., their land). On this front, the commercial rivalry extended beyond competition for market share and productivity and included contests over legal prerogative, with each company seeking to dictate the terms of access to and movement across the lands.

3
Honour and Duplicity
Debts of Rivals, Dreams of an Aristocrat

IF ECONOMIC RATIONALIZATION and a nobleman's benevolence suffice as explanations of the Hudson's Bay Company's pivot to settler colonialism, then there is no need to proceed further. But such an account does little to detail why a company enjoying the vestiges of its monopoly ceded land to Lord Selkirk after the British government itself had refused so often to do so. Four related considerations shed some light on this matter. First, there was significant volatility in the trade. Under pressure to secure more raw materials, the HBC committee was keen to extend operations westward toward the Pacific Ocean.[1] However, interest in that region was hotly contested: John Jacob Astor's American Fur Company was incorporated in 1808 and competed directly with the North West Company, there were strong Russian holdings farther north,[2] and the British conflict with the French continued into the nineteenth century.[3] Second, related to Anglo-Franco enmity,[4] access to foreign markets was curtailed by the Napoleonic Wars, which also had an inflationary effect on the cost of goods.[5] Specifically, when the Continental Blockade of 1806 limited the export of furs to Europe from Britain, Russian imports increased,[6] but this demand was not enough to offset HBC losses through to 1808 – leading the company to borrow more than usual from the Bank of England.[7] Third, the number of beavers was in decline.[8] In his description of the period leading up to 1821, Arthur Ray explains that "by the end of the period many sections of central and southern Manitoba and Saskatchewan had been nearly depleted of these resources."[9] Fourth and most importantly, the depletion of resources in the area combined with the waves of death caused by diseases provided a new opportunity to exert force over Indigenous peoples' land and labour.[10] In blunt terms, the conditions of the dispossession of Indigenous peoples were simultaneously the conditions of the first step in clearing the way for a settler colony.[11]

At first glance, the base ingredients that led the Hudson's Bay Company to part with what it understood as its most valued asset – land – included a modest amount of guile on behalf of Selkirk, a considerable degree of luck, and heaps of social capital in the form of access that a peerage can provide.[12] Stock accounts of Selkirk's ambitions tend to address an amalgam of these three elements when explaining the company's settler colonial turn in the early nineteenth century. But a more persuasive analysis examines the circumstances that led the directors of the company to see the land as theirs to give to Selkirk – "white possessive logic" par excellence. In other words, the principal focus must be on the company's taking rather than giving; after all, this supposed concession by the company was an act of dispossession, one that both arose from and precipitated a host of changes to Indigenous peoples' lives.

Early Jurisdictional Disputes

In the colonial context, "jurisdictional jockeying and disputes were pervasive."[13] Although officials from Upper Canada, Lower Canada, the North West Company, and the Hudson's Bay Company all claimed to be operating in the service of the British crown, doffing to the same sovereign did nothing to alleviate the jurisdictional conflicts on the ground. Among the principal concerns of HBC officers was the breach of the company's exclusive right to direct profits from the furs. Sanctions and restrictive contracts that attempted to prevent private trade proliferated as a consequence, but the problem of enforceability lingered,[14] which made it difficult to execute formal punishments in response to desertion among its servant ranks.[15] What prevailed, however, was a far-from-centralized administrative approach despite the nominal authority of the Hudson's Bay Company and presumed backing by the crown. Accused individuals rarely benefited from due process and instead faced disciplinary measures akin to those used on insubordinates in the British Navy.[16] This privately enforced, militaristic system of summary punishments exemplified the considerable discretionary power of HBC officers, but it extended only to those members of the company within their purview of control. With the movement of the Montreal merchants' outfits into the northwestern terrain, the Hudson's Bay Company's jurisdictional claim was at stake as more agents hostile to its commanding force began to infiltrate the terrain claimed as Rupert's Land.

Criminal sanctions were sometimes deployed,[17] and this was no less the case during the period up to and including this aggressive interval of the commercial fur trade. For example, one zone of acute enmity was Island Fort (Fort de l'Isle), which in 1802 was the site of many overlapping claims along the North Saskatchewan River. The XY Company, North West Company, and Hudson's Bay Company each had a post at this location; in their contest for favour with Indigenous producers, some disgruntled NWC men apparently attempted to rob an XYC member, who, to protect himself and his property, shot dead one of the would-be thieves.[18] Joseph Maurice Lamothe was indicted for murder by a grand jury in Montreal, but he was freed because it was not clear that the matter fell within Canadian jurisdiction.[19] Similarly, earlier murder charges against NWC partner Peter Pond never went to trial; the charges were dropped in 1782 because the events ostensibly occurred within the jurisdiction of the Hudson's Bay Company. One case that did make it to trial in 1788 ended in the acquittal of two NWC men, and again ambiguity surrounding jurisdictional authority was cited as the reason.[20]

Although the Hudson's Bay Company had the nominal authority to administer legal decisions, the committee never established a court system. Perhaps it was the blend of too much concentrated legal authority and limited action; in any case, the outcome made for confusing encounters. To address this quandary, the Privy Council struck a committee, which found that the governor of Lower Canada "could issue a special commission" that would "authorize the trial of cases from the Indian country."[21] The remedy that ensued was supported by members of the grand jury at Lamothe's trial – consisting of many active agents in the fur trade – who saw "no real distinction ... between Rupert's Land and the Indian Territories farther to the north and west."[22] With the passing of the contentious Canada Jurisdiction Act in 1803, the British Parliament took an additional step to clarify how disputes regarding transgressions should be settled. The act included provisions that made it possible to bring criminal matters to Lower or Upper Canada "on a case-by[-]case basis," and it allowed lesser offences to fall under the purview of magistrates appointed by the governor of Lower Canada.[23] Authority was granted to the courts of Lower Canada, in which criminal disputes could be heard or remitted to Upper Canada at the discretion of magistrates.[24] Still unresolved was the extent to which this legislation should be interpreted as a curtailment of the authorities granted in the original HBC charter. From the perspective of HBC directors, it "had no application to the north-west, since it was intended to deal with crimes committed in 'Indian territories' not already under the governance of a recognizable authority."[25] NWC partners disagreed.

Even in the absence of a formal charter securing their own monopoly on trade, the Montreal merchants acted as though such a privilege existed – a "ruthlessness" that A.S. Morton brings to light in his comments on Duncan McGillivray's journals.[26] In the rivalry, McGillivray assumed the role of agitator. He was the target of a civil suit stemming from actions in 1801 when, at Grand Portage, he confronted a Mr. Hervieu, who was in charge of a small expedition financed by a competing Montreal merchant.[27] Apparently, McGillivray, accompanied by fellow partner Archibald Norman McLeod, had a dagger in hand and "struck it into Hervieu's tent, and tore it from top to bottom," and he threatened that "he would cut his [Hervieu's] throat" if Hervieu dared to tread any farther into the interior.[28] At the civil court in Montreal, the merchant won £500 in damages to cover some of the losses associated with having to abandon the trade expedition.[29] Despite being named in the suit, McGillivray was appointed as justice of the peace with the passing of the Canada Jurisdiction Act of 1803.[30] This violent rift between the Montrealers continued even after the merger of the North West Company and the XY Company. It was not until 1805 that those stationed near the Mackenzie River learned of the consolidation,[31] so they would not have been aware of the negotiations when, in the fall of 1804, three men from the "old" North West Company attempted to trade with two Indigenous men at Great Bear Lake. John McDonald from the XY Company tried to forestall what he viewed as an incursion given that it was likely that at least one of the Indigenous producers owed a debt to that company.[32] When John Steinbruck of the North West Company ignored McDonald's notice, he was shot in the arm and died three weeks later as a result of the wound.[33]

The HBC officers were aware of the North West Company's track record of "ruthlessness" and the possibility of mutual destruction, and they attempted to avoid outright conflict with their Montreal-based rivals. This was the nature of the contest that informed the "passive" period, a policy of conflict avoidance that remained in place even after settlement at Red River in 1812. Reluctance to engage in outright conflict stemmed as much from a keen understanding of the legal precariousness of their exclusive privileges and the prevailing geopolitical climate as it did from any combination of economic considerations. Even so, a policy of conflict avoidance is not the same as actual passivity.

The Hudson's Bay Company faltered in the opening decade of the nineteenth century as it was outpaced in the northwest and the cost of competition had an impact on profits.[34] Meanwhile, competition among the Montreal merchants in the Athabasca region, principally between the North West Company and the XY Company, reached a heightened level of "extravagance"[35] in 1802–03 when "both companies expended trade goods far beyond the value of the furs they purchased."[36] This spending by the Montrealers coincided in 1802 with the return of the Hudson's Bay Company to the Athabasca region, which it had left ten years prior and would leave again by 1806 following "unrelenting harassment."[37] As the North West Company's own financial stresses made it even more crucial that the company establish a shorter westward route other than through Montreal, a direct confrontation with the Hudson's Bay Company was on the horizon. When, controversially, the North West Company staked its claim to Kaamischii (Charlton Island) in James Bay in 1803,[38] HBC directors sought the advice of lawyers to see if they might have recourse to the British court system to try this as a civil dispute.[39] The lawyers found that, "the trade monopoly was probably void, the grant of the soil ... was good," yet they advised against pursuing a case in court and suggested that the better remedy would be a statutory correction to address the jurisdictional morass.[40] The legal standing of the chartered company was not strong in terms of being able to substantiate its exclusive privileges to trade, but it did appear to buttress its standing as a jurisdictional authority in the region.[41] The key for HBC directors was to find a way of leveraging this authority for economic benefit, a balance that became even more delicate since the Canadas had been extending their own jurisdictional reach westward since the late 1700s.

For the North West Company, the HBC monopoly had a chafing effect on relations. Once the former company was large enough, it could tackle the chartered privileges of the Hudson's Bay Company through unrelenting competition, although the Montrealers were interested in "the easier path of purchasing or leasing those privileges for themselves," which led them to negotiate access with their rivals.[42] Negotiations were led by Duncan McGillivray,[43] who sought a shorter access route by offering £103,000 to the Hudson's Bay Company plus a 5 percent annuity. The salvo was denied. He then proposed that the North West Company withdraw from certain posts along the bay and offered £2,000 per year as rent for their use,[44] an offer that did not tempt his HBC counterparts given their own shift inland two decades earlier. As part of their counteroffer, the HBC negotiators suggested that the North West Company either buy out the Hudson's Bay Company, which would ensure that its shareholders received dividends, or merge with it under its own structure.[45] Among other stipulations was the HBC officers' attempt to ensure that with any type of agreement – even if it amounted to informal collusion – the North West Company would operate under the same restrictions as the chartered Hudson's Bay Company, which required sending all furs to Britain before they were distributed elsewhere.[46] However, having just undertaken the capital-intensive acquisition of the XY Company, the North West Company was not in a position to purchase the Hudson's Bay Company.[47] Also, the North West Company was already exporting furs to China and enjoying the vestiges of its access to the French territories of the United States, which made the idea of diverting furs through Britain a non-starter. Negotiations ran aground in 1805 when neither party offered concessions that the other found sufficient, and the ensuing six-year stalemate opened the door for less than formal resolutions to both new and old conflicts.

In addition to negotiating access, attempting to secure their own privileges, and making a presumptive claim in James Bay, the NWC partners challenged the provision of 1670 curtailing the exclusive right of the Hudson's Bay Company on lands already occupied by allies. The principal stake extended back to 1738, when Fort Rouge was established by much earlier iterations of the North West Company at the junction of the Red River and the Assiniboine River ("the Forks"), although there was some disagreement about whether this was just a wintering fort or a more permanent claim.[48] This dispute over privileges and jurisdiction went unresolved, even as the situation was becoming dire in the face of sliding share values. Without a successful way to reduce costs, the NWC partners implemented a series of cuts, including to salaries, such as for clerks, which were reduced by 40 percent in the first year of their contracts.[49] This likely curtailed any further agitation by the workers, who showed a willingness as early as 1803 at Kaministiquia to withdraw labour for better pay.[50] As another cost-cutting effort, the partners in charge of the amalgamated North West Company implemented new provisions barring the voyageurs from making private trades with members of local Indigenous societies, a practice that until that point (unlike the HBC directors) the Montreal merchants did not expressly forbid.[51] The effectiveness of these restrictions was ensured in part by one of the consequences of the merger: the new reserve army of labour. This had an important disciplinary effect on the voyageurs as they became aware of the precarity of their employment.[52]

The number of exploitable people and the extent of terrain extended northwest and access at the southern border became more restrictive, the North West Company's profit margins narrowed, and arguments for reduced salaries were rationalized. Because of this, the company might not have reaped the same level of profits that it once did, but trade activity itself did not diminish. Despite mounting legal, economic, and geopolitical pressure on the NWC partners to find a transit route that would cut costs drastically, it is erroneous to interpret the company's devaluation as evidence of the abatement of its exploitative measures of dispossession. Likewise, the HBC committee's policy of conflict avoidance is synonymous with neither stasis nor cooperation, demonstrating that it is possible to adopt a policy of conflict avoidance but still practise rampant exploitation. Processes of dispossession continued in neither a uniform nor a linear way. Alongside pockets of relative autonomy, the way that the truck system operated to gradually domesticate aspects of customary reciprocity eventually became the basis for more exploitative measures of dispossession with the founding of the Red River Colony.

Debt Intolerance

Impatience was escalating, which did not make for even-tempered encounters. Yet some historians refer to the six-year period between 1804 and 1810 as a relatively "passive" phase because of edicts from the HBC upper echelons instructing company men to avoid direct conflict with the newly consolidated North West Company.[53] It is argued that open hostilities were the exception to the rule – more personality driven and local than a general pattern.[54] However, this characterization sits strangely beside A.S. Morton's commentary on the "ruthlessness" that the NWC partners "showed to all who crossed or threatened to cross their path,"[55] as well as some legal histories that look less to economic data as an indication of predatory competition and more to instances of homicide to determine levels of manifest hostility. And, although the HBC committee wanted to avoid outright conflict while the NWC partners were anxious about the imminent dissolution of their company,[56] describing this as a "passive" phase only makes more glaring the tendency to ignore the agency of, and effects on, Indigenous peoples.

In his *Sketch of the British Fur Trade*, then principal HBC shareholder Lord Selkirk offers his biased take on select events during this phase. The incidents that fill the pages are meant to prove the North West Company's predilection toward violent territorialism, what Selkirk describes as "the most unprovoked aggression,"[57] all recounted in a fashion that served his interest in presenting the Hudson's Bay Company as a passive victim of the North West Company. One such incident occurred in 1806 at a locale called Bad Lake, which he deems "within the limits of Albany Factory, (in the Hudson's Bay territory)." The conflict arose between William Corrigal of the Hudson's Bay Company and NWC partner John Haldane[58] when five men under Haldane's charge broke into Corrigal's house and robbed Corrigal of his furs and guns.[59] Similar clashes occurred that spring at Red Lake: once in the fall, when an HBC officer suffered violent retribution after being accused of trading with an Indigenous producer who had a debt with the North West Company, and once more in February 1807.[60]

Other historical records speak of the North West Company's James McKenzie.[61] He was willing to exalt what others considered deplorable; among other acts, he trafficked Indigenous women and beat members of the competing XY Company.[62] Shortly after his promotion to partner in 1802, McKenzie was "responsible for implementing the policy of harassment" in the Athabasca region,[63] which escalated after the NWC and XYC merger in 1804 and culminated with the chasing away of HBC surveyor Peter Fidler in 1806. Fidler's journals report that McKenzie erected a "watch house" close to the HBC post, robbed hunters of their furs, and incited certain members of a local Denesuline group to kill members of his own company.[64] In more polite language, though dismissive in its own right, Davidson describes McKenzie as possessing "a certain animus against the ways of the North West Company and of its Canadian *engagés*."[65] Where Davidson concedes that there was a violent tendency, he goes only as far as to indict McKenzie; Selkirk, for his part, flatly rejected the notion that NWC aggression was attributable to one bad actor.

To advance his case, Selkirk recounted two more incidents that involved Fidler. First, he was followed and beaten by a member of the North West Company in 1807.[66] Second, from 1809–10 through 1811, Fidler was on the receiving end of more interference from NWC men when he attempted to "establish a trading post at Isle a la Crosse, near the borders of the Athabasca country, but within the territories of the Hudson's Bay Company."[67] His efforts were trounced by the rivals, who, according to Selkirk, pilfered Fidler's firewood, ruined the supplies, and exercised such a "terror" on the local Indigenous population that it discouraged any trade in the Hudson's Bay Company's favour. As before, Fidler and the HBC servants were driven away.[68]

In another exemplary clash, it was James Swain of the Hudson's Bay Company who escalated the conflict. While at Beaver Lake House in present-day northern Ontario in March 1809, Swain attempted to acquire four furs from an Indigenous producer; however, when four nearby free Canadians saw him try to take what they claimed they were owed by the Indigenous man, Swain ended up quite outnumbered. As Burley recounts, "Swain managed to free himself, drew his pistol, and challenged his Canadian counterpart to a duel, which the latter declined."[69] Perhaps the greater blow to Swain was the fact that this altercation occurred in the vicinity of several HBC men; some feigned ignorance of the event, while others watched from inside the house – the only one who wilfully came to Swain's defence was his wife.[70]

Among the more controversial incidents, however, was a murder charge against the Hudson's Bay Company's John Mowat stemming from events in 1809 at Eagle Lake, 300 kilometres northwest of Lake Superior. Selkirk conceded that this was the "one case [that] has been brought to trial under the Act of 1803." William Corrigal of the Hudson's Bay Company was implicated when an NWC camp was established under the charge of Aeneas MacDonnel near the HBC post, and a dispute surfaced between the two companies over the debts owed by an Indigenous producer. Already having promised a canoe to Corrigal as payment of his debt to the Hudson's Bay Company, the unidentified Indigenous man was then set upon by an armed group of NWC men led by a sword-wielding MacDonnel. Corrigal, with two of his men, rushed to intervene, and one was injured by MacDonnel, a scene witnessed by a nearby group from the Hudson's Bay Company who joined the escalating affair and quickly added to the tally of injuries.[71] As MacDonnel was once again about to strike Mowat with his sword, the latter shot MacDonnel.[72] Out of fear of retaliation, Corrigal and his complement took refuge in the house, only allowing entrance to the NWC men after they threatened to kill everybody in the house if they were not allowed inside. Mowat eventually admitted to the shooting and shortly thereafter left for Montreal to be brought to trial.[73] He was shackled in a windowless cell at Fort William (formerly Kaministiquia) – an "Indian territory" facility by then under the jurisdiction of the NWC partners/magistrates – where he was denied medicine.[74] Mowat did not arrive in Montreal until September 1810, a year after the event itself,[75] and even then the HBC committee members in London were ignorant of the trial until late November.[76]

Selkirk punctuated his disdain by comparing what occurred in Mowat's case to the standards of British adjudication: "In the course of the trial circumstances occurred, which could not have taken place in a court of justice in England, without exciting indignation from one end of the kingdom to the other."[77] Here he adopted a duplicitous legal position: while he extolled the high principles of English law, he remained reticent about the actual extension of such principles beyond the northern borders of Upper Canada. In his analysis of the historical records associated with this case, legal historian Hamar Foster refers to Selkirk's entry as "bitterly critical" but agrees with the general sentiment that the Canada Jurisdiction Act of 1803 gave the North West Company an obvious advantage in Montreal courts.[78] With the provision that magistrates would be appointed at the pleasure of the governor of Lower Canada, the chances were high that these appointees would hold prominent positions in the fur trade. Furthermore, given the modest population of Montreal at the time, there was an equally modest likelihood that any jury assembled there would be composed of men whose livelihoods were not entwined with the interests of the city's merchant class.[79] Despite the act of 1803, therefore, the formal extension of adjudicative authority to the plains and beyond did nothing to alleviate the tensions between the two companies, but what remains shrouded is exactly what was at stake for these companies: That is, over what were they fighting?

Note what many of these events had in common: they began as disputes over debts purportedly owed by Indigenous producers. In other words, what scholars widely accept as evidence of economic hostility between the two companies are violent episodes that had the decisions and actions of Indigenous peoples as their genesis. When it comes to an analysis of these circumstances, it is not a lack of clarity about legal authority that precipitated violent clashes, nor is it merely a question of the manifest anxiety of shrinking market shares or profit margins that spurred brutal acts; rather, these were symptoms of an even greater transformation in which the two sides struggled to assert themselves. With the combination of customary reciprocity and debt-based obligation, the latter became the basis for action in times of duress. The truck system amalgamated so effectively with customary practices that it was not until the credit-granting capacity of the merchants was in peril that the creditor-debtor relation revealed itself to contain little of the socially minded obligation that generally accompanies relations of reciprocity. Instead, "credit ... necessitated reduced mobility," amounting to a foundational challenge to the social relations of land among Indigenous peoples:[80] by influencing the scope and terms of Indigenous peoples' mobility across the lands, the companies distorted the "political practices, exchanges, and development of new relationships" between Indigenous societies.[81] This reveals the clash of two monopolizing companies as both a cause

82 *A Legacy of Exploitation*

and a consequence of the relative autonomy of Indigenous producers at the centre of the industry.

The companies' shared desires to exert economic and juridical control over the "Indian Territory" were really contests over control of Indigenous peoples. This fact is overlooked by Carlos, who states that "from 1804 to 1810 the relationship [between the two companies] is better described as passive rather than aggressive."[82] Without any definitive sense of what might qualify as "passive" or "aggressive," the implicit claim suggests, on the one hand, that there were not enough aggressive acts in an absolute numerical sense to warrant characterizing the nature of competition as such and, on the other hand, that some officers' journal entries and committee-level discussions reference the mostly amicable nature of relations. Carlos relies on a quantity over quality argument to support the notion that relations were not that aggressive and a quality over quantity argument to support the notion that relations were passive. But one party's formal adoption of a position of passivity in the abstract sense does not discount the need to examine the actual instances of exploitation and conflict;[83] left unchecked, this characterization girds the idea that it was an era of complicity and equanimity. The HBC officers' concerns about passivity were in line with Selkirk's worries about the violation of the high ideals of British justice; in neither instance do the actual circumstances of exploitation, distortion, or differentiation carry significant weight. This take is compatible with laudatory commercial campaigns that celebrate the adventurers' conquest of "territory," yet all fail to recognize that what was really occurring was a dispossession of other humans – their histories, their cultures, their knowledges, their labours, their skills, and their lands.

By studying the examples of aggression as a group, one notices that what was troublesome to both companies was the relative autonomy of Indigenous producers. As the distorted customary means of influence yielded returns insufficient for unabated growth, a brand of conflict arose that led to further transformations in the processes of dispossession. This was a symptom of changing social relations of land, which could be achieved by making more favourable adjustments to the companies' standards in a manner that emphasized the commercial value of gifts; by incentivizing demand with regard to specific goods, such as alcohol and rifles, which influenced exchanges and interactions between Indigenous societies; by laying claim to debt, which restricted the mobility of Indigenous producers; and, principally, by distorting the core tenet of reciprocity at the bases of these exchanges. On each front, the companies stood to increase their respective profit margins – especially so if the means of production could be appropriated from the Indigenous producers. When the Hudson's Bay Company shifted its operations inland, and with the voyageurs' documented adoption of hunting and trapping skills, the companies were well positioned to undermine the existing terms of labour and the relative autonomy of Indigenous producers. Again, it was because of the dynamism of their extant networks of reciprocal exchange that certain Indigenous societies involved in the fur trade could include the European traders, and the same dynamic social relations of land fortified their capacity to resist a relation of absolute dependence on the colonizers. At the same time, these processes of dispossession had a deleterious effect on the stocks that the Indigenous peoples required in order to sustain their relative degree of autonomy – this meant that there was a ceiling to the productivity within any given territory.

Laura Peers highlights the pressures that these changes were having on the Saulteaux at the time, observing that competition among hunters increased after the merger of the XY Company and the North West Company, which increased the number of Métis hunters in the region where the Saulteaux were already active.[84] John Milloy stresses a similar point about competition with respect to the Nēhiyawok and Métis, which intensified into the mid-nineteenth century with the decline in the buffalo population.[85] Despite these tensions, as Robert Alexander Innes observes, "it is surprising that there are no accounts of the Plains Cree, Assiniboine, and Saulteaux waging war on the Métis," adding later that "the reason for the lack of warfare was likely kinship ties between the groups."[86] On and around the plains, the labouring Indigenous societies were strained, yet their labour was still vital as hunters and providers of food for the companies, not to mention as possible allies in the event of war. These considerations informed many of the HBC officers' and governors' decisions in the years to come, and by the close of the first decade of the 1800s the directors had a new course that they hoped would offset the company's dependencies while bolstering its claim to Rupert's Land.

Retrenchment

The NWC partners were not alone in their concern about their financial fortitude or the cost of transportation; the HBC men also sought measures to abate shrinking profit margins. There was a degree of urgency, and officers' journals included more accounts of "disobedience and insolence" among servants; although there was no prospect of an outright mutiny, a careful balance was sought.[87] On the one hand, "the committee could not risk alienating potential recruits"; on the other hand, there was a sense of the need for a stronger hand in order to bolster productivity and at least keep pace in the competitive era. Against this backdrop in 1809, HBC committee member Andrew Wedderburn – Selkirk's brother-in-law – developed a retrenchment plan.[88] To offset dependence on Indigenous peoples' labour, in-house agricultural production provided by a settlement was under consideration, attractive in large part because it could mitigate the expenses of trucking goods from England.[89]

After the move inland, the Hudson's Bay Company required a larger volume of trade items since more goods were either in stores or in transit.[90] Transportation concerns were unrelenting: costly transportation meant less capital to invest elsewhere, and obstacles in bringing the item to market meant delays in the realization of profit.[91] Along with this increased outlay was a need to catalogue the movement and consumption of goods, leading to more scrupulous accounting methods.[92] Touted as an "innovative plan," increased attentiveness to accounting methods was one of the key outcomes of this retrenchment effort, which included moving away from made beaver as the standard of measuring value and adopting pounds sterling.[93] With seemingly improved record keeping came a new disciplinary outlook: "Costs could be calculated more precisely and the men's efficiency, diligence, and honesty more easily judged."[94] Remuneration structures were revised accordingly as salaried work began to look less favourable compared with a flexible pay scale that reflected output.[95] This signalled a shift toward piecework, in which workers' livelihoods were linked directly to their productivity in a more quantifiable sense.[96]

To accommodate this change, the HBC committee deemed it necessary to restructure the company by dividing it into a Northern Department and a Southern Department,[97] with each department assigned a superintendent who, in turn, oversaw the workings of the chief factors of the assigned posts.[98] Ostensibly, this was implemented in the name of efficiency, which would afford the company a basis on which to ensure greater returns through increased austerity when it came to salaries and bonuses.[99] In this regard, internal restructuring recognized that the short-term hope for higher profits lay in effective management. The change also underscored the importance of hierarchy, an obvious attempt at improving accountability across the company without having to establish enforcement and dispute resolution measures, such as sheriffs, deputies, or a court system.[100]

According to Burley, these were not entirely new measures. Although she concedes that the techniques might have become more sophisticated, the conservative-minded objectives and the feudal attitude that underpinned them were not.[101] The officer-servant relation retained its feudal quality thanks to the still predominant belief that rigid contracts and trucking were the best means of exercising control; however, the internal structure of the Hudson's Bay Company had to be improved in order to reinforce the disciplinary functions of contractual obligations – "laxness was to stop."[102] Servants already on contract responded to the new terms of labour compulsion by protesting at Brandon House in 1811,[103] and other disaffected former employees became "free men," increasing the competition among Indigenous hunters and trappers in the region.[104] Another way to expunge bad habits among the existing servant class was to hire new servants recruited under terms that better suited the company's plan,[105] and this was done when contracts were terminated or not renewed.

The feudal relation between HBC officers and servants demonstrates the extent to which the internal corporate structure relied on vestigial social customs to maintain obedience. But changes to the officer-servant relation are at least related to, and at most symptomatic of, the ongoing transformations to the social relations of land with respect to the surrounding Indigenous societies. Indigenous producers remained outside the scope of direct HBC authority and control in both an economic and a legal sense.[106] Even the expanding web of debt-based obligations that the company established through an elaborate and durable truck system did not eradicate the networks of reciprocity among the Indigenous peoples, whose labour remained the linchpin of the commercial fur trade. Nevertheless, the retrenchment plan included a measure to mitigate this dependence by introducing a step toward the formal alienation of land. Specifically, the company used land grants to incentivize employee performance, making 100 acres available to select servants "retiring with a good character." As demonstrably worthy retirees, they would be familiar with both the land and the company, and as such they would further ease the need for a formal system of legal administration,[107] which underscored a long-standing reliance on the efficiency of internal and/or informal resolutions as opposed to external and/ or formal remedies.

The site where, in later decades, many would eventually retire was the Red River Colony. This settler colonial initiative was thought of as a possible solution to several problems, all of which were connected to the company's ongoing dependence on Indigenous peoples' labour: the lack of steady provisions, the high cost of transportation of those provisions, and the difficulties hiring workers. As such, the origins of the settler colony are intrinsically connected to the economic rationalization that informed the retrenchment plan overall,[108] with the relative autonomy of Indigenous producers as a key driver. At the heart of the Hudson's Bay Company's incentivized distribution, meanwhile, was a presumptive claim on the land itself. A century and a half of unequal trades gave HBC aristocrats enough confidence to take these relations of dispossession to new heights, eventually using the same distorted practices of customary reciprocity that facilitated the exploitative exchanges to execute an agreement for land use.

Selkirk's realization of a settler colony occurred at a pivotal moment of transition as it pertained to Britain's broader imperial campaigns. The Royal Proclamation of 1763 followed the suppression of the Jacobite Rebellion and preceded the US Revolutionary War, ostensibly marking a turn to a more "centralized (that is, London-based) approach towards aboriginal policy."[109] For Paul McHugh, this portended "the final disappearance of the old feudal notions of the personal relationship between ruler and subject" in favour of "the more modern, secularizing notion of independent state sovereignty that had been emerging through the seventeenth century."[110] Abstracted, this might have been the aim of new legal arrangements enacted by the British Parliament; in practice, however, there was a measure of continuity in the combination of feudal relations, truck economy, and customary reciprocity. Attempts to launch more formalized and centralized policies came not just from London but also from Montreal and eventually the governors of the Red River Colony itself – with every new measure clashing with the established practices on the ground.[111]

Monopoly or Colony?

The HBC royal charter of 1670 granted "true and absolute Lords and Proprietors" the authority "to have, hold, possess and enjoy the said Territory, Limits and Places."[112] Privileges were also afforded to "all Governors of Colonies, Forts and Plantations, Factors, Masters, Mariners, and other Officers" to "make, ordain and constitute ... Laws, Constitutions, Orders and Ordinances,"[113] and elsewhere the charter stated that the company retained the right to erect "Castles, Fortifications, Forts, Garrisons," as well as "Colonies or Plantations, Towns or Villages."[114] However, given the sparseness of a population with transferable currency, the most valuable HBC asset remained the territory itself and the exclusive privileges that the company retained in Rupert's Land.

In legal terms, the monopoly right was assumed by the British sovereign and transferred to the chartered companies, which then wielded these royal ordinances primarily as weapons of private accumulation, especially through resource extraction. For British investors and merchants in the pre-industrial era, these companies "were powerful levers for the concentration of capital," and later settler colonies were attractive as potential "market[s] for the budding manufactures."[115] By the mid-eighteenth century, the HBC committee's refusal to establish settlements was the focal point of controversy. In a charged condemnation of the company, Arthur Dobbs penned a document in 1744 intended to "implore" the king to undertake colonial settlement in Rupert's Land,[116] and he attested that a duty to encourage settlement was a condition of the chartered monopoly itself. The speciousness of his position could not be ignored insofar as Dobbs was appealing to a document that he believed was baseless – a paradox that occasioned an absurd turn of phrase: "But supposing they had a legal Right, they have forfeited their Right."[117] To prop up his claim, he relied on the Lockean argument that, by failing to initiate "proper Improvements" to the land,[118] the

Hudson's Bay Company had "forfeited their Right to all these Countries except their present Factories."[119] After the legal and moral entreaties were made, economic appeals then took hold. With the emergent manufacturing industries in England, Dobbs's appeal to King George II explained that colonies abroad provided ready-made consumer markets for British goods. Such markets had three advantages: first, they would ameliorate the lives of the colonists; second, they would have a "civilizing" effect on the Indigenous peoples; and third, they could provide "full Employment to our Manufacturers."[120] Bound up with the vision for Rupert's Land, therefore, was the potential for a consumer market – the prospects of which would not appeal to the HBC directors until the early nineteenth century.

The royal charter gave the HBC committee leeway to found colonies, but it possessed little ambition in this regard. Most company men intended to return to their homeland;[121] as Jennifer Brown notes, "they were not colonists."[122] Despite the overtly colonial mandate of the HBC charter, Brown avers that, by not having to tend to settler colonists and their array of needs, the company could concentrate on the fur trade itself.[123] Historian Nicholas Rogers offers a slightly different take but arguably makes a comparable point, remarking that the term "British Empire" was not commonly used up to 1770.[124] On this basis, we should not be surprised that there was little desire for colonial settlements in Rupert's Land until the nineteenth century. The suitable conclusion, however, is not to deny the Hudson's Bay Company its colonial essence; the absence of settler colonists from the outset does not mean the absence of a manifest colonial relation. Socio-legal scholar Russell Smandych explains that the "difference between 'colonizers' and 'settler colonizers' is that they want different things; while the 'colonizer' comes to the land of the colonized and tells them 'you, work for me,' the 'settler colonizer' takes over the land of the colonized and tells them 'you, go away.'"[125] The truck system embodied the former, whereas the Red River Colony embodied the latter; so, although a transformation took place, it was both a continuation and a modification of the processes of dispossession under way.

The practical capacity to compel productivity was uneven, as evidenced by the disparate nature of autonomy that certain Indigenous producers continued to wield, yet the truck system set the stage for the more overt measures of dispossession that flourished over the next century and beyond. This exhibits one of the marked characteristics of dialectical transformation: the shift from quantitative to qualitative change.[126] One simplified analogy is the transition from water to ice, which occurs through quantitative changes as the temperature of the liquid decreases at measurable intervals, resulting in qualitative change in the substance as it solidifies.[127] With respect to the establishment of the Red

River Colony by the Hudson's Bay Company, a comparable process occurred as small changes over time led to a qualitative shift toward settler colonialism. The Canada Jurisdiction Act of 1803 is held as a watershed piece of legislation in this regard, representing an early attempt to establish formal legal authority over Indigenous peoples and rival traders alike. Although feudal norms, the truck economy, and Indigenous customary practices reigned in the century following the founding of the company – all of which were characterized by the prevalence of informal obligation and swift retributive punishment – the act of 1803 was both an expression of formal authority from the perspective of the British Parliament and an attempt to initiate more centralized authority abroad with its insistence that disputes be settled by the courts of Upper and/or Lower Canada. Despite this notion that there was a sweeping move away from customary, private, and feudal norms toward the impersonal formalism of British law, the reality was much less uniform and linear.

The supposed exercise of more direct and formal authority did not apply to everybody in Rupert's Land, which I aver is better understood as a site of "decentralized administration."[128] Crucially, this decentralized nature of colonial governance cannot be reduced to problems of distance, geography, and lack of personnel;[129] as Mahmood Mamdani explains, practices of "indirect" and "mediated" rule were purposeful measures of colonial control and not inadvertent by-products of circumstance. Architects of these strategies established a bifurcated structure of governance in which certain laws applied to "citizens," whereas the "subject population of natives" was governed by a separate but related and malleable set of customary measures.[130] In advance of the founding of the Red River Colony, such strategies were evinced in the enactments of factors' discretionary power, namely the practice of identifying "trade captains"; in the HBC committee's presumptive claims to the lands for redistributive purposes, which made it possible to produce the category of "settler"; and in the practical limits of parliamentary statutes, in which the formal delineation of British subjecthood was most obvious.

Indigenous peoples in this area and at this historical juncture of the fur trade continued to rule themselves, although the practices that constituted the truck system entailed differentiation as both a means and an outcome of dispossession. Modified means of differentiation that accompanied the Red River Colony applied to those already considered "citizens" within Rupert's Land and amounted to a crucial step in institutionalized segregation that culminated (legislatively speaking) with the Indian Act of 1876. Plainly, the decision to establish a settler colony at Red River marked a departure from the perspective of the Hudson's Bay Company, whose officials had a long track record of resistance to planned settlements of the territory. On the ground, however, this qualitative change was the outcome of quantitative increments of dispossession occurring in the context of a rapidly changing geopolitical landscape. The man who won the concession from the company, Lord Thomas Selkirk, was immersed in these geopolitical intrigues.

The Malthusian Candidate

The Fourth Earl of Selkirk, Dunbar Douglas, was considered during his lifetime to be "one of Scotland's major agricultural improvers,"[131] and he fathered a presumably secure line of male heirs: six sons, with Thomas as the final addition.[132] Born in 1771, Thomas would be a university-educated (though not degree-holding) Scot.[133] Adam Smith had as significant an influence on the youngest Selkirk's worldview as did the plight of the Highland tenant farmers, forced

Figure 3.1 Thomas Douglas, Fifth Earl of Selkirk (1771–1820) | *Source:* Library and Archives Canada published holdings project, c-001346

from their lands after lending support to the losing side in the Jacobite Rebellion in 1745.[134] His childhood was marked by his father's growing support for the American cause in the Revolutionary War, a rather abrupt shift from the elder's earlier alliance with the English during the Jacobite Rebellion.[135] Thomas's early adulthood was coeval with the French Revolution, the occasion of a trip in 1791 to Paris, where Thomas bore witness to the social and political consequences of aristocratic intransigence.[136] By 1799, following the death of his father and all of his brothers, he became the unlikely Fifth Earl of Selkirk, inheriting associated land and investments that allowed him to turn to North America to build his own legacy.[137]

Selkirk was convinced that emigration was the best solution to the difficulties of the era, which many learned men simplified as a crisis of overpopulation, a theory popularized in a 1798 essay by Reverend Thomas Malthus.[138] Malthus surmised that food scarcity and death by starvation were inevitable,[139] and though at various periods there would be an "excess of births above ... burials"[140] seemingly "natural" checks (e.g., starvation) would thwart a growing population – and, if these corrections failed, then there would be "great and ravaging epidemics to repress what is redundant."[141] Redundancy for Malthus is a measure of productivity, with periods of higher population redundancy understood as a natural phenomenon. Karl Marx later countered this view by pointing out that redundancy is derivative of the emergent capitalist mode of production: "Development of machinery and the exploitation of the labour of women and children, inevitably made a great portion of the working class 'redundant.'"[142] Not mincing words, Marx accused Malthus of stumbling into success because his theory served the reactionary ideals of the aristocratic agenda.[143] That Selkirk was such a proponent of the Malthusian thesis might be expected given that population redundancy informed his vision of incentivized resettlement and allowed him to champion a type of betterment campaign that did not threaten his own status.

Redundant workers were only one sign of the swath of changes under way, and vengeful British policy bent on the pacification of the Highlands later combined with the clearances to great consequence.[144] Subsistence farming was the standard of production in the Highlands, and it was characterized by customary agreements between landlord and tenant, but this way of life could hardly escape the pressure of food scarcity, internal power struggles, and external economic influences.[145] The clearances represented concerted initiatives to "improve" the agricultural industry, mainly with the objective of obtaining higher profits by changing small tenant holdings into pastures, which meant dispossession through eviction.[146] Sheep and deer-hunting forests materialized where previously there were tenant farmers, with demand for Highland property leading to an upswing in the commercial value of land by the mid-nineteenth century.[147]

"Depopulation, the great Malthusian panacea,"[148] enlivened the capitalist colonizers and speculators of the day, including Selkirk, who proposed in 1802 to Lord Pelham (then the home secretary for Ireland) to resettle Irish people in Louisiana – later revising the proposal with Rupert's Land as the preferred destination.[149] To make his case, Selkirk offered to engineer the removal of the most "turbulent and disaffected" among the Irish, "whose habits of idleness and irregularity render them most difficult to be converted into useful and industrious subjects."[150] He suggested that it would be in the interests of the British government to relocate the Irish from areas "where the increase of Population is so rapid" to a land "deficient in numbers," claiming that upon arrival they might discover within themselves a spark of industriousness, whereas "at home they would be worse than useless."[151] Personal sacrifice was also on offer, with Selkirk willing "to devote his personal exertions and the best years of his life" to this pursuit as an added assurance.[152] He suggested that the lands just south of "Lake Winnipeck" were especially worth settling given the fertility of the soil and a climate that he described as comparable to that of Germany, Poland, and parts of Russia.[153] It remained his opinion, however, that the HBC monopoly was "the greatest impediment to a Colony in this quarter,"[154] yet a mere decade later he became the staunchest defender of that very privilege.

Denied a government agreement for a colony in the west, Selkirk received approval for a settlement on Prince Edward Island in 1803 and another in Upper Canada in 1804,[155] and he travelled to these locales to select the best sites in person.[156] In a publication in 1805, he again pleaded his case to the deep pockets of London regarding "the necessity of active interference,"[157] and he did so by prematurely celebrating the success of the settler colonies already established.[158] Within a year, however, illness, mismanagement, and miscommunication appeared to question the viability of these two settlements, though this did not diminish his pursuits in a publication in 1806 in which Selkirk again favourably cited Malthus.[159]

Traces of the same Malthusian crutch are perceptible in an unpublished "Advertisement and Prospectus of the New Colony." It is undated; however, given his pronounced interest in military matters and parliamentary politics at this juncture, the advertisement was likely written in haste around the time that Selkirk wrote his "Observations": that is, when he was still campaigning the government for a land grant.[160] Although uncirculated, this document yields insight into why he wanted to pursue this "experiment."[161] Explicit in his concern about those British jurisdictions "most overburdened with inhabitants, viz. the Highlands of Scotland, and some parts of Ireland," Selkirk rejected the option to open the colony to settlers from the United States because they were not likely to behave as loyal subjects of the crown.[162] Other controversies associated with this pamphlet centre on the extent to which Selkirk misrepresented the climate and soil quality,[163] as well as his glaring omission of a substantive account of the Indigenous societies in the area. This might have been a shrewd omission since this was an advertisement, which can also be read as a telling measure of his sense of entitlement. Selkirk admitted that the settler colony would be an expensive undertaking and that no investor who expected swift returns should consider it,[164] but then he quickly injected an air of confidence by amplifying the favourable prospect of significant returns in the form of rent or payment for land title. He also understood that especially attractive incentives – in the form of lower prices for alienated land – would be necessary to recruit the first wave of settlers and that it would be at least up to twelve years before those settlers would have "purchase money."[165]

As a Scottish peer elected to the House of Lords, Selkirk was eager to impress his colleagues with his skills as an orator. But his political ambitions began to stagnate in 1807, around the time that Alexander Mackenzie approached him with a business arrangement to expand the fur trade into the northwest.[166] Mackenzie's famed *Voyages*, which includes an account of the land and people in the area of the Red River,[167] perhaps caught the eye of Selkirk some years earlier.[168] Mackenzie might have inspired Selkirk's vision, yet there was little in Mackenzie's account that would have turned Selkirk's mind to the Red River area in particular.[169] Instead, historian Barry Kaye finds "quite the opposite: references to sand, gravel, short grass, and timber scarcity would more likely have raised the spectre of sterility and low agricultural potential."[170] Selkirk's overselling in "Advertisement and Prospectus of the New Colony" of the agricultural prospects suggests that, against on-the-ground evidence, Selkirk was willing to disclose to the government "what he thought it wanted to hear."[171] After multiple rejections to his requests for a land grant, perhaps he recognized that the better, if not the only, way to realize his aspirations was to align himself with one of the fur trading companies competing for territorial control.[172] Whereas his earlier proposals might have suffered from promising too much, Selkirk learned from his settler colonial efforts in Upper Canada and Prince Edward Island.[173] He eventually accepted that, if the HBC monopoly was the "greatest impediment to a Colony," then he might be better served by working with the company and using its monopoly to achieve his goals.[174] Mackenzie, for his part, wanted to agitate for access to HBC trade routes on behalf of his Montreal-based fur company.[175]

Mackenzie and Selkirk, "two promoters of grandiose schemes,"[176] thus joined forces and began to buy large quantities of depreciating HBC stock.[177] They hoped that by joining efforts their combined pressure might sway the HBC committee to agree to grant land for a colony (Selkirk) and ease the North West Company's transportation burdens (Mackenzie). By 1811, however, it became plain that these objectives were incompatible to a significant extent.[178]

The Grant and Instructions for Settlement

Mackenzie and the other NWC partners were aware of the advantage that their competitor held, so they sought a like privilege. In an 1810 pamphlet originally scribed by Duncan McGillivray (though the 1811 publication was attributed to Nathaniel Atcheson or John Henry), the case was advanced to the British government for a monopoly charter that would grant an exclusive right to the North West Company to trade furs in the northwest. The pamphlet emphasized the hardships of the company and painted a dire picture of its chance for survival without a monopoly.[179] High transportation costs met with restrictions on territorial access that accompanied the tête-à-tête with the Hudson's Bay Company,[180] sending into doubt the likelihood that the North West Company could continue its operations for both economic and legal reasons. The plea warned of a looming incursion from "a foreign people" (i.e., American settlers) and insisted that, should the latter company be dissolved, "the Indian Territory becomes the theatre of contention."[181] By appealing to British authorities, the hope was that the company's exclusive claim to the area would be formalized, stemming the threat from the United States and ending the vague jurisdiction of the "Indian Territory," which remained unresolved by the act of 1803.[182] The NWC men presented themselves as the natural, deserving, and capable standard bearers for British interests in North America.[183]

This appeal to the British government failed, just as the negotiations between Mackenzie (along with other Montreal merchants) and the Hudson's Bay Company stalled. Consolidated and digitized anthologies, which include copied and archived letters under the heading "Selkirk Papers," attest to the aimless nature of the exchanges between the high-ranking men of the two companies. A letter dated June 3, 1811, from prominent Montrealers to William Mainwaring (then the HBC governor), cited recent and ongoing violence as a reason to renew negotiations,[184] which they presented as an attempt to "prevent the recurrence of such melancholy results from a violent competition in the trade of a country so far removed from the protection of Justice."[185] Deterrence served as "the greatest inducement," but "another great motive" was "the mutual Interest of both parties ... to curtail expence [sic] in the competition."[186] The HBC response, on June 26, 1811, hinted that the Montrealers' letter could be interpreted as an ultimatum – that is, if the Hudson's Bay Company should ignore these attempts at rapprochement, then there would be more violence.[187] The HBC

94 *A Legacy of Exploitation*

representatives also referred to "the limits specified in our charter," which stipulated that they must be the sole claimants of "the country lying on the waters which run into Hudsons [sic] Bay."[188] Here the charter returned as a minimum guarantee for the Hudson's Bay Company – a statement less of privilege than of duty – precisely what the Montrealers were attempting to curb in their efforts to gain access to the bay. By August 28, 1811, negotiations deteriorated again, with the HBC directors stipulating that the Montrealers could have the Athabasca region, being prepared to grant them an informal monopoly as long as the Hudson's Bay Company kept its authority over Rupert's Land.[189] Mackenzie's efforts were therefore once again thwarted, and by 1812 he returned to Scotland, married a girl aged fourteen, and died eight years later.[190] His retreat also happened to coincide with the arrival of the first settlers at Red River under Selkirk's charge.

To decide whether to issue the land grant requested by Selkirk, a "general court of proprietors" convened in accordance with the conditions of the HBC charter of 1670.[191] The terms of the grant stipulated the governance structure but also contained a clause requiring that within ten years Selkirk and his heirs or agents settle "one thousand families, each of them consisting of one married couple at the least," or the company could undertake to "revoke the grant."[192] Another revocation clause made it prohibitive for Selkirk, his agents, and the settlers to encroach on the "exclusive rights, power, privileges, and immunities of commerce, trade and traffick [sic]" of the Hudson's Bay Company, citing the charter as the basis for this restriction.[193] At the same time, all objects of production with regard to cultivation of lands and livestock were destined for use or consumption by the company, and all goods entering the territory had to travel via its own ships, effectively securing a captive market for HBC-procured goods.[194] In terms of the company's obligations, the final clause of the grant stipulated that the company would commit to the "well-being" of the settler colony by establishing and maintaining, as needed, courts and police in addition to systems of communication and public offices.[195] Even in the concessions listed in this grant, the contract can be read as a testament to, and a girding of, the exclusive rights and authorities that the company had long enjoyed. What is more, with the founding of a settlement under the purview of the company's authority (albeit at arm's length), commercial and legal interests converged in plain sight.

A shareholders' petition was submitted to the HBC directors in protest of this conveyance, signed by six men with glaring conflicts of interest in the matter: most were closely aligned with the North West Company, and two purchased HBC shares just prior to the general court.[196] The petitioners listed eight reasons the grant should be denied: the considerable size and value of the land; the lack of a public auction of the land; the paltriness of the punitive clauses should Selkirk fail; the likelihood that this grant was a vanity project for him; the prospect of incursions by the United States through private trading that would inevitably occur; the potential for the colony to be a haven for deserters; the proximity to the United States that would undermine HBC interests in the north; and the ongoing "sacrifices" that the company would need to make in order to stabilize the settlement, namely in the form of the promise to establish a court system and maintain police.[197] To Selkirk's delight, the petition was not successful, but the eight grievances did strike at the core of the HBC committee's gravest concerns: private trading, desertion, and the westward advances in the US territories. Officials attempted to account for these concerns in drafting the terms of the grant, awarded to Selkirk in 1811.

The grant encompassed the southern half of present-day Manitoba and beyond, amounting to an area of 186,000 square kilometres.[198] The official name of the area was the District of Assiniboia,[199] derived from the Assiniboine River that begins in Saskatchewan and terminates where it meets the Red River (the site of the eponymous settler colony) and from the name given by the French to the group of Indigenous peoples on the plains. Multiple contracts comprised the legal foundation of the settlement, which included a contract between the Hudson's Bay Company and Selkirk outlining the terms of the transaction; another contract between the settlers and the company that legally secured the exclusive rights of English goods; and many individual servant contracts that stipulated precise conditions to be met before they would retain their segments of land. In this scheme, the company conceded title to a portion of "the most enduring of all possessions,"[200] but this was only in exchange for formal legal control over the economic activities of its inhabitants. The furs in the area of the Red River had depleted, so from the perspective of the HBC committee the land had little value in that regard; however, one of its greatest features was its geographical placement at the juncture of two key rivers. As "the hub of the competing NWC's transportation network,"[201] it encompassed a major portion of the NWC trade route and was the site of a sizable herd of buffalo, which sustained both Indigenous societies of the region and the men of rival trading outfits.[202] In claiming this site, the Hudson's Bay Company made an aggressive choice, to say the least.

The Red River Colony was a double-fronted imposition: economic and legal. On the economic front, the settlement was intended to become a site of both production and consumption to minimize the Hudson's Bay Company's dependence on Indigenous producers, and it became one of the means by which the company undermined NWC control of the area. On the legal front, it was the gateway to the official dispossession of the lands of the Indigenous peoples in the region, which undergirded further changes to their social relations. Formal law's apparent reach into the "Indian Territories" did not portend the end of customary reciprocity, though the distortion of customary practices deepened the exploitative relations and laid the groundwork for institutionalized segregation.

The import of this initiative is underscored by the details contained in the instructions that Selkirk sent to the freshly appointed governor of the District of Assiniboia, Captain Miles Macdonell, who acted as the designated manager of the Red River Colony on behalf of Selkirk.[203] Between Selkirk's vision and on-the-ground reality sat Macdonell, tasked with "interpreting, modifying, and implementing policy in light of local conditions."[204] Common sense would have it that the bearer of such responsibilities would have some connections or more than a passing familiarity with the terrain and peoples in it, but Macdonell lacked these basic qualifications. His journal entries were laden with exclamations of surprise at what he saw, but it was in his descriptions of the Indigenous peoples whom he encountered in the first weeks that his naïveté was most prevalent. Unsure about customs and ignorant of consequences, he operated on appearances – on one occasion identifying the supposed leader of an Indigenous party based upon how long it took the man to dress himself.[205]

In establishing the settlement, Macdonell was expected to identify suitable candidates: Scottish were preferred, some Irish were permitted, and in all instances married men were favoured.[206] The men were expected to sign three-year contracts, and each was to have an account opened in his name to facilitate the tracking of goods and dues, a continuation of established trucking practices.[207] Selkirk's instructions also emphasized the need for a distinctly military type of discipline: "It is of great importance to introduce and keep up from the first habits of exact subordination, and implicit obedience to command," yet Macdonell should avoid "exciting the jealousy of the people, who might think they were kidnapped if the forms of military service were prematurely introduced."[208] Selkirk, by this account, was making soldiers on the sly. Macdonell was to introduce the standards of military service on the ship, naming guardsmen to warn "against surprise from Indians," and eventually establish quarters in the form of garrisons.[209] That the Red River Colony was to be fashioned in this manner is significant since a military garrison, compared to a permanent settlement, would not arouse as much immediate suspicion among the locals.

It was not until the penultimate paragraph of the document that Selkirk turned his attention to the Indigenous peoples – and this was perhaps the boldest expression of his colonial ambitions. The objective was to dupe them into believing that the settlement was just "an ordinary trading post," and for that purpose the overall number of men at the site should not exceed what had come to be

Honour and Duplicity 97

expected as the normal complement for a post.[210] There was some sense that this ruse would not be convincing for long, but it was necessary "at least till the post is well established and fortified."[211] And here was the crux: "When it can no longer be concealed that the establishment is to be permanent, if the jealousy of the Indians appears to be roused, the proposal of purchasing the land must be brought forward."[212] Palpable in this directive was Selkirk's intention to conceal insidious actions that amounted to theft in plain sight.

There was no expectation that a permanent settlement would be welcomed, and, although the settlers and governor anticipated eventually having to account for their presence, they did not doubt that they could easily quell disturbances by offering to "purchase" the land – again on terms in their favour. Selkirk emphasized the custom of gift-giving by insisting that Macdonell secure sufficient provisions to sustain the expedition, and he encouraged his appointee to bring goods to trade with members of the nearby Indigenous societies. Selkirk explicitly acknowledged the importance of "obtaining the friendship of the Indians," but then he stated that "it would certainly be wrong to trust very much" in that friendship, adding that "better security will be in the awe which they will entertain for so strong a post, if they see it guarded with unremitted vigilance."[213] To indict the untrustworthiness of Indigenous peoples while scheming a grand deception was indicative of the prevailing sense of entitlement. This was stressed by the reference in the instructions to a "vaccine," which can be inferred was designed to curb the spread of smallpox,[214] a disease that had greatly diminished many Indigenous populations in the area surrounding Cumberland House thirty years earlier.[215] Among Red River societies farther south, the consequences of the outbreak in 1781 were similarly severe, as James Daschuk remarks: "Assiniboine losses in the community that came to be known as Dead River led to an invitation of Anishinabe to occupy the region."[216] The mention of a "vaccine" in Selkirk's instructions was no small matter for those Indigenous societies that suffered such grave losses, but that it was referred to as a "gift" to be exchanged for favour is remarkable.[217]

An appreciation of the gravity of this offering is clear in the passages of the document itself. Selkirk wrote that "[a] boon of immense consequences may be held out in the communication of the vaccine."[218] He was far from ignorant of its value. As likely the earliest record explicitly connecting the Hudson's Bay Company to the existence of the smallpox vaccine,[219] his direction that Macdonell be prepared to offer the vaccine in exchange for the alienation of land disclosed a genocidal dimension of this early colonial settlement – the underlying assumption being that, if the company just waited long enough, the disease would clear the plains for it. However, there is also evidence of the lengths that the company went to in order to curb the spread of the disease through quarantine and to ensure that as many as possible would be immunized as the vaccine became more readily available two decades later.[220] Whether or not the latter efforts offset the malevolent intentions that this singular document made explicit is not a point that should be conceded too hastily, especially when these specific instructions are considered in their broader context. Even the most generous attribution of magnanimity to the Hudson's Bay Company fails to explain in a convincing way why it took almost a decade before the vaccine was made available at all.[221]

Selkirk's prescriptions show how this instance of settler colonialism grew out of the processes of dispossession that became common in the truck system, but the waves of death and displacement among Indigenous societies in the region increased the stakes of customary exchanges. Macdonell was instructed to ready a "payment" in which land would be alienated in exchange for life-saving medicine, and he was told that the transaction should take the form of an annuity as opposed to a lump sum. There is no need to guess at the rationale because Selkirk again stated it plainly: "An annuity to be annually distributed among the tribes and families, who have a claim to the lands, will form a permanent hold over their peaceable behaviour, as they must be made to understand that if any individual of the tribe violates that treaty, the payment will be withheld."[222] Pacification on top of dispossession – quite in keeping with the exploitative terms of previous transactions, whereby the Hudson's Bay Company assured itself of the more favourable outcome by consenting to an exchange if the relative value of the items served its advantage.

As a landed aristocrat, Selkirk had the confidence bred of material relations of exploitation, reflected in his certainty that the lands would be alienated successfully. In a letter that he wrote the same year, he informed Macdonell that he would receive £500, shares in the company, and 50,000 acres for his troubles, to be delivered upon the successful establishment of the settlement. These were substantial incentives on top of Macdonell's salary of £3,000 per year as the manager of the settler colony,[223] but economic enticements were not enough. Given the absence of a centralized government in the area, on December 12, 1811, the Provincial Secretary's Office published a notice in the *Quebec Gazette* announcing the instalment of Macdonell as a civil magistrate and justice of the peace "for any of the Indian Territories."[224] It is worth pausing here to comment on the convergence of commercial responsibility as a salaried agent working for the largest shareholder of the Hudson's Bay Company and administrative responsibility as a magistrate appointed by the governor of Lower Canada of supposedly lawless territories. The overlap is so significant that it becomes difficult to distinguish instances when decisions were made for the well-being of the company versus the well-being of the population of the lands that Macdonell was assigned to govern.[225]

Principled Hypocrisy

Even before he reached Red River in the fall, Macdonell wrote a letter of heightened urgency to Selkirk on the eve of the War of 1812 requesting "some kind of judicature in the Colony," perhaps realizing that impending war would be a convenient pretext to make the case for military support. Also worried about depending on the Indigenous peoples "or other external enemies," Macdonell wished to guard against internal mutiny. As an added measure, he used the occasion to propose that a licence system be established in which anyone who wanted to engage in trade had to apply for permission. On this last point, he suggested that this would be a way of bringing the North West Company to heel and outlined the commercial benefit of a bureaucratic imposition on the rival company.[226] In his reply dated a full year later, Selkirk agreed with Macdonell regarding the necessity of a "Judicature for the Colony," but he also admitted a lack of "legal knowledge" about how to achieve it.[227]

One of the persistent complications had to do with where grievances should be heard. The nature of the competition with the North West Company pushed this matter to the forefront for Selkirk, for the precise processes by which disagreements should be decided had serious consequences for how disputes in his settler colony might be treated. The legal line was fine: Macdonell, a colonial governor and an appointed magistrate of "Indian Territories," also executed the HBC charter of 1670, and Selkirk assumed that any land where the company conducted business was automatically within the sovereign purview of the company thanks to its charter. Anywhere that Macdonell conducted business as an agent of the company expanded the reach of the charter and as such was not subject to the Canada Jurisdiction Act of 1803, which required grievances to be heard in the provincial courts of Upper or Lower Canada. From the reigning logic, Macdonell was a magistrate in charge of "Indian Territories" that were simultaneously the vanishing grounds of his responsibilities as an agent of the Hudson's Bay Company; although a single jurisdiction could not be both in this instance, Macdonell had been delegated authorities that applied in either. Legal ambiguity, it must be said, can benefit commercial interests as much as the predictability afforded by established order – that legal developments occur in a straightforward manner as though moving from murkiness to clarity at the service of emergent capitalism is not supported by the evidence of this historical moment.

Selkirk was not oblivious of the nuances of this predicament, but it was in the broader interests of the Hudson's Bay Company to exercise – if subtly – its jurisdictional monopoly for as long as possible, which supposedly shielded it from external grievances and allowed its government-appointed agents to leverage in a strategic manner a range of empowering ordinances. Selkirk therefore instructed Macdonell to avoid confrontations with the North West Company that would draw attention to the precarious boundaries of this legal latitude, a continuation of the policy of conflict avoidance that obscured the real aggressiveness of exploitation exemplified by the violent clashes over Indigenous peoples' debts and the imposition of the settlement itself. He advised that the Hudson's Bay Company adopt a "defensive" position in relation to its rival, and Macdonell was to assume "all the powers that are necessary for maintaining the internal police of the settlement," even referencing the original charter to assure him that he had the "authority to act as a Judge."[228] The ideal in Selkirk's mind was to import the trial procedure formalized in England for criminal cases, but the small population of the settlement would not have been able to ensure the constitution of an impartial jury. In this case, Selkirk again instructed Macdonell to proceed cautiously: "If no doubt can be entertained of your having acted right to the best of your judgment, and kept as nearly as you could to the essential principles of the law of England, there can be no risk of your conduct being afterwards impeached."[229] The desire to punish but not be punished was the defining feature of Selkirk's hypocritical approach to the legal dilemmas of this era, a time depicted in concurrent moral and political philosophical works as fraught by contradictory impulses and a host of geopolitical intrigues.

Revolutionary wars in France and the United States were within his recent memory, and newly stoked democratic appetites clashed with the realities of the slave trade – manifested most pointedly in the Haitian Revolution fought from 1791 to 1803. As C.L.R. James makes plain, "the slaves had revolted because they wanted to be free. But no ruling class ever admits such things."[230] Decades earlier, at the time of the US Revolutionary War, stalwarts of the republican cause claimed the high principles of liberalism in the name of its independence even while they defended their reliance on slavery, and British loyalists saw themselves as the source of these liberal tenets in their most pure form at the same time that they advocated suppressing the American fight for freedom.[231] Neither could reconcile its position with any coherent force in relation to its actions. Domenico Losurdo remarks that, "like that of the blacks, the Indians' fate had not in the slightest unsettled the deep conviction of the English on either side of the Atlantic that they were the chosen people of liberty."[232] George Washington believed that the Royal Proclamation of 1763, which the British government had imposed to curb unruly land grabbing, was "immoral" because it prevented the capacity to civilize "'an unenlightened race of men,'"[233] words reminiscent of Jodi Byrd's remarks on how the "merciless Indian Savage" became the civilizational counterpoint on which "imperial desires" were exercised.[234] London was accused of having "incited these savage, bloodthirsty 'tribes,'" and it was in keeping with this logic that Thomas Jefferson insisted that it was

London's problem to undertake "'the extermination of this race in our America.'"[235] This stance echoes Grotius's claim about "just war," a position that justified slavery in the service of God and provided righteous armour for the violent campaign that centred on civilizing the "wild beasts."[236]

With the US Revolutionary War waged within his lifetime, and with the Haitian Revolution less than a decade old, Selkirk would have known about these events. That the HBC instructions to Macdonell expressed such worry about the potential threat posed by the Indigenous societies in the area of the Red River settlement is in keeping with these views. Even though these correspondences were laced with mistrust of Indigenous peoples, also palpable was a certain confidence that they could and should be pacified. This certainly had to be done with some measure of consideration to guard against any uprising, as had recently occurred in Haiti among the slaves, but notable is the nonchalance with which the Hudson's Bay Company was already divvying up the lands even before "purchasing" them from the Indigenous societies in question. That they had rights to the lands was a foregone conclusion; all barriers to realizing this truth were secondary and could be overcome on site with the right offering of gifts on company terms or in post hoc claims to humanitarian impulses. From Selkirk's perch, the company was doing the good work of the British Empire.

Harmony within the colony was a goal that Selkirk considered vital and attainable with a balanced political and juridical cocktail consisting of coercive order and individual right. He wanted to instill in the settlers the requisite level of respect for British legal principles and rules, but he did not want the actual laws to apply to his domain. Far from linear fatalism ushering in the predictability of a centralized system of formal law, Selkirk exploited the shifting legal grounds in the service of his twin interests in commercialism and settler colonialism. In this instance, where returns on investments were not guaranteed and a formal penal system was lacking, imported feudal norms plus a combination of customary reciprocity and debt-based obligation provided the crucible for obedience and exploitation. Perhaps counterintuitively, the original charter gave a degree of legal recourse to the use of force, yet it was with the unique combination of various elements of the overlapping modes of production that the fur trade companies succeeded. Note that the instructions from Selkirk to Macdonell counselled on the use of deception and urged a defensive posture. Even when it came to the large-scale dispossession of land, Selkirk initially relied on the distortion of customary reciprocity and the upper hand of unequal exchange, motivated as he was to avoid outright conflict.

Violence within the commercial fur trade was rife, but violent depravity was not officially tolerated. That it was considered reprehensible is clear in the breathless disdain of agents of the two fur trade companies whenever they accused each other of violent acts.[237] Honour and civility were performatively exalted as ways of bolstering the moral fortitude of their own position. Meanwhile, gift-giving and reciprocity were distorted as principal conduits of dispossession, proven by the fact that companies used these exploitative exchanges as primary means of profit extraction. Obligations extended to company men, requiring them to act in accordance with the prevailing social relations of land, expressly upheld but practically eroded in the course of these exchanges. Righteous disregard for their own responsibilities arising from these exchanges became the standard, upheld whenever Indigenous peoples attempted to claim what the companies owed them.

The lack of violent, direct force as a norm of labour compulsion denotes not a virtuous type of colonialism-lite but just one way of achieving the same end. As Glen Sean Coulthard remarks,

> In the specific context of Canadian settler-colonialism, although the *means* by which the colonial state has sought to eliminate Indigenous peoples in order to gain access to our lands and resources have modified over the last two centuries ... the *ends* have always remained the same: to shore up continued access to Indigenous peoples' territories for the purposes of state formation, settlement, and capitalist development.[238]

Customary reciprocity and debt-based obligation were modified and combined in the more overt practices aimed at the dispossession of the Indigenous societies of the prairies. Yet in 1794 NWC partner Duncan McGillivray was impressed by the relative autonomy of the Indigenous peoples along the North Saskatchewan River, whose access to meat and skins afforded an important degree of self-sufficiency.[239] The nature of transformation on the prairies initially involved a remarkable lack of forceful incursion by the companies, which exercised instead a truck system that accommodated a degree of autonomy among Indigenous producers. It was not until certain changes to Indigenous social relations of land materialized that performances of apparent reciprocity subsided, at which point there was an increasing reliance on force. One such measure involved the execution of a key component of Selkirk's instructions: the militarization of servants coming to settle at Red River – yet even this has a long history in how the Hudson's Bay Company conducted transactions because of the naval training of its earliest traders.[240]

4

Servitude and Independence
The Settler Colonial "Experiment" Begins

ON THE GROUND in the early quarter of the nineteenth century, the inhabitants of the Red River Colony were not capable of independent subsistence, nor was there an established market where they could purchase life-sustaining goods. This realization raises doubts about the purpose, structure, viability, and legacy of this settler colony. From one angle, the HBC committee's economic objectives were straightforward: "to establish at Red River a commercial agricultural colony that combined cropping and livestock rearing" with the hope that this production would reduce importation and transportation costs for provisions,[1] thus giving the company an edge in its competition with the North West Company for dominance in the Athabascan fur trade.[2] From another angle, the settlement represented a qualitative shift in course for the company.

Animosity would be expected with this belligerent move into the area by the Hudson's Bay Company, but in the initial months of this settler colonial foothold on the plains there was some degree of cooperation. The looming War of 1812 between the United States and Britain (including the Canadas, several Indigenous allies, and eventually Spain) had direct resonances on the circumstances of the settlement, aggravated all the while by the unresolved matter of jurisdictional authority between the two fur trade companies. Both sides claimed to act in the service of the crown, but their clashes evoke what Lauren Benton refers to as "the fluid jurisdictional politics of colonial settings."[3] Such disputes entailed challenges to ownership and strategies of dispossession; for Benton, this shows that "legal institutions emerged *with* capitalist relations of production through repetitive assertions of power and responses to power."[4] To build upon her deft study of "jurisdictional politics" within the context of the historical emergence of capitalism, it is necessary to study the entwined transformations of legal and economic relations rather than focus mainly on the legal and political spheres.[5]

Long fattened on the informalities and inequities endemic to the merchant credit–backed truck system, many investors were habituated to the exploitative terms of exchange. Gone was the creditor's brash assuredness that seemed to reign in the late eighteenth century. By the time the Hudson's Bay Company was willing to gamble on a settler colonial strategy, confidence was replaced by a growing appetite for direct, violent extra-economic force through more formal means. However, the extension of such formalism "was rarely simple"[6] or evenly applied. With the company's officers attempting to exercise their jurisdictional privileges in new ways, established processes of dispossession became alloyed with increasingly legalistic claims. This began to formalize a type of segregation between Indigenous peoples as "subjects" on whom legality was exercised in highly variable ways and settlers as eventual "citizens" with associated political freedoms and duties.[7]

The Enforcement Question

"With the settlers came the first treaty in the Canadian West and the first missionary and 'civilizing' efforts aimed at Native people there," remarks Laura Peers, highlighting the magnitude of changes that the settler colony both represented and unleashed.[8] At base, the settlement was simultaneously an economic strategy of preventing the further loss of profits by the Hudson's Bay Company and a legal strategy that reflected the changing nature of social relations of land at that time. Rosa Luxemburg provides even greater context for these transformations, explaining that the extant mode of production is anathema to capitalism because of its limited production and consumption capacity.[9] In the case at hand, limited production was evident in the lack of willingness, need, means, or capacity to produce surplus furs for the market, and limited consumption occurred thanks to the localized, intersocial practices of reciprocity that buttressed autonomy and stemmed growing demand for imported goods. Yet the distortion of these practices remained the primary means of labour compulsion for the companies.

An archetypal account of settler colonialism tells of how the ballooning number of settlers became self-sufficient, which in turn undermined dependence on Indigenous peoples and eroded the earlier "peaceful coexistence."[10] The events at Red River revealed even more troublesome developments. The notion that relations shifted from "relative equality between peoples to a colonial relationship" miscasts this as a break from, not a continuation of, actual processes of colonial dispossession that animated the fur trade prior to settlement, and it overlooks the exploitative nature of the truck system especially as it pertained to Indigenous peoples' labour.[11] Against this narrative, I detail the extent to which settler colonial relations at Red River dovetailed with long-established practices of dispossession, revealing that in fact it was the growing dependence of settlers on Indigenous peoples' labour that frustrated relations, paving the way for new measures of control.

As a commercial enterprise coeval with the slave trade, the fur trade might seem to be comparatively benign, but there was no sharp demarcation between the two. Economically speaking, intercontinental commodity trading required seaworthy vessels, which demanded capital, lumber, and labour on a scale that would have been unachievable without the slave trade. In his study of the social and economic history of slave ships, Marcus Rediker comments that "each phase of the process, from exploration to settlement to production to trade and the construction of a new economic order, required massive fleets of ships and their capacity to transport both expropriated labourers and the new commodities. The Guineaman [i.e., slave ship] was a linchpin of the system."[12] Again, it is imprudent to draw too deep a divide between the two trades, which could amount to externalizing "the intertwined histories of slavery, patriarchy, racism, colonial subjugation and exploitation so fundamental to the making of capitalist modernity."[13] Unequivocally, the sugar, rum, metals, and textiles readily exchanged as gifts or given as compensation in the truck system of the fur trade were all directly linked to the slave trade.[14]

Preferences for less forceful means of exerting control appeared in even the most imbalanced power relations, such as on the slave ship. Rediker offers an inkling of why some captains opted for a more measured approach to their management of slaves.[15] While extolling the benefits of the slave trade to British parliamentarians in 1788, Captain Robert Norris claimed that "good treatment ... was in the captain's self-interest, as he stood to make a 6 percent commission over and above his salary on the slaves delivered healthy and alive" – this was meant to bolster the notion that "'Interest' and 'Humanity' were perfectly united in the slave trade."[16] Even where there was veritable free rein to terrorize their human cargo, Rediker's study shows, captains might have had self-interested reasons to quell that impulse.

Similarly, in the Canadas, there was reason for British colonial officials to show goodwill. This was the prevalent sentiment in 1812 when Governor-in-Chief of British North America Sir George Prevost penned a directive to Superintendent and Inspector General of Indian Affairs Sir John Johnson. Prevost, head of the military on the eve of the War of 1812, outlined measures by which day-to-day order was to be maintained with respect to the Indigenous societies in the provinces.[17] Reminiscent of Selkirk's instructions to Macdonell, Prevost's duplicity scarcely masked his disdain and self-entitlement. This is clear in the explicit paternatism of Prevost's explanation that it made good economic and legal sense to have the Indigenous peoples believe that nothing nefarious was afoot – a means of ensuring that they would act like "good & obedient children."[18] This rationale resonated in his first prescription: "These people consider themselves free & independent and are in fact unacquainted with control and subordination," and because of their lack of amenability to external authority "they are alone to be governed by address & persuasion & they require the utmost attention to ceremonies & external appearances."[19] Attentiveness to ceremonial rites, principally the custom of gift-giving and associated displays of respect, was considered critical. From these instructions, the calculated administration of what was referred to throughout as "Presents" became distorted in an attempt at controlling the Indigenous peoples themselves.

There was an obvious economic advantage to less coercive means of labour compulsion, as W.L. Morton crassly states: "The only good Indian was not a dead one; he was, on the contrary, a live one who would follow his trap line."[20] In addition to being integral to the productive labour of the fur trade, Indigenous producers were obliged to pay debts since they operated in the truck economy. Importantly, the transference of debt to the family was not a promising option since several Indigenous societies engaged in mourning rituals ensuring that nothing could be recovered. In his essay on the Nēhiyawok and Saulteaux, Paul Hackett explains that, "in addition to disposing of the deceased's personal possessions, relatives were also expected to destroy or rid themselves of their own property," noting that "on some occasions furs, clothes, and goods were said to have been given to others, while in many other cases they were burned, thrown in a river, or simply abandoned."[21] Evidence that the worldly possessions of the deceased were sometimes discarded as part of a mourning ritual is also cited by Laura Peers regarding the Saulteaux and by Victor Lytwyn with respect to the Maškēkowak,[22] adding insight into the prevailing social relations of land in a manner that reinforces the connection between the material world and "the rest of Creation."[23] Death therefore led both to a decrease in the front-line production of furs and sometimes to the need to absorb the deceased producer's debts – a twofold loss for the company that resonates in W.L. Morton's crassness.

Strategies of effective enforcement were therefore an abiding concern, not only in terms of day-to-day labour compulsion, but also in a punitive capacity. When it came to punishment for misdeeds, however, the preferred recourse was to engage in "immediate and equivalent retaliation."[24] Hamar Foster comments on the violent reflex among fur traders against "what they perceived as the Indians' penchant for stealing axes, horses, and other items of personal property," and he notes that traders routinely failed to appreciate how their own acts of despoliation "may have appeared just as felonious to the chiefs and tribes whose traditional resources these were."[25] Such events occurred at Henley House in 1754–55 and again in 1759 when "hostile Natives" destroyed an HBC store and killed nine company men in the process.[26] Practised judiciously among certain Indigenous societies, these were rarely spasms of wanton reactionary violence[27] but selectively undertaken measures "governed by customary expectations and principles of liability."[28] Individual acts of violence committed by a named Indigenous person, however, were scarcely detailed in the accounts from that place and time. Until the violence of 1816 in the Red River area at Seven Oaks, many colonizers' records suggest that the threat from Indigenous peoples was atmospheric and *in potentia* born from a general mistrust.[29]

If an Indigenous individual did commit an offence against an HBC representative after 1803, company officials were not inclined to acknowledge the jurisdiction of the courts of Upper or Lower Canada, where criminal offences would be tried.[30] At a minimum, this would require granting Indigenous peoples formal legal standing, which arguably HBC officers had the prerogative but not the will to do.[31] With no recourse to offload an Indigenous accused to Britain for trial, the company was caught between its own claim to exclusive authority and its commercial impetus to maintain good relations. In this instance, the formal extension of British law clashed with the limits of its own enforcement capacity and the customary practices that grounded exchange and conflict resolution.[32] This conundrum was palpable in Macdonell's journal entries of 1812–13. In one entry on November 11, 1812, Macdonell expressed surprise that one of the Indigenous traders with whom he had exchanged the day before "wantonly murdered 3 Canadians" in the past.[33] However, by March 9, 1813, he recorded having "received a present of dried meat from the Murderer,"[34] perhaps an indication that "vengeance-in-kind" was not an absolute maxim, especially when "compensation" of some sort better served the interests of all parties.[35] Indeed, the preferred approach for the company in the short term was distortion through the adoption of Indigenous customs[36] and differential treatment of the accused, as opposed to the self-defeating invocation of the Canada Jurisdiction Act.[37]

But as I have shown, the capitalist-in-waiting is not always so patient. Because of the fur trade's multi-pronged though sometimes unhurried erosion of the social relations of land, more overt measures were exercised.[38] Luxemburg states that "the accumulation of capital, seen as an historical process, employs force as a permanent weapon, not only at its genesis, but further on down to the present day."[39] The settlement was a testament to the growing impatience among HBC officials, who wanted more than tenuous, nominal control of the region, and though I concur with Luxemburg's statement on force as a "permanent weapon" in capitalism two caveats are warranted. First, the turn to direct, violent extra-economic force was concurrent with the growing formalization of legal processes associated with dispossession; consequently, where the means of control were consolidated at a formal level, they advanced the segregation of Indigenous peoples: that is, neither their complete eradication from the capitalist mode of production nor their total proletarianization. Second, it was not merely a matter of sluggish trade but also the dynamic aspects of Indigenous peoples' social relations of land and their adaptations in the process. That Indigenous

108 *A Legacy of Exploitation*

peoples retained some measure of relative autonomy remained a problem for the companies, and the growing spectre of overtly coercive force was meant to address this.

The exploitative dimensions of the commercial fur trade are indisputable, but the one-sided exercise of direct, violent extra-economic force was not its principal characteristic at the time and place in question, especially when it came to interactions with Indigenous producers. This historical analysis demonstrates that, where economic matters predominated, legal concerns could be relegated to the background, and when legal authority needed protection economic cravings could be consigned. In this interplay dwelled the dialectical facets of historical transformation, which in the early years of the settler colony had serious but discrete consequences for servants, settlers, and Indigenous peoples alike, as evident in the prohibition in 1814 on specific Indigenous hunting practices and the deaths of twenty-one HBC men in 1816.

"The Council of the Governor in Assiniboia"

More than a reaction to the imperatives of commercial competition, the Red River Colony was a symptom of the uneven and combined nature of legal and economic transformation in which the customary practices of the truck system contributed to the normalizing of the processes of dispossession, leading to this "embryonic 'institutional segregation.'"[40] In the previous chapter, I accounted for the reasons that the HBC committee ultimately conveyed the sizable land grant to Selkirk. These considerations – legal, economic, and geopolitical alike – were all reflected in a statement written by company men and sent to Lord Bathurst, then the secretary of state for war and the colonies, and as such someone who was immersed in both the War of 1812 and the Napoleonic Wars.[41] In the statement, the HBC committee members wrote about unsustainable levels of expenditures associated with importing and transporting provisions from England, and they contended that, because of the nonarable quality of bayside land, the company had to go farther into the interior to begin setting up the system necessary to supply provisions from within it.[42] They then suggested that the servants already contracted to the company were unlikely to be able to cultivate the land "with sufficient care and attention"; however, "independent settlers" with land tenures would ensure that the Hudson's Bay Company could receive "moderate price[s]" for the goods produced.[43]

Guidance and competence were in short measure from the earliest days of this settler colonial initiative, so it is fitting that the authors of the statement referred to this undertaking as "the experiment." The legal basis for it was likewise unproven from the outset and often fretted over as a result – tellingly, in this regard, the forty-fourth volume of the Selkirk Papers begins with a section titled "Law Opinions on Red River." The first entry is dated December 18, 1813, and speculatively attributed to a William Cruise, notable because it consists of a collection of questions that evaluate HBC claims to jurisdictional authority from a number of angles.[44] This source indicates that the letter of opinion was signed on February 22, 1812, some months prior to the first colonial settlement at Red River.[45] Accordingly, Cruise's opinions were indispensable in addressing the ambiguity of the legal viability of the experiment.

The first question – "does the right of the Company to the property of the soil appear to be open to any material objection?" – pertained to the legitimacy of the charter. Answering in the affirmative, Cruise cited the precedent set in 1683 by *East India Company v Sandys*, in which Thomas Sandys sought to outfit a merchant vessel and sail to the East Indies to conduct trade despite the monopoly held by the East India Company.[46] The case was decided in favour of the monopoly-holding company, and the lawyers for Sandys argued that, in upholding such a broad scope for crown prerogative, the company might eventually be emboldened to take on the role of a "formidable martial government."[47] Cruise explained that the reasoning offered in the *Sandys* decision would likely fail in his era given the fresh emphasis on statute law as the means by which these privileges could be decided. He also asserted that the East India Company had only a trade monopoly, whereas the HBC governors were designated as "proprietors of the soil, to hold to them and their successors forever,"[48] on which basis he confirmed the legitimacy of the latter company's right to the land. Deciding the first question in favour of the HBC charter gave him direction in terms of how to answer the subsequent eight questions. Responses amounted to logical enactments of authority emanating from the exclusive right to the land; for instance, Cruise acknowledged the Hudson's Bay Company's right to expel any transgressors, writing that the company "may certainly dispossess the Canadian traders by legal process, of the posts occupied by them, & may pull down any buildings erected by them."[49] Although Selkirk sought other opinions,[50] and continued to do so for a number of years,[51] he used Cruise's comments as leverage in the ongoing competition with the North West Company.[52]

By Cruise's logic, the HBC claim to the land was legitimate: it was held to the exclusion of other interests; it included all waterways linked to Hudson Bay; and Cruise affirmed that, even beyond the exclusive right to trade, the HBC governors were legally considered "proprietors" of the soil and had the "right to protect & preserve their property."[53] Perhaps most crucially, these rights and privileges carried with them dispute resolution and enforcement authority encompassing both civil and criminal matters, an authority that "may be exercised by the Company by authorizing their Governor and Council to hold a Court of Justice in which the English Law may be administered."[54]

Cruise also opined that deference to the courts of Lower Canada would be fundamentally incompatible with the English legal system given that the former operated more in line with French legal procedures. He admitted that actions could be brought to Upper Canada, and for NWC partners who resided in England there was recourse to the British courts, akin to what occurred in *Sandys*.

But there remained a degree of confusion about whose interests the institutions of the Red River Colony would serve. The revolving door of accountability was evident in the discrepant and cumulative nature of legal transformation, and the HBC committee was reluctant to expedite the establishment of legal dispute processes for overlapping claims to authority. Selkirk's campaign for a measure of recognition and support from the British government for the experiment would have gone some distance toward offsetting the costs of establishing a more formal legal body at Red River. In the absence of this commitment, however, Selkirk was in no rush to bankroll institutions to the detriment of his own ambitions. The legacy of this quandary is that the legislature in Manitoba is celebrated as "the first legislative body in western Canada," but its seed, the Council of Assiniboia, was a bureaucratic body beholden to company interests from the start.[55]

In a letter to Macdonell dated June 13, 1813, Selkirk wrote that, "by the Charter, the Governor of any of the Co.'s Establishments *with his Council* may try all causes, civil or criminal, & punish offences according to the Law of England. You have, therefore[,] authority to act as a judge; but to do this correctly, it is necessary that you have a council to sit as your assessors."[56] This exhibits the continuity of logic between the opinions rendered by Cruise and the instructions regarding judicial proceedings that Selkirk wished Macdonell would follow. Selkirk noted that what was needed was an assembly of members who would convene on matters pertinent to the judicial affairs of the colony; as "assessors,"[57] their duties recalled those associated with the courts of assize that operated across England during that era. To ready Macdonell, Selkirk provided him with an excerpt from a 1755 work titled *The Justice of the Peace, and Parish Officer* by Richard Burn – known as "the standard manual of the day for magistrates."[58] Burn advised that the assize was an ancient type of court "where the judges or assessors heard and determined causes" and where the sheriff was responsible for notifying justices of the peace and constables of their duties to attend the proceedings.[59] These courts were administered semi-regularly by travelling judges tasked with the responsibility of hearing and deciding civil cases. Characteristic of "decentralized administration," assizes were vital to local judicial administration and a system of dispute resolution that the British exported to colonies across the empire.[60] In the remote setting of the District of Assiniboia, appointees were vital intermediaries between local practices and the principles of British justice.

Selkirk's letter of June 1813 condensed and repeated many of Burn's ideas to Macdonell, underlining that the appointment of a sheriff was significant since it was up to him to "execute the judgements of the court," and the sheriff should be supported by "a few trusty men" – in this case settlers who, if "well officered, & trained to exact obedience ... will give you nearly as much security, as you could derive from a more regular military force."[61] Before such a court could be established, therefore, Macdonell had to make the requisite appointments – populating the district with settlers was congruent with populating the council. Selkirk instructed Macdonell on this matter as well, carefully outlining who should be appointed. Records do not provide a clear indication of who actually served on the council versus whose names were merely recommended;[62] however, based upon his journals and letters, Macdonell made appointments to the council in 1814, including John Spencer, who also became the sheriff.[63] These appointments were made in haste, and the first recorded meeting of the council did not take place until June 1815, though an ad hoc version met in 1813 without Macdonell's knowledge,[64] which hints at the suspicion of the appointed governor among many in the district.

Legal historian Edmund Henry Oliver recognizes the complicated origins and purposes of the council: "The first Council of Assiniboia was appointed to safeguard the judicial functions of the Governors. It was not so much a council *of* Assiniboia ... as the Council of the Governor *in* Assiniboia, not so much a legislative or administrative body as a judicial tribunal."[65] Oliver's wording is significant. By design, the Council of Assiniboia did not pretend to be a representative body, which would have extended the scope of its accountability; instead, it processed disputes as a means of legitimizing the governor's legal and economic claims. Perhaps to soften the hard truth of this imposing design, Selkirk stressed the sanctity of procedural justice with the hope that it would help to inoculate the system from the gravest accusations of bias. The membership of the council was therefore a delicate matter, and in a letter to Macdonell he ordered that "a few of the most respectable persons in the Settlement must be named as your Council, of which not less than two ought to sit along with you on any important case."[66] But it was also imperative that such a case not require punitive measures much beyond that of confinement. Any charge that carried with it "capital punishment or any other of great severity" was to be tried in Britain, and Selkirk emphasized that this channel was acceptable only as a last resort. Cases of this magnitude "must be very few indeed,"[67] he explained, adding that "nothing is to be gained by sending home any offenders to be tried in England, except in the single case of murder."[68] This condition divulges why

112 *A Legacy of Exploitation*

Selkirk was so deliberate in seeking legal opinions and drafting these instructions for his manager.

"The *appearance* of impartiality was essential" in the settler colonial context,[69] and the preponderance of procedural fairness was evident from Selkirk's insistence that serious cases be tried by a jury, the members of which would both witness and lend legitimacy to the display of authority that Macdonell was tasked with conducting. He was to call on the people of Red River to help decide such cases, and he had to gather the most suitable people as possible while recognizing that "some of them must be very illiterate."[70] Their competence aside, this arrangement was preferred because Selkirk sought a minimum guarantee of the enforcement of law rather than the prospect of having transgressions "go unpunished."[71] He wanted to empower Macdonell enough to ensure that he would not make a habit of deferring to the courts of England to oversee disputes but not so much that he might upset the North West Company before the settler colony was established with reinforcements. This judicial framework, however, remained an abstracted ideal that more than anything soothed Selkirk's mind regarding the legalities of the Red River Colony. It is easy enough to concoct schemes from afar, but it is another matter to put them into practice.

Selkirk was concerned with boosting his legal case through subtle manoeuvrings, yet when it came to executing his juridical responsibilities Macdonell's record was "unimpressive."[72] To a degree, that is explicable. According to his journals and letters, Macdonell was busy with basic tasks, such as procuring food for his charges, which included entertaining traders and assigning hunting parties. Also, he did not think highly of his colleagues, and such factious relationships meant that finding suitable appointees was not so straightforward. He abhorred delegating tasks to those whom he considered incompetent, and he relished his paternalistic status as one who could exercise discretionary power without having to defer to anyone other than Selkirk.

Clashes en Route

Opposition to Selkirk's grant continued, with efforts by the NWC partners to derail the lord's settler colonial goals. Their opposition took the form of a letter by Simon McGillivray published in 1811 and distributed in Scotland. It claimed that the recruits were being led to "an infertile region subject to an intemperate climate" and that the initiative was led by a man "who had already exerted himself to depopulate his native land."[73] Yet it was not the letter alone that complicated recruitment efforts. A basic though critical point was not clearly articulated to the recruits: Were they signing up as settlers, as workers under the private enterprise of Selkirk, or as employees meant to labour for the Hudson's Bay Company in the fur trade?[74] Since they had to sign servant contracts with the company prior to their arrival, they had a hybrid status. For this reason, I refer to the initial waves of newcomers as "servant-settlers."[75]

In July 1811, they left for Hudson Bay, making the sixty-one-day journey across the Atlantic Ocean and arriving at York Factory on the bay's coast by September 24; they then wintered there before heading toward the interior.[76] Sixty-six of the eighty-one men onboard were workers, and among them thirty-five were supposed to continue to Red River as servant-settlers: that is, men contracted as servants and expected to remain at the settlement at the end of their term.[77] Throughout this time, it remained unclear to whom they owed their obedience as servants and what they were expected to do. The blurred legal and economic standing of these servant-settlers carried consequences for the viability of the settler colony, especially when they were asked to take up arms in service of the experiment.

As the group travelled away from the bay, they stopped at company posts to trade for provisions, sometimes facing a harsh reception from officers and servants upset at the new tack that the Hudson's Bay Company was pursuing with this settler colonial initiative.[78] Macdonell's claim to have authority over so many of the men was one of the first clashes between Macdonell and Superintendent of the Northern Department William Auld, especially after being left with just thirty-five new servants to service the company's most expansive department.[79] And though Auld's scorn for Macdonell was palpable – at one point, Auld called him "a fool of the first magnitude"[80] – they shared contempt for the newcomers.[81] Within the complement of would-be settlers, matters were no better. The journey, which placed Scots and Irish in close quarters, proved to breed hostility to the point that some of them refused to travel together[82] and culminated in an open fracas between the two groups in January 1812.[83] Such discord seemed to fuel a more far-reaching mutinous spirit,[84] and in one case a servant-settler rebuffed his work orders and was punished, only to have his countrymen burn down the hut that served as a makeshift jail.[85] There was also an attempted uprising by servant-settlers at York Factory. Some men, including a group from Glasgow, "rebelled and could not be forced back to work until June,"[86] the culmination of growing distrust toward the HBC officers that prompted Auld to pen a "Notification to the Insurgents" in May 1812, telling the servant-settlers that they must obey Macdonell or face "evil consequences."[87]

Among such consequences were two possible outcomes. First, the "Glasgow Insurgents" had the option to return to service as soon as possible on the understanding that they would not receive any remuneration for the time spent withholding their labour.[88] Auld explained that any further punitive measures would be left to the "Honourable Committee's decision," effectively submitting the servant-settlers to the discretionary power of the HBC directors.[89] Second, for those who still refused to return to service, they could be forcibly confined on the HBC ship as prisoners and sent back to Britain to be tried by the court system there. On the one hand, these options point to an implicit divide regarding how violations of different degrees would be addressed by the company; the latter option, reserved for the most serious offences, not only was the most expensive but also gave company brass the least control over the outcome. On the other hand, the choices confirmed the HBC committee's position when it came to the jurisdictional authority of the Canadian courts since both were in opposition to the Jurisdiction Act of 1803. Each option therefore reinforced the company's claim to be the legitimate authority, superseded only by the juridical right of Britain itself.

Eventually, the risk of a widespread mutiny was quieted, and the trek to Red River continued in the spring. Some historians attribute this fragile peace to Macdonell's decision to arm himself and the others in the group, which prevented their ship from being commandeered by the insurrectionists,[90] yet it was just as likely that further agitation from below was difficult to sustain in such an alienating setting, in which the newcomers were poorly outfitted for the weather and their sustenance was controlled by the company itself. From Macdonell's perspective, such obstinacy represented more than a lack of respect for authority; it also pointed to an inborn thirst for independence among the stock of servant-settlers and the lack of a credible authoritative presence that could tame this tendency. Worried about what this might lead to if it were to continue unabated, Macdonell made multiple requests to Selkirk up to and following the establishment of the settlement for some form of "martial law."[91]

Even if the reports that Selkirk was receiving from abroad were causing him to lose faith in Macdonell's capacity for sound judgment, he might have thought that any possibility of a severe blunder could be mitigated by upholding a set of procedures that were both familiar and logical, and further, that the HBC supervisory hierarchy that resulted from the retrenchment could be relied on for its internal disciplinary mechanisms. In Auld, Selkirk thought that he had an overseer of Macdonell who could act as a guide and backstop against mischief, but he was disappointed. In a June 1813 letter to Auld, Selkirk admonished him for complaining about Macdonell and accused him of failing to act based upon his considerable experience to guide Macdonell's decisions, especially during the insurgency at York Factory the previous year.[92] Selkirk thought that Auld showed too much "lenity" to those who had "aided and abetted the mutineers."[93] Meanwhile, in letters to Macdonell, Selkirk encouraged him to adopt a more moderate stance. He argued that martial law would likely invite more problems than it would solve and emphasized the merits of "delicate management" in executing the legal authority of the Hudson's Bay Company.[94] Selkirk's taste for retribution paired well with his belief in the necessity of effective (i.e., enforced and enforceable) law, but it was at odds with his apparent taste for a defensive, less martial stance. That Selkirk continued to promote judicial proceedings that nourished the perception of impartiality suggests that he understood the value of law as spectacle – a spectacle that made it possible to curb leniency and perform fairness at the same time.

First Reception

The first wave of servant-settlers, sometimes referred to in militaristic terms as "the first brigade,"[95] arrived with Macdonell at the mouth of the Red River from Lake Winnipeg at noon on August 29, 1812.[96] Custom demanded a formal flag raising, a display of colours that signalled both the presence and the allegiance of Macdonell's party while announcing to their neighbours that they were prepared to receive traders.[97] Macdonell invited "freemen, servants, Indians," as well as "the gentlemen here of the NWC," all of whom took part in the ceremony,[98] and by outward appearances these measures were consistent with the usual practices undertaken when setting up a trading post. However, the flag raising coincided with the date of the formal conveyance of the grant: September 4, 1812. This confirmed that it was more than just another trading outlet, marked as it was by a signed declaration testifying that "peaceable possession of the land and hereditaments by the within-written indenture, granted and enfeoffed."[99] With this, the experiment officially commenced.

Already the end of summer upon arrival, there was no time to work the land for the next year's harvest, a situation that raised immediate concerns about the provisions that could sustain the servant-settlers through the winter.[100] With no likelihood of erecting habitable buildings prior to the onset of the colder months, the servant-settlers remained, for the most part, in the area of the Pembina Post (in present-day North Dakota, where the Pembina River joins the Red River), and some were put to work hunting buffalo,[101] which added still more competitors in a region already swollen with hunters. By this time, the group consisted of only seventeen men and one woman, mostly general labourers with an average age of about twenty-four. Macdonell made his urgent appeal to Selkirk for more coercive authority because of his concern about a mutiny, but it also reflected his apprehension about the means of compulsion at his disposal to control the labour of this meagre group of servant-settlers. "The present state of the country requires strong power to bring it to order," Macdonell

116 A Legacy of Exploitation

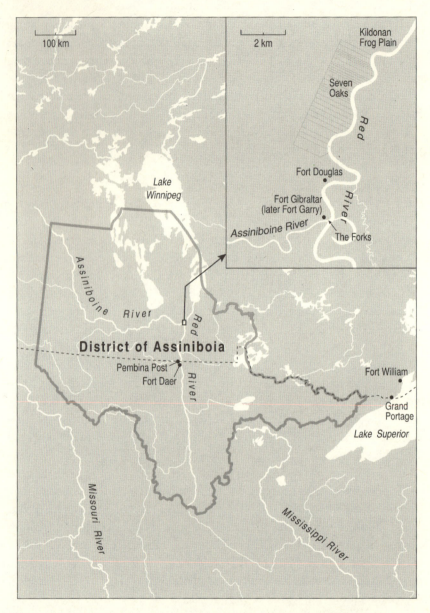

Figure 4.1 Map of the District of Assiniboia, 1811 | *Cartographer:* Eric Leinberger

wrote, "and if we are to have Glasgow weavers, or others of similar principles among us ... we may all be overturned by one tumultuous onset of our own people."[102] His disdain for the supposedly incorrigible servant-settlers was aggravated when they did not exhibit certain skills that he thought all individuals should naturally possess – such as the handling of arms[103] or a degree of agricultural know-how.[104] These apparent deficiencies became a recurring theme in his lamentations.

With a flair for confrontation through imposition, Macdonell's tendencies "were not encouraging signs in a man who was to be governor of a frontier settlement."[105] Initial discord over provisions occurred not between the two rival companies, as would have been expected, but between two HBC officers.[106] It did not take long for Macdonell to present himself indelicately to his colleagues, mainly by inserting himself in the established trade networks among the Indigenous producers, the North West Company, and the HBC men stationed at the Pembina Post. By his account from September 21, he bought meat from a freeman, and later he wrote that this "meddling" upset the officer of Pembina, Hugh Heney.[107] Tensions between Heney and Macdonell escalated, especially as the latter accepted dinner invitations from NWC officers within weeks of his arrival.[108] Some of Macdonell's relatives were active in the upper echelons of the North West Company, which might have enhanced his trust in the bitter rival.[109] So trusting was Macdonell that he kept his provisions in the NWC fort "for security," a rapport that made Heney anxious since he claimed that "it had a bad effect on the Indians."[110] This continued into the spring of 1813, to the point that Heney was one of the officers that Macdonell suspected of conspiring against him in the events that led to the first ad hoc meeting of the Council of Assiniboia, which expressly excluded the governor himself.

Macdonell also enjoyed amicable relationships with members of certain Indigenous societies in the region. Nearby Saulteaux were engaged in hunting, fishing, and agriculture (potatoes and corn), and the products of these activities helped the members of the "first brigade" to survive.[111] Among certain Saulteaux previously aligned with the North West Company, there was incredulity at the encroachment of the Selkirk settlers. This was exemplified by a derisive yet historically disputed[112] reference by the Premier (or Grandes Oreilles)[113] to the servant-settlers as "'makers of gardens,'" at which point he asked, "'who gave them our lands?'"[114] Others seemed to be less threatening at first sight, at least according to Macdonell's reading of the situation. Detailed in his journal is one encounter with Canard Noir, "a Soto Chief of Portage de Prairie,"[115] who arrived one morning looking "to be advised and instructed by me in what manner he and his people were to live and conduct themselves," and he "hoped I would not take all the soil from them."[116] His account of this exchange suggests that Canard Noir and his party were looking for assistance to alleviate their dire situation,[117] the cumulative effects of disease, displacement, and scarcity.

118   *A Legacy of Exploitation*

Even if contorted by his sense of self-importance, Macdonell's reply to Canard Noir offers insights into the HBC position with respect to the local Indigenous groups:

> I informed them that I was sent out here by the proprietor of the soil – to establish regulations for them & others in the country to furnish the bad & reward the good – that lands would be allotted them & that they should be instructed in the cultivation thereof for their own benefit ... I would endeavour to prevail on the Sieux [sic] to make peace with them or otherwise would assist to repel & reduce them to the necessity of suing for peace.[118]

When the passage is parsed, a few salient points surface. Macdonell claimed to have been sent to the area by "the proprietor of the soil," implying Selkirk, but more revelatory is the assertion of proprietorship in the first instance. Whether he made the true scope of this declaration clear is questionable, but Macdonell recorded Canard Noir's plea as an expression of deference. By explaining that "lands would be allotted them & that they should be instructed in the cultivation thereof," he both assumed and exercised his own jurisdictional authority as the agent of the "proprietor," unabashedly promising the Indigenous peoples allotments of land – as though it was his to redistribute – and peace with the Sioux.

Flashes of an eager paternalism were demonstrated again in 1813 when the Premier visited Macdonell on March 12. He noted in his journal that the Premier was pleased with the prospects of more regular trade that would certainly accompany a settlement and that this would be beneficial to the nearby Indigenous peoples.[119] The Premier had high expectations and received assurances from Macdonell that the "fire of [Macdonell's house at Pembina] will not be extinguished." In turn, the Premier's perceived enthusiasm gave Macdonell some relief in the face of growing worries about the possibility that another group at Red Lake – possibly Saulteaux but not named by Macdonell – was threatening to attack the burgeoning settlement. The impression left by the Premier was profound, as Macdonell penned: "They are by far the most decent Indians I have yet seen in the Country," and he honoured the Premier by raising the flag after they shared breakfast.[120]

The more arrogant dimensions of this relationship were not manifest until March 16 after Macdonell learned that the Premier and his counterparts referred to him as "our Father" when they visited the nearby NWC post after leaving him.[121] That the use of "Father" by the Premier so charmed Macdonell suggests that he understood it in its most superficial sense: namely, as an expression of submissiveness. However, the term has a complicated history in the British

North American context. Mark D. Walters explains that "the Anishinaabeg did not have a word for king," noting that the use of "father" reflected the custom of using "kinship terms" to reinforce obligation and loyalty, explicitly stating that "one thing that they were *not* doing was submitting to Crown sovereignty."[122] It was understood that the father figure owed "duties of care" within the framework of customary reciprocity and that the father figure "gave their relations resources and advice, but not commands."[123] Among British company men, however, paternalism bred fondness and strengthened trust, understood as having utilitarian value.[124] Gratified as Macdonell was to be called "Father," it was not long before his skewed meaning of the term was obvious;[125] as he became frustrated by the kinship-type duties attached to this term, care gave way to commands.

As matters of custom in the course of the fur trade, the gesture of flag raising and the extension of kinship were meant to encourage commercial and social bonds, but at this juncture such performances scarcely convinced either party. Peers contends that the first indication of a souring relationship between the HBC men at Red River and the nearby Saulteaux did not appear until 1817,[126] but Macdonell's recordings show that the seeds might have been sown much earlier during the spring of 1813, mere months after their initial exchange. The paternal figurehead was exasperated by the expectations attached to his status, in particular the level of accountability that the Premier demanded of him after learning that Macdonell had abandoned Pembina Post despite his assurances otherwise.[127] The Premier, wrote Macdonell on June 19, was "much disappointed at my leaving Pembina … [T]hey now came to see their father for his advice"; in response to this appeal, Macdonell tempered his promises: "Perhaps another year we should be able to render them assistance."[128] He explained that they left because there were not enough resources to maintain both Pembina and nearby, newly established Fort Daer. In an effort to mend relations, he provided the Premier with items needed for the battle against the Sioux – though Macdonell added that this was done "against my will."[129] The feeling of being obligated to provide supplies could also account for his receding patience when the Premier and his family returned in October, twice referring to their presence and requests as "troublesome."[130]

But the sense of danger from rival Indigenous groups and the struggling settlement might have provided sufficient reason at least to pay lip service to the ongoing alliance, so much so that, despite using the term "troublesome," Macdonell was again pleased to have the Premier make speeches to others about the importance of "respecting the establishment of the Colony."[131] Macdonell's uneasy offerings reveal an underlying truth about the Red River Colony: even with his conferred title and land grant in hand, Macdonell could not avoid relying on Indigenous producers. At the outset and throughout the lean years, local Indigenous peoples provided vital assistance to the members of Selkirk's settler colony,[132] ill prepared for the harsh climate. The nearby groups of Saulteaux were the primary points of contact, and they supplied the colonists with provisions as well as shelter in their time of need – acts that "made the difference between survival and starvation for the settlers."[133] These interactions were noteworthy because their assistance extended to defensive aid when the colonists faced threats from the North West Company.[134]

Peers sheds light on some of the possible reasons for the generosity that the servant-settlers received from some local Saulteaux, especially from Peguis. Although others left the region after the decline of the beaver population and game, some remained.[135] Peers, citing archival documents from 1814–15, notes that the sudden presence of traders buoyed spirits among remaining Indigenous parties, who hoped to benefit from the Europeans in some fashion since the fur trade was proving to be less fruitful than in previous years. An entry in Macdonell's journal dated September 30, 1812, supports this contention and likewise shows some measure of relief with the new HBC presence, as Macdonell remarked after his first meeting with Peguis: "The Cutnosed chief of the Forks a Soto had arrived last evening and came this morning with 5 attendants to visit me. He advanced with much apparent joy and took me by the hand."[136] Based upon these accounts, Selkirk's grand deception in having the settlers pretend to be innocuous fur traders never would have been feasible. As the parties that undertook the primary labour of trapping and hunting, local Indigenous peoples were well aware of the declining stocks of fur and game, and they were not likely to have been duped by Selkirk's pretense of establishing a new trading post.

The ruse was also improbable because the "first brigade" arrived when the War of 1812 was already about two months old. Although Selkirk could not have known this when he was writing his instructions to Macdonell in 1811, the war might have provided an advantageous backdrop to the otherwise obvious territorial incursion at the foot of Lake Winnipeg. Peers suggests as much, explaining that Saulteaux acceptance of and assistance to the servant-settlers indicated their own desire to have "access to the European's potential material wealth and military power."[137] With the commercial promise of the fur trade waning on the plains alongside a growing consumer market in the United States[138] – which stoked the appetite among British capitalists for "free trade"[139] – the Saulteaux were well aware of such changes, and this diplomatic compact was evidently more forthcoming as a result. Favourable relations were "created and maintained by gift-giving, and involved reciprocal physical and military support," Peers observes, noting too that these were not strictly altruistic acts, for the Saulteaux "fully expected their actions to be later rewarded and reciprocated."[140] Although

Macdonell was pleased at the initial expressions of deference and joy, he continued to resent the "reciprocal obligations of care."[141] He surmised that local Indigenous peoples could be pacified in the short term with "Indian rum" – but only up to the point that they became troublesome by wanting more,[142] not just rum but also protection and assurances.

Geopolitical upheavals related to the War of 1812 provided Macdonell and the Hudson's Bay Company with an opportunity to play a more overtly colonial role as peacemaker. By adopting a paternalistic stance, they presented themselves as just proprietors and under this guise formed alliances, but the economic entanglements of the settler colony were never far from Macdonell's mind. On this point, Peers comments that "the Company and the colony officials were not about to conform to Saulteaux terms of alliance at the expense of profit."[143] Such were the discrete effects of geopolitical changes during this founding period of the Red River Colony, which helped to shape not only the terms of the transition to a capitalist mode of production but also its legal elements.

Differentiation as Means and Ends

Despite the willingness of the HBC directors to gamble on the settler colony, the British government did not share Selkirk's optimism regarding the prospects for settlement at Red River. While Macdonell was busy in November 1812 cajoling the servant-settlers to bend their religious convictions and agree to work on the Sabbath,[144] Selkirk was engrossed by the task of winning the British government's approval of the initiative. Without such recognition and support, the Red River Colony remained outside "the ambit of official colonial status,"[145] meaning that it could not be established as effectively or efficiently as Selkirk would have liked since there was no public purse from which to draw.

It was during this period that he again turned his mind to the resettlement of "ignorant & distrustful" Irish.[146] Selkirk pleaded for some assistance at least in the form of the removal of statutory obstacles to the success of the settler colony. Such was the case with the Passenger Vessels Act of 1803, from which he desired an exemption that would allow the company to authorize the transportation of servant-settlers to British North America without having to submit to the restrictions stipulated in the act.[147] He also leveraged the circumstances of the War of 1812 to ask for "a small armed force, to serve as a Police guard, and to support the authority of the Governor."[148] Without government backing, private funds were essential. Selkirk sought subscriptions for land parcels, and the money was held in trust by three "well-known Evangelicals and humanitarian reformers" who gave a sheen of credibility to the experiment.[149] Again touting honour among creditors, Selkirk described the money as a "fund for defraying the charges of establishing the Colony."[150] For the servant-settlers, the allotment process did not take place until some time after their arrival. Selkirk's instructions from 1811 dictated the terms of land redistribution, which would not be possible until some proof of the soil's fertility could be obtained. Only once there was a "tolerably abundant" crop[151] could Macdonell grant lands to individual family units, who would then cultivate them and live off the yields. However, as often the case with Selkirk's vision, the simplicity of the directives belied the difficulty of their execution.

Macdonell was instructed to allocate lands to individuals who, by virtue of their initial contract, were technically servants. Regardless of whether the colonists expected to work directly for the Hudson's Bay Company, or whether they made the voyage as settlers strictly speaking, all were contracted as servants using the terms long established by the company.[152] For Selkirk, this contract was integral to establishing a permanent foundation for the colony. Legally speaking (per the contract) and economically speaking (per the terms of the truck system), Selkirk wanted them "under complete command," for that way they "may be employed in the most systematic manner, in distinct lands allotted for different branches of the work."[153] At the same time, he knew that the prospects of continued recruitment depended on the servant-settlers sending favourable news back to their friends and family members,[154] which at some stage required breaking the servile yoke to ensure more glowing reports.

Incentives to prospective settlers had to be great enough to make the prospect tempting, and feudal servitude – be it in support of the company or the colony – was unlikely to pique much interest. So Selkirk advised Macdonell that, should the crops prove to be adequate to allot the lands, the servant contracts should be terminated, with the expectation that "from the time that any man is thus set free, to work for himself, his wages ought to cease."[155] Unleashed from servitude, the individual would then be "free" to "be charged as a debtor to the establishment" on occasions when supplies or provisions were still required. Title to the land, meanwhile, would be granted to the settler only once his debts were paid in full.[156] This was in line with what Mamdani identifies as the basis of legal order in the settler colonial context: "appropriation of land, destruction of communal autonomy, and establishment of the 'freedom' of the individual to become a wage worker."[157] The instructions also implored caution when allocating lands, for Selkirk worried about how local Indigenous peoples would react to the sight of "scattered settlers" each claiming up to 100 acres. He recommended granting a maximum of 10 acres at the time until the worry subsided, and he reassured Macdonell that, as the population of the colony grew, it would have greater clout and not have to worry about upsetting the members of nearby Indigenous societies.

Tensions in the first years of the Red River Colony appeared almost as a mirror image of the dispute that occurred decades earlier in the Scottish Highlands. At the time of the clearances, the tenants were driven from the land by the lairds seeking to turn their holdings into sheep pastures; whatever approximation to subsistence farming that once existed was undermined by the wave of agricultural "improvements." At Red River, tenants were needed on the land to execute the labour essential not only to a self-sustaining community but also to a community of producers of provisions for export and a consumer market for imported goods. Tenants driven from farms were given the opportunity to undertake their own brands of improvements as freeholders of lands in their own right – ostensibly moving from tenants to landowners in the space of a single generation. Such a vision of freedom might have been proffered by recruiters in accordance with Selkirk's colonial agenda, but in reality the servant-settlers faced circumstances reminiscent of those that they had struggled against in their countries of origin. Contracted servants and the extensive truck system had long given the Hudson's Bay Company the type of exploitative relations needed to profit from the fur trade, and it was thought that the same arrangement was necessary in order to overcome the obstacles facing the experiment.

Given all of Selkirk's instructions and interventions, some historians might see strategic adeptness, but the heights of duplicity that Selkirk was capable of suggest that he was an opportunist with a shifting position on certain matters that made him seem feckless. This was on display in a letter in August 1812 to the Chancellor of the Exchequer when Selkirk appeared to want to rescue the Irish Catholics from themselves.[158] He sought to benefit from the colonial devastation of the Irish masses, people displaced and exploited by the anti-Catholic British government. Outwardly sympathetic to their plight, he recognized it as a rich source of potential settlers who could serve his colonial charge. This echoed his stance on the abolition of slavery. Although ostensibly against the commercial trade of slaves, Selkirk "blamed the existence of the trade on the petty needs of African leaders," and he thought that the solution would be to establish a "confederation of African nations" led by those who were "civilized," "disinterested," and in possession of "superior knowledge": that is, the British.[159]

Discourses of freedom were in the air, as E.P. Thompson notes, for "it was a time in which the plebeian movement placed an exceptionally high valuation upon egalitarian and democratic values."[160] However, that liberation might be agitated for from below was difficult to countenance from the perspective of a well-ensconced member of the aristocracy. As made plain in Selkirk's correspondence, freedom was not a birthright but a bestowment measured by one's utility in the establishment and maintenance of order.[161] For this reason, such an ideological devotion to the precepts of freedom could operate in concert with the continued exploitation of those without freedom. Events at Red River lend weight to Lisa Lowe's astute observation that "the abstract promises of abolition, emancipation, and the end of monopoly often obscure their embeddedness within colonial conditions of settlement, slavery, coerced labor, and imperial trades."[162] At the settler colonial site in question, Selkirk's false sympathy for the Irish cause led to some problems for Macdonell. The terms of the contracts under which early Irish servant-settlers laboured at Red River reflected this duplicity; as Macdonell explains, "the Indentures of the Irishmen are not well made out & give ill disposed men room to be troublesome."[163] Broadly stated guarantees were made to them regarding minimum levels of housing and food but were not in concert with the "general contracts" of the Hudson's Bay Company; although such guarantees might have won some servants over to Selkirk's cause, they presented impediments to their wholesale exploitation by Macdonell and the company.[164] Yet, as Burley notes, the Irish servant-settlers "were as disappointed with the HBC as it was with them."[165] Before long, they fell out of favour in terms of a resource for the labour needs of the company.

Macdonell proposed that the servant-settlers' insurrectionary appetites had roots in the "principles" of the colonists themselves, yet the obvious lack of preparation by Selkirk could have also stoked their recalcitrance. Not only were their terms of recruitment and employment ambiguous, but also their journey was so delayed that they arrived at their destination only to have to winter again offsite, all the while doing so without "suitable garments."[166] Upon their arrival at Red River, there were no horses on hand to facilitate "the stalking of buffalo for their subsistence,"[167] and there were only hand tools to break the ground and sow the wheat crop for the next year.[168] The explicit expectation of obedience hints at the feudal mindset; however, the servant-settlers were not cast in the same servile mould that the company had relied on in previous centuries. They had expectations of their own – nurtured perhaps by Selkirk's own recruitment campaign – for a new way of life once they arrived at Red River. As the lack of preparedness exposed itself as a chronic problem, there was little reason for the servant-settlers to follow the governor's orders.

Macdonell sensed this resistance early and instituted an ad hoc system of adjudication that hinted at juridical order but mostly relied on old-fashioned pecuniary and corporal punishment. On a few occasions, and for reasons never countenanced by Macdonell, the workers refused to perform their assigned tasks. His response on November 23, 1812, was to withhold food, a cruelty in any circumstance but especially so at a time when provisions were already scarce.[169] He noted his logic in his journal on December 12: "We only feed those men who continue to work."[170] Macdonell expressed this sentiment even more starkly in a letter to Selkirk in which he strained to comprehend why he should feed those unable to work since "their labour is not equivalent to the victuals they consume."[171] By denying them food, he saved provisions, rendered the men weak, and exercised his authority over them. Not surprisingly, this refusal had the intended effect, and Macdonell deemed that the "idle men" could have their breakfast, "they being now brought to a due sense of their error"; as an added assurance, the men sent somebody "to apologise for them & promise never to quit work again without orders."[172] But Macdonell's triumph was short lived. On February 3, five men refused to report for work in the morning, and Macdonell reacted by denying them meat and fining them ten shillings.[173]

By the middle of that month, two men who deserted some weeks earlier appeared at his camp; Macdonell had them "put in Irons," and then they were "tried," "found guilty," and "fined 3 month's [sic] pay."[174] Once the verdict was issued, Macdonell ordered the men to "resume work," which they refused to do apparently because of a dispute regarding the terms of their contract, at which point he "ordered them into confinement."[175] The familiarities associated with British due process were performed, though as a charade, with Macdonell operating simultaneously as prison warden, prosecutor, and police – not to mention employer and provider of sustenance. Notably, these admonishments were not confined to the male servants, with one incident involving his cook. When Mrs. Smyth, an American, once again refused to prepare his breakfast, he had her removed from his kitchen and wrote in his journal that she was "of Republican principles, does much mischief among the people – talking to them of the U. States – liberty & Equality."[176] The governor could hardly tolerate the idea of his labourers discussing liberty, an affront to the mixed feudalist and military campaign that he was leading.

The confused legal and economic standing of the servant-settlers was an extension of the lack of clarity as it pertained to the status of the settler colony and those tasked with overseeing its success. Overt coercion was certainly the predominant means of compulsion within the colony in those early years. However, by reflecting on five interrelated considerations, it is possible to untangle the web of legal and economic intrigues, helping us to gain a more coherent perspective that links these coercive practices to other goings-on.

First, from atop the hierarchy, Selkirk promoted an approach to judicial authority that was subject dependent, not "blind" in the idealized manner that saturates discourses of contemporary legal administration. This perspective does much to move the analysis past a superficial tautology – which maintains that the authority of Macdonell and the Hudson's Bay Company was ineffective because their claims were unenforceable – and offers a better understanding of the purposes and effects of social differentiation. With respect to servants, insubordination was to be punished categorically and immediately; this approach underscored the fact that as servants they had meagre grounds to contest the authority of their masters, so this was the one area where more severe force could be exercised. However, regarding voyageurs, the men of the North West Company, and members of nearby Indigenous societies, the Hudson's Bay Company's and settler colony's claims to authority were contestable. Where Selkirk's directives to Macdonell and Auld oscillated in terms of their tolerance of transgressors, it is important to consider the identities of the legal subjectivities in question, for Selkirk seemed to appreciate most of all the limits of enforcement when it applied to those not under the direct control of the company. This differentiation therefore reflected both the complicated legal terrain that the company had been occupying for over a century and a justifiable circumspection among those at the edges of control regarding the legitimacy of the company's prerogative.

Second, the settlement was a type of nascent proprietary government, and Selkirk's subject-dependent confidence in its legal authority conveys this reality. The Hudson's Bay Company's authoritative hold on the land emanated from the original terms of the charter,[177] a brand of governance that was a relic of the late fifteenth to late seventeenth centuries, an era when crown prerogative gave rise to chartered monopolies and attendant proprietary claims.[178] The HBC endowment was more than a corporate charter, strictly speaking, as evident from the permissions granted to the company and its governor to establish administrative and adjudicative bodies – powers that extended beyond the exclusive rights to trade.[179] For this reason, the Hudson's Bay Company as a whole had a type of "figurative possession,"[180] making the Red River Colony a type of proprietary government.[181] In the era after royal prerogatives, the preference was for centralized parliamentary authority over trade and commerce,[182] a reflection of the more concerted colonial agenda. The Hudson's Bay Company, however, remained a relic of the prerogative era, and confusion about its legal authority was attributable to its "company-state" status, which informed how its directors approached settlement.[183] Despite the decision to undertake the experiment, the HBC officers rarely diverged from the primarily profit-driven motives of the company, as Oliver argues, and the "chief achievement of the Council of Assiniboia" was that it could legislate and establish institutions while "under the patriarchal supervision of a company interested in trade rather than in colonisation."[184] This emphasis on trade aggravated the difficulties that Macdonell faced in founding the settler colony and attending to the long-term welfare of its inhabitants since the company provided minimal guidance to or support for the enterprise.

Third, Selkirk's political wavering tells its own story. On the one hand, Selkirk was an aristocrat who bore witness to two major revolutionary insurrections against aristocratic entitlement, one in France and the other in the United States. He could appreciate then that the struggle for freedom from below was a threat to his class interests but that this craving for freedom might be useful for his personal gain. Destitute people hungry for freedom could be viewed through the Malthusian lens, emptying it from any substantive claim to universal humanitarianism and making it the basis for policy making on how to deal with "difficult" or "redundant" populations. A strong punitive government that included certain feudal sensibilities remained Selkirk's preference, and paternalism still trumped individualism as the guiding principle of governance. On the other hand, Selkirk was living in an era when codifications and written constitutions were the predominant modes of ordering newly established realms. The written declarations of France and the United States set the benchmark for rethinking the nation within a constitutional framework, and the Napoleonic Code was either influencing or being adopted across continental Europe and in Haiti as the basis for organizing national governments.[185] In Rupert's Land, the clearest effect of this nineteenth-century wave of codification was the Code of Penal Laws released by the Hudson's Bay Company at Moose Factory in 1815,[186] evidence of a willingness to combine common law principles with the rationalization of a written code. Each of these developments supports a type of institutional proceduralism as the foundation for governance, which Selkirk might have found appealing in his highly selective efforts to import and apply British legal principles.

Fourth, these clashing elements in Selkirk's logic reflect the contradictions endemic to law itself. In theoretical terms, law can be seen as a conduit for justice, freedom, and equality even while it serves retributive objectives and the maintenance of order through coercive power. This dynamism is the crux of law's flexibility insofar as it can operate variably as a fetter and a catalyst in relation to economic growth in the context of a range of modes of production.[187] Throughout the time frame in question, it is possible to see appeals to legality as serving both aims, even simultaneously.

Fifth, for the servants to become settlers, they needed to possess land, which assumed the dispossession of lands belonging to Indigenous peoples; the relative autonomy of these two groups therefore moved in opposite directions, a core point of differentiation. For his own part, Macdonell was not ignorant of the confusion regarding ownership of land. At one point, he admitted that he was "at a loss" about how to approach members of the Indigenous societies inhabiting the area of the grant, explaining that "those here do not call themselves owners of the Soil, although long in possession it belonged originally to the Crees."[188] This lack of certainty was in contrast to the assuredness that Macdonell and Selkirk routinely exhibited when it came to the legal authority of the company in Rupert's Land, and it was a moment of bewilderment – if not accidental restraint – when it came to the experiment. Although Indigenous peoples were hardly treated with the utmost forbearance, it is significant that the legitimacy of their claims to the lands was not immediately dismissed. The Red River Colony relied so heavily on Indigenous peoples' labour to survive, yet their productivity remained beyond the scope of HBC control.

Fleetingly disquieted by the matter of land ownership, Macdonell suggested a simple solution – "a small annual present" – to the Indigenous peoples with the strongest claim to the land, and he added that "should the others make a claim a present will satisfy them also."[189] After making this suggestion, he asked Selkirk for guidance on the best way to manage relations with the Indigenous societies of the area. Macdonell explained that he was "liberal to them" when it came to offerings and that this generosity was favourably received to the extent that the Premier himself was agreeing to his requests and seeking his guidance.[190] The reason for such concern, however, had little to do with barbed ethical issues and more to do with a lack of conviction about the best legal and economic strategies given the manifest autonomy of Indigenous peoples.

The gulf was growing between the governance of the settler colony at Red River and the activities intrinsic to the fur trade. Auld expressed as much in a letter in which he noted that the "colonists do not perhaps consider or understand" the fur trade in general, let alone their particular relationship with the Hudson's Bay Company's primary profit-making enterprise. The more the settler colony struggled, the more resources – in terms of both labour and provisions – it required from surrounding Indigenous societies; the more resources were diverted to sustain the experiment, the more it and its proponents were blamed for causing losses to the company in general.[191] Dissonance between the settler colonial activities and the commercial fur trade was also evident in the fact that no factor was appointed to the Red River Colony, ostensibly leaving it without anybody with the expertise to negotiate exchanges for furs in accordance with established practices.[192] Macdonell stated as much and admitted to exchanging provisions for furs as a way of building allegiances among Indigenous producers because he believed that it was better that the furs ended up with him as opposed to the North West Company. But he also complained about the "trouble & inconvenience" of having to play the role of factor, and he did not appreciate having to barter away the settlement's provisions.[193] For the HBC directors, however, the worry seemed to be the opposite: it was unthinkable that the fur trade would be secondary to the sustenance of a group of servant-settlers who should have been well on their way toward self-sufficiency. That which for 150 years had been the sole objective of the company was at this juncture, for

Macdonell at least, a nuisance. From the company's perspective, the longer the experiment absorbed energies and resources, the settler colony itself was troublesome. For a venture meant to buttress the company's position, each quantifiable loss and every psychological defeat had a lasting impact, which in turn served as a justification for even grander measures that might finally reverse the fortunes at the Red River Colony.

For the servant-settlers, there were no halcyon days in the years immediately following the establishment of the District of Assiniboia – Eden remained a future promise and not an antediluvian dream. Even when the weather was more accommodating and the hunt more gainful, scarcity combined with competition made it difficult to establish a regimen conducive to reliable outputs of any variety but especially so in agricultural production. Before long, the welcoming acts that greeted the servant-settlers were less the norm and more the promising gloss that Macdonell strained to apply, and his accounts of the development at Red River began to look more ludicrous than hopeful. In the winter months of 1812–13, Macdonell was forced to source food from the North West Company, which at this time benefited from more established connections to Indigenous producers, while the lack of any significant agricultural harvest in the fall also forced the servant-settlers to hunt despite being so inexperienced at it.[194] This impressed on Macdonell the need to exert greater control in the area,[195] but that attempt was met with swift and violent responses by the North West Company.

5

Menace and Ally

Proclamation as Provocation

IN KEEPING WITH the commitment to austerity at the core of its retrenchment plan, the HBC committee intended to reduce by three-quarters the amount of meat that it sent to the Red River Colony, "and [it] expected pemmican from the Winnipeg and Saskatchewan districts to make up the difference."[1] When setbacks occurred in 1812–13, the HBC officers had to purchase provisions for a settler colony that they expected to be self-sufficient.[2] By 1814, the production, movement, and procurement of pemmican became the flashpoint in the District of Assiniboia, precipitated by the rush by both sides to stockpile as much as possible. Consequently, the matter of legal prerogative became even more heated in the years preceding the violent clash at nearby Seven Oaks in 1816.

With the establishment of the district boundaries per the terms of Lord Selkirk's grant, the next steps involved delineating which acts were deemed punishable within the scope of this territory pursuant to the Hudson's Bay Company's exclusive privileges. Selkirk continued to exude confidence in his company's claim to authority. In his correspondence, however, that certainty was often buttressed by an unconvincing humanitarian imperative – the "just foundation" of his enterprise.[3] At this critical juncture in the economic and legal transformation of both the area and the company, Miles Macdonell relied on direct, violent extra-economic force in an attempt to bring to an abrupt end the commercial and customary practices that prevailed to the benefit of his rivals. It was in response to some of these shifts that the NWC partners proceeded to exert their own legal prerogative, leading to an internecine dispute in which both parties claimed to be executing orders "in the King's name."[4] These conflicting claims to royal prerogative were made as the Napoleonic Wars continued to rage in Europe, while the proxy War of 1812 in North America led to renewed clashes over borderlines.

By examining the confluence of such events, we can see why Macdonell turned to force and how that decision arose yet diverged from established practices. With the events of 1814, a new basis for HBC supremacy was emergent – one that brought to the foreground how formal procedures could be used to gain advantage even while the foundation of the charter was eroding. What I excavate are the roots of the long-standing practice of harnessing formal legal means to undertake the most destructive measures of dispossession – or what Glen Sean Coulthard refers to as the use of formal legality "as a wrecking ball" against the relative autonomy of Indigenous producers.[5] By doing so, I highlight the measures of distortion and differentiation at the core of these transformations, and I show that the expansion of the capitalist mode of production was not the vanishing ground of violent extra-economic force in this settler colonial context.

The Pemmican Proclamation

In a letter of July 22, 1813, McGillivray, McLeod, and McKenzie derided Macdonell's order for the removal of two NWC men from their posts and disputed the HBC claim to the area, specifically targeting Macdonell's own authority and the legitimacy of the grant.[6] In their response to Macdonell's attempted expulsion, they quipped that "we are at a loss to divine the grounds on which this requisition is founded."[7] Should Macdonell wish to test their legal liability, they argued, he would be obliged to recognize the jurisdictional authority of Lower Canada in Rupert's Land by sending them to trial there.

The same month Macdonell wrote to Selkirk to update him on the settler colony. He emphasized the dearth of provisions, especially pemmican,[8] and the balance of the letter contained a chorus of prevalent concerns melded with a shrewd narrative: he claimed that the people were in "want of experience," he bemoaned the "extraordinary" lack of support from the HBC officers, and he stated that "it is not in my power to describe to your Lordship all that I suffered last winter" before launching into a defensive account of the "rudeness" that he had to put up with from the other HBC men.[9] To be sure, Macdonell had no need to exaggerate his despondency in the first eighteen months of the settler colony – the hardships were real, and there was no appreciable hope for a quick turnaround. But all these divulgences acted as an overture to his request for greater discretionary power and coercive force. Macdonell hastened to note that the actions of the NWC men were a grave impediment to the welfare of the servant-settlers and that more drastic measures would be necessary in the future: "I think that in consideration of the number of people for whom I have to provide subsistence," he pleaded, "I shall be fully justified in laying an Embargo on all provisions within our territory."[10] Written after the gruelling winter of 1813 and in the midst of a less than adequate summer hunting and fishing season, these were the words of a man fed up with being undermined by his counterparts and nature alike. To him, the success of the Red River Colony was incompatible with the interests of the North West Company in the region, and this justified the harsh measures. But Selkirk did not support this tack. Again he advised a more measured approach rather than outright belligerence at a moment when there was little likelihood of victory given the lack of military reinforcements.[11] However, perhaps because of weather, distance, and even third-party meddling, his counsel did not reach Macdonell in time.[12]

With mistrust mounting among all parties, Macdonell became more desperate. The conflict between the two fur trading companies became frenzied, especially over access to food stocks, which precipitated what has since been referred to as "the first food wars."[13] In *Pemmican Empire*, George Colpitts explains why this was primarily a problem arising from competition and not one of depletion-caused undersupply. By about 1810, food scarcity had less to do with environmental factors and more to do with the desire by both companies to secure an abundance of provisions that would allow each to prevail in the Athabasca region.[14] To offset its dependence on imports, for instance, the Hudson's Bay Company stockpiled pemmican at its posts along the bay; meanwhile, the North West Company relied on pemmican from Red River to supply its traders in the Athabasca region,[15] and Métis peoples were "dominant players" in this regard.[16] Despite the spike in demand, however, there was an abundance of buffalo and favourable weather, and Colpitts notes that in 1813, "the Assiniboine just above the elbow of the Saskatchewan killed 700 animals on one occasion."[17] Although the supply was greater than that of recent years, it would never be enough, particularly in light of William Auld's order in the spring of 1812 to acquire as much stock as possible.[18] The NWC men would not take long to realize that the Hudson's Bay Company was drastically undermining their supply of pemmican, and "their reprisals could be expected."[19]

With advice from Richard Burn's "do-it-yourself" tome on legal administration at hand, Macdonell acted. For the uninitiated, the manual provided pat definitions of concepts such as "lands" and "warrant,"[20] offered some insights into the basis and limits of the authority granted to justices of the peace and constables,[21] and included an array of templates that would be useful in any number of circumstances. In the most formal language at his disposal, Macdonell crafted a proclamation.[22] Issued on January 8, 1814, the "Pemmican Proclamation" forbade the export of pemmican from the buffalo herds of Assiniboia, with the reasoning that there was a food shortage and implying that such an aggressive measure was necessary in order to protect the welfare of the settler colony.[23] The proclamation was intended to change by decree unfavourable existing economic practices, and from his viewpoint, it was all the better for operating also as a legal fetter on the North West Company.

Macdonell noted in his journal that the proclamation "had been some time in contemplation,"[24] and, although it is not mentioned explicitly in his daily entries, the frequently registered worry about provisions provided something akin to a logical precursor.[25] The terms of the proclamation are also interesting, particularly with respect to how the price of and the compensation for pemmican were determined. In the original text, Macdonell assured that "no loss may accrue to the parties concerned" and that "they will be paid for by British Bills at the Customary Rates."[26] Compensation was decided according to rates established by the Hudson's Bay Company in concert with its retrenchment plan of 1810; moreover, these rates were measured not in MB but in British currency.[27] On this occasion, the formalization of the means of exchange and the formality of the proclamation were mutually reinforcing.

In terms of the rationale for the proclamation, Auld provided what seemed to be a sound post hoc version in 1814: "The NWC supply their distant trading posts with the provisions procured in the district whilst we to whom the soil belongs are obliged to go to the expence [sic] & trouble of importing from Britain a considerable part of the subsistence of our people."[28] Colpitts echoes Auld's reasoning, considering the proclamation "as part of a larger imposition of the HBC's presumed jurisdictional authority and Lord Selkirk's proprietorial claim to 'Assiniboia.'"[29] Duress might have hastened the order and lent a "humanitarian" dimension, but underlying it was the presumption of privilege that accompanied the original charter.[30] Others meanwhile refer to this move by Macdonell as "a mistaken act," suggesting that, rather than securing the colony against further privation, it might have precipitated the events "of the disastrous year 1814."[31]

The first hurdle in executing the edict had to do, again, with enforcement.[32] The language of the proclamation set the foundation for possible penalties if the conditions were not followed;[33] it was in the service of the latter aim that Macdonell appointed John Spencer as "Sheriff for the District of Ossiniboia" on February 1, 1814. Another move involved extending the scope of his delegation through a more formal mechanism, the installation of the council that would constitute the "gov't of the District of Ossiniboia," marked by the swearing in of George Holdsworth as council member alongside Spencer on February 8.[34] In terms of its legal legacy, therefore, the proclamation was a step toward the bureaucratization of the region's governance structure. The swearing in of officials and the granting of formal powers arguably strengthened the hierarchical order in general and buttressed their allegiances to the company and the settler colony in equal measure. By the spring of 1814, Macdonell increased enforcement and "swore in 4 Constables & sent off a guard in the evening to watch the river," and they reported seeing "Frenchmen ... in numbers armed" and waiting for a shipment of pemmican.[35] Macdonell instructed the sheriff to intercept and accompany the boat, and on May 25 he learned from two men held on suspicion that the pemmican was already removed and hidden.[36] Still unsatisfied with the level of compliance, he ordered a seizure of provisions from the North West Company on May 30, going so far as to issue a warrant himself.[37]

In quick succession during the spring days of 1814, Macdonell built his own law-making and -enforcing authorities, issued appointments, and adopted the formal practices now recognizable as the basis of policing. NWC men did not sit idle as these blockades were coordinated but undertook their own series of seizures of both pemmican and Deputy Sheriff Joseph Howse.[38] Macdonell contested these acts on the grounds of their lack of legitimate authority to execute seizures and keep prisoners.[39] Unmoved, the NWC men threatened to send Howse to Lower Canada for trial, arguing that "'the Laws of our Country will determine which of the two parties … took up arms first,'"[40] a threat that Macdonell considered incredulous given his conviction that the courts of the Canadas had no legal grounds to try officials of his council.[41]

Alienation of the Métis

Ramifications associated with this edict are of particular interest since they relate to the broader legal and economic changes in the area. As previously established, after Britain gained control over New France and Montreal-based partnerships emerged among prominent Scottish families, companies competing in the fur trade at the end of the eighteenth century pushed ever northwestward.[42] Consequently, more freemen (also known as "free Canadians," usually former servants) ended up on the plains and beyond working for the North West Company or its rivals, with some choosing to remain in the area after their commitments to the companies expired.[43] The Red River Colony was a crossroads in the fur trade, and it functioned like a headquarters as families in the area migrated,[44] providing opportunities for men to operate more like independent producers. At a time when demand was increasing, local Nēhiyawok and Assiniboine did not "increas[e] their efforts" to supply the trading companies and the settler colony with the foods that they desired,[45] and Saulteaux in the area were suffering hardships in part because of their ongoing battles with the Sioux. Those who attempted to fill the seemingly insatiable need were the free Canadians and the Métis, the latter referred to by Colpitts as a distinct group of emergent "market hunter[s]."[46]

They were not usually bound by strict or expansive contracts, allowing them a considerable measure of control over their mobility; as "free agents," they took "their excess foodstuffs to whoever was convenient or paying [the] most."[47] When the demand for pemmican and other provisions increased, the hunters in the region – principally these freemen and the Métis – were in a position to command higher wages and favourable terms if they had contracts.[48] One man who did work under contract was the freeman Jean-Baptiste Lagimodière,[49] whose payment of thirty pounds "and Equipment of clothes" was three times as much as a clerk's salary after a year of working for the settlement.[50] Working without a contract was the preferred approach of another freeman, François Enos (Hénault or Delorme; Francois De Lorme in Macdonell's journal[51]), though there was a dispute between Delorme's recollections of his time hunting for the settlement and Macdonell's claim to having formally "engaged" Delorme.[52] Notably, both of these free Canadians married Indigenous women and had children and grandchildren that became Métis leaders at Red River in later decades.[53] In addition to hiring Delorme's Métis son, Macdonell regularly bought provisions from a man from an established Métis family, Tranchemontagne,[54] and attempted at one point to hire as an interpreter a man who would soon become one of the settlement's greatest adversaries, Pangman (or Bostonais).[55]

Given the changes to the social relations of land in the area – evident (*inter alia*) in the corrosion of the principle of mutual accountability and debt-based restrictions on Indigenous peoples' mobility – the Pemmican Proclamation had serious consequences for these free Canadians and Métis. The ill-advised edict stipulated restrictive conditions on the movement of provisions, but among the more disconcerting facets of this order was that it alienated the Métis communities largely aligned with the North West Company as its principal suppliers of pemmican.[56] At the time of the proclamation, there were approximately two hundred families in the region engaging not only in the provision of pemmican but also fishing and agriculture.[57] Macdonell wrote to Selkirk about the strong presence of Métis,[58] and in his journal he recorded multiple instances of having to hire them for tasks that his servant-settlers were not able to execute.[59] At the same time, there was a dearth of forethought from either Macdonell or Selkirk when it came to building more substantive inroads between the Hudson's Bay Company and the Métis.[60] Consistent with the general contempt for Indigenous societies of the area, Macdonell and his company made no effort to "win the allegiance of the Métis" prior to the promulgation of the proclamation,[61] a blunder that provided sufficient ground for retaliatory advances by year end.

Historians still disagree about whether a singular event led to the coalescence of a distinctive Métis identity in the region, but there is some acknowledgment that the Métis made more overtly political demands following Macdonell's restrictive decree.[62] The proclamation, therefore, was a significant albeit reactionary turning point. Not only was the settler colony itself under threat of starvation, but also its legitimacy was at stake – and by extension so was the HBC monopoly. The NWC forts and posts built in the region in the previous decades were an affront to the HBC claim, and the failure of the Red River

Colony to thrive was hard evidence that the Hudson's Bay Company had limited control over the commercial activities that it deemed within its domain. The Pemmican Proclamation was an attempt by Macdonell to use formal means to alter extant practices in an effort to enforce what he referred to as the "letter of the law."[63] It was a coercive measure of differentiation insofar as it empowered some, targeted others, and alienated the Métis altogether, setting the groundwork for a series of administrative and enforcement measures that leveraged the growing segregation, all in the name of further dispossession.

Six months after the proclamation was issued, NWC representatives negotiated with Macdonell to allow greater quantities of pemmican to be exported by their company, and in making their case they explained the inconveniences wrought by the War of 1812, which forced them to make detours to avoid interference from their American counterparts.[64] Macdonell agreed to relief, albeit on the condition that the North West Company assist the Red River Colony servant-settlers in the next year.[65] With these new terms and the nominal acknowledgment of the rights and interests of the settler colony, Macdonell believed that he gained the legal edge. Records from the annual NWC meetings suggest otherwise. The partners saw the proclamation as an offensive manoeuvre and had no intention of upholding the newly negotiated terms; rather, they "were committed to defending their property at all costs as well as to the destruction of the colony."[66] While the upper echelons of the Hudson's Bay Company were still relatively ignorant of the events surrounding the Pemmican Proclamation, the NWC wintering partners at Fort William were already planning their next move.[67] Tellingly in this regard, each NWC officer who worked in the district left the meeting "with military appointments, swords, and uniforms."[68] George Prevost reinstated William McGillivray's military commission at the rank of lieutenant-colonel and delegated to McGillivray the authority to grant new commissions as he saw fit in order to populate the "Corps of Voyageurs in the Indian & Conquered Countries."[69] Among the commissions granted by McGillivray was the appointment of Duncan Cameron to the rank of captain, and his first order in the summer of 1814 was to conduct arrests and disperse the colonists at Red River "in the King's name."[70]

If Macdonell was only beginning to appreciate the consequences of his edict, Auld's letter in March 1814 would confirm such thoughts. Auld chastised Macdonell and saw the proclamation as a display of ineptitude, and he proceeded to reproach him for not pursuing a more measured tack. Auld also wondered why neither he nor the Métis were told in advance, explaining that "a *notice* in my opinion, & I speak feelingly, would have pleased them & us better."[71] Additional consequences of the order therefore included internal strife among the men of Macdonell's own company, as well as the souring of relations with the

Figure 5.1 Fort William, an establishment of the North West Company, on Lake Superior, 1811, artist Robert Irvine, 1792–1823 | *Source:* Library and Archives Canada, Peter Winkworth Collection of Canadiana, e000756944

Métis population – who, Auld explained, were in a "humiliated condition" and appeared to "propagate among the natives a very unfavourable idea" of the HBC representatives in the district.[72]

Dissatisfied with the lack of cooperation, worried about ruined relations, and perhaps even emboldened by Auld's tepid commitment to the cause, Macdonell took further action. By the midway point of 1814, he attempted to flex the force of his command with added restrictions, such as on July 21, when he recorded that he had issued another proclamation, this time "prohibiting the running of Buffaloe [sic] with Horses."[73] The rationale was that this method of hunting ran the risk of driving buffalo to the outer limits of the district and thus beyond the reach of the handful of servant-settlers taking part in the hunt.[74] In their study of these events, Gerhard Ens and Joe Sawchuk explain that this latest prohibition "had little effect other than to raise the ire of the Métis, who in any case did not heed it."[75] The North West Company was pleased with this development and fanned the animosity that resulted by encouraging deserters among the servant-settlers and trying to break Saulteaux allegiances to the settler colony in the process.[76] Yet this second proclamation was a curious one: Macdonell knew that

138 *A Legacy of Exploitation*

he did not have the numbers that the North West Company had and that his meagre enforcement capacity was far from dependable. Perhaps he was momentarily reassured by the news that the Americans were forced to retreat from Upper Canada and the defeat of Napoleon in Europe,[77] or maybe he was heartened that both Peguis and the Premier seemed to be equally dismayed by the activities of the North West Company and were keen to maintain their allegiances to the Hudson's Bay Company.[78] However, if the first proclamation was a qualified success at best in terms of curbing the outflow of pemmican, the second one was an unmitigated failure from Macdonell's point of view.

Before Macdonell could attend to one matter, boatloads of new servant-settlers were arriving on the banks of the still temporary settler colonial establishment.[79] In his journal entry for June 18, Macdonell wrote in passing that Spencer had resigned "his office [of] Sheriff & Counsellor," which once again left Macdonell without an effective means of enforcement,[80] a concern aggravated by the resignation of Holdsworth on July 19[81] and by growing resentment among the servant-settlers.[82] In between these events, Auld – an avowed skeptic of the experiment – visited the settlement[83] and criticized Macdonell's negotiated capitulation to the North West Company with respect to pemmican.[84] These chiding remarks did much to undermine Macdonell's spirits. His journal entries during these weeks detailed his increasing misery as they became shorter and less effusive in his positive assessment of the outcome of his efforts: new land allotments were assigned, and people were pleased,[85] but horses were stolen, other newcomers were discouraged, and workers were resisting their orders.[86]

Macdonell's Anguish and the War of 1812

In a letter to Selkirk dated July 25, 1814, Macdonell took the opportunity to justify the Pemmican Proclamation and his ordering of retaliatory acts, eager to boast that his men "cheerfully followed" his orders.[87] He depicted his side as relatively few in number fighting back the NWC Goliath, and it was because of the likelihood of a devastating defeat that he brokered a peace with the rival side, thus achieving a cessation of actions in what he vaingloriously referred to as the "Pemican [sic] war."[88] Macdonell felt abandoned by the Hudson's Bay Company and unfairly criticized by Auld, which led him not only to request permanent leave from his responsibilities as governor of the District of Assiniboia[89] but also to experience what J.M. Bumsted refers to as a "nervous breakdown" while visiting York Factory in August 1814.[90]

The list of sixty-seven points of instruction that Selkirk wrote for Macdonell in April 1814 had yet to arrive in Rupert's Land, and had Macdonell received it by mid-summer he would have known that Selkirk advised against travelling to meet the boats upon their docking at York Factory – labourers, not governors, were most needed to help move cargo.[91] But by August 22, Macdonell arrived at the bay.[92] Within a week, he wrote of feeling "distracted on account of the state of [Red River settlement] matters here," and then for three consecutive days thereafter his daily entry mentioned that he was "unwell."[93] To HBC surgeon Abel Edwards, it was clear that Macdonell was "depressed" and "dejected," noting at one point that he was "convulsed with agony"; Macdonell confided to Edwards that "he had ruined Lord Selkirk as well as the Colony" and that "nothing but death could relieve him."[94] Measures were under way to find a suitable replacement, which Macdonell consented to in a letter dated September 2.[95] Yet by September 9, in a letter written to Selkirk by Macdonell while still at York Factory, there was no indication of any intent to resign from his duties.

En route back to the settlement, accompanied by Peguis and his group, as well as some freemen, Macdonell learned that Spencer had been "taken prisoner by the NWC on a warrant."[96] Although Macdonell mentioned it briefly in his journal, the arrest of Spencer was one of the outcomes associated with Duncan Cameron's August 1814 order to move in on the Red River Colony. Cameron donned regalia, borrowed from Archibald McLeod, and in his assumed authority as "chief of the country"[97] he "was authorized to move as many settlers as possible to Upper Canada free of charge" and take Macdonell into custody.[98] Less obvious, however, were the geopolitical facets of this offensive, specifically the connections to the War of 1812.

From the outset of the war, the British military benefited from the fact that the North West Company not only had a number of vessels available in the Great Lakes but also established lines of communication.[99] It was in the interests of the NWC partners to contribute to the defence of British holdings to ensure the integrity of their trade routes.[100] As early as the summer of 1812, the NWC partners agreed that they should stockpile munitions and provisions; they took this step in part to serve better the military cause and to make sure that they were in decent stead should the British fall to the Americans.[101] In one notable manoeuvre ordered by then head of the Upper Canada forces, Major-General Isaac Brock, the North West Company played a leading role in the attack on Michilimackinac by assembling "an army of fur-trade-hardened voyageurs" and Indigenous allies.[102] In less than two days and without any casualties, the fort was taken over from the Americans, who agreed to evacuate the island and relinquish their control.[103] The fort remained a site of contention, and in the winter of 1814 a series of American successes in battle threatened both the NWC and British transportation routes in the northwest of Upper Canada at the same time that Macdonell's proclamations curtailed the movement and procurement of pemmican in the western reaches of the NWC transportation network.[104]

With the defeat of Napoleon and the capture of Paris in the spring of 1814, American forces were wary that reinforcements would soon arrive in the Canadas, causing them to quicken their plans to regain control of Michilimackinac.[105] It was in this context that Prevost appointed NWC agents to the military. The militarization of the North West Company underscored not only the close relationship between that company and the Canadas but also worry about the possible effects of the war on access to supplies. By providing agents aligned with the Montreal merchants with military appointments, Prevost – perhaps unwittingly – was stoking an internecine conflict between the two companies.

Into this barely contained morass strode Macdonell, returning from his ill-advised trip to York Factory. With minimal fanfare other than six men in military dress, he arrived at the Red River Colony by October 19; modest as it was, this pose spoke both to his waning spirits and to his commitment to martial order.[106] Shortly after his return, Macdonell found the stores in disarray, both physically and with regard to accounting records, aggravated by the arrest of Spencer.[107] That year Selkirk was still canvassing the learned legal practitioners in London for their opinions on judicial matters. He eventually heard from the then governor of the Hudson's Bay Company, Joseph Berens, Jr., who reiterated the need to ensure that technical matters and formal procedures were upheld so that decisions rendered could withstand the scrutiny of the appeals process, should a dispute ever go so far.[108]

The Prerogative to Exploit

With manifest disdain for the more monotonous responsibilities of chief administrator, Macdonell was drawn to the dramatics of command. Spencer alluded to this bombastic tendency in Macdonell. Spencer, in executing Macdonell's order to seize the pemmican from the North West Company, appeared to realize only later – after being taken into custody by the North West Company for executing the warrant – that the matter of jurisdictional authority was far from settled.[109] Further evidence of this tendency can be seen in the eviction notices that Macdonell sent to at least seven NWC men in October 1814.[110] His motivation to order the evictions had to do with his goal of breaking up the bonds between the "Canadian freemen" and the North West Company and to turn the former into allies of the Hudson's Bay Company by offering them "*gratis* all the lands they could cultivate for 3 years & to furnish them with seeds."[111] This offer of property was also his attempt to "wean" the freemen from the "Indian manner of living" and to bring them "quickly to a regular mode of living."[112] Conspicuously, Macdonell wished "to dispossess [the North West Company] forcibly," but he could not do so because of his compromised enforcement capacity.[113] Instead, he invoked a chain of dispossession: appropriating access to buffalo from the Métis, usurping the labour of the freemen, and seizing the NWC posts and provisions.

Each instance of dispossession was intrinsic to the exploitative practices that made up the core of the HBC profits in the fur trade and essential to the viability of the experiment as a primary measure of exerting control over people and resources. The HBC committee's insistence on the establishment of a settler colonial holding signalled its commitment to find new ways of conducting its central business: by domesticating resource production to minimize the costs associated with purchasing and transporting imported provisions. This facet of the retrenchment plan also heralded further changes among the societies in the surrounding areas, announced most pointedly by Macdonell's expressed desire to undermine the way of life of the freemen and have them turn instead to agricultural production. The common element of these associated dispossessions was the increased reliance on coercive force to engineer a more dependent relationship between the HBC/colonial agents and the servants, settlers, Métis hunters, and would-be Canadian farmers.

In December 1814, Selkirk wrote to Macdonell informing him that, though he thought the Pemmican Proclamation impulsive and contrary to his instructions, the compromise brokered between the two fur trading companies was an appropriate secondary measure.[114] Again Selkirk insisted that the defence of the settlement should take priority, this time disparagingly referring to the NWC men as "*white* savages" to underscore the gravity of the threat that they posed.[115] Hints that the HBC directors were becoming impatient with the experiment became more pronounced, as evident in the instructions sent to Thomas Thomas in preparation for his taking over the role of superintendent of the Northern Department. The expectation was that the Red River Colony should be self-sufficient by the end of 1816; no more imports should be necessary, allowing the Hudson's Bay Company to ease expenditures.[116] Where punitive efforts proved to be incapable of achieving much more than an inducement to desertion, economic means were increasingly resorted to as a way of squeezing more labour out of the workers for less remuneration. The introduction of "piecework" was suggested as a measure of "exciting some emulation in the workmen who are employed by the year; & enabling the officers to judge more correctly whether these men do fair days work."[117] This change to the employment status and remuneration structure of workers represented the gradual disintegration of the feudal hierarchy that was the hallmark of the HBC structure. With the officer-servant system, the company was under contract to ensure some minimum standard of living for its workers, but without such a contract the company could avoid being blamed for any deficiency in this minimum standard – the men would be "free."

By the spring of 1815, it was eight years since the Hudson's Bay Company had issued dividends to shareholders.[118] The climate of austerity was apparent in orders to the newly installed Superintendent Thomas to cut the workforce by three-quarters yet still be prepared somehow to mount a forceful defence against the North West Company.[119] Concerns about reliable labour did not abate as new commercial ventures were developed. In May 1814, the HBC committee announced its intention to "form a large Establishment in Athabasca"; beyond this presence in what had long been the NWC domain, the committee also intended to employ Canadians as their primary labour force.[120] By hiring Canadians, a number of objectives appeared to be within reach: it was one way of circumventing the restrictions imposed by the Passenger Vessels Act, which limited the number of men who could be brought over; it undermined the established expectations among Orkneymen, who made up the core of the HBC workers, were not likely to fight for the company, and were accused of "lacking in backbone";[121] and it facilitated the breakdown of the officer-servant relationship, making space for new exploitative measures such as the planned introduction of piecework. Based upon these plans, it appeared that the workers were to shoulder the burden of this new phase of the retrenchment plan, but again what they did not seem to consider was the agency of Indigenous peoples.

Defining the "Menace"

Threats, disobedience, and desertion became dominant themes in Macdonell's journal, especially after learning that partners of the North West Company offered an option to the Red River servant-settlers to relocate to the Canadas. Against a backdrop of the enveloping prairie winter and dwindling resources, optimism would have been hard to come by; still with insufficient dwellings to winter at the settlement, the colonists were forced to scatter to the posts.

It was a visit from Indigenous allies – namely a group of Saulteaux led by L'Homme Noir, whom Macdonell "made a Chief" in 1814[122] – that bolstered Macdonell, which in turn reinforced the terms of the reciprocity, the nature of which Laura Peers distills as "you help me when you can and I'll help you when I can."[123] Up to this point, Macdonell supported the Saulteaux in their wars with the Sioux by providing munitions, and he was glad to be on the periphery of these violent clashes.[124] As relations with the North West Company, the Canadians, and the Métis soured into 1815, HBC agents had heightened expectations of their allies, even as the servant-settlers themselves would "refuse to take up arms in support of the laws."[125] Perhaps it was the absence of a groundswell from the servant-settlers to defend the colonial holding that prompted Macdonell to send McLeod "to the Freemen on a Mission of Peace" on February 9, 1815.[126] First, the lack of devotion suggests that there was not much to fight for from the servant-settlers' perspective. Allotments were still being granted, private dwellings were planned only once the communal structures were erected, and just a modest amount of land was cultivated – that Cameron could entice many servant-settlers to desert to the Canadas is a testament to the indifference bordering on contempt that they felt for the Red River Colony.[127] Second, there remained practical limits on labour compulsion. As servants, they were occasionally permitted to terminate their contracts early and settle on their allotments, thereby forgoing any future promise of pay from the Hudson's Bay Company. This suited the company insofar as it led to reduced costs, but the transition from servants to "free" workers also interrupted the authority of the company to compel them to perform specific tasks as needed. Unless the advantages of joining the company's campaign were readily apparent, however, "free" settlers had few incentives to submit once again to the authority of HBC officers. And third, it could be taken as an implicit understanding that the land was not theirs to fight over, lacking perhaps the impervious sense of territorial entitlement rife among officers and aristocrats.

With rumours crisscrossing the land of an imminent attack by the North West Company on the settler colony, efforts were ongoing at the highest echelons of the Hudson's Bay Company to confirm the legal authority long assumed to be valid.[128] Governor Berens wrote to Lord Bathurst to inform him of the dangers facing the settlement, and Selkirk was just beginning to learn of those dangers; however, on both counts, the information given and received was not altogether accurate since it identified the "Indians" as the "menace."[129] Eventually, Selkirk made a direct appeal to Bathurst seeking "military protection to the settlement" and challenging his opinion that this was foremost a commercial dispute between two rival companies.[130] Bathurst's interpretation of this conflict was as telling as it was deft. By denying that this was anything more than a matter of "pecuniary interests between two commercial bodies,"[131] Bathurst blunted the claims made by both companies that their warrants, seizures, and arrests were carried out in the name of the British sovereign. The upshot of this stance was that he had no responsibility to provide military support despite Selkirk's contention that such protection was needed in order "to secure the lives of a number of British Subjects, who without having done anything to provoke hostility, are threatened with a massacre by the Indians."[132] When Selkirk chose not to identify the North West Company as the primary "menace," he tried to press Bathurst into action by undermining the notion that it was a commercial feud, but presenting the conflict in this manner only emphasized the link between Selkirk's own deficient understanding of the situation and his tendency to be duplicitous as a means of gaining favour.

Right after deflecting Bathurst's reading of the conflict by referring to "a massacre by the Indians," however, Selkirk went on to describe the conduct of NWC agents. He emphasized the structure of the two companies in order to suggest that, by being headquartered in London, HBC officers' conduct exhibited greater "personal responsibility" than that of the unaccountable NWC partners who remained in the farthest reaches of the territories.[133] Even after a diatribe against the North West Company, Selkirk concluded the letter with a final plea that returned to the theme of his opening salvo: "If the danger does exist your Lordship will not think of leaving British Subjects at the mercy of the Savages."[134] Be it the weight of this final appeal or the positive outlook prompted by the recent ratification of the Treaty of Ghent (which brought the War of 1812 to an official end), a week after Selkirk's letter Bathurst consented to notify the governor of British North America that some military protection "to the Settlers at Red River" should be provided.[135] His lukewarm support for the cause took the form of a commitment to notify the governor of the Canadas that there was no guarantee of actual protection – even had he come through with a military deployment, it would have been too late given the rapid developments in the district.[136]

By the end of the War of 1812, the land mass that Selkirk had been granted by the HBC committee was being reassessed because of the newly established northern border of the United States stipulated in the Treaty of Ghent. This eventually resulted in the loss of the Pembina site to the south.[137] Around the same time, Selkirk wrote to Macdonell to inform him of the impending arrival of troops to protect the servant-settlers[138] and advocating for a "shift in the Justification of the Pemmican Proclamation."[139] Increasingly, Selkirk sensed that the strength of his position lay in making it clear that he was acting in the best interests of the settler-colonists. He therefore distanced himself from the proclamation, twice referring to it in the letter to Macdonell as "your Proclamation," placing the blame for the clashes on his governor's shoulders, with some culpability to spare for Auld.[140] Selkirk contended that it aggravated relations with "these Indians" (likely implying the "Ossiniboyns" [Assiniboine] whom he mentioned in the preceding paragraph), causing them to believe that their livelihoods were threatened.[141] Then came the about-face from his earlier rationale – "the legality of the prohibition rests upon the apparent necessity of the case" – so the legitimacy of the proclamation stemmed not from Selkirk's "rights as Proprietor" but from Macdonell's responsibility as governor to protect his charge from starvation.[142] The preponderant concern that led Selkirk to seek legal clarification in 1812 – namely the Hudson's Bay Company's proprietary rights in the region that comprised the cornerstone of his and Macdonell's manoeuvrings – was strategically relegated in this letter. To leverage the humanitarian angle, Selkirk insisted that, once the threat of famine had subsided, the prohibitions that Macdonell had ordered should be lifted.[143]

By invoking this agenda, Selkirk sought to ensure that nobody would question either Macdonell's motives in issuing the proclamation or the claim that the settler-colonists deserved protection as British subjects. Of course, this downplaying of the economic rationale for the edict sat uncomfortably beside the multiple eviction notices sent to NWC officers in 1815, not to mention the fact that the early settlers signed servant contracts in the pecuniary interests of the Hudson's Bay Company. Most interestingly, the need to modify the motivating logic sheds light on the extent to which the company was not in a position to dismiss the relative autonomy of the Indigenous peoples in the area. The ultimate test for determining the legitimacy of the prerogative of either fur trading company was not in calculating how many warrants were issued and executed against each other or how many of the competitor's men were held as prisoners. Rather, the legitimacy of the prerogatives was best measured by examining in what manner, if at all, the reciprocal obligations with nearby Indigenous societies were considered.

When Macdonell dispensed the proclamations and evictions, he might have overplayed his hand, but in doing so he revealed the eagerness of the Hudson's Bay Company to make pronouncements that would allow it to realize the full scope of its exclusive privileges. As the company moved into the Athabasca region, its vision for the future was even more expansive. Fundamentally, the social relations of land had to change in the company's favour to an extent that could realize this new regime, and that the Premier, Peguis, and Canard Noir conferred with Macdonell for reasons other than to trade furs suggests that these changes were under way. However, though the social relations of land were transforming (through commercial incentives, shirked accountability, mobility restrictions, and unequal exchange), the Hudson's Bay Company was not yet in a position to claim as much autonomy as it thought it could with respect to the everyday functions of its business, which still centred on the labour of Métis and Saulteaux producers and a patchwork of allegiances.

By the end of the March 23 letter to Macdonell, Selkirk finally agreed to visit the Red River Colony, and he planned to time his journey with the spring thaw of 1816 since he preferred to travel from Montreal rather than via Hudson Bay. His worries about "the threats of Indian hostility" likely spurred his decision to visit the colony, and he expressed a desire to be there in person to conduct negotiations with the "Ossiniboyns" for the land.[144] The peculiarity of this position, as before, was the mix of assumed prerogative and material dependence.

146 *A Legacy of Exploitation*

Selkirk seemed to be confident that "small presents" and future promises of greater quantities of tobacco and alcohol – subject to the ability of the agricultural settlement to produce its own tobacco and a grain crop with "surplus for distillation" – should "keep them quiet."[145] Yet he also recognized that how the negotiations were conducted was crucial, and he insisted that he be the one to undertake the discussions, which I argue in the next chapter was a model performance of distortion and differentiation, with little inkling of humanitarian intent.

To the Brink

The gap between Selkirk's instructions and the events at the settler colony was widening still. For all the efforts by both the North West Company and the Hudson's Bay Company to legitimate their respective claims to exclusive authority, it was a matter that seemed to concern only themselves – a contest over supremacy that ostensibly occurred in a vacuum. On the ground, a new and growing segment of the population belied the revolving assertions of prerogative and staked its own position.

McLeod, captured while on a "Mission of Peace" to the Métis camp,[146] was eventually "released at the request of the Indians," namely the settler colony's Saulteaux allies,[147] which highlights the complicated web of shifting allegiances, further discredits Selkirk's notion of the "menace," and reveals the scope of influence that these local Indigenous groups retained. Detentions and desertions became more frequent, with Macdonell recording in his journals the intensification of threats, dispersals, and regroupings taking place across the district.[148] In mid-March 1815, two weeks after learning about the NWC plan to arrest him,[149] Macdonell took Métis leader Bostonais prisoner and made a speech to all in the vicinity.[150] He recorded that one of the responses to his speech was an appeal to release Bostonais, a request that was denied only to be issued anew a few days later after the Premier and his allies gathered for a council of local leaders.[151] Macdonell again denied the release and carried on issuing orders dealing with deserters.[152] While on his way back to the settlement in early April after spending most of the winter months at the forts throughout the District of Assiniboia, Macdonell learned that the stores and shelters had been robbed,[153] causing most of the servant-settlers to disperse north toward Lake Winnipeg, with some of the single men remaining at a nearby NWC fort.[154] Much like the North West Company almost a year earlier, Macdonell made military appointments (appointing himself as the captain and making the men in his charge soldiers), and soon after they began to transform the buildings at the site into battle-ready bunkers.[155]

With the fortitude of his position resting on Selkirk's proprietorship, the same line of accountability that Selkirk himself was playing down, Macdonell adopted all the habits of a military guard, with parades, drills, and sentries. To prevent future desertions, he also wanted to make the men in his company "take the oath of allegiance and to swear to defend the premises" – but they refused.[156] Such a refusal is understandable coming as it did from this slapdash military company consisting of servant-settlers with no substantive claim to defend. Desertions continued throughout the spring, and emissaries journeyed between Cameron and Macdonell, each carrying letters that accused the other of acting out of order.[157] This wrangling persisted as each faction assumed legal preroga-tive in its favour, and it was becoming clear that it was precisely because such assumptions were acted on without regard to the material condition of their application – that is, the relative autonomy of the Indigenous producers – that "a sort of civil war" percolated.[158]

Concurrently, other important developments were afoot in the Canadas and beyond. On April 12, 1815,[159] the HBC committee in London appointed Robert Semple to the position of governor-in-chief to act as its representative in the District of Assiniboia.[160] He would answer to the committee directly rather than an appointee of Selkirk's alone whose accountability was more compli-cated.[161] This did not mean that Macdonell was dismissed from his responsibility as the district's governor,[162] but it represented another bureaucratic layer in the legal administration of the area. The HBC directors were also attempting to advance the company into the Athabasca region, an undertaking that it con-sidered the fulcrum in determining the outcome of its competition for furs with the North West Company.[163] Colin Robertson, formerly of the latter company, championed this cause to Wedderburn and Selkirk while in London in 1810, and he attempted to convince them that an aggressive position would better serve the quest of the Hudson's Bay Company to gain advantage over its rival,[164] which would entail a definitive step away from the nominal passivity of years past. Robertson's argument did not convince the two principal share-holders at the time, but it was given new life when the struggles of the Red River Colony came to light in 1814. With the company's financial backing, Robertson and a sizable group of fur traders departed from Lower Canada in May 1815 to commence their work exploiting the northern region. Along the way, he met settlers headed in the opposite direction, which is how he learned about the tensions in the district.[165]

During this time, Macdonell was visited by various Indigenous parties, includ-ing Captain Grant and his brother, an unspecified group from Leech Lake, as well as a group of Nēhiyawok from farther north, each concerned about the events taking place and reluctant to get involved in them, and in each case Macdonell boasted about his diplomatic skills in subduing their concerns.[166] In his journal, he assessed that "the general feeling of the Indians" is that "they dislike the NWC but are still afraid of them."[167] As before, Macdonell prided himself on being magnanimous, but he took the time to mention instances when he found these Indigenous allies "troublesome."[168] Other allegiances, those wrought by the forced fealty of the servant's contract, were also waning as the men brought into the service in 1812 were to be released as of June 1. Macdonell met with them individually, most of them Irish, and with empty promises as incentives he asked that they remain after the end of their contracts.[169] Come June 1, none of the men desired renewal of the terms, and Macdonell felt the effects immediately, not only when they did not report to work the next day, but also when they and a handful of deserters sought to settle their accounts and take what they were owed by the Hudson's Bay Company.[170] Without any contracts, the ex-servants were able to withdraw all of their labour, agricultural and military; however, they still had to act in a manner that ensured subsistence for them, which forced them to choose a side. On June 5, 1815, the men admitted to Macdonell that they wanted to depart for the Canadas under the terms stipulated by Cameron, and they appeased their former master by assuring him that they would not take up arms against him or his company.[171] Within two days, some of these men were back at the site, this time as NWC emissaries.[172]

The letter that these ex-servants brought with them was from Cameron, still not satisfied with the number of deserters who had already left the Hudson's Bay Company for his camp. In this letter, he made an appeal to those who remained, the force of which was derived once again from an assumption of legal prerogative. He intimated that they were "deluded" and compelled into acting "contrary to Law"; he also advised them "to pay due respect[,] submission and obedience to the Law of our blessed Constitution."[173] Within a week, a reply was sent to Cameron signed by four HBC officers – Fidler, Sutherland, McDonald, and White. They chastised the boldness of their adversary, but they also appealed to the humanitarian measures that had to be adopted to ward off the "hostility" of Cameron and his company.[174] They pleaded with him, asking that "people [be] allowed to follow their lawful callings without any one to disturb them."[175] With their position weakening by the day, this was a late-stage attempt to secure a peaceful solution to the conflict.

While he was beseeching the Saulteaux allies for support, Macdonell was mostly on the defensive by this time.[176] The Pemmican Proclamation was a by-product of the processes of dispossession set in motion when Europeans arrived on the continent and adopted exploitative practices that made the fur trade a profitable enterprise. In practical terms, it was the result of the frustration of an ineffectual formal claim on jurisdictional authority, which materially emboldened and nominally undermined the relative autonomy of the Métis, Saulteaux, Nêhiyaw, and Assiniboine producers in the area. They were still the primary providers of support for the District of Assiniboia in general and the Red River Colony in particular, and the experiment made this dependence on Indigenous producers more acute. Military manoeuvres, prohibitions, and humanitarian overtures, therefore, were symptomatic of the irregular and partial transformations of the social relations of land of Indigenous peoples, and the stunting of Selkirk's colonial ambitions had everything to do with the variableness of these changes, which no claim to prerogative could hasten or make absolute. The particularities of uneven and combined customary and commercial practices were essentially bound up with the segregation of Indigenous communities (eventually most starkly onto federal reserves), the rise of Métis nationhood, and the disputes over proclamations and treaties that continue to this day.

6

Consciousness and Ignorance

New Nation, Old Grievances

THE PARTNERS OF the North West Company began their plotting against Miles Macdonell and the "troublesome settlement" at their Fort William meeting in the summer of 1814.[1] For proponents of the Red River Colony, this meeting was the genesis of the violence that ensued. The NWC partners then incited antagonism against their rivals, moving among Indigenous parties and spreading rumours of Selkirk's intention to enslave them.[2] In one account, the NWC men offered "all the goods or merchandize [sic] and rum" to a group of Saulteaux if they would attack the settlement, which they refused to do.[3] Macdonell, meanwhile, sought dependable allies among the surrounding Indigenous peoples, such as with L'Homme Noir, swayed not only by Macdonell's promise to bring a bounty of tobacco, cattle, and whisky to the area as a measure of enlivening the settler colony as a trading hub, but also by his commitment to support that group of Saulteaux's ongoing battles with the Sioux.[4] Similar offerings were later extended to "Cayach Cobion," the leader of an Anishinaabe group from Leech Lake who came to trade furs in February 1815.[5] To Macdonell's additional relief, Colin Robertson quit his Athabasca-bound complement and headed straight for the settlement on learning about the threats of violence in the district earlier in the spring, and as he gathered deserted settlers along the way he extended his protection to them if they would agree to return to the Forks.[6]

Not forgotten were the proclamations of the previous year since the effects of the restrictive pronouncements continued to reverberate across the District of Assiniboia. The economic advantage of each company became even more entangled in the race to claim legitimate prerogative, with each side turning to formal legal pronouncements and proceduralism as means of breaking the mutually destructive economic competition that showed few signs of relenting. Only after the destruction of the site and the killing of HBC men at Seven Oaks did any politician in London intervene, which happened to coincide with Selkirk's first trip to the Red River Colony in 1817.

On Allegiance and Autonomy

The first scattering of the servant-settlers from Red River occurred after a series of clashes between the two companies, initially rhetorical in nature through an exchange of pointed letters between Cameron and Macdonell,[7] then performative in the form of parades and posturing,[8] and later physical through an exchange of gunfire. Crops were ruined and buildings set afire by the combined efforts of NWC men, HBC deserters, freemen, and Métis. By June 16, 1815, around the same time of the Battle of Waterloo in Belgium, Macdonell surrendered to the North West Company[9] and was taken to Montreal to face a felony charge associated with the Pemmican Proclamation.[10] Within days, Peguis and thirty-three men arrived on the scene after Peter Fidler sent two emissaries in a desperate attempt to leverage the reciprocal social obligations cultivated in the preceding years. In their plea to Peguis, they acknowledged that it was Saulteaux land, and as such the servant-settlers were not required to leave on the orders of the NWC partners; moreover, they referred to "the gift-giving aspect of their relationship with the Saulteaux," reminding them of the mutual obligations stemming from Macdonell's past exchanges with Peguis.[11] At this moment of crisis, it was the Red River Colony officials who relied on established practices of customary reciprocity as a defence mechanism.[12] In doing so, they stretched the boundaries of logic: to protect their claim to the land, they admitted that it did not belong to Selkirk – a blunt reversal of the charter and legal opinions selectively amassed to date. The distortion of the principle of reciprocity here is obvious in the fact that it both reinforced customary allegiances and advanced the cause of dispossession. Even if it was a strategic concession and not a principled reconsideration, the malleability of title and ownership, as well as the reciprocity-based social relations germane to exchange, lent the party in retreat some degree of protection. Peguis acknowledged the terms of the allegiance and approached NWC officials on behalf of his allies.[13] Although the gesture did not halt aggressions, Peguis accompanied the settler-colonists as they deserted the site.[14]

These years were difficult for many, including Peguis and his group. The ever-changing allegiances and conflicts with the Sioux, Blackfoot, and Mandan peoples in addition to the dwindling population of animals made it difficult for them to trap furs.[15] As Laura Peers recounts, much of their conflict with the Sioux was over territories still viable for the fur trade, but the cost of battles began to offset the advantages of hunting and trapping in those areas.[16] It was at this juncture that more Saulteaux in the region – especially women – turned to agricultural production, specifically wild rice, potatoes, and corn, crops that they would rotate depending on the potential for flood or drought in any given year.[17] As a consequence of spending less time hunting and trapping, they not only had new items to trade but also relied less on the truck system in order to secure the items necessary for their productive labour – in other words, they took on fewer debts. As demonstrably adaptable as Saulteaux peoples were, Peers warns against interpreting this as a sure sign of their "independence," suggesting instead that these adaptations were more indicative of the ongoing pressures that they were facing from increased competition and scarcity.[18] Although they were certainly not liberated from hardships, debts, or obligations, it is nevertheless feasible to interpret these practices as both evidence of ongoing transformations of their social relations of land and, by extension, their relative autonomy. These changes were evident in the wider adoption of agricultural activities, fluctuating alliances, and territorial displacements. But perhaps the best measure of the resilience of the Saulteaux in the region was the fact that they were the ones Fidler turned to for help when the settler colony was facing its most difficult tests.

In addition to the adaptations and shifting allegiances among groups of Nēhiyaw, Assiniboine, Saulteaux, Sioux, and Blackfoot in the area, all had to adjust to the growing fortitude, both economic and political, of the Métis. Jennifer Brown comments on the frequency with which the term "halfbreed" began to appear in the letters of the era, often complicated by the fact that some of the leaders of the Métis at Red River – Grant, Bostonais, Bonhomme, and Shaw – were the sons of high-ranking NWC men: Cuthbert Grant, Peter Pangman, Nicholas Montour, and Angus Shaw (respectively).[19] The difficulties arising from these circumstances had to do with deciphering the intentions of the parties in question: Were these sons NWC men, or did they represent the interests of their own distinct society? For clarity, it is useful to consult the documents exchanged between the Métis representatives of the North West Company and the HBC agents who remained at the Forks in the wake of Macdonell's surrender. Although Hugh McKenzie of the North West Company previously agreed to cease further actions against the Red River Colony, new negotiations commenced once Fidler was left as the highest-ranking HBC officer in the district. Significantly, these talks included Métis leaders. On the relevance of the negotiations, Brown comments that "these demands make clear that the Red River metis already identified themselves with a distinctive lifestyle and with values emphasizing the freedom to claim the benefits and privileges of both their maternal and paternal heritage."[20] More than allies of the North West Company but less than fully aligned with its objectives, the Métis exercised an important degree of autonomy and were recognized accordingly albeit selectively.

Although Peguis could not forestall the dispersal of the remaining servant-settlers, he was tasked with informing Fidler of the order to vacate. Instead of obeying the directive, Fidler responded with a list of proposals.[21] Included in the document was an agreement to cease hostility, retraction of the terms of the Pemmican Proclamation, amnesty for Métis from future flexing of the settlement's administrative powers, and an equal share of gifts in relation to those offered to their other Indigenous allies.[22] This offer would have unravelled all that Macdonell had attempted in putting the settler colony on a path toward self-sufficiency. Where Macdonell sought to bring all transactions within the purview of the governor's mandate and alienate the Métis, Fidler relinquished further control – especially with respect to the procurement and movement of pemmican. With the HBC agents still unable to exercise control over production, they finally had to acknowledge the relative autonomy of the producers. Moreover, that the agreement was being negotiated with the Métis, and not Nēhiyaw, Saulteaux, or Assiniboine leaders, shows that a transformation had occurred in the standing of the latter Indigenous peoples – not because the Métis had replaced the traditional fur trading societies but because of the historically specific ways that practices endemic to the fur trade transformed. The Métis peoples in the region emerged as a force in the context of economic instability, legal uncertainty, and geopolitical volatility; they were a manifestation and a facilitator of these changes.

Their genesis in many respects was bound together with the particular nature of labour compulsion characteristic of the early commercial fur trade. Unable to exercise direct control over the means of production from the outset, the trading companies inserted themselves into customary networks and facilitated economic access through merchant credit–backed obligations. Carolyn Podruchny and Nicole St-Onge argue for the need to adopt a narrative of Métis ethnogenesis that sheds notions of territorial originalism and mono-ethnicity, observing that the Métis had "economic niches within the fur trade" and that "the ever-expanding fur trade's water and land routes became the geographic architecture for Metis ethnogenesis because Metis communities emerged around the constantly opening and closing fur trade posts."[23] Agents at the heart of changing social relations of land – driving new alliances, traversing territories, adopting new political practices – it is understandable that they were at the centre of a dispute over what might be termed "upstream" activities: namely, the labour that supplied the expansion of the fur trade across the continent. Ron Bourgeault likewise points to the nature of the commercial fur trade itself, observing that "the consciousness of being Metis is not the product of a primordial instinct that arises out of intermarriage ... It's the rise of consciousness within the political economy of the mercantile capitalist fur trade."[24] The Métis of the Red River area were not unique in the sense of being the offspring of mixed race or interethnic unions;[25] their emergence as a force especially at this time and place was inseparable from the legal, economic, and geopolitical transformations associated with this trade.

While communities across the region continued to adapt to these changes in various ways, the Pemmican Proclamation was the boldest attempt to wrench autonomy away from the producers themselves. Despite Fidler's efforts to mute the effects of Macdonell's edict, the Métis took any imposition of a settler colony as an attack on their autonomy, and for this reason they refused Fidler's terms. In reply, they presented a six-article agreement that required the dispersal of the servant-settlers and the removal of the settlement; peaceful relations among "traders, Indians, and freemen"; limited access to the river for the Hudson's Bay Company; absolution for both the company and the Métis; freedom from molestation during the dispersal; and restrictions on trading at posts in the area of the former settler colony.[26] This was issued to the HBC representatives less as a point of negotiation and more as an order. Upon receipt of it, dispersal of the remaining settlers commenced, as did the destruction of the colonial structures and crops to discourage any resettlement.[27] Although the measures contained in the 1815 agreement from the four Métis leaders were beneficial to the commercial and political interests of the North West Company, the stipulations themselves suggest that the document was an "occasion to formulate and express their own demands."[28] The Métis leaders were the ones setting the ground rules and taking action, a testament to what was at stake in the conflicts at Red River and a reflection of the scope of changes that had occurred up to that point.

"New Nation," "New Régime"

Despite the abstract principles of legal subjectivity being stoked in the transformation of servants into "free" settlers, Selkirk's legal instructions and learned advice could not discipline this class faction of aspiring independent agricultural producers. They were caught by the pressures of an increasingly capitalist-oriented company that needed them to be instantly productive but withheld any investment in the form of fixed capital that might have served this vision. As a testament to the durability of the truck system, everything was done on credit: the building of houses and the planting of crops had to be done through a system of debt obligation in which the servant-settlers drew on accounts to establish the infrastructure that eventually would provide the Hudson's Bay Company with the bounty that it sought and the self-sufficiency that it needed to offset its dependence on Indigenous producers. The rapaciousness of this plan found its highest watermark in the fact that Selkirk likely had every intention of making the settlers repay their debts[29] – a plan foiled by NWC agents who nullified the debts of those who deserted to the rival company.[30]

These concerns about finances were reflected in a letter to Selkirk on September 19, 1815, that Macdonell wrote after arriving in Montreal for his court proceedings. From the outset, Macdonell detailed his repeated attempts to save on expenses and gird the budding community, always with an eye on giving Selkirk a sense of his commitment to frugality and the long-term welfare of the settler colony.[31] On the subject of the Pemmican Proclamation, meanwhile, he insisted that the order "had no bad effect ... on the Indians," even claiming that the local Indigenous peoples "understood well that the provisions of a Country belong to those in it."[32] He also mentioned Bostonais and Cuthbert Grant by name and identified them as principal agitators acting on behalf of the North West Company while also taking care to make himself out as the cool-headed leader, having insisted "that the past should be forgiven" upon releasing Bostonais from custody.[33] On the same theme, he intimated that his own surrender was not an act of cowardice or mere self-preservation but done in order to spare the settler colony – futile, as it was, since everything was burned down after Macdonell was taken away.[34]

Just as the remaining "free" settlers made their way northward to escape the violence,[35] and the last of the HBC representatives capitulated to the North West Company,[36] a vessel launched from Scotland with a new wave of colonists destined to become the latest addition to the settlement.[37] Coincidental to this, Selkirk was empowered by the HBC committee to undertake direct negotiations with the North West Company and given a firm directive as part of this charge: access would be permitted via Hudson Bay in exchange for some advantage in the Athabasca region, or the Hudson's Bay Company would surrender the region if its rival would acknowledge the legitimacy of the charter-backed monopoly.[38] But as Selkirk was finally preparing for his first trip to the Red River Colony, he remained unaware that it was deserted.[39]

Heightened activity in the fall of 1815 proved that the first dispersal was only temporary, however. Robertson arrived with a group of settlers whom he had convinced to return, and they were eventually joined by 120 of the latest servant-settlers from Scotland in November.[40] Included in the new party was Robert Semple, the company's appointee for governor-in-chief, and James Sutherland from the Church of Scotland, who was to administer the ecclesiastical rites that Macdonell had been grudgingly tending to until then.[41] Semple was quick to populate the council, swearing in four members in August while at York Factory and two more (Sutherland and Peter Fidler) in September, en route to the Red River Colony.[42] Despite the new administrative and spiritual leadership, however, accounts of the servant-settlers' experiences were remarkably harmonious in relation to those of the "first brigade": the newcomers were poorly clothed, food was scarce, and there was nothing upon arrival. Once more it came down to the generosity of the local Indigenous societies to save them from perishing, and again their reliance on the "rude savages" caused resentment among the colonists.[43] The undertone of this resentment was a frustrated impotence, the result of an idealized sense of superiority clashing with the reality of their dependence on peoples they considered inferior. Domination was difficult to practise from such a powerless position; this was the relation that the experiment was tasked with dismantling, but at every turn it seemed to entrench the circumstances further.

The North West Company officials noticed the growing number of arrivals at the briefly abandoned site, as did the Métis. In the waning days of the winter of 1816, Alexander Macdonell of the North West Company wrote to Cameron that "the New Nation under their leaders are coming forward to clear their native soil of intruders and assassins."[44] The HBC men might not have been cognizant of them prior to 1815, but by this time it would have been difficult not to be aware of the growing clout of the Métis. To Selkirk, Miles Macdonell made the matter plain by admitting that his Pemmican Proclamation had negative ramifications for the Métis. He wrote that the edict and its enforcement provided the NWC partners with the grounds to "irritate the half-breeds against us," but still seeking to evade outright blame he suggested that his own peacemaking efforts through direct negotiations with the Métis and freemen had left the parties "well satisfied."[45] In reality, these overtures had not had the effect that he believed. As much as the return of the servant-settlers to Red River was unanticipated, it was also unwelcomed by the North West Company and Métis alike – and Robertson took great pride in that.

Robertson was determined to reinvigorate the colony, which included a shift in tactics from a defensive to a more offensive approach – or at least a similarly aggressive approach less the veil of legal prerogative.[46] Robertson began by undertaking smaller gestures to aggravate the North West Company, including hiring a Métis man by the name of Batis, which he thought was a good first step in "breaking the chain of connection that is formed between the NWCo and the Halfbreeds."[47] He also wrote of having in tow an abundance of provisions from Montreal, and he commented that he would present these riches to the Métis, knowing that the North West Company would have few items at its disposal to make good on its promises to the colonists, the Métis, and its own servants made during the height of the conflict in previous months. Robertson surmised that the Métis were not satisfied with the paltry offerings received in exchange for their efforts, and he intended to corrode relations between the North West Company and its allies by engaging in tactics similar to those that Cameron used in the previous year: luring people away with the promise of more.[48] Less salient was any allusion to the legitimacy of the monopoly, a commitment to establish the semblance of an administrative body, or a claim to be acting in accordance with legal prerogative; rather, Robertson engaged in direct antagonism and a more personal vendetta against Cameron.[49] This plan had roots in Robertson's familiarity with the NWC rival,[50] having been employed by it until the fall of 1815.

Beyond the strategic downplaying of his claim in past letters to Bathurst and Macdonell, however, Selkirk never abandoned the matter of legal prerogative, as confirmed by the substance of negotiations with the North West Company. As the representative of HBC interests in the dispute, he sought a resolution through arbitration, a proposal much scoffed at by the NWC partners since, from their perspective, it amounted to an ultimatum: either accept the terms of the charter monopoly or lose the advantages gained in the Athabasca region.[51] Negotiations between the two companies failed to reach a resolution by the start of 1816, with Selkirk maintaining that matters of legal authority were paramount and his counterparts prioritizing matters of mutual economic interest in the cessation of hostility.[52] Meanwhile, the cases against Spencer and Macdonell were likewise pivotal in substantiating Selkirk's claim. If they were found guilty of acting beyond the scope of their authority, then the HBC committee's assumption of prerogative would have unravelled. It ended up that this question did not have to be answered since the charges against them were dropped once the prosecuting officials realized that they would not be able to prove *"felonious intent."*[53] As was the case fifteen years prior, the legal matter went unresolved one way or the other.

A fatalistic understanding of the circumstances might lead to the opinion that the lack of a more amicable solution made the violent outbursts of 1816 inevitable, but this perspective ignores the agency of the Métis, who – despite having a significant interest in the outcome of any negotiated agreement – were scarcely given a second thought by Selkirk. Robertson's brinkmanship aside, there seemed to be relatively little risk of any significant clash – at least it appeared this way in the fall when Semple and the new settlers arrived.[54] What Robertson did not heed was the British government's aim to avoid an outright military conflict,[55] and the appointment of Selkirk as the HBC negotiator could serve as primary evidence of a preference for a peaceable solution. His unsuccessful petitions to the government for military support just as feasibly could have filled Robertson's mind with doubt about the prospects of obtaining, by force, a monopolistic stronghold on the disputed territories.

Although a fresh cast of figures was in place in this "new régime,"[56] events unfolded much as they had before: an appointee operating on site under misinformation, a lord failing in his petitions for a legal resolution and state-sponsored military support alike, misled servant-settlers, and Indigenous peoples' labours both coveted and degraded. The rival companies understood the need to fortify allegiances among the Indigenous peoples, which is not to imply that they accepted the relative autonomy of Indigenous societies beyond their utility in conflict. But it was the relative autonomy of local Indigenous peoples that protected the population of the settler colony from death by starvation; it was the relative autonomy of the same peoples that the Hudson's Bay Company sought to banish by approving the experiment.

Benevolence or Ignorance?

In a letter written by William McGillivray dated November 1815, there was some mention of the incompatibility between colonization and the welfare of Indigenous peoples. It was a strategic ploy – a defensive posture meant to advance the claim against the feasibility of the Hudson's Bay Company's settler colonial enterprise – but it is worth noting as a measure of rebuffing the notion that individuals of that age were of uniform consciousness when it came to Indigenous peoples and colonialism:

> Colonization, and Indians with their trade, cannot to any great extent co-exist. The fatal experience of the *Indian nations* in the neighbourhood of the United States proves this; and that unfortunate people now see (when too late) the ruin with which they are thereby threatened. Had they resisted, in the first instance, the occupation by any colonists of any spot beyond the Ohio, the natives would still have been independent and happy, instead of having to apprehend, as they now have, a universal spoliation of their lands, and the extermination of their persons by the unbounded rapacity and injustice of the United States ... What a lesson for Indians, yet beyond American control![57]

McGillivray then proceeded to claim that the only way that Selkirk's settler colonial experiment differed from the example just mentioned was that the former lacked military support, thankfully so, he argued, or the British government would have found itself as hated as the US government.[58]

Around the time that this correspondence was enclosed and sent to Sir Gordon Drummond (Prevost's replacement as governor-in-chief of British North America), altered customary practices formed the template of colonization. Per Selkirk's original instructions to Macdonell, presents and reciprocity-informed obligations remained key in the processes of dispossession, as had been the case throughout the commercial exchanges of the fur trade. As a result, the Hudson's Bay Company's and by extension the British government's lack of an overtly militaristic campaign in the first phase of western settlement afforded a benevolent gloss that continues to obscure the exploitative reality of settler colonialism in Canada today. However, it should not be taken as a given that there were no acts of resistance in response to such encroachments, which McGillivray's account intimates was the norm.

Within a year of his calculated but in some respects prescient letter, a group of Métis acted in response to the HBC impositions. Among the most decisive actions came from a group whose fortitude was a testament to the historical particularities of the previous century and a half and whose own transformations both mirrored and drove the changes occurring. Because of the agency of the Métis, one cannot assume that the inaction of the British government in the face of the disputes over legal prerogative and commercial competition had as an inevitable outcome the violent clash at Seven Oaks in 1816. Such an assumption speciously suggests that the politicians could have devised some fix comprehensive enough to address the grievances of all parties. As the correspondence among politicians, aristocrats, and merchants makes plain, the Métis were rarely on their minds as anything other than a vague threat, even while both companies were still deeply dependent on the labour of the Métis and other Indigenous producers in the region. Any resolution that would have been satisfying to the companies' men likely would have involved either legislated subordination of the Indigenous peoples or some version of the status quo: that is, practices of exchange that expanded the network of dispossession through often a one-sided, intermittent, or grudging reciprocity.

At no discernible point, other than summarily in McGillivray's letter, were the interests of Indigenous peoples taken into serious consideration in a manner that reflected the scope and depth of the obligations consented to during the exchanges. The indelible presumption was that the claims to the land were beyond contest, and all that was left to be decided was which of the companies should be permitted to have the balance of power. Those who subscribe to the premise that violence at Seven Oaks was inevitable – either because of the lack of a legal declaration regarding the inviolability of the HBC charter or because of the lack of a military assignment benefiting one side or the other[59] – unwittingly buttress the view that the conflict was the result of an impotent British government. But the perspective that the violence was caused by aristocratic ambivalence or self-interest loses sight of the degree to which (even in dithering) the company officials were reacting to the relative autonomy of Indigenous producers, which remained a key factor during these transformative years.

After his arrival in the fall of 1815, Semple wintered at the posts north of the Red River Colony situated along the Saskatchewan River;[60] meanwhile, Robertson's attempts to insert himself between the Métis and the North West Company seemed to be having the desired effect, with Grant becoming nervous about the reliability of his allies, causing him to mount a countercampaign to reinstate his influence.[61] Also that fall, Selkirk arrived in New York and finally learned about the sacking of the settler colony, which precipitated a new urgency in his efforts to assemble a military complement. Negotiations with the North West Company were ongoing throughout December from Montreal, and when they dissolved by the new year Selkirk turned his attention to gathering accounts from former servant-settlers of the previous spring's dispersal. These accounts were made before Selkirk, who as the official witness of the depositions signed the transcripts with the title of "Civil Magistrate for the Indian Territories,"[62] an expansive judicial assignment received while in Montreal that granted him authority in all of the territories not deemed within the remit of the Canadas.[63] He continued gathering information in Upper Canada and eventually concluded that neither the ill-advised Pemmican Proclamation nor the militancy of Miles Macdonell was the primary target of the servant-settlers' grievances prior to their dispersal. From his investigation, Selkirk surmised that the servant-settlers detested the expectation that they should have to bear arms on behalf of their lord.[64] Conveniently, this strengthened his case for military assistance, which Drummond finally granted by allowing Selkirk a modest number of soldiers recently released from their duties following the War of 1812.[65]

At Red River and in the surrounding areas, the winter months were difficult because of the increased number of inhabitants vying for provisions. In some instances, food was obtained by negotiating with NWC agents, and present needs were met by promising future advantages; in other cases, nothing could be done to ward off starvation, as at Peace River, where sixteen people died.[66] In the months between their arrival and the spring of 1816, Robertson and his party began to lose whatever goodwill had been achieved with regard to the Métis and freemen in the region the previous fall.[67] With the subsequent arrival of Semple, the NWC men needed no further inkling of what was afoot in the region on the HBC side, recognizing that "the spirit of our People particularly the half breeds would require to be roused."[68] At this point, Grant's campaign to reassert himself as a leader among the Métis was well under way.

By March 13, 1816, Grant declared that the Métis would not submit to Robertson and the Hudson's Bay Company. As proof of his ability to summon his people and their willingness to heed his call, he confirmed to J.D. Cameron that "the half-breeds ... are all to be here in the spring, it is to be hoped we shall come of[f] with flying colours & never to see any of them again in the colonizing way in Red River. In fact the Traders shall pack off with themselves also for having disregarded our orders last Spring."[69] Stated plainly by Grant, the desire to see the end of the Red River Colony, as well as to repel any trace of the Hudson's Bay Company in the area, was greatly informed by the sense of betrayal with the breach of the six-article agreement of June 1815. But Grant's letter was intercepted by Robertson, who within less than a week led a band of men to the North West Company's Fort Gibraltar (situated on the east side of the Red River, just north of where it joins the Assiniboine River, it later became Fort Garry). This occasioned the arrest of Cameron, the seizing of the NWC communications, and a range of destructive acts that rivalled those that befell the Red River Colony nearly a year earlier.[70]

Selkirk, while still in Montreal, wrote to Robertson that he would be heading to Red River in the spring and that Macdonell would make a return, lending some "Official Character" to proceedings.[71] Remarkable about this letter, however, was the flagrancy of Selkirk's personal claim to the lands in question. For all of the gesturing toward humanitarianism, legal process, and formalism, the lord betrayed his mounting frustration with what he saw as encroachments on his private domain, and he insisted that the "troublesome"[72] North West Company "be compelled to quit all their intrusive possessions upon my lands and particularly the Post at the Forks," adding that "it will no doubt be necessary to use force for this purpose, [and] I am anxious that this should be done in a regular manner under a legal warrant from the Governor."[73] As the Métis were cementing their position by hoisting their now iconic flag at the Forks and vowing to rid the terrain of the English,[74] Selkirk stayed true to his formal claims and personal ambitions, not once paying attention to the Métis.

Throughout April, the Métis ranks were growing as Grant's allies began to appear along the Qu'Appelle River, west of the Forks.[75] Sutherland, meanwhile, was fretting over the effects of Robertson's actions at Fort Gibraltar: "Whatever just cause Mr Robertson has had for such a step, will not persuade either Indians or Half-Breeds that we are in the right, particularly the latter who absolutely threaten us with extermination."[76] Faced with mounting tensions, an NWC agent attempted to distance his party from the Métis and their demands by urging Sutherland and the HBC men at Qu'Appelle River to meet with him and arrive at a peaceable solution.[77] Sutherland refused, ostensibly not convinced that the NWC agent had the authority to negotiate, and he attempted to gather those at Qu'Appelle River to join the others at the Forks. Outnumbered, he was captured by the Métis on the way and held as a prisoner.[78] By then, news that Robertson had previously taken Cameron prisoner reached the NWC men at Qu'Appelle River, which likely informed this act of retribution against Sutherland. While at Brandon House, Fidler learned of the destruction of the HBC's Qu'Appelle River post, and despite Sutherland's plea that he should send a warning to Semple at the Forks, Fidler knew that any attempt at such communication would be intercepted.[79]

In the preparations for his trip to the Forks, Selkirk was pleased to secure his small lot of mercenaries (a mix of Swiss, German, French, and Italian men) from the Regiment de Meurons,[80] although Drummond emphatically stated that "the Military guard which I have been induced to give your Lordship is intended solely for the purposes of your *Personal Protection*" – implying that this should not be interpreted as a commitment of military support for the Hudson's Bay Company or Selkirk's colonial experiment.[81] Drummond underlined this caveat a few weeks later – the military escort was only for Selkirk's "personal safety" and not meant to be understood as sanctioning a military offensive against the North West Company.[82] When

Drummond eventually wavered even on this modest commitment, Selkirk took it upon himself to negotiate the terms of service with the military men and successfully used the promise of land to lure over one hundred men (an additional twenty coming from the Watteville Regiment)[83] for his westward campaign.[84]

At the Red River Colony that May, the Premier gave a speech to Semple in the presence of Cameron, still in custody. The Premier expressed gratitude to Semple for "having come on our lands" and derided Cameron and the North West Company for "having spoiled our lands," for reducing his people to a "Pitiful" state, and for keeping the Premier's own son "in Slavery" at Lac La Pluie (in present-day northern Ontario along the US border).[85] Despite Macdonell's earlier feeble commitment to this group of Saulteaux, the allegiance remained roughly intact following the first dispersal. Two further considerations are also noteworthy: first, the Premier referred to Semple as "Father," as he did when Macdonell was in charge of the Red River Colony; second, on two occasions in the brief text, the Premier claimed the land as "our land," a potentially contentious matter in the context of the Métis peoples' growing presence, not to mention the Nēhiyawok and Assiniboine who inhabited the area in the previous century.

The events in the spring of 1816 were still unravelling according to a pattern like that in 1815: the factious parties were again exchanging threats and grandstanding, neither wanting to be the first to engage in belligerence and risk having all liability held against it.[86] By June 2, Fidler wrote from Brandon House to Semple at the Forks and mentioned being suddenly surrounded by "about 48 Halfbreeds with a few Canadians all on horseback" and having all of their supplies pilfered in the process.[87] In the letter, he remarked how "all the Ind[ians] here was [sic] greatly exasperated" by the occurrences but were too outnumbered to resist the intrusions.[88] A telling indicator of changes in the region was the fact that everything was taken from the main storehouse "except the furs"; arms and provisions were the most valued, and items that were once the primary fuel for the trade, furs, were left as an afterthought.[89]

As evidence of both the scale of the transformation and the breadth of the Métis peoples' influence on the situation, it was clear that HBC and NWC men alike relied on outmoded or ill-suited processes of dispute resolution and commercial gamesmanship, and as such they were outdone by the Métis. Steeped in ignorance of their own limits, neither side "'had a handle' on who these Mixed-bloods really were."[90] The nonchalant way the HBC men dismissed the six-article agreement established with the Métis was one facet of this wilful neglect. What the resettlement also disclosed was the belief that the Red River Colony was more important to the Hudson's Bay Company than the terms of this agreement in particular and the Métis in general. Dismissed but not dispirited, the Métis at Red River responded.

From the rubble of the NWC structures at Gibraltar, fortifications were built along the riverbanks, and what remained at the site was incinerated.[91] With a vital site lost to the Hudson's Bay Company, the news made its way to the North West Company and its Métis allies around the region; efforts were then mounted to send provisions and support to the NWC agents that remained in the area, with partners committing themselves to joining Grant and his party at the Forks.[92] The landscape was rapidly shifting, and the prospect of direct conflict was mounting as each side sought retribution for wrongs.

Seven Oaks

Grant and a party of no more than thirty traversed behind Semple's station at the area known as La Grenouillère (Frog Plain) in late June 1816,[93] and on detecting their movements nearby Semple readied his men. Grant noticed the rush to arms at Fort Douglas (situated at the junction of the Red and Assiniboine Rivers, across the Red from Fort Gibraltar) and ordered one of his own men to the other side to explain that they were simply planning to encamp and wait for the arrival of canoes in order to offload their provisions. Semple reached for the emissary's horse and gun and attempted to take the man prisoner, but he resisted, fired a shot, and then jumped from his horse to run back to his side. Semple issued an order to shoot at the retreating man, and although he was not hit another one of Grant's men was struck. Grant's group quickly opened fire on Semple and his party, killing twenty-one.[94] In a narrative published by three NWC men a year after the events in question, they reported that "a Saulteaux Indian, in defiance of [Grant's] efforts and entreaties to spare Mr. Semple's life, shot him through the head."[95] The same account states that no settler was killed in the clash,[96] but later reports indicate that three of the dead were settlers, and the rest were employed at various levels by the Hudson's Bay Company.[97]

Accounts more sympathetic to the HBC cause note that Grant was positioning his group in an antagonistic manner intending to meet the reinforcements making their way to the Forks after the sacking of Fort Gibraltar. They were initially encamped farther away from Semple's station but marched toward the Forks and were discovered by the HBC men that evening[98] in an area where there was "a bend in the river, in a grove of trees known as Seven Oaks."[99] The decision to halt the march put Semple and the settlers on edge, with some of the latter fleeing in fear of an imminent attack.[100] In an account from a century after the conflict, Chester Martin writes that Semple was injured but had his life initially spared by Grant, at which point "an Indian, seeing the Governor down[,] 'shot him in the breast and killed him on the spot'"; Martin also explains

164 *A Legacy of Exploitation*

that the first shot might have been fired by a panicked settler and that the bodies on the ground after the gunfire were "stripped," with some being "barbarously mutilated," as the "half-breeds carried off as plunder even the blood-stained clothing."[101] In an interview published in 2016, Bumsted concurs – to a degree – with Martin's understanding of the role of the Métis in the clash, and he states that "the *massacre* of course comes because Cuthbert Grant cannot control his mixed bloods."[102] Meanwhile, Peers recounts that Semple was warned of a looming attack some weeks earlier by the Saulteaux allies of the settler colony but dismissed them and their offer of aid.[103] Still, they remained nearby; Peguis and his group went to Seven Oaks following the battle to recover the bodies of the fallen, burying some in the wake.[104]

The conflict has come to be known as "The Seven Oaks Incident" or "The Battle of Seven Oaks," and some refer to it as a "massacre" or downplay it as a "skirmish."[105] How the event was depicted in primary and some secondary literature up to 1970 is especially useful in terms of charting the racist discourses about the agency of the Métis peoples,[106] with some scholars more critical of how Seven Oaks became "usable history" in the service of a Métis mythical narrative.[107] Gerhard Ens, for one, contends that "the reasons for the Battle of Seven Oaks are not to be found in the national aspirations of the Metis but, rather, in the attempts of the NWC to keep the HBC out of the Athabasca District."[108] For what he considers the real reasons for the violence, Ens offers an economic rationale that emphasizes the circumstances of competition for furs.[109] Against the twenty-first-century views of Seven Oaks that interpret the event as the source of a liberation narrative, he argues that the impetus for action came not from visionary leaders of the "Metis Nation" but from profit-mongering company men all too willing to instrumentalize the Métis as a means of securing their market share. In his reading, instead of acting in response to the HBC agents' flouting of the six-article agreement in the name of their own "freedom dreams,"[110] the Métis were duped by the North West Company. That they were made to shoulder the blame for the violence has been evident across many accounts over the past two centuries, especially in the aftermath of the Métis uprisings of the late nineteenth century.[111] Not wanting to tread that particular racist path, Ens instead interprets the historical exclusion of the Métis from the subsequent negotiations as evidence of their having been instrumentalized.[112]

Cast as pawns of the North West Company, the Métis are denied either the mature intent or the fully formed awareness that would allow their actions to be seen as emancipatory in any legitimate sense. Whether the objective is to villainize the Métis to serve the "imperial desire" of the Canadian state or to infantilize them to dispute the liberation narrative, the outcome in both instances amounts to denying the agency of the Métis in a manner not wholly supported by a broader assessment of the events in question.

There are several counterpoints worth explicating, not simply to interrogate Ens's challenge to the narrative of Métis nationhood, but also to underscore the utility of a more comprehensive framework of historical analysis that resists focusing on economic competition as the primary driver of actions. By understanding it as one occurrence in a sequence of related events, it is possible to place it in a historical relation to other changes ongoing in the region at the time. More than just a conflict born from vengeance, it reflects the fact that commercial advantage and legal prerogative were entwined campaigns but, even more importantly, that the lack of a resolution on either the economic or the legal front did not make the violence an inevitable occurrence. The violence was not a consequence of the failure to negotiate a compromise between the rival outfits, nor was it the result of a lack of forceful intervention by the British government; such explanations misleadingly shield the rivalry from the sphere of influence of Indigenous peoples and make it seem feasible that the only solution to avoid violence was one designed by aristocrats imbibing their magisterial power. The specifics of the settler colonial context are vital to understanding the effects of the rivalry on the Indigenous peoples in the area and how the peoples themselves influenced the direction of the competition.

It is also a dubious undertaking to link the genesis of Métis nationhood to one event versus seeing it as part of a sequence of ongoing transformations. The ethnogenesis of Métis identity cannot be comprehended in either a territorial or a temporal vacuum but is tangled up with a host of changes associated with the fur trade. Consequently, Ens is convincing in his claim that the violent conflict at Seven Oaks had to do with the competitive appetites of the rival companies; however, the company men themselves were reacting to the relative autonomy of Indigenous producers leading up to and including Seven Oaks. With the terms of the Pemmican Proclamation and the dismissal of the six-article agreement, the Red River Colony proved to be an existential threat to the Métis. To interpret Seven Oaks as anything less than pivotal in the consciousness raising of the Métis is to ignore that threat. As an added disservice, it denies integral connections to coeval campaigns for liberation waged in other parts of the world. Although it is tempting, for the purposes of pat conclusions, to look at the incidents at Red River as occurring within "the great political vacuum of the early northwest,"[113] this parochialism is baneful. There are elements worth excavating that place Seven Oaks firmly in a global context.

For a Métis recollection that validates these connections, there exists a ballad written by Pierre Falcon, a witness of the conflict at Seven Oaks. His piece has been variably titled "Chanson de la Genouillère," "Chanson des Bois Brûlés," and "La Bataille des Sept Chênes," and in it he commemorates the victory of the Métis over the English forces at Red River. The stanzas cover the main elements of the conflict: they reference the intention of the foreigners to pillage their land; note that the English fired the first shot; celebrate the admirable conduct of the Métis in the conflict; and express joy in having taken down the false emperor, Semple.[114] On close inspection, Falcon's ballad also echoes the themes common to battles of that era. The stanzas are animated by anger at British rule; they are interwoven with the hallmarks of romanticist flair that accompany the early days of nationalist fervour that champions a collective-possessive claim to "our country"/"notre Pays";[115] and they culminate in a tale of success in repelling an encroaching "Empereur."[116] This last point has resonances with Napoleon's campaign at Waterloo fought one year earlier, almost to the day, and might have been an ironic way of maligning the British, themselves attempting to halt an emperor's overreach.[117] Much like how Seven Oaks was one event in a string of other circumstances germane to the commercial fur trade, it can likewise be thought of in geopolitical terms as in congruence with a range of other battles fought in the same era.

Rare insofar as it is one of the few eyewitness accounts, it is difficult to deny it as an expression of exuberance in the kinship that congealed in the defeat of the foreign interloper.[118] Ens, however, observes that it was "hardly a national anthem" and might have had more humble objectives, namely as a way of memorializing "the feat of a particular group of men."[119] His main charge against reading the ballad as an expression of fomenting Métis nationhood, in addition to the Métis having been coaxed into action by the North West Company, has to do with the fact that it did not develop its anthemic status until later in the century, after the HBC-NWC merger in 1821 up to and including the disputes over trading rights in the District of Assiniboia in the 1840s.[120] Ens concludes that the Métis could not have had a "conscious" nationalist awakening during the dispersals of the Red River Colony;[121] therefore, it is misleading to infer a liberation narrative from their actions, and those who do so are liable to engage in mythmaking.

Even if it was an embryonic consciousness in 1816, it was a consciousness nevertheless. It would require bending the historical details to the point of warping them to isolate Seven Oaks as neither indicative of the consciousness of the Métis nor quintessentially of its time in a broader geopolitical sense. As historian Eric Hobsbawm observes, "even the arts of a small minority in society can still echo the thunder of the earthquakes which shake all humanity."[122]

Seven Oaks can be thought of as one incident among many integral to the qualitative changes underway. On this occasion, it was the Métis who were challenging the practices of dispossession directly undermining their own relative degree of autonomy over the production and transportation of pemmican and other provisions. The fallout from Seven Oaks further reveals the extent to which Indigenous peoples continued to exercise an important degree of ownership over the means of production as it related to these upstream activities associated with the still-expanding fur trade.

Act Three

With the pending arrival of the NWC reinforcements from Fort William on June 22, 1816, the settler colony was deserted once again. In his chronicle of the events, Peter Fidler lamented "thus has a Colony which has cost the Earl of Selkirk near £40,000 founded for the cause of humanity been totally destroyed, through the means of the NWCo."[123] That the failure of the so-called cause of humanity was measured in monetary terms and not according to the human costs is significant. Meanwhile, at the northern end of Lake Winnipeg, the servant-settlers consented to remain for up to a year and wait for further instructions from Selkirk, which included the possibility of obtaining a military escort back to the Forks.[124] Yet Fidler himself was warned by the NWC partners that, "should any of the HBCo Traders go back this season to Red River, they should be shot."[125] Although the NWC partners were in control at the Forks, their position was severely curtailed farther east.

On receiving news of the deaths at Seven Oaks in late July, Selkirk was in Sault Ste. Marie and opted not to go to Red River straightaway, but to Fort William, arriving there by August 12.[126] With his mercenaries in tow, according to the NWC account of the proceedings, he camped just north of the NWC establishment and mounted cannons on the banks, aimed at the fort in preparation for an attack.[127] Eager to flex his precariously vested authority, Selkirk ordered the arrest of several NWC men for wrongs arising from the 1814–15 conflicts and the first dispersal,[128] and he relieved the fort of its provisions and arms.[129] During the summer and into the fall of 1816, he was still gathering evidence for his case against the North West Company while he was also receiving detailed ledgers that attested to the quantifiable losses at the various posts in the District of Assiniboia.[130] By the end of August, it was his understanding that the violence at Seven Oaks was the fault of "the Half Indian Servants of the North West Company,"[131] effectively collapsing the Hudson's Bay Company's most threatening adversaries into a single identity, and Selkirk responded with the authority of both righteousness and military might on his side. He did so with a degree of reckless impunity, which one effusive historiographer softens as two "technical legal errors."[132]

168 *A Legacy of Exploitation*

The first "error" was a business agreement with a discredited NWC partner, Daniel McKenzie, who – in an attempt to settle his own debts – spoke with Selkirk to put an end to the hostilities as a whole. The emboldened McKenzie promised to sell all of the NWC stores to Selkirk[133] and agreed to submit the company to a process of arbitration in Britain for the violent exchanges.[134] In the fall of 1816, the NWC partners denied their colleague's standing within the company, which sapped the legitimacy of any purported agreement. The partners used this dubious arrangement as proof of Selkirk's rapaciousness, asserting that the lord went to great lengths to punish the North West Company by taking advantage of McKenzie, who later claimed that he was too drunk at the time to be of sound mind.[135] The second "error" was that Selkirk believed he was beyond judicial reproach.[136] That fall he received a warrant for his arrest, which he refused because of its origin from a magistrate of Lower Canada,[137] the lack of the arresting constable's credentials, and "irregularities" with the warrant itself.[138] Again he disputed the NWC claim to legal prerogative and scoffed at the "pretended arrest."[139] In objection, the NWC partners submitted a letter of protest against Selkirk's actions in which they questioned the lord's intentions and doubted the finer distinction between what constituted "legal" versus "illegal" business in the context of competition in disputed territories.[140] The case that the North West Company was mounting was one in which it could prove jurisdictional overreach for economic gain; if Selkirk was truly making arrests at Fort William on the suspicions of wrongdoing in June 1815, then the additional orders to seize provisions and take over command of NWC forts were spurious.

From a wider perspective, Selkirk's actions – in any given instance – can be traced back to at least one of four overlapping rationales: belief in his unimpeachable authority, the apparent inferiority of his enemy's character and/or intellect, duress caused by the looming prospect of the enemy "excit[ing] the Indians against us,"[141] and his colonial ambition shrouded in the thin veil of a humanitarian cause. The two so-called errors that Selkirk committed were not blunders or exceptions arising from momentarily poor judgment but a continuation of the duplicitous positions and arguments previously attempted in order to secure dominance, be it his own or the company's. From these events, it is clear that the more presumed legal prerogative, commercial voracity, and paramilitary force converged, the weaker the legitimacy of Selkirk's position became.[142] In effect, his actions were a by-product of a company with the nominal right and will to execute a monopoly but an actual incapacity to do so, not only because of the rivalry as such but also because of the relative autonomy of Indigenous producers that spurred commercial activity and legal frustration alike.

After the NWC partners at Fort William were searched, arrested, and sent to Montreal,[143] Selkirk ordered his assemblage of soldiers ahead to the Red River Colony.[144] When these dispatched troops, led by Miles Macdonell, arrived in the District of Assiniboia, it was thought that the best way to "establish themselves" was to capture Fort Douglas.[145] Given that these actions took place by Selkirk's orders and with a regiment of soldiers, it is difficult to see them as defensive manoeuvres.[146] Macdonell had his own take, much more aggrieved. In another one of his loquacious letters, he defended his character against the rumours that it was his fault that the Red River Colony failed and that the only reason he was leading this company of sixty back to the scene was to exorcise his personal demons of that defeat.[147] Undaunted, Macdonell had an air of superiority about him arising from acquired knowledge of the region, and he concentrated on executing a surprise attack on Fort Douglas. As an added measure, he dispatched a messenger to seek assistance from a seasoned ally, Peguis.[148] Although initially out of reach, he and nine of his men intercepted Macdonell and offered some provisions at the encampment the night before the planned attack.[149]

By daybreak, Macdonell wrote, the "Company's flag was hoisted on the staff" at Fort Douglas; within a few days, he took on some of the former NWC servants[150] and recalled the male settlers from their post-dispersal encampment at Jack River (later Norway House) at the northern end of Lake Winnipeg.[151] Convinced that the threat of "disturbances" loomed, however, he planned buildings "for the protection of the Settlement."[152] He also set out to reinforce alliances with various Saulteaux leaders, namely Peguis and La Robe Noir, met with a group of Assiniboine,[153] and attempted to win over a Nēhiyaw leader, Le Sonnat.[154] With the third resettlement at the Forks, the narrative of hardship became more emphatic: after a difficult winter at Jack River, some saw no hope and left for their homelands, whereas others suffered through a now familiar dearth of provisions in order to resurrect their settler colonial base.[155] For the third time, the survival of the new and returned settlers could not have been without the support of Peguis and his allies.[156] This reflects what Robert Alexander Innes identifies as "the close relations between the Métis and Plains Cree, Assiniboine, and Saulteaux bands," underscoring the strength of these allegiances despite the tense circumstances.[157]

Meanwhile, the pamphleteering for the sake of persuading the court of public opinion was rampant. Each side was amassing observations and recollections related to the recent clashes, imputing blame, and populating the pages of Montreal newspapers in turn.[158] This was "a war of words," with vested businessmen and relatives on either side seeking to spin the events in their favour.[159] Lord Bathurst, concerned by the expanding scope of liability that Selkirk faced by rebuffing the warrants, wrote from London in February 1817 that he deemed it "necessary ... for the remedy of existing as well as for the prevention of further evils" that the rule of law should be applied and that Selkirk be arrested.[160] In a letter to Bathurst, HBC Governor Joseph Berens reinforced the company's claim that "the Crown has vested the sole jurisdiction within the limits of their charter," at the same time performing magnanimity by agreeing to instruct officials across the company to cooperate with a newly established commission.[161] Struck in May 1817 by Sir John Sherbrooke (governor general of the Canadas as of 1816) on orders from Bathurst, the initiative had appointed two commissioners and instructed them to visit the district with a military escort "to support their authority and that of the laws."[162] It was led by William Bachelor Coltman, who reviewed documents submitted by both parties in order to understand what occurred at Seven Oaks and attempt to avoid reprisals. The Coltman Commission represented the most formal juridical overlay to apply to the district since the earlier attempts by Macdonell and Semple to establish the Council of Assiniboia, and Selkirk initially welcomed this as a relief from the burdens of being the uppermost-ranked authority in the region.[163]

This intervention by London in the affairs of the Red River Colony could be interpreted as a victory for Selkirk, who had spent years courting the government's favour. But the circumstances of this long-awaited involvement suggest that these measures might have been taken in part because of a lack of confidence in Selkirk himself,[164] not to mention the increasingly embarrassing public airing of grievances. Still, he remained unaware of the commands issued by Bathurst out of London intent on bringing "law and order into the territories."[165] All of his recent activities were in direct contravention of a royal proclamation issued by Sherbrooke in Quebec on May 3, 1817, that aimed to stop hostilities and prevent future violence by ordering an end to all "unauthorized Military Force" by immediate disbandment; the "Restitution of all Forts, Buildings, or Trading Stations, with the Property which they contain, which may have been Seized or Taken Possession of by either Party"; and the removal of "any Blockade or Impediment" to the free movement of traders, subjects, and Indigenous peoples, as well as their goods, furs, and provisions.[166] Sherbrooke informed Selkirk directly of these latest orders in a letter and assigned to the commissioners the responsibility of promulgating and exercising these terms throughout the territories;[167] heeding these directives, Coltman made the prince regent's proclamation known by reading it aloud at the Forks during his visit.[168]

After passing the winter at Fort William, Selkirk arrived at the settlement by June 21, with Coltman arriving just over a week later on July 1,[169] a meeting that brought to a head the matter of jurisdictional authority expressed in their divergent expectations of the commission itself. The process by which to undertake the restitution of property – whether wholesale or by region – was one problem for Selkirk, and so was Coltman's unwillingness to entertain the possibility of retribution in the name of the men killed at Seven Oaks.[170] Faced with what he perceived as forced restitution and unjustifiable impunity, Selkirk attempted to tighten his grip on the lands even further by conferring directly with the Indigenous allies of the settler colony.

Before arriving at Red River, he received reports about local Indigenous men working to build roads to service the Red River Colony,[171] construction activity that made use of their intimate knowledge of the lands and waterways of the district and surrounding areas. "The triumphant march of commodity economy thus begins in most cases with magnificent constructions of modern transport," Rosa Luxemburg reminds us.[172] The Indigenous builders worked through that spring, labouring to give a more permanent shape to the settler colony by constructing the physical circuits of the "commodity economy." This coincided with the repopulation of the Red River Colony, among other important changes. After the third resettlement, for instance, the colonizers were permanently relieved of their requirements to pay rent for the title to property.[173] Either as incentive or as reward for their return, such alms reflected the combined quasi-feudalist and early capitalist quality of the settler colony. More than an opportunity for Selkirk to display his benevolence, it was also a gesture that reinforced fidelity and rendered more freely disposable money that would otherwise have gone to rent – a step in the shift from dependent retainers to independent consumers and producers.

A comparable type of generosity was afforded to the military men offered land should they choose to stay, and many did, including some officers from the regiment subsequently appointed to the Council of Assiniboia.[174] Order was still paramount for Selkirk as he erected the administrative and enforcement institutions that he instructed Macdonell to undertake six years earlier. Selkirk's brand of genteel exploitation did not rely on direct force; rather, these more refined measures had been honed in the course of the fur trade itself. Those cumulative changes led to this direct reckoning between the proprietorship of the settlers and the relative autonomy of the Indigenous peoples.

The Treaty

Lord Selkirk's visit to the settler colony was the occasion for more sycophantic commentaries about his character. Finally able to act as the sovereign over his long-desired settlement, he was announced as "the enlightened colonial administrator";[175] he "was able to restore order and confidence to the beleaguered community," and his "presence and decisive leadership at Red River that summer ensured the settlement's survival."[176] But none of these statements speaks to the

172 *A Legacy of Exploitation*

most important historical reality: Selkirk's formal but contested dispossession of lands from the Indigenous peoples in the district. Also worth emphasizing is that this dispossession occurred without overt force and during a time of relative peace, a feat not attributable to his character or cunning but to the fact that the Treaty of 1817 was a continuation and culmination of exploitative practices that both relied on and further distorted relations of customary reciprocity.[177]

Reports from John Fletcher (Coltman's associate commissioner[178]) to Sherbrooke in the summer of 1817 raised suspicions regarding Selkirk's attempt to draw up a peace pact among some of the warring Indigenous parties in the region, noting the lord's ill-conceived idea of inviting a group of Sioux peoples into their enemies' territories in order to undertake negotiations.[179] There was some speculation that Selkirk's overture to win the favour of the Sioux was an arrogant attempt to draw near the enemies of the rival North West Company and its Indigenous allies. But his offerings were insufficiently enticing, and Selkirk likewise rejected the Sioux peoples' demand that he cease agricultural activity and withdraw the military force from the area.[180] Still, it is significant that Selkirk's first move was to confer with Sioux leaders – those at war with the allies of the Red River Colony – and that he did not meet with any Métis leaders.

A week after Selkirk's much anticipated arrival,[181] Macdonell joined a council at the Premier's camp; there he communicated his expectation that "they would cede us a grant of land which would belong to us, that we should then take care of it."[182] Two weeks later, a three-day public meeting between Coltman and principally Saulteaux parties took place,[183] with Macdonell noting that the latter "wish the Colony to remain & offer a gratuitous grant of Land of a considerable extent, the Crees as well as Sauteaux."[184] His journal entry the next day states that "the Indians concluded the land business to-day with his Lordship & signed the conveyance in the Mess room each Chief making his mark – or distinction of his tribe – which we all witnessed."[185] Such was the context for the July 18, 1817, signing of a document that was then variably referred to as a "conveyance,"[186] an "Indian Grant,"[187] "Deed,"[188] or an "Indenture,"[189] but has since come to be identified as "the first treaty in the Canadian West."[190] Four Saulteaux leaders were named – including Peguis, the Premier (Ouckidoat or Grandes Oreilles of the Bear Clan),[191] L'Homme Noir (the Black Man, or Kayajieskebinoa, from Turtle River), and La Robe Noir (the Black Robe, Blue Robe, or Mechkaddewikonaie, from beyond Portage la Prairie) – and a sole Nēhiyaw leader, Le Sonnant (Mache Wheseab or Senna of the Wapucwayanak).[192] The documented terms of the treaty stipulated that the identified Saulteaux and Nēhiyaw groups would receive, in addition to the gifts offered during the signing, a present on an annual basis in exchange for specific tracts of land along the Red and Assiniboine Rivers. The area of land included the swath within a six-mile radius around Fort Douglas, Fort Daer, and the Forks, as well as two miles on each side of both rivers.

At the time, Selkirk had in mind "not a Sale but a Gift" to the treating parties as an "acknowledgement of their right," and sensed that this type of "Deed" would survive even if the HBC charter and his own land grant were dismissed.[193] To this end, he committed a "Present or Quit Rent" at the rate of "one hundred Pounds weight of good and merchantable Tobacco, to be delivered [to the Saulteaux] on or before the tenth Day of October at the Forks," and the same amount was to be delivered to the Nēhiyawok at Portage la Prairie. These deliveries were conditional on the settlers not being "molested."[194] While the stipulated annuity and caveat amounted to a means of pacification in line with Selkirk's instructions in 1811 to Macdonell,[195] as with many compacts of the era, the terms and intentions of the Treaty of 1817 remain in dispute. On the one hand, this caveat lent a disciplinary dimension to the agreement, but on the other hand, the stipulation of the annual meeting constituted "a similar ceremonial honouring of a valued business associate or relative," effectively reinforcing accountability as the basis of mutual obligation.[196] The established practices of customary reciprocity suggest that the five Indigenous leaders saw it as an extension of this kinship relation, not one in which sovereign authority was granted to Selkirk in perpetuity, which would have amounted to a curtailment of their own autonomy to a degree antithetical to established customs of exchange.[197] Even the term "quit rent" was an indication of a pact that did not transfer ownership but leased a right to use – similar to how a tenant might pay quit rent to a landholder in place of the usual obligations owed by a servant.[198] The actual language of the document from 1817 and the customary practices that framed it converge on the point that there was no formal sale of land.

The terms of the treaty did not abolish the ongoing self-sufficiency of the Indigenous societies in the area but shifted it in a new direction by appearing to establish the Indigenous signatories as *de jure* "landlords of the Red River region."[199] This amounts to both a deviation from the customary principles and a key step in the processes of formalized segregation. It restricted where Indigenous peoples could go and how they could use the land with the stipulation that they were not allowed to encamp within or too close to the settlement, but they were permitted as visitors in order to conduct trade.[200] What one party might have interpreted as the continuation of past practice – perhaps even an assurance of their special standing in relation to the company – actually heralded more changes.[201] The most convincing proof of this was the dispute about who had the authority to sign the document and who was excluded from it.

174 A Legacy of Exploitation

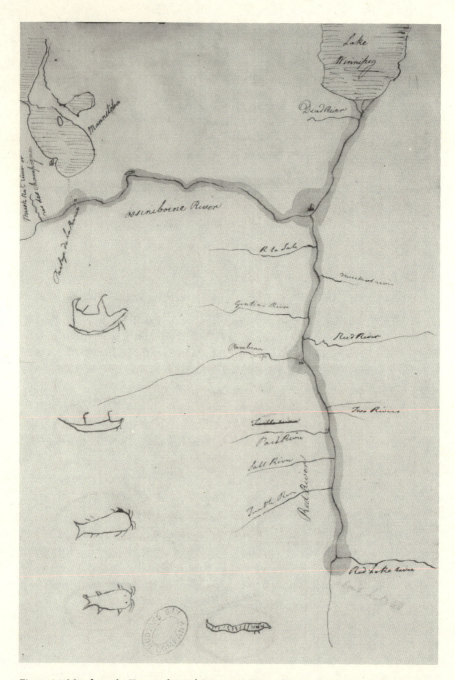

Figure 6.1 Map from the Treaty of 1817 | *Source:* Archives of Manitoba, Hudson's Bay Company Archives, HBCA E.8/1 fo. 11, https://www.gov.mb.ca/chc/archives/hbca/spotlight/selkirk_treaty.html

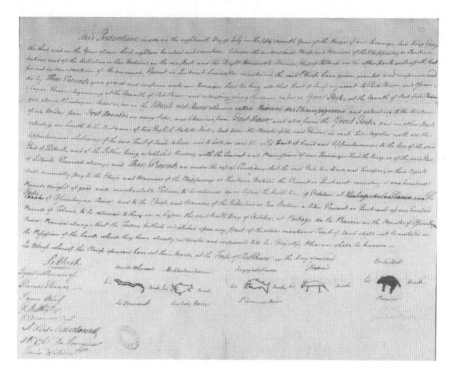

Figure 6.2 Text from the Treaty of 1817 | *Source:* Archives of Manitoba, Hudson's Bay Company Archives, HBCA/AM E.8/1 fo. 9d, https://www.gov.mb.ca/chc/archives/hbca/spotlight/selkirk_treaty.html

Peguis's preferential status among the HBC officers and colonial agents afforded his Saulteaux group some deference,[202] but the document was called into question in the decades that followed – by private businessmen, the Métis, and Peguis himself.[203] In a 1857 letter to the *Colonial Intelligencer* in London, Peguis noted that in 1812, "the lands along the Red River ... were taken possession of, without permission of myself or my tribe, by a body of white settlers." He explained that the 1817 agreement was temporary, to be finalized in 1818, yet in the meantime the settler colonists' claim swelled to "nearly double of what was first asked from us."[204] In another statement published in 1860, Peguis argued that "we never sold our lands to the said Company, nor to the Earl of Selkirk."[205] In 1863, he recounted the circumstances of the negotiations of the agreement, and he noted that, when Selkirk conferred with the leaders of the five Indigenous parties, he asked them which sections of land they were willing to give to him to be cultivated by the settlers. Each offered some section, except Le Sonnant, who balked, according to Peguis, at the prospect of an agricultural settlement – a revelation that raised questions about Le Sonnant's mark on the document itself.[206] Peguis reiterated that a final agreement was never reached. Selkirk was in a rush to leave the area,[207] but he wanted some type of documented confirmation that an arrangement was under consideration. "The Earl said – if your names were down, it would be easier for me to conclude the affair when I get back," Peguis stated, adding that "we did not see why he pressed us to sign; but I now think it was in order to have us in his power, should he not do what he promised. He did not tell us what was in the paper ... Lord Selkirk never came back."[208] Peguis explained that presents received were consistent with the practices that became standard between his group and the Red River Colony.

A challenge to Peguis's account was published in 1860 in the *Nor'Wester*, written by businessman and high-ranking member of the Council of Assiniboia Andrew McDermot.[209] In an attempt to clarify the circumstances of the signing in 1817, he argued that, when Selkirk initially approached the Saulteaux leaders, their first comment was that they were not the original peoples of the land in question, and they named the Nēhiyawok in their stead. McDermot then indicted the character of Peguis by intimating that it was his eagerness for the gifts promised upon signing the document that compelled him to make frequent trips to see Le Sonnant to encourage him to sign it. In McDermot's version, while Le Sonnant agreed to allow Peguis to sign on his behalf,[210] without the Nēhiyaw leader's mark by his own hand the land use agreement remained in dispute.[211]

Recall, however, Peguis's words from two years prior to the Treaty of 1817: "These are not my Lands – they belong to our Great Father – for it is he only that gives us the means of existence, for what would become of us if he left us to ourselves?"[212] It is possible to see how Peguis understood his relationship to the land at the time of Selkirk's visit. Layered and transformative social relations of land were clear from the outset since his was a position not "fixed in some pre-contact context."[213] Peguis knew that the lands were not his and could not be "sold": they were inherited, and in ongoing transformative acts of exchange, what he was agreeing to were terms that reflected the responsibilities endowed by this inheritance. Given all that he had done to support the fledgling Red River Colony in its most trying years, it is more than feasible that he saw any agreement with Selkirk as an extension of this ongoing relationship founded on distinct social relations of land. Since "the principles of respect, responsibility, and renewal ... are foundational in Anishinaabe political thought and practice," Peguis's letters from decades later can be read as his response to breaches of these principles.[214] It is clear that he and the other signatories "reserved their sovereignty in their treaty relationships" and did not give away absolute authority over and ownership of the land to Selkirk or the Red River Colony.[215]

In the same year of these articles in the *Nor'Wester,* Métis groups of various backgrounds also gathered to discuss the validity of the Treaty of 1817. The Métis were mostly left out of the negotiations despite their prominence in the region and the fact that the HBC officers – in the context of negotiating a peaceful resolution to the conflict in 1815 – had previously entered into an agreement with Métis leaders, recognizing their standing in the area. The conference participants in 1860 produced five conclusions, each highlighting a different controversy related to the treaty: first, they found that the one with "the best claim to this country" was Le Sonnant, recognizing further that he never relinquished his land to Selkirk or the company; second, they disputed the rumour that the Hudson's Bay Company was paying a monetary annuity to the five leaders; third, the group recognized that the annual presents "were not given in the way of payment for lands; but merely to keep them friendly towards the Company," in both a political sense and an economic sense; fourth, they underscored the continuity of this practice insofar as it was in line with the norms of exchange established in previous decades; and fifth, in the absence of a formal agreement regarding the lands, the Métis expected to be included in any future discussions on the matter.[216]

The exclusion of the Métis is a symptom of the complicated historical time frame, and the Treaty of 1817 reflects the multi-dimensionality of the ongoing transformations. The Saulteaux occupied terrain once populated by Nēhiyawok and Assiniboine, while the Métis were likewise growing in number; by recognizing Peguis as having a foremost claim to the land, and by invoking the customs of exchange in the process, "ritual powers" of established practices of exchange became "confused with proprietary rights"[217] for the sake of what Selkirk hoped would be an expedient resolution. Where the legitimacy of the treaty was concerned, he invoked the ceremonial rituals that he likely believed would lend the most authenticity from the perspective of his Indigenous counterparts. The type of convenient authenticity that Selkirk sought was another attempt at socially differentiating the producers in the region as a measure of exercising some control over them.

What does not result from the Treaty of 1817 is "absolute private property,"[218] a crucial point. Intrinsic to the origins (and, I hypothesize, to the maintenance and expansion) of capitalism in the settler colonial context in question is this treaty, the terms of which do not confer private ownership but bind all parties to an ongoing relationship of mutual accountability. Without a "real" claim to alienated land, therefore, a core condition of a capitalist mode of production cannot be said to exist: control over land is not dictated by "impersonal exigencies of machine production" but remains contested, partial, and highly political.[219] Such is the value of a frame of analysis that adheres to the idea of social relations of land. By insisting on an idea of land not reducible to property, it is possible to resist slipping into the facile stagism in which so-called pre-capitalism is characterized by direct, violent extra-economic force and capitalism by indirect, "purely 'economic' coercion."[220] The core insight is that capitalism cannot undertake the assumed transition to "purely 'economic' coercion" precisely because the social relations of land – reflected in the treaty – still inhere in the relative autonomy of Indigenous peoples. To deny this and to insist on the paramountcy of "purely 'economic' coercion" is to assume that "absolute private property" supplanted social relations of land, which amounts to believing that the processes of dispossession endemic to settler colonialism have ended and voiding the principle of customary reciprocity at the centre of the treaty.

The contentiousness of the terms and circumstances of the Treaty of 1817 encapsulates the legacy of exploitation overall: the treaty represented continuity as much as it signalled change. As a legal document, it both grew out of and further entrenched economic unevenness; as an economic contract, it borrowed from the customary traditions of feudalism and practices long established as the terms of exchange with Indigenous producers. It simultaneously recognized and undermined their relative autonomy. Understood in relation to the changes that came before it and those that occurred in the decades that followed, the Treaty of 1817 is an invaluable cipher for comprehending the scope of transformations wrought by the processes of dispossession. Significantly, it set the terms of what became an increasingly racialized framework of segregation, but it did so not through primarily violent, direct extra-economic force, strictly speaking. "Forged in response to the ever present dilemma of how to secure political order," Mamdani observes, "the bifurcated state was like a spidery beast that sought to pin its prey to the ground, using a minimum of force – judicious, some would say – to keep in check its most dynamic tendencies."[221] The creation of the "free and equal" servant-turned-settler was contingent on the fragmentary effects of the processes of dispossession, which show that the making of the "bifurcated state" is not a stagist tale of the transition out of extra-economic force or, what amounts to the same, a product of the violent moment of original accumulation. Rather, it is a more inscrutable history that reveals the extent to which dispossession involved the seemingly counterintuitive dependence of the colonizing agents on those social relations of land that nourished the relative autonomy of those peoples being dispossessed. Dispossession took root, but "the oxygen of autonomy remained."[222]

Conclusion
Continuity and Change

> As the colonial machine grinds forward through time and space, the law tends to repress alternatives rejected by power, sometimes even to deny that these alternatives ever existed. If this "legitimating" enterprise is so effective that it makes what was once a coherent and competing view unthinkable, then it has succeeded most admirably. And by succeeding, distortion ceases to distort: bad history becomes good law.
>
> – HAMAR FOSTER[1]

THE LAND USE agreement of 1817 was drawn up in haste and is remarkable in that it betrays both Selkirk's desire for a swift resolution to the question of title and his negligible understanding of Indigenous peoples themselves. Like other early European traders, Selkirk misapprehended his power in believing that he had the capacity to "make chiefs" among a people who had existed for millennia prior to his arrival. The exclusion of the Métis and the exploitation of the settlement's preferential terms with Peguis are evidence of this ignorance and presumption. Although the treaty was not the cause of these transformations, it certainly reflected changes already under way and facilitated the decline of the settler colony's dependence on Indigenous producers.

Report, Trials, and Merger

Disagreement about the Treaty of 1817 amounted to criticism of the legitimacy of not just the Hudson's Bay Company's claim to the land but also the crown's prerogative in the decades prior to Confederation in 1867. There was a sense that a firm and timely resolution to the conflict was necessary "in order to avoid troublesome disputes."[2] By the time Alexander Ross was writing in 1856 about his experience as a Red River settler, however, he saw it fit to condemn the Saulteaux as "vagrants and evil-doers ... [Al]though fed, clothed, and nursed by the benevolent hand of charity, they are, after all, the most debased, vicious, and criminal of all the tribes."[3] Such a harsh judgment of former allies offers an idea of the transformative fractures that occurred in the aftermath of the treaty. One change was the arrival of missionaries on the prairies by 1818 – a major offensive in the attempt to "civilize" Indigenous peoples that entrenched even stronger "racist and assimilationist sentiments in the region."[4] A second change occurred in the wake of another outbreak of disease in 1819–20, which caused deaths especially among the Nēhiyawok, Assiniboine, and to a lesser extent the Saulteaux.[5] A third change was the decision by the HBC directors to establish a store to service the settlement;[6] this meant that the colony could begin to fulfill one of its purposes as an export market for British goods, and it signalled a step away from having to rely so heavily on Indigenous producers. In addition to the store, a fourth change of note was the hasty establishment of a permanent guard, which became a core objective in William Coltman's plan to introduce stability in the Red River Colony.[7]

The findings from the commission were published in 1818 in what has come to be known as the Coltman Report. Although the timeline of the report began in 1810, decades after the Métis families of the area were established, Coltman presented Selkirk's claim to the territories as arising principally from his becoming a major shareholder in the Hudson's Bay Company – a clinical assessment that breached the logic of the charter's supremacy and separated Selkirk's humanitarian claims from his commercial and settler colonial motivations.[8] Coltman recognized that, although the company had an exclusive right, it lapsed in its establishment of legal authority by not inaugurating any administrative institution in the preceding 150 years, which in turn afforded a legitimate basis for the North West Company's claim and gave clout to the Jurisdiction Act of 1803.[9] In view of the "generally unreserved compliance" with the terms of the commission, Coltman concluded that both of the fur trading companies acted in accordance with "the utmost submission to the Commands of the Prince Regent."[10] Ultimately, the commission embodied a supposedly superior authority that corroborated facts and, by not laying blame on any single party, rewarded each side for its allegiance to the crown. On the basis of this conclusion, Coltman stated that the conflict at Seven Oaks was variably "foreseen"[11] and "not foreseen."[12] As "foreseen," it was difficult to assign blame since both parties appeared to have acted rationally in the context of "private hostilities or acts of war,"[13] and they did so according to their respective prerogatives – the legitimacy of which Coltman questioned but never voided in either case. As "not foreseen," the conflict was a matter of "chance,"[14] a parade of inexperience alloyed with miscalculation that made it impossible to establish the level of guilty intent necessary for further criminal proceedings.

For the nearly two weeks that Coltman and Selkirk were both at Red River, more than fifty pieces of correspondence were sent between them. Coltman acted on the warrant against Selkirk, requiring him to pay a steep bail with the added condition that he and his colleagues involved in the capture of Fort William appear before the courts in Upper Canada.[15] The commissioner noted in a letter to Sherbrooke that, notwithstanding all of the violence, Selkirk had acted with restraint in the face of many opportunities for "retaliation."[16] Like Macdonell and Selkirk before him, Coltman saw in the ongoing tensions a need for the aforementioned system of law enforcement; as a consequence, he requested from Sherbrooke that "a small body of the King's troops" be established at the settler colony "as a most excellent check on the colonists themselves, as well as a defence against the natives."[17] This "watch and ward" strategy of governance, which in England dates back to 1233,[18] involves constables, watchmen, sunset curfews, and surveillance in what amounts to a mix of martial law and open-air confinement. Deployed by colonial administrators at historical sites and eras such as in India during the late 1800s and in New England in the mid-1600s,[19] the strategy also divulges the lengths that Coltman was willing to go to in order to find legal grounds for the institution of a more formal and coercive system of extra-economic order.

Direct extra-economic force was neither the fateful outcome nor the calamitous starting point of settler colonial relations of dispossession. While "watch and ward" diminished the settlement's need to conform to the established standards of loyalty for the sake of securing Indigenous peoples' allegiance in the time of conflict, and the eventual construction of a store where settlers could incur their own debts in exchange for imported goods curtailed the need for Indigenous producers to provide daily sustenance, the Saulteaux were still able to exercise their agency when it came to taking on or refusing debts up to the termination of this "credit system" in 1821.[20] Close scrutiny of this era demonstrates that the processes of dispossession were well under way, for pacifying measures (e.g., restrictions on mobility by proclamation or debt, commercial incentives, and the devaluation of gifts and customary reciprocity) were routinely deployed and transformed social relations of land with the aim of wrenching from Indigenous producers their relative autonomy. Much like how they were held to be both existential threats and invaluable allies to both settlers and officials, Indigenous peoples were a means to an end in either respect. As the legal trials related to mutual recriminations by the men of both fur trading companies began in the late fall of 1817 – trials that might once and for all have settled the matter of jurisdictional authority – the interests and opinions of (as well as the obligations to) Indigenous peoples remained outside the parameters of the proceedings.

Selkirk wished that the trials related to his conduct would occur in London; Sherbrooke, meanwhile, saw fit to move some proceedings from Lower Canada to Upper Canada,[21] though the suits and countersuits brought by each company often meant shifting between the two jurisdictions.[22] On arrival at York in January 1818, Selkirk faced a number of criminal charges, including theft of arms, resisting arrest, and false imprisonment; the first was quickly dismissed, and others were quashed or delayed,[23] and the only verdict against him came in civil proceedings in the form of a suit filed for false imprisonment related to his conduct at Fort William, for which he owed £2,000 in damages.[24] Among the related proceedings, men of the North West Company faced over one hundred charges, with the murder of Semple being among the more grievous, while the men of the Hudson's Bay Company and the settlement faced twenty-nine charges. Each of the NWC men was acquitted on all counts, except for Charles de Reinhard, held liable for Owen Keveny's murder.[25] The movement between the two jurisdictions complicated and confused many involved, with delays leading to dismissals of some charges, departures of certain witnesses, and disappearances of key figures such as Cuthbert Grant.[26] The failure to win convictions for Semple's death on top of financial losses set Selkirk down a path of vindication through the final two years of his life, writing in his own defence and penning new schemes as a way of rehabilitating his financial standing.[27] At the same time, the settlers themselves were driven from the site, this time by swarms of locusts that destroyed the vegetation in 1818 and 1819, forcing them to import wheat seed from a US colony at the expense of Selkirk.[28] The hardships endured by the remaining settlers, however, compelled them to become more self-sufficient, learning to hunt and lead teams of dogs, adopting Indigenous peoples' own means of production, and reducing the need for new or extended reciprocity-based agreements between them.[29]

Treaty-making, new hunting skills, and free socage aside, Selkirk did not see the colony prosper in his lifetime, for he died in April 1820 (just weeks after Sir Alexander Mackenzie).[30] Selkirk's estate was saddled with £160,000 worth of debt, and the Hudson's Bay Company incurred debts from the mounting costs of conducting business in an era of muted returns, with all of this occurring in the midst of the expiration of the founding contract of the North West Company.[31] Gone with Selkirk, however, was the thirst for retribution against the rival company, which made a merger more feasible.[32]

Importantly, one of the prescriptions that Coltman offered in 1818 was that a monopoly was the best way to conduct trade with Indigenous societies, although there is little explanation of why he thought that to be the case.[33] Obviously, the high cost of competition was one impetus for a merger, but that alone does not explain why Coltman thought that offering an exclusive right to trade with Indigenous peoples was the best way forward. Based upon the analysis contained in the preceding chapters, I aver that the relative autonomy of the Indigenous producers was a primary factor in the merger. Neither company could claim total authority over Indigenous producers, and in exercising their agency the producers themselves played one company off the other. With the merger in 1821, the terms of the charter of 1670 remained, and a twenty-one-year agreement was established that expanded the Hudson's Bay Company's exclusive

Figure C.1 "Winter fishing on ice of [Assiniboine] and Red River," 1821, artist Peter Rindisbacher, 1806–34 | *Source:* Library and Archives Canada, Peter Rindisbacher Collection, e011161354

rights to trade from the Atlantic to the Pacific and from Athabasca to Oregon.[34] Under the leadership of George Simpson, the company became even more rigidly hierarchical and bent on internal efficiencies: he closed many posts, cut the workforce, and discouraged gift-giving and the extension of credit.[35] Racism underpinned many of these initiatives, for Simpson thought that Indigenous women were acceptable playthings, but entirely unfit for marriage,[36] whereas select Métis – with the right pedigree and education – could climb the HBC ranks.[37]

These racialized policies constituted further steps in the process of differentiation and firmly debunk "the theory that the fur trade was a mutually beneficial partnership between merchants and Natives."[38] The racial divide between subject and citizen was in the process of being institutionalized, and violent forms of compulsion were becoming the preferred means of ensuring productivity among Indigenous producers. These sentiments became clear after Simpson's first tour of the region in 1822, specifically in a letter that he wrote to Andrew Colvile (formerly Wedderburn). Simpson found the Indigenous peoples from the woodlands to the bayside to the plains upset by the new efficiencies wrought by the merger, so much so that they were not as productive as in previous years. "I am convinced that they must be ruled with a rod of Iron to bring and keep them in a proper state of subordination," Simpson concluded, "and the most certain way to effect this is by letting them feel their dependence upon us."[39] Restricted access to tobacco, arms, and alcohol was one way of making Indigenous producers "feel their dependence," except that the Hudson's Bay Company under Simpson could not entirely undermine the relative autonomy of Indigenous producers, especially in regions where their labour was still vital to the commercial trade, such as on the plains.[40]

Simpson knew this. In the same paragraph in which he called for "a rod of Iron," he also stated that "in the plains however this system will not do as they can live independent of us, and by witholding ... the Staple Articles of Trade for one year, they will recover the use of their Bows and spears and lose sight of their smoking & Drinking habits."[41] This differential treatment caused Simpson to consider "mild and cautious measures" in his approach to the prairie populations.[42] Autonomy, though variable and fragmented, did not inoculate Indigenous peoples against exploitation but reflected the uneven and combined facets of historical transformation.

Troublesome Legacy

In the decades leading up to and following Confederation of the Dominion of Canada, the signing of numbered treaties matched a growing law enforcement presence. It was in the immediate aftermath of the Louis Riel–led Métis rebellion and the signing of the Deed of Succession in 1870 that the Royal North West Mounted Police was formed.[43] The police moved onto the plains in 1874, an offensive described in a poem published in the *Saskatchewan Herald* in 1878 and titled "The Riders of the Plains":[44]

> Our Mission is to plant the right
> Of British freedom here –
> Restrain the lawless savages,
> And protect the pioneer.
> And 'tis a proud and daring trust
> To hold these vast domains
> With but three hundred mounted men –
> The Riders of the Plains[45]

Celebrated are the "proud and daring" who "protect the pioneer" – but from whom?[46] These mounted police drew their valour from controlling the "lawless savages" of the plains, the legacy of which has deep resonance in the present day.

Two centuries after the Coltman Commission, and following years of pressure and activism,[47] a set of commissioners was appointed to lead the National Inquiry into Missing and Murdered Indigenous Women. On June 3, 2019, the final report, *Reclaiming Power and Place*, was released. Contributors to the truth-gathering process speak to the same matters that appear throughout this book. On the intersection of law and economics, Barb Manitowabi comments that "Canada has built a system of rules and laws stemming from greed, racism, and hate; this system continues to devour our families today. Canadians cannot deny the facts, as ugly as they may seem: this is genocide."[48] On mutual accountability, Norma Jacobs states that, "today, all of our demands are about respecting our values and principles. Settlers should respect Turtle Island from our perspective, as visitors in our homes. We have to speak out and instill responsibility and accountability in each and every living person."[49] Rebecca Moore, meanwhile, highlights the matter of autonomy: "The Canadian government prevents Indigenous women and their families from having the autonomy to earn a moderate livelihood and achieve their own safety and security. Until Indigenous women are given the power and authority to self-determine what happens within their own territories, we will always be at risk under Canada's 'Rule of Law.'"[50] Notions of the "lawless savage" lurk behind claims to the "Rule of Law," and Indigenous peoples' autonomy continues to be curtailed while settler colonial agents deny the "responsibility and accountability" terms of the treaties. But most of all the outcry over the report's findings of genocide – steeped in a willingness to deny the evidence – shows how far members of the Canadian settler colonial enterprise will go to defend the mythical narrative of the "proud and daring" and the "adventurers."

In the foregoing chapters, I stressed the importance of confronting the "uncomfortable" foundations upon which the Red River Colony was built, which I view as a microcosm of the larger transition to capitalism that occurred in the settler colonial context of Canada. I showed that, though distortion and social differentiation pervaded the exploitative practices of the commercial fur trade, the relative autonomy of Indigenous producers was a key driver of change. The concurrence of exploitation and autonomy, as well as continuity and change, obscures the troublesome legacy of exploitation. Colonial processes of dispossession during the commercial fur trade were often incongruous and always layered, a claim that I supported by examining the relative autonomy of Indigenous producers from 1763 to 1821. On closer study, the connection between relative autonomy and social relations of land came to light, revealing that any change to the latter implicated the former and that how these changes happened is of paramount importance. What became clear is that exploitative practices entailing distortion and social differentiation had intersecting legal, economic, and geopolitical dimensions; moreover, associated transformations occurred in an uneven and combined manner. By making sense of – without simplifying – the essential contradictions that constituted the transformations, one is simultaneously making sense of that which most effectively veiled the exploitative facets of the commercial fur trade. Such is the troublesome legacy: the contradictions and complexities abetted a malevolent innocence that miscast relative autonomy as complicity in dispossession, fomenting a settler colonial fantasy of Canada as a "proud and daring" nation of "adventurers."

Each step of this book excavates these dynamics and casts off this stunted fantasy: the apparent conformity between merchant credit–backed debt and customary reciprocity; the conflict over Indigenous producers' debts; the principled hypocrisy of Selkirk's instructions to Macdonell; the conditions of the emergence of the "free" worker; the eager yet resentful paternalism of Macdonell; the alienating effects of the Pemmican Proclamation and the violence that ensued; and, most quintessential of all of these confounding relations, the Treaty of 1817. Parochialism, reductionism, and stagism thus sloughed, no longer is it feasible to believe that the history of the commercial fur trade is the story of the movement from absolute freedom to outright conquest, extra-economic force to "purely 'economic' coercion," or lawless violence toward lawful non-violence. Based upon these findings, it is possible to reject the notion that "absolute private property" reigns in this particular setting – as such, this definitive if idealized feature of the capitalist mode of production cannot be said to exist in this settler colonial context.[51] That is because assuming the total alienation of land as a given amounts to a denial of settler colonialism and treats the ensuing violence not as fundamental but aberrational in the capitalist mode of production. Consider the genocidal legal measures that followed Confederation (e.g., the Dominion Lands Act of 1872 and the Indian Act of 1876), as well as subsequent amendments and policy decisions (e.g., the residential school system[52] and the Sixties Scoop[53]). It defies logic to proclaim that "purely 'economic' coercion" defines capitalism in a settler colonial context that requires the quotidian enforcement of such measures and the management of their effects.

By examining specific ways that the "free" worker emerges as a legacy of the exploitation of Indigenous peoples' labour, what becomes visible is an understanding of "how the transfer of whiteness to the threshold of nationality actively links freedom with the management of public authority, specific mechanisms of violence, and an operational notion of (racial) nemesis."[54] Importantly, these more overtly violent means of coercion represent both the continuation and the transformation of established processes of dispossession. They are neither "pre-capitalist" nor means of "purely 'economic' coercion," yet they are intrinsic to the transition to (as well as the maintenance and expansion of) capitalism in the context discussed. Patently, the existing Marxist framework for understanding capitalism as a mode of production requires a foundational rethink when it comes to the settler colonial context, and my close study of the Red River Colony lends veracity to this thesis. By modifying my framework to centre a non-reductive notion of land, a dynamic understanding of the relative autonomy of Indigenous producers was possible. From this perspective, it became clear what drove transformations in the era and area in question, which not only underscored the extent to which legal relations are intrinsic to economic relations but also revealed the limits of the facile transition thesis.

This book is a historical, critical, and theoretical study, but above all – as a commentary on exploitation and autonomy – it is a political intervention. To borrow from the late Ellen Meiksins Wood, the objective of such a perspective is to "illuminat[e] the principles of historical movement and, at least implicitly, the points at which political action can most effectively intervene."[55] As much as this has been a critical historical and theoretical undertaking, modifying the standard Marxist framework has helped to identify "the principles of historical movement" in the settler colonial context and marks a political intervention that breaks from stagist developmentalism and the fatalist mindset that it engenders. For final insights into how to learn from this past and continue to make and support meaningful interventions, we should heed the words of Audrey Siegl, as quoted in *Reclaiming Power and Place*:

> Yes, we have a shit ton left in front of us to do, but look at how far we've come and look at whose shoulders we're standing on to keep carrying ourselves with dignity and respect, and to keep knocking down those walls, to keep shining the light, to keep leading with love, to keep leading with medicine, to keep reconnecting to ourselves while we're surviving a genocide and being accountable to the Canadian government for legalities that they're using against us to carry on that genocide.[56]

Notes

Introduction

1 Aileen Moreton-Robinson, *The White Possessive: Property, Power, and Indigenous Sovereignty* (Minneapolis: University of Minnesota Press, 2015), xxiv.

2 Elizabeth Vibert offers an insightful assessment of the "heroic hunter" of this era: "Traders' actions were grounded in a vision of manhood that was clearly British middle-class." Elizabeth Vibert, *Traders' Tales: Narratives of Cultural Encounters in the Columbia Plateau, 1807–1846* (Norman: University of Oklahoma Press, 1997), 275, http://archive.org/details/traderstalesnarroooovibe_i7n8. It is noteworthy that the HBC History Foundation promotes this vision two hundred years later under the banner of Canadian heritage.

3 Hudson's Bay Company, *HBC History Foundation – The Country of Adventurers: Dr. John Rae Narrated by Les Stroud*, 2015, https://www.youtube.com/watch?v=n-b_MaltYD4; Hudson's Bay Company, *HBC History Foundation – The Country of Adventurers: David Thompson Narrated by Rick Hansen*, 2015, https://www.youtube.com/watch?v=m_vzybpOiIM.

4 Martha Troian, "After Tina Fontaine: Exploitation in a Prairie City," APTN National News, August 22, 2018, https://aptnnews.ca/2018/08/22/after-tina-fontaine-exploitation-in-a-prairie-city/.

5 "Injustice Is a Way of Indigenous Life, Say Advocates Dismayed at Verdict in Tina Fontaine Murder Trial," *The Current*, CBC Radio, February 23, 2018, https://www.cbc.ca/radio/thecurrent/the-current-for-february-23-2018-1.4547552/injustice-is-a-way-of-indigenous-life-say-advocates-dismayed-at-verdict-in-tina-fontaine-murder-trial-1.4548471.

6 I refer to the inquiry and its report in detail in the Conclusion.

7 National Inquiry into Missing and Murdered Indigenous Women and Girls (Canada), *Reclaiming Power and Place: Final Report of the National Inquiry into Missing and Murdered Indigenous Women and Girls* (Ottawa: Privy Council Office, 2019), 44, http://epe.lac-bac.gc.ca/100/201/301/weekly_acquisitions_list-ef/2019/19-23/publications.gc.ca/collections/collection_2019/bcp-pco/CP32-163-2-1-2019-eng.pdf.

8 Troian, "After Tina Fontaine."

9 To borrow from Linda Tuhiwai Smith, I see settler colonialism as a facet of colonialism, while "colonialism is but one expression of imperialism." Linda Tuhiwai Smith, *Decolonizing Methodologies: Research and Indigenous Peoples* (London: Zed Books, 2012), 60. The multiple uses of imperialism speak to its economic, coercive, ideological, and intellectual/psychological facets, while colonialism is the material manifestation of these various facets as "a particular realization of the imperial imagination" (64). Meanwhile, Allan Greer insists that colonialism was one facet of, but not reducible to, "empire building." Allan Greer, *Property and Dispossession: Natives, Empires and Land in Early Modern North America* (Cambridge: Cambridge University Press, 2018), 6. I underscore that point in the third chapter by demonstrating how the term "British Empire" postdated the colonialism of the Hudson's Bay Company. See Nicholas Rogers, "From Vernon to Wolfe: Empire and Identity in the British Atlantic World

of the Mid-Eighteenth Century," in *The Culture of the Seven Years' War: Empire, Identity, and the Arts in the Eighteenth-Century Atlantic World,* ed. Frans De Bruyn and Shaun Regan (Toronto: University of Toronto Press, 2014), 42. I also discuss in the third chapter how "conventional" colonialism does not assume the establishment of "settler societies." See Daiva K. Stasiulis and Nira Yuval-Davis, "Introduction: Beyond Dichotomies – Gender, Race, Ethnicity and Class in Settler Societies," in *Unsettling Settler Societies: Articulations of Gender, Race, Ethnicity and Class,* ed. Daiva K. Stasiulis and Nira Yuval-Davis (London: SAGE, 1995), 2. Although in the longer sweep of history it is worth differentiating between capitalism and colonialism, because I focus on the conjuncture of settler colonialism and the transition to capitalism, I do not heed a strict delineation. However, I am clear about what might be considered the "pre-capitalist" tentacles of colonialism.

10 See, for example, Miles Macdonell, who uses the term "troublesome" in journal entries to describe the behaviour of a newly encountered group of Indigenous people to whom he gave liquor in exchange for skins, dried meat, and fish. Miles Macdonell, "Journal: 6 July 1812 to 22 April 1813," Library and Archives Canada [hereafter LAC] – Selkirk Collection, 16735, http://heritage.canadiana.ca/view/oocihm.lac_reel_c16/207?r=0&s=1; "Journal: 22 April 1813 to 7 April 1815," LAC – Selkirk Collection, 16861–62, http://heritage.canadiana.ca/view/oocihm.lac_reel_c16/207?r=0&s=1. This term appears throughout the records to denote a nuisance or an obstacle alike; notably, in "Journal: 6 July 1812 to 22 April 1813," 16706, 16714, Macdonell also describes as "troublesome," respectively, the Irish and mosquitoes. My use of the term in this book serves two functions: as a means of drawing attention to the instances when "troublesome" was deployed and as a description of the processes of dispossession in general. The last point is a nod to Howard Adams, who notes that "the process of trading was always troublesome." Howard Adams, *Prison of Grass: Canada from a Native Point of View,* 2nd ed. (Saskatoon: Fifth House Publishers, 1989), 27. Vibert, *Traders' Tales,* 120–21, writing about the fur traders of the Columbia Plateau in the first half of the nineteenth century, offers a comparable commentary on the term "indolent." I should add that, though I use the term "Indigenous" throughout, I focus on the peoples in the subarctic and do not address the history of Inuit peoples.

11 When I use the general term "Indigenous producers," I refer to hunters, trappers, and trade captains as well as those within communities engaged in the quotidian labour of social reproduction, who tended to be women. At various points in the book, however, I speak more specifically about certain types of producers and groups.

12 W.L. Morton, "The North West Company: Pedlars Extraordinary," *Minnesota History* 40, no. 4 (1966): 161.

13 At base, both of these essentialisms "disqualified" Indigenous peoples "not just from civilization but from humanity itself." Tuhiwai Smith, *Decolonizing Methodologies,* 67. These types of essentialism reappear in later centuries, such as with respect to Ukrainian Canadian immigrants, especially in the context of early-twentieth-century enfranchisement. See Susan Dianne Brophy, "Freedom, Law, and the Colonial Project," *Law and Critique* 24, no. 1 (2013): 39–61; and Susan Dianne Brophy, "The Emancipatory Praxis of Ukrainian Canadians (1891–1919) and the Necessity of a Situated Critique," *Labour/ Le travail* 77 (2016): 151–79.

14 Thomas Douglas Selkirk, *A Sketch of the British Fur Trade in North America with Observations Relative to the North-West Company of Montreal* (London: Printed for James Ridgway, 1816), 4.

15 E.E. Rich, "Trade Habits and Economic Motivation among the Indians of North America," *Canadian Journal of Economics and Political Science/Revue canadienne d'economique*

190 Notes to pages 4–6

et de science politique 26, no. 1 (1960): 46. Adams, *Prison of Grass,* 11–12, names these racist views as the motivating factor for both the emergence of capitalism in Canada and his work.

16 Ann M. Carlos and Frank D. Lewis, "Trade, Consumption, and the Native Economy: Lessons from York Factory, Hudson Bay," *Journal of Economic History* 61, no. 4 (2001): 1038–39, https://doi.org/10.1017/S0022050701042073.

17 Arthur J. Ray, *Indians in the Fur Trade: Their Role as Trappers, Hunters, and Middlemen in the Lands Southwest of Hudson Bay, 1660–1870,* 2nd ed., ACLS Humanities E-Book (Toronto: University of Toronto Press, 1998), xiii.

18 Carlos and Lewis, "Trade, Consumption, and the Native Economy," 1039.

19 I have in mind works that span the past two centuries, including corporate histories such as George Bryce, *The Remarkable History of the Hudson's Bay Company, Including That of the French Traders of North-Western Canada and of the North-West, XY, and Astor Fur Companies,* 3rd ed. (New York: Charles Scribner's Sons, 1910), and Morton, "The North West Company," and more recent works on economic history, such as a range of essays by Ann Carlos from 1981 to 2001. A common thread across these and other works is the distortion of Indigenous peoples' autonomy, casting it in support of some notion of linear developmentalism.

20 Heidi Kiiwetinepinesiik Stark and Gina Starblanket, "Towards a Relational Paradigm – Four Points for Consideration: Knowledge, Gender, Land, and Modernity," in *Resurgence and Reconciliation: Indigenous-Settler Relations and Earth Teachings,* ed. Michael I. Asch, John Borrows, and James Tully (Toronto: University of Toronto Press, 2018), 182. I detail these social relations of land in the first chapter, which becomes the foundation for the analysis that I undertake throughout the book.

21 I share a few core motivations with Greer. The most significant commonality is that we both seek to resist "reifying 'property' or 'land'" by bringing into focus specific practices of dispossession. Greer, *Property and Dispossession,* 3–4. Given this commonality, I endorse his conceptual objectives in the general sense and cite this text accordingly. His book does much to advance a more nuanced understanding of the history of legal transformation in Canada, specifically by examining the "fragmented" facets of land grant processes in seventeenth-century Quebec (177). However, his work is still focused on land as such, whereas I adopt a more expansive approach to the social relations of land from the outset. Moreover, I am explicit about the political objectives of my book and see myself as being accountable to different interlocutors and intellectual traditions. Divergence on this front is best illustrated in his avoidance of sources by Indigenous scholars and elders, such as in the opening chapters, where Greer explicitly discusses Indigenous forms of property in New France. This aversion informs his still-too-narrow attention to land as such (evidenced by his focus on maps, surveyors, and Locke) and leaves the impression that he overpromises when he states (in the first sentence of the book) that he "proposes a new reading of the history of the colonization of North America and the dispossession of its indigenous peoples" (1). I am wary of any "new reading" of dispossession that retains old blindspots.

22 Tuhiwai Smith, *Decolonizing Methodologies,* 81.

23 Rauna Kuokkanen, *Reshaping the University: Responsibility, Indigenous Epistemes, and the Logic of the Gift* (Vancouver: UBC Press, 2007), xvi.

24 Karl Marx and Friedrich Engels, *Collected Works of Marx and Engels – Engels: Anti-Dühring; Dialectics of Nature,* vol. 25 (New York: International Publishers, 1987), 135.

25 Marx and Engels, *Collected Works,* 25: 58.

26 Marx and Engels, *Collected Works,* 25: 56.

27 Marx and Engels, *Collected Works,* 25: 135.

Notes to pages 6–7 191

28 Vladimir Ilyich Lenin, *Materialism and Empirio-Criticism* (Beijing: Foreign Languages Press, 1972), 267.
29 Marx and Engels, *Collected Works*, 25: 34.
30 I have given much thought to this framework in other works, which informs my approach here. See, for example, Susan Dianne Brophy, "An Uneven and Combined Development Theory of Law: Initiation," *Law and Critique* 28, no. 2 (2017): 167–91; and Susan Dianne Brophy, "The Explanatory Value of the Theory of Uneven and Combined Development," *Historical Materialism* (blog), 2018, http://www.historicalmaterialism.org/blog/explan atory-value-theory-uneven-and-combined-development. This theme, in keeping with the general tradition of exploring the gap between law and society, is also given much consideration in the legal history literature on property in settler colonial contexts. See, specifically, John McLaren, A.R. Buck, and Nancy E. Wright, "Property Rights in the Colonial Imagination and Experience," in *Despotic Dominion: Property Rights in British Settler Societies*, ed. John McLaren, A.R. Buck, and Nancy E. Wright (Vancouver: UBC Press, 2004), 4. Rather than just note the gap between idea and practice, I account for how the two evolve in a dialectical relationship and explore this tension to explain the generative yet relative autonomy of Indigenous producers in the transition to capitalism.
31 Lenin, *Materialism and Empirio-Criticism*, 260.
32 Lenin, *Materialism and Empirio-Criticism*, 262.
33 Lenin, *Materialism and Empirio-Criticism*, 325.
34 Leon Trotsky, *History of the Russian Revolution*, trans. Max Eastman (Chicago: Haymarket Books, 2008), 4.
35 Useful because this practice of identification facilitates but does not dictate historical study, yet there is a risk that it becomes a mechanical classification of dialectical processes. See Lenin, *Materialism and Empirio-Criticism*, 329. Built into the frame of analysis, however, is a way to avoid such an outcome. Dialectical materialism carries with it an implicit obligation to interrogate the "why" of human life as it is, not just to catalogue the "how" of history as it was, and as long as this imperative grounds historical study a descent into vulgar materialism or formulaic dialectics can be avoided. See Elleni Centime Zeleke, *Ethiopia in Theory: Revolution and Knowledge Production, 1964–2016* (Leiden: Brill, 2019), 251.
36 Rosa Luxemburg, *The Accumulation of Capital*, 2nd ed. (London: Routledge, 2003), 398.
37 Adams, *Prison of Grass*; Charles A. Bishop, "The First Century: Adaptive Changes among the Western James Bay Cree between the Early Seventeenth and Early Eighteenth Centuries," in *The Subarctic Fur Trade: Native Social and Economic Adaptations*, ed. Shepard Krech III (Vancouver: UBC Press, 1984), 21–54; Ward Churchill, ed., *Marxism and Native Americans* (Boston: South End Press, 1983); Ron G. Bourgeault, "The Indian, the Métis and the Fur Trade: Class, Sexism and Racism in the Transition from 'Communism' to Capitalism," *Studies in Political Economy* 12, no. 1 (1983): 45–80; Eleanor Leacock, "Relations of Production in Band Society," in *Politics and History in Band Societies*, ed. Eleanor Leacock and Richard Lee (Cambridge: Cambridge University Press, 1982), 159–70. Worth also acknowledging are the prejudicial statements made by Engels in his short entry on the Haudenosaunee, specifically where he refers to their constitution as "wonderful in all its childlike simplicity!"; see Karl Marx and Friedrich Engels, *Collected Works of Marx and Engels: General Works 1844–1895*, vol. 26 (New York: International Publishers, 1987), 203.
38 Vanessa Watts, "Indigenous Place-Thought and Agency amongst Humans and Non-Humans (First Woman and Sky Woman Go on a European World Tour!)," *Decolonization: Indigeneity, Education and Society* 2, no. 1 (2013): 22.
39 Luxemburg, *The Accumulation of Capital*, 337.

192 Notes to pages 7–9

40 Luxemburg, *The Accumulation of Capital*, 397; Patricia A. McCormack, *Fort Chipewyan and the Shaping of Canadian History, 1788–1920s: "We Like to Be Free in This Country"* (Vancouver: UBC Press, 2011), 34.

41 Karl Marx, *Capital: A Critique of Political Economy*, trans. Ben Fowkes, vol. 1 (New York: Vintage Books, 1977), 714. The controversy stems from the use of "primitive" instead of "original," which would have been a more literal translation of the German term.

42 Marx, *Capital*, 1: 875, 873. In the balance of this book, I challenge this cursory interpretation of Marx and the stagist notion of historical transformation that it can promote. Importantly, however, I challenge stagism by insisting on a more rigorous application of dialectical materialism. In other words, I make use of his own methodology to attenuate the worst readings of his thesis and to add new facets specific to a settler colonial context.

43 Marx, *Capital*, 1: 474.

44 Marx, *Capital*, 1: 505–6. David Harvey famously challenges the implicit stagism of this approach by reconceptualizing the notion of primitive accumulation as an ongoing process of "accumulation through dispossession." My use of the term "dispossession" can be read as concurring with Harvey in that respect. See David Harvey, "Notes towards a Theory of Uneven Geographical Development," in *Spaces of Neoliberalization: Towards a Theory of Uneven Geographical Development*, vol. 8, Hettner Lectures (Stuttgart: Franz Steiner Verlag, 2005), 70. On the dangers of stagist developmentalism, see Tuhiwai Smith, *Decolonizing Methodologies*, 74–76.

45 William Clare Roberts, *Marx's Inferno: The Political Theory of Capital* (Princeton, NJ: Princeton University Press, 2016); Werner Bonefeld, *Critical Theory and the Critique of Political Economy: On Subversion and Negative Reason* (New York: Bloomsbury, 2014); Robert Nichols, "Disaggregating Primitive Accumulation," *Radical Philosophy* 194 (2015): 18–28.

46 Silvia Federici, *Caliban and the Witch* (Brooklyn: Autonomedia, 2004); David Harvey, *The New Imperialism* (Oxford: Oxford University Press, 2005); Glen Sean Coulthard, *Red Skin, White Masks: Rejecting the Colonial Politics of Recognition*, Indigenous Americas (Minneapolis: University of Minnesota Press, 2014); Samir Amin, *Accumulation on a World Scale: A Critique of the Theory of Underdevelopment, Volume 1* (New York: Monthly Review Press, 1974).

47 Marx, *Capital*, 1: 899.

48 Greer, *Property and Dispossession*, 155–56.

49 Henry Heller, *The Birth of Capitalism: A 21st Century Perspective* (London: Pluto Press, 2011), 12.

50 Scott P. Stephen, *Masters and Servants: The Hudson's Bay Company and Its North American Workforce, 1668–1786* (Edmonton: University of Alberta Press, 2019), 21.

51 Marx, *Capital*, 1: 719.

52 By "discipline," I have in mind measures of control, which can vary in degrees of coercion and source, that act on the individual in a manner that habituates that person into or toward certain behaviours or relations.

53 Maurice Dobb, *Studies in the Development of Capitalism* (London: Routledge and Sons, 1946), 17.

54 Kahente Horn-Miller, "Distortion and Healing: Finding Balance and a 'Good Mind' through the Rearticulation of Sky Woman's Journey," in *Living on the Land: Indigenous Women's Understanding of Place*, ed. Nathalie Kermoal and Isabel Altamirano-Jiménez (Edmonton: Athabasca University Press, 2016), 33.

55 Marx, *Capital*, 1: 729–30.

56 Heller, *The Birth of Capitalism*, 51.

57 Adams, *Prison of Grass*, 14.

Notes to pages 9–11 193

58 Frank Tough, "From the 'Original Affluent Society' to the 'Unjust Society': A Review Essay on Native Economic History in Canada," *Journal of Aboriginal Economic Development* 4, no. 2 (2005): 54. Slave labour was also used, which included some people from Inuit communities who were bought or gifted in the seventeenth and eighteenth centuries; see Stephen, *Masters and Servants,* 159–60.

59 Ellen Meiksins Wood, "The Separation of the Economic and the Political in Capitalism," *New Left Review* 127 (1981): 89.

60 Coulthard, *Red Skin, White Masks,* 9. By "normative developmentalism," I infer from Coulthard a linearity and a normative imperative to economic and social development.

61 Mahmood Mamdani, *Citizen and Subject: Contemporary Africa and the Legacy of Late Colonialism* (Princeton, NJ: Princeton University Press, 1996), 147.

62 Marx, *Capital,* 1: 899.

63 Luxemburg, *The Accumulation of Capital,* 343.

64 Moreton-Robinson defines "possessive logics" as "a mode of rationalization ... that is underpinned by an excessive desire to invest in reproducing and reaffirming the nation-state's ownership, control, and domination," adding that "white possessive logics are operationalized within discourses to circulate sets of meanings about ownership of the nation." See Moreton-Robinson, *The White Possessive,* xii.

65 Bonita Lawrence and Enakshi Dua, "Decolonizing Antiracism," *Social Justice* 32, no. 4 (2005): 123.

66 Lawrence and Dua, "Decolonizing Antiracism," 123.

67 To a degree, and with a different inflection, Stephen, *Masters and Servants,* 26, offers a comparable observation regarding the alienation of land in Canadian settler colonial history.

68 Coulthard, *Red Skin, White Masks,* 9.

69 Winona LaDuke, "Preface: Natural to Synthetic and Back," in *Marxism and Native Americans,* ed. Ward Churchill (Boston: South End Press, 1983), ii.

70 Russell Means, "The Same Old Song," in *Marxism and Native Americans,* ed. Ward Churchill (Boston: South End Press, 1983), 26.

71 Alexander Anievas and Kerem Nişancıoğlu, *How the West Came to Rule: The Geopolitical Origins of Capitalism* (London: Pluto Press, 2015), 4–5.

72 Tough, "From the 'Original Affluent Society' to the 'Unjust Society,'" 54.

73 Robin Brownlie and Mary-Ellen Kelm, "Desperately Seeking Absolution: Native Agency as Colonialist Alibi?," *Canadian Historical Review* 75, no. 4 (1994): 545.

74 Brownlie and Kelm, "Desperately Seeking Absolution," 545.

75 Wood, "The Separation of the Economic and the Political in Capitalism," 67, 89.

76 Robert Brenner, "The Origins of Capitalist Development: A Critique of Neo-Smithian Marxism," *New Left Review* I/104 (1977): 59.

77 I do undertake some degree of class analysis in this book, specifically pertaining to the master-servant relation germane to the feudalist hierarchies of fur trading companies. However, I do not use the term "class" when accounting for the relative autonomy of Indigenous producers, except when referring to the emergence of the settler/citizen as an independent agricultural producer. It would be conceptual overreach (at least) and an act of distortion (at worst) to cast Indigenous producers as a "class" in relation to the colonists. Among the main reasons to reject that approach is the fact that it hastily disintegrates the principled nation-to-nation framework that best defines their relations at the time and place in question, evidenced by the expectation of reciprocity in the treaty process and trade in commodities alike. See John Borrows, "Canada's Colonial Constitution," in *The Right Relationship: Reimagining the Implementation of Historical Treaties,* ed. Michael Coyle and John Borrows (Toronto: University of Toronto Press, 2017), 30.

194 Notes to pages 12–13

78 Brenner, "The Origins of Capitalist Development," 82.
79 Wood, "The Separation of the Economic and the Political in Capitalism," 91.
80 Wood, "The Separation of the Economic and the Political in Capitalism," 89.
81 Nikhil Pal Singh, "On Race, Violence, and So-Called Primitive Accumulation," *Social Text* 34, no. 3 (2016): 33.
82 Jairus Banaji, *Theory as History: Essays on Modes of Production and Exploitation*, 1st trade paper ed. (Chicago: Haymarket Books, 2011), 140. This approach supports Brenna Bhandar's argument that "those communities who lived as rational, productive economic actors, evidenced by particular forms of cultivation, were deemed to be proper subjects of law and history; those who did not were deemed to be in need of improvement as much as their waste lands were." See Brenna Bhandar, *Colonial Lives of Property: Law, Land, and Racial Regimes of Ownership* (Durham, NC: Duke University Press, 2018), 8.
83 Evgeny Bronislavovich Pashukanis, *General Theory of Law and Marxism*, ed. Chris Arthur, trans. Barbara Einhorn, 2nd ed. (Piscataway, NJ: Transaction Publishers, 2007), 114.
84 This focus on Indigenous peoples' labour sets my approach apart from that offered by Scott P. Stephen in his recent book *Masters and Servants*. Notably, the first mention of Indigenous peoples in that text is from the vantage point of the company men, who, he argues, viewed the Indigenous communities in the vicinity as "neighbours." Stephen, *Masters and Servants*, 24. Although I do see the value of this framing in that it underscores the import of the principle of reciprocity in the social and economic relations of the day, it sidesteps the kernel of exploitation that pervaded these relations, leading Stephen to assert misleadingly that "the HBC's colonial world during this period appears less as an empire than a neighbourhood" (25). I explore the tension between reciprocity and dispossession at length in the first chapter.
85 Instead of a fetter on economic growth that must be overcome in processes of capitalist expansion, direct coercion becomes institutionalized in principle and practice. For instance, the idea of "sovereignty-without-a-doubt" permeates judicial reasoning in cases where Indigenous peoples' practices challenge Canadian state sovereignty. This judicial principle informs decisions that delineate the scope of Indigenous peoples' claims to land, dictates what practices within Indigenous societies are deemed acceptable by the settler state, and by extension, grants the institutions of the settler state the power to stipulate the thresholds of justifiability for infringements on Indigenous peoples' rights. See Mark D. Walters, "'Looking for a Knot in the Bulrush': Reflections on Law, Sovereignty, and Aboriginal Rights," in *From Recognition to Reconciliation: Essays on the Constitutional Entrenchment of Aboriginal and Treaty Rights*, ed. Patrick Macklem and Douglas Sanderson (Toronto: University of Toronto Press, 2015), 37.
86 Adams, *Prison of Grass*, 26.
87 Brenda Macdougall, *One of the Family: Metis Culture in Nineteenth-Century Northwestern Saskatchewan* (Vancouver: UBC Press, 2010), xii.
88 This type of thinking is evident in relatively recent fur trade literature. Frank Tough, for instance, veers in the direction of economism, arguing that "the market was ahead of any legal/administrative 'frontier.'" Tough, "From the 'Original Affluent Society' to the 'Unjust Society,'" 31.
89 Karl Marx and Friedrich Engels, *Collected Works of Marx and Engels: 1857–61*, vol. 29 (New York: International Publishers, 1987), 264.
90 Marx and Engels, *Collected Works*, 25: 137, 152.
91 Marx, *Capital*, 1: 536.
92 Luxemburg, *The Accumulation of Capital*, 349, 376.
93 Brophy, "An Uneven and Combined Development Theory of Law."

94 Brophy, "Freedom, Law, and the Colonial Project."
95 John Haldon, "Mode of Production, Social Action, and Historical Change: Some Questions and Issues," in *Studies on Pre-Capitalist Modes of Production*, ed. Laura da Graca and Andrea Zingarelli (Leiden: Brill, 2015), 213.
96 E.E. Rich, for one, emphasizes the social and not the economic dimensions of these exchanges. See Rich, "Trade Habits and Economic Motivation among the Indians of North America," 42.
97 Lauren Benton and Richard J. Ross, "Empires and Legal Pluralism: Jurisdiction, Sovereignty, and Political Imagination in the Early Modern World," in *Legal Pluralism and Empires, 1500–1850*, ed. Lauren Benton and Richard J. Ross (New York: New York University Press, 2013), 4.
98 Brian Z. Tamanaha, "The Folly of the 'Social Scientific' Concept of Legal Pluralism," *Journal of Law and Society* 20, no. 2 (1993): 192–217.
99 Some texts that elaborate on this connection include Lisa Lowe, *The Intimacies of Four Continents* (Durham, NC: Duke University Press, 2015); Lauren Benton and Benjamin Straumann, "Acquiring Empire by Law: From Roman Doctrine to Early Modern European Practice," *Law and History Review* 28, no. 1 (2010): 1–38; Christopher Tomlins, *Freedom Bound: Law, Labor, and Civic Identity in Colonizing English America, 1580–1865* (Cambridge: Cambridge University Press, 2010); and more recently, Maïa Pal, *Jurisdictional Accumulation: An Early Modern History of Law, Empires, and Capital* (Cambridge: Cambridge University Press, 2020).
100 "Law of nations," "law of nature," and "land belonging to nobody," respectively. See Tomlins, *Freedom Bound*, 117.
101 Ian Hunter, "Global Justice and Regional Metaphysics: On the Critical History of the Law of Nature and Nations," in *Law and Politics in British Colonial Thought: Transpositions and Empire*, ed. Shaunnagh Dorsett and Ian Hunter (New York: Springer, 2010), 17. See also Brian Slattery, "Paper Empires: The Legal Dimensions of French and English Ventures in North America," in *Despotic Dominion: Property Rights in British Settler Societies*, ed. John McLaren, A.R. Buck, and Nancy E. Wright (Vancouver: UBC Press, 2004), 54–56.
102 Christopher L. Tomlins, "The Legalities of English Colonizing: Discourses of European Intrusion upon the Americas, c. 1490–1830," in *Law and Politics in British Colonial Thought: Transpositions and Empire*, ed. Shaunnagh Dorsett and Ian Hunter (New York: Springer, 2010), 53.
103 Peter Fitzpatrick, "Ultimate Plurality: International Law and the Possibility of Resistance," *Inter Gentes* 1, no. 1 (2016): 9.
104 Val Napoleon, "Living Together: Gitksan Legal Reasoning as a Foundation for Consent," in *Between Consenting Peoples: Political Community and the Meaning of Consent*, ed. Jeremy Webber and Colin M. Macleod (Vancouver: UBC Press, 2010), 45.
105 Robert Gordon, "Critical Legal Histories," *Faculty Scholarship Series*, January 1, 1984, http://digitalcommons.law.yale.edu/fss_papers/1368; Lauren Benton, *Law and Colonial Cultures: Legal Regimes in World History, 1400–1900* (Cambridge: Cambridge University Press, 2002); Benton and Straumann, "Acquiring Empire by Law."
106 Alan Hunt, "The Ideology of Law: Advances and Problems in Recent Applications of the Concept of Ideology to the Analysis of Law," *Law and Society Review* 19, no. 1 (1985): 26.
107 Hunt, "The Ideology of Law," 33.
108 As Jean Barman observes, "the global and the local jostled up against each other time and again in the fur economy." See Jean Barman, *French Canadians, Furs, and Indigenous Women in the Making of the Pacific Northwest* (Vancouver: UBC Press, 2014), 70.

196 *Notes to pages 15–20*

109 Lisa Ford, *Settler Sovereignty: Jurisdiction and Indigenous People in America and Australia, 1788–1836* (Cambridge, MA: Harvard University Press, 2010), 3, 4.
110 Ford, *Settler Sovereignty,* 3.
111 With respect to the relation between theory and history, I take seriously Neal Wood's observation that "history is not discovered ... but instead created in a critical way on the basis of our theorizing, conceptualizing, and hypothesizing within the limits, of course, set by the documents and other evidence that is to be assessed. In effect history and theory are one." See Neal Wood, "The Social History of Political Theory," *Political Theory* 6, no. 3 (1978): 346.

Chapter 1: Reciprocity and Dispossession

1 Lorenzo Veracini, "Containment, Elimination, Settler Colonialism," *Arena Journal* 51–52 (2018): 19.
2 "Territoriality is settler colonialism's specific, irreducible element." Patrick Wolfe, "Settler Colonialism and the Elimination of the Native," *Journal of Genocide Research* 8, no. 4 (2006): 388. Notable in this respect are Wolfe's statements connecting the racist dimensions of settler colonialism and the dispossession of land. As it applies to the Canadian context, see, for example, Michael McCrossan, "Contaminating and Collapsing Indigenous Space: Judicial Narratives of Canadian Territoriality," *Settler Colonial Studies* 5, no. 1 (2015): 20–39.
3 For an example of this approach and how it privileges a white possessive notion of property, see Thomas Flanagan, Christopher Alcantara, and André Le Dressay, *Beyond the Indian Act: Restoring Aboriginal Property Rights* (Montreal and Kingston: McGill-Queen's University Press, 2010), 18.
4 Heidi Kiiwetinepinesiik Stark and Gina Starblanket, "Towards a Relational Paradigm – Four Points for Consideration: Knowledge, Gender, Land, and Modernity," in *Resurgence and Reconciliation: Indigenous-Settler Relations and Earth Teachings,* ed. Michael I. Asch, John Borrows, and James Tully (Toronto: University of Toronto Press, 2018), 182.
5 For an extensive discussion about "the idea of property in land," see Allan Greer, *Property and Dispossession: Natives, Empires and Land in Early Modern North America* (Cambridge: Cambridge University Press, 2018), 11–18.
6 Zoe Todd, referencing Vanessa Watts, notes that "the appropriation of Indigenous thinking in European contexts *without Indigenous interlocutors present to hold the use of Indigenous stories and laws to account* flattens, distorts and erases the embodied, legal-governances and spiritual aspects of Indigenous thinking." See Zoe Todd, "An Indigenous Feminist's Take on the Ontological Turn: 'Ontology' Is Just Another Word for Colonialism," *Journal of Historical Sociology* 29, no. 1 (2016): 9. I offer this work as an expression of my desire for further interlocution in order to bolster decolonization initiatives within and beyond the academy.
7 Stark and Starblanket, "Towards a Relational Paradigm," 189.
8 Toby Morantz, "Economic and Social Accommodations of the James Bay Inlanders to the Fur Trade," in *The Subarctic Fur Trade: Native Social and Economic Adaptations,* ed. Shepard Krech III (Vancouver: UBC Press, 1984), 55.
9 Audra Simpson and Andrea Smith, "Introduction," in *Theorizing Native Studies,* ed. Audra Simpson and Andrea Smith (Durham, NC: Duke University Press, 2014), 5.
10 Stark and Starblanket, "Towards a Relational Paradigm," 190.
11 Janna Promislow, "One Chief, Two Chiefs, Red Chiefs, Blue Chiefs: Newcomer Perspectives on Indigenous Leadership in Rupert's Land and the North-West Territories," in *The Grand Experiment: Law and Legal Culture in British Settler Societies,* ed. Hamar Foster, Benjamin L. Berger, and A.R. Buck (Vancouver: UBC Press, 2008), 59.

Notes to pages 20–22   197

12   Mahmood Mamdani, *Citizen and Subject: Contemporary Africa and the Legacy of Late Colonialism* (Princeton, NJ: Princeton University Press, 1996), 39.

13   Peter Kulchyski, *Like the Sound of a Drum: Aboriginal Cultural Politics in Denendeh and Nunavut* (Winnipeg: University of Manitoba Press, 2005), 79.

14   Winona LaDuke, "Preface: Natural to Synthetic and Back," in *Marxism and Native Americans*, ed. Ward Churchill (Boston: South End Press, 1983), ii.

15   James Daschuk, *Clearing the Plains: Disease, Politics of Starvation, and the Loss of Aboriginal Life* (Regina: University of Regina Press, 2013), 6; J. Colin Yerbury, "Protohistoric Canadian Athapaskan Populations: An Ethnohistorical Reconstruction," *Arctic Anthropology* 17, no. 2 (1980): 17–33.

16   Harold Adams Innis, *The Fur Trade in Canada: An Introduction to Canadian Economic History* (Toronto: University of Toronto Press, 1999), 12.

17   Arthur J. Ray and Donald B. Freeman, *"Give Us Good Measure": An Economic Analysis of Relations between the Indians and the Hudson's Bay Company before 1763* (Toronto: University of Toronto Press, 1978), 23.

18   Most of the fur trade literature uses Cree or Ojibwe (pluralized as Ojibweg). At various points, more specific groups are referred to, such as the Lowland Cree or Eastern James Bay Cree with respect to the former and Chippewa, Bungi, and Saulteaux with respect to the latter. As Laura Peers explains regarding Ojibwe names, "the names by which they refer to themselves differ from community [to community]." Laura L. Peers, *The Ojibwa of Western Canada, 1780 to 1870* (Winnipeg: University of Manitoba Press, 1984), xv. Wherever possible, I include the Indigenous names for specific groups for more accuracy.

19   This book is explicitly about the lead-up to and establishment of the Red River Colony, so my use of the name Métis throughout refers to peoples associated with that specific time and place. I acknowledge that there are ongoing debates about Métis identity in different contexts; see, for example, Adam Gaudry and Darryl Leroux, "White Settler Revisionism and Making Métis Everywhere: The Evocation of Métissage in Quebec and Nova Scotia," *Critical Ethnic Studies* 3, no. 1 (2017): 116–42; Brittany Hobson, "'They're Stealing Our Identity': Métis National Council Calls Out Eastern Métis Groups," *APTN News* (blog), November 26, 2018, https://www.aptnnews.ca/national-news/theyre-stealing-our-identity-metis-national-council-calls-out-eastern-metis-groups/; and Michel Bouchard, Sébastien Malette, and Guillaume Marcotte, *Bois-Brûlés: The Untold Story of the Métis of Western Quebec* (Vancouver: UBC Press, 2020).

20   Harold Hickerson, *The Chippewa and Their Neighbors: A Study in Ethnohistory* (New York: Holt, Rinehart and Winston, 1970), 39.

21   William Whipple Warren, *History of the Ojibway People*, ed. Theresa Schenck, 2nd ed. (St. Paul: Minnesota Historical Society, 2009), 9.

22   Peers, *The Ojibwa of Western Canada*, xvi. In the seventeenth century, the *engagés* were identified as servants employed by *voyageurs*, with the latter being understood more as independent producers. See Allan Greer, "Fur-Trade Labour and Lower Canadian Agrarian Structures," *Historical Papers* 16, no. 1 (1981): 198. With respect to labelling, I use *engagés* when the original author does and *voyageurs* in reference to a larger category of fur trade workers that eventually came to include servants, per Carolyn Podruchny, "Baptizing Novices: Ritual Moments among French Canadian Voyageurs in the Montreal Fur Trade, 1780–1820," *Canadian Historical Review* 83, no. 2 (2002): 166.

23   Warren Cariou and Niigaanwewidam James Sinclair, "Peguis," in *Manitowapow: Aboriginal Writings from the Land of Water*, ed. Warren Cariou and Niigaanwewidam James Sinclair (Winnipeg: Portage and Main Press, 2011), 13.

198 Notes to pages 22–24

24 Peguis, "A Reply to the Selkirk Settlers' Call for Help," in *Manitowapow: Aboriginal Writings from the Land of Water,* ed. Warren Cariou and Niigaanwewidam James Sinclair (Winnipeg: Portage and Main Press, 2011), 14.

25 Vanessa Watts, "Indigenous Place-Thought and Agency amongst Humans and Non-Humans (First Woman and Sky Woman Go on a European World Tour!)," *Decolonization: Indigeneity, Education and Society* 2, no. 1 (2013): 27.

26 Jill Doerfler, "A Philosophy for Living: Ignatia Broker and Constitutional Reform among the White Earth Anishinaabeg," in *Centering Anishinaabeg Studies: Understanding the World through Stories,* ed. Jill Doerfler, Niigaanwewidam James Sinclair, and Heidi Kiiwetinepinesiik Stark, American Indian Studies Series (East Lansing: Michigan State University Press; Winnipeg: University of Manitoba Press, 2013), 180.

27 Heidi Kiiwetinepinesiik Stark, "Nenabozho's Smart Berries: Rethinking Tribal Sovereignty and Accountability," *Michigan State Law Review* 2 (2013): 350.

28 Stark, "Nenabozho's Smart Berries," 353.

29 Sara J. Mainville, "Manidoo Mazina'igan: An Anishinaabe Perspective of Treaty 3" (LLM, University of Toronto, 2007), 16. For an overview of various origin stories, see Warren, *History of the Ojibway People,* 45–47.

30 Quoted in Michael Relland, "Saulteaux Indigenous Knowledge: Elder Danny Musqua," *Native Studies Review* 13, no. 2 (2000): 94.

31 Carolyn Podruchny, "Trickster Lessons in Early Canadian Indigenous Communities," *Sibirica* 15, no. 1 (2016): 67.

32 Peers, *The Ojibwa of Western Canada,* xvi.

33 Nicole St-Onge, "Uncertain Margins: Métis and Saulteaux Identities in St-Paul des Saulteaux, Red River 1821–1870," *Manitoba History* 53 (2006), http://www.mhs.mb.ca/docs/mb_history/53/uncertainmargins.shtml. For the sake of consistency with the sources cited, I use the term "buffalo" instead of the more zoologically precise term "bison" throughout.

34 Laura L. Peers, "Subsistence, Secondary Literature, and Gender Bias: The Saulteaux," in *Women of the First Nations: Power, Wisdom, and Strength,* ed. Christine Miller and Patricia Marie Chuchryk, Manitoba Studies in Native History 9 (Winnipeg: University of Manitoba Press, 1996), 45. See also Joan A. Lovisek, Leo Waisberg, and Tim Holzkamm, "'Deprived of Part of Their Living': Colonialism and Nineteenth-Century Flooding of Ojibwa Lands," in *Papers of the Twenty-Sixth Algonquian Conference,* ed. David H. Pentland (Winnipeg: University of Manitoba, 1995), 228.

35 David Goodman Mandelbaum, *The Plains Cree: An Ethnographic, Historical, and Comparative Study* (Regina: Canadian Plains Research Center, 1979), 7.

36 Mandelbaum, *The Plains Cree,* 20.

37 John S. Milloy, *The Plains Cree: Trade, Diplomacy, and War, 1790 to 1870* (Winnipeg: University of Manitoba Press, 1988), especially 72–77.

38 Milloy, *The Plains Cree,* 5.

39 James G.E. Smith, "The Western Woods Cree: Anthropological Myth and Historical Reality," *American Ethnologist* 14, no. 3 (1987): 435.

40 Dale R. Russell, *Eighteenth Century Western Cree and Their Neighbours* (Hull, QC: Canadian Museum of Civilization, 1991), 1.

41 James Daschuk, "Who Killed the Prairie Beaver? An Environmental Case for Eighteenth Century Migration in Western Canada," *Prairie Forum* 37 (2012): 152; Russell, *Eighteenth Century Western Cree and Their Neighbours,* 25.

42 Smith, "The Western Woods Cree," 438.

43 David Meyer and Paul C. Thistle, "Saskatchewan River Rendezvous Centers and Trading Posts: Continuity in a Cree Social Geography," *Ethnohistory* 42, no. 3 (1995): 403–44; David

Meyer, Terry Gibson, and Dale Russell, "The Quest for Pasquatinow: An Aboriginal Gathering Centre in the Saskatchewan River Valley," *Prairie Forum* 17, no. 2 (1992): 201–23.

44 Scott P. Stephen, *Masters and Servants: The Hudson's Bay Company and Its North American Workforce, 1668–1786* (Edmonton: University of Alberta Press, 2019), 11.

45 Daniel Francis and Toby Elaine Morantz, *Partners in Furs: A History of the Fur Trade in Eastern James Bay, 1600–1870* (Montreal and Kingston: McGill-Queen's University Press, 1983), 11.

46 Philip Awashish, "A Brief Introduction to the Eeyou Traditional System of Governance of Hunting Territories (Traditional Eeyou Indoh-Hoh Istchee Governance)," *Anthropologica* 60, no. 1 (2018): 1.

47 Francis and Morantz, *Partners in Furs*, 7. More inland, away from the bay, beavers were primarily hunted for food; for the purpose of trading, the mid-winter period meant better beaver pelts, though in general the beaver population varied depending on climate and scarcity (8).

48 Greer, *Property and Dispossession*, 45–46.

49 Toby Morantz, "Foreword: Remembering the Algonquian Family Hunting Territory Debate," *Anthropologica* 60, no. 1 (2018): 12. This piece and Awashish's introduction are part of a special issue of *Anthropologica* that revisits the research on "family hunting territories" among the Eeyou, specifically as it pertains to the governance practices of these varied Indigenous societies and their corresponding land claims.

50 Awashish, "A Brief Introduction," 3.

51 Hans M. Carlson, *Home Is the Hunter: The James Bay Cree and Their Land* (Vancouver: UBC Press, 2009), 13.

52 Michael Witgen, *An Infinity of Nations: How the Native New World Shaped Early North America* (Philadelphia: University of Pennsylvania Press, 2011), 177. Winipeg-athinuwick is also spelled Winnipeg Athinuwick.

53 Victor P. Lytwyn, *Muskekowuck Athinuwick: Original People of the Great Swampy Land* (Winnipeg: University of Manitoba Press, 2002), 7.

54 Louis Bird, *The Spirit Lives in the Mind: Omushkego Stories, Lives and Dreams*, ed. Susan Elaine Gray (Montreal and Kingston: McGill-Queen's University Press, 2007), 8.

55 Bird, *The Spirit Lives in the Mind*, 42.

56 Lytwyn, *Muskekowuck Athinuwick*, xii.

57 Lytwyn, *Muskekowuck Athinuwick*, 17.

58 Lytwyn, *Muskekowuck Athinuwick*, 20.

59 Quoted in Lytwyn, *Muskekowuck Athinuwick*, 11–12.

60 Michel Hogue, *Metis and the Medicine Line: Creating a Border and Dividing a People* (Chapel Hill: University of North Carolina Press, 2015), 16–17.

61 Gerhard John Ens, *Homeland to Hinterland: The Changing Worlds of the Red River Metis in the Nineteenth Century* (Toronto: University of Toronto Press, 1996), 17.

62 Ens, *Homeland to Hinterland*, 15.

63 Scott Berthelette, "The Making of a Manitoban Hero: Commemorating La Vérendrye in St. Boniface and Winnipeg, 1886–1938," *Manitoba History* 74 (2014): 17. Worth noting, however, is a tendency in the study of Métis history to focus on the Red River area, often at the expense of other sites, a point that Brenda Macdougall addresses in *One of the Family: Metis Culture in Nineteenth-Century Northwestern Saskatchewan* (Vancouver: UBC Press, 2010), 2.

64 Carolyn Podruchny and Nicole St-Onge, "Scuttling along a Spider's Web: Mobility and Kinship in Metis Ethnogenesis," in *Contours of a People: Metis Family, Mobility, and History*, ed. Nicole St-Onge, Carolyn Podruchny, and Brenda Macdougall (Norman: University of Oklahoma Press, 2012), 65. Mobility was not an absolute, for there were also some who engaged in farming; see Hogue, *Metis and the Medicine Line*, 26.

200 *Notes to pages 26–27*

65 Podruchny and St-Onge, "Scuttling along a Spider's Web," 69; Hogue, *Metis and the Medicine Line*, 5–6, 21.
66 Podruchny and St-Onge, "Scuttling along a Spider's Web," 67; Hogue, *Metis and the Medicine Line*, 35.
67 Podruchny and St-Onge, "Scuttling along a Spider's Web," 67–68; Arthur J. Ray, *Aboriginal Rights Claims and the Making and Remaking of History*, McGill-Queen's Native and Northern Series 87 (Montreal and Kingston: McGill-Queen's University Press, 2016), 209–10.
68 Chris Andersen, *"Métis": Race, Recognition, and the Struggle for Indigenous Peoplehood* (Vancouver: UBC Press, 2014), 5.
69 Daniel Voth, "Her Majesty's Justice Be Done: Métis Legal Mobilization and the Pitfalls to Indigenous Political Movement Building," *Canadian Journal of Political Science/Revue canadienne de science politique* 49, no. 2 (2016): 247.
70 Andersen, *"Métis,"* 6, 11; Hogue, *Metis and the Medicine Line*, 7.
71 Elizabeth Vibert provides a deft overview of these debates in *Traders' Tales: Narratives of Cultural Encounters in the Columbia Plateau, 1807–1846* (Norman: University of Oklahoma Press, 1997), 11, http://archive.org/details/traderstalesnarroooovibe_i7n8.
72 For a most skilled assessment of the notion of *terra nullius*, see Christopher Tomlins, *Freedom Bound: Law, Labor, and Civic Identity in Colonizing English America, 1580–1865* (Cambridge: Cambridge University Press, 2010), 119n81.
73 Aileen Moreton-Robinson, *The White Possessive: Property, Power, and Indigenous Sovereignty* (Minneapolis: University of Minnesota Press, 2015), 11.
74 Bradley Bryan, "Property as Ontology: On Aboriginal and English Understandings of Ownership," *Canadian Journal of Law and Jurisprudence* 13 (2000): 4.
75 Bryan, "Property as Ontology," 5.
76 Isabella Bakker and Rachel Silvey, "Introduction: Social Reproduction and Global Transformations – From the Everyday to the Global," in *Beyond States and Markets: The Challenges of Social Reproduction*, ed. Isabella Bakker and Rachel Silvey (London: Routledge, 2012), 2–3.
77 Hogue, *Metis and the Medicine Line*, 22–23.
78 *The Fur Trade: Our People's Story* (Edmonton: University of Alberta, 2014), https://www.youtube.com/watch?v=2HHGmxQ2C4w; Rauna Kuokkanen, "Globalization as Racialized, Sexualized Violence: The Case of Indigenous Women," *International Feminist Journal of Politics* 10, no. 2 (2008): 8.
79 Sylvia Van Kirk, "The Role of Native Women in the Fur Trade Society of Western Canada, 1670–1830," *Frontiers: A Journal of Women Studies* 7, no. 3 (1984): 10.
80 Peers, "Subsistence, Secondary Literature and Gender Bias," 42, 45–47.
81 Basil Johnston, *Ojibway Heritage* (Toronto: McClelland and Stewart, 1987), 66.
82 Eleanor Leacock, "Relations of Production in Band Society," in *Politics and History in Band Societies*, ed. Eleanor Leacock and Richard Lee (Cambridge: Cambridge University Press, 1982), 167. Her mid-twentieth-century research on the Cree of northern Quebec/Eastern James Bay led Leacock to argue that this shift entailed a movement away from "primitive communism," which Toby Morantz rejects for a number of substantive reasons captured by her view that Leacock tended to make "sweeping generalisations covering all northern Algonquians." See Morantz, "Foreword," 12.
83 Rauna Kuokkanen, "The Politics of Form and Alternative Autonomies: Indigenous Women, Subsistence Economies and the Gift Paradigm," Working Paper Series – Globalization Working Papers, McMaster University, 2007, 2.
84 Jean Barman, *French Canadians, Furs, and Indigenous Women in the Making of the Pacific Northwest* (Vancouver: UBC Press, 2014), 162. However, when discussing childbirth a

Notes to pages 27–29   201

few pages later, citing recorded observations from the 1800s, Barman does not confront the racism behind the idea that women of colour have higher pain thresholds. On the long history and contemporary consequences of this view, see Kelly M. Hoffman et al., "Racial Bias in Pain Assessment and Treatment Recommendations, and False Beliefs about Biological Differences between Blacks and Whites," *Proceedings of the National Academy of Sciences* 113, no. 16 (2016): 4297.

85 Van Kirk, "The Role of Native Women in the Fur Trade Society of Western Canada," 11.

86 Lytwyn, *Muskekowuck Athinuwick*, 107.

87 Peers, *The Ojibwa of Western Canada*, 35.

88 Brian Gallagher, "A Re-Examination of Race, Class and Society in Red River," *Native Studies Review* 4, nos. 1–2 (1988): 35.

89 Van Kirk, "The Role of Native Women in the Fur Trade Society of Western Canada," 9.

90 Barman, *French Canadians, Furs, and Indigenous Women*, 107, 122.

91 Van Kirk, "The Role of Native Women in the Fur Trade Society of Western Canada," 10.

92 Lisa Ford, *Settler Sovereignty: Jurisdiction and Indigenous People in America and Australia, 1788–1836* (Cambridge, MA: Harvard University Press, 2010), 18.

93 Andersen, "*Métis*," 122, 206–7. Among the main sources consulted pertaining to the settlement at Red River, the Assiniboine figure less prominently around the site until the negotiations and commission in 1817; however, they do appear more frequently in the HBC officers' journals from posts further west along the Assiniboine River. See, for example, the many references to "Asniboils" by John Linklater, "1795–1796," Archives of Manitoba, Brandon House Post Journal, http://pam.minisisinc.com/DIGITALOBJECTS/Access/HBCA%20Microfilm/1M17/B22-A-3.pdf. In scholarly accounts of the history of the Red River Colony, the Assiniboine are not afforded the same amount of attention compared to the other members of the Iron Alliance, which means fewer sources to draw on for this study; see Nathan Hasselstrom, "An Exploration of the Selkirk Treaty" (master's thesis, University of Ottawa, 2019), 28. To offset their wholesale erasure and to gesture to their import, I mention the Assiniboine as they appear in the primary sources at specific times and places.

94 Robert Alexander Innes, *Elder Brother and the Law of the People: Contemporary Kinship and Cowessess First Nation* (Winnipeg: University of Manitoba Press, 2013), 59.

95 Edward Ahenakew, *Voices of the Plains Cree*, ed. Ruth Matheson Buck, 2nd ed. (Regina: Canadian Plains Research Center, 1995), 17. With respect to the Innu, see Greer, *Property and Dispossession*, 47.

96 Innes, *Elder Brother and the Law of the People*, 59–60.

97 Innes, *Elder Brother and the Law of the People*, 61. The leaders of these various groups negotiated what has come to be known in Canada as the "numbered treaties." See James Rodger Miller, *Compact, Contract, Covenant: Aboriginal Treaty-Making in Canada* (Toronto: University of Toronto Press, 2009), 150. The numbered treaties refer to the agreements made across what was until 1869 "Rupert's Land," from present-day northern Ontario to northern British Columbia and up to the Northwest Territories. Negotiations between the crown and various Indigenous groups took place from 1870 to 1921, establishing agreements from Treaty 1 in 1871 to Treaty 11 in 1921.

98 Laura Peers and Jennifer S.H. Brown, "'There Is No End to the Relationship among the Indians': Ojibwa Families and Kinship in Historical Perspective," *History of the Family* 4, no. 4 (2000): 532.

99 Innes, *Elder Brother and the Law of the People*, 65.

100 Innes, *Elder Brother and the Law of the People*, 30.

101 Innes, *Elder Brother and the Law of the People*, 29, 31.

202 Notes to pages 29–31

102 Innes, *Elder Brother and the Law of the People*, 34. See also John Borrows, "Constitutional Law from a First Nation Perspective: Self-Government and the Royal Proclamation," *UBC Law Review* 28, no. 1 (1994): 7.

103 Innes, *Elder Brother and the Law of the People*, 38.

104 Innes, *Elder Brother and the Law of the People*, 39–41. There is also a story from Saulteaux society called "Nänibozhu and the Wolves," in which Nänibozhu becomes a brother to the wolves and ends up taking the youngest off as his nephew. See Alanson Skinner, "Plains Ojibwa Tales," *Journal of American Folklore* 32, no. 124 (1919): 283–84.

105 Borrows, "Constitutional Law from a First Nation Perspective," 8.

106 John Borrows, "Heroes, Tricksters, Monsters, and Caretakers: Indigenous Law and Legal Education Special Issue – Indigenous Law and Legal Pluralism," *McGill Law Journal* 61 (2016): 826.

107 Innes, *Elder Brother and the Law of the People*, 35. In addition to Nanbush, Borrows, "Heroes, Tricksters, Monsters, and Caretakers," 831, notes that this figure is referred to as Nanaboozho or Nanabush in Anishinaabe society.

108 Deanna Christensen, *Ahtahkakoop: The Epic Account of a Plains Cree Head Chief, His People, and Their Struggle for Survival, 1816–1896* (Shell Lake, SK: Ahtahkakoop Publishing, 2000), 13. Although reciprocity and kinship were significant principles, there was also concern about the loss of identity. Elder Danny Musqua expresses such a concern in his account of Saulteaux from the Sault Ste. Marie region; he states that the combination of certain Ojibweg and Cree produced "a distinct tribe," and he notes that "some of the old people are worried that we are going to be swallowed up by the Cree or swallowed up by the Ojibwa," quoted in Innes, *Elder Brother and the Law of the People*, 11.

109 Mark D. Walters, "'Your Sovereign and Our Father': The Imperial Crown and the Idea of Legal-Ethnohistory," in *Law and Politics in British Colonial Thought: Transpositions and Empire*, ed. Shaunnagh Dorsett and Ian Hunter (New York: Springer, 2010), 94; Heidi Kiiwetinepinesiik Stark, "Respect, Responsibility, and Renewal: The Foundations of Anishinaabe Treaty Making with the United States and Canada," *American Indian Culture and Research Journal* 34, no. 2 (2010): 145–46.

110 John Milloy, "'Our Country': The Significance of the Buffalo Resource for a Plains Cree Sense of Territory," in *Aboriginal Resource Use in Canada: Historical and Legal Aspects*, ed. Kerry Abel and Jean Friesen, Manitoba Studies in Native History 6 (Winnipeg: University of Manitoba Press, 1991), 62, 66.

111 Milloy, "'Our Country,'" 62.

112 Milloy, "'Our Country,'" 63.

113 D.G. Mandelbaum and Fine Day, "Fine Day Interview #2," August 8, 1934, http://ourspace.uregina.ca/handle/10294/1768.

114 Walters, "'Your Sovereign and Our Father,'" 94.

115 Cary Miller, "Gifts as Treaties: The Political Use of Received Gifts in Anishinaabeg Communities, 1820–1832," *American Indian Quarterly* 26, no. 2 (2002): 223.

116 Karl Marx, *Capital: A Critique of Political Economy*, trans. Ben Fowkes, vol. 1 (New York: Vintage Books, 1977), 131.

117 Miller, "Gifts as Treaties," 223; emphasis added.

118 Lytwyn, *Muskekowuck Athinuwick*, 107.

119 Leacock, "Relations of Production in Band Society," 162.

120 Leacock, "Relations of Production in Band Society," 159–60.

121 My working understanding of the term "band" comes from Robert Alexander Innes, "Challenging a Racist Fiction: A Closer Look at Métis–First Nations Relations," in *A People and a Nation: New Directions in Contemporary Métis Studies*, ed. Jennifer Adese

and Chris Andersen, 92–114 (Vancouver: UBC Press, 2021). Innes uses the term to refer to distinct "social, cultural, and political" societies, which "were semiautonomous, kin-based entities that came together in times of need, such as in buffalo hunts and warfare"; see Innes, "Challenging a Racist Fiction," 94, 96. I use the term "group" in a similar respect throughout to avoid confusion with the many versions of the term "band," specifically post–Indian Act.

122 Arthur J. Ray, "Periodic Shortages, Native Welfare, and the Hudson's Bay Company 1670–1930," in *The Subarctic Fur Trade: Native Social and Economic Adaptations,* ed. Shepard Krech III (Vancouver: UBC Press, 1984), 3.

123 Ray, "Periodic Shortages, Native Welfare, and the Hudson's Bay Company," 3.

124 Promislow, "One Chief, Two Chiefs, Red Chiefs, Blue Chiefs," 70.

125 Frank Tough, "From the 'Original Affluent Society' to the 'Unjust Society': A Review Essay on Native Economic History in Canada," *Journal of Aboriginal Economic Development* 4, no. 2 (2005): 34. To a degree, this perspective is implicit in the thesis on the transition to capitalism in *Capital,* but it is more explicit in accounts of the fur trade by mid-century authors such as W.L. Morton, as I detail in the chapters that follow.

126 Readers more familiar with debates in Marxist theory will note that I do not adhere to a strict differentiation between the sphere of exchange and the sphere of production. A too rigid divide does not allow for an understanding of the totality of social relations intrinsic to historical transformation. Moreover, such a division is especially imprudent when discussing the truck system, which collapses remuneration (a lever of labour compulsion for the purpose of productivity) and consumption (an activity often confined to the realm of money circulation in the form of consumer demand).

127 Ray and Freeman, *"Give Us Good Measure,"* 236.

128 Richard White, *The Middle Ground: Indians, Empires, and Republics in the Great Lakes Region, 1650–1815* (Cambridge: Cambridge University Press, 2011), 96.

129 André Le Dressay, Normand Lavallee, and Jason Reeves, "First Nations Trade, Specialization, and Market Institutions: A Historical Survey of First Nation Market Culture," Aboriginal Policy Research Consortium International, 2010, 109–10. The authors go so far as to argue that "market characteristics" were evident among "pre- and early contact First Nations in Canada," including "public infrastructure, standards, mediums of exchange, and property rights" (125). The danger, of course, is going too far by reading into history certain prototypically capitalist relations – a "manifest destiny" of market rationalization. This danger underscores the importance of the modifications that I undertake in this book.

130 Kuokkanen, "The Politics of Form and Alternative Autonomies," 3.

131 Glen Sean Coulthard, *Red Skin, White Masks: Rejecting the Colonial Politics of Recognition,* Indigenous Americas (Minneapolis: University of Minnesota Press, 2014), 40. I borrow this terminology from Coulthard's study of the government of Canada in the twentieth and twenty-first centuries, which Coulthard uses to describe the bureaucratization of land claims processes that offers formal rights to land in exchange for more substantive rights to self-determination.

132 John Sutton Lutz, *Makúk: A New History of Aboriginal-White Relations* (Vancouver: UBC Press, 2009), 20.

133 Christopher L. Tomlins, "The Legalities of English Colonizing: Discourses of European Intrusion upon the Americas, c. 1490–1830," in *Law and Politics in British Colonial Thought: Transpositions and Empire,* ed. Shaunnagh Dorsett and Ian Hunter (New York: Springer, 2010), 60.

134 Ian Hunter, "Vattel in Revolutionary America: From the Rules of War to the Rule of Law," in *Between Indigenous and Settler Governance,* ed. Lisa Ford and Tim Rowse (London:

204 Notes to pages 32–34

Routledge, 2012), 2. For interpretations of this phenomenon along the lines of legal pluralism, see Lauren Benton, *Law and Colonial Cultures: Legal Regimes in World History,
1400–1900* (Cambridge: Cambridge University Press, 2002), 2.

135 Tough, "From the 'Original Affluent Society' to the 'Unjust Society,'" 32.

136 Mamdani, *Citizen and Subject,* 49.

137 Kahente Horn-Miller, "Distortion and Healing: Finding Balance and a 'Good Mind'
through the Rearticulation of Sky Woman's Journey," in *Living on the Land: Indigenous
Women's Understanding of Place,* ed. Nathalie Kermoal and Isabel Altamirano-Jiménez
(Edmonton: Athabasca University Press, 2016), 33.

138 Coulthard, *Red Skin, White Masks,* 63.

139 David Nugent, "Property Relations, Production Relations, and Inequality: Anthropology, Political Economy, and the Blackfeet," *American Ethnologist* 20, no. 2 (1993): 344–45.
Nugent's notion of a rather idealized "reciprocal period" lends itself to a more stagist
understanding of economic and legal transformation.

140 Coulthard, *Red Skin, White Masks,* 63. I explain this in much more detail later in this
chapter after I provide more context regarding the truck system and the corporate structure of the Hudson's Bay Company.

141 Patricia A. McCormack, *Fort Chipewyan and the Shaping of Canadian History,
1788–1920s: "We Like to Be Free in This Country"* (Vancouver: UBC Press, 2011), 34.
McCormack does well to adopt a more dialectical framework, and though the lack of
engagement with key texts and debates in Marxist political economy is understandable
(given the orientation of her book) it does make her deployment of Marxist terms for
analytical purposes rather imprecise. In particular, her dialectical tendencies sit awk-
wardly beside her dated adoption of the base-superstructure metaphor (27).

142 Paul McHugh, *Aboriginal Societies and the Common Law: A History of Sovereignty, Status, and Self-Determination* (Oxford: Oxford University Press, 2004), 103.

143 Marx, *Capital,* 1: 915–16.

144 Arthur J. Ray, J.R. Miller, and Frank Tough, *Bounty and Benevolence: A History of Saskatchewan Treaties* (Montreal and Kingston: McGill-Queen's University Press, 2000), 4.

145 Edith I. Burley, *Servants of the Honourable Company: Work, Discipline, and Conflict in
the Hudson's Bay Company, 1770–1879* (Toronto: Oxford University Press, 1997), 2.

146 Cole Harris, "Arthur J. Ray and the Empirical Opportunity," in *New Histories for Old:
Changing Perspectives on Canada's Native Pasts,* ed. Theodore Binnema and Susan Neylan (Vancouver: UBC Press, 2007), 258.

147 Robert Brenner, *Merchants and Revolution: Commercial Change, Political Conflict, and
London's Overseas Traders, 1550–1653* (London: Verso, 2003), 11.

148 Brenner, *Merchants and Revolution,* 21, 28.

149 Karl Marx, *Capital,* vol. 2 (New York: Penguin Group US, 1993), 312; John Smail,
"Credit, Risk, and Honor in Eighteenth-Century Commerce," *Journal of British Studies*
44, no. 3 (2005): 440; Elizabeth Mancke and Rupert's Land Research Centre, *A Company
of Businessmen: The Hudson's Bay Company and Long-Distance Trade, 1670–1730* (Winnipeg: Rupert's Land Research Centre, 1988), 7.

150 Rosa Luxemburg, *The Accumulation of Capital,* 2nd ed. (London: Routledge, 2003), 340.
For a more recent account of these global effects, see Alexander Anievas and Kerem
Nişancıoğlu, *How the West Came to Rule: The Geopolitical Origins of Capitalism* (London: Pluto Press, 2015). Their work examines the rise of world capitalism and makes
particularly astute use of the theory of uneven and combined development in doing so;
however, I do depart from their assessment of "the Americas," in which they conclude
that the "colonialists annihilated indigenous populations, communities, modes of life
and production," referring to this as a "scorched earth policy" (168). My objective in

this book is to challenge such sweeping assertions and highlight settler colonialism as ongoing and partial, with particular emphasis on the abiding autonomy of Indigenous producers in the face of these threats.

151 Henry Heller, *The Birth of Capitalism: A 21st Century Perspective* (London: Pluto Press, 2011), 25.

152 Karl Marx and Friedrich Engels, *Collected Works of Marx and Engels: 1844–45*, vol. 4 (New York: International Publishers, 1975), 471.

153 Anievas and Nişancıoğlu, *How the West Came to Rule*, 170. Anievas and Nişancıoğlu dispute Brenner, arguing that merchants could have a direct influence on production and citing the plantations in the United States as an example. Although the particularities of the fur trade meant that influence on production could not take the same form as was the case on slave plantations (e.g., investments in fixed and variable capital and direct labour compulsion), merchant credit was nevertheless important to the production of furs for the commercial trade (see 170–73). The specifics of the relation between production and merchant credit in the fur trade require more attention in order to comprehend the transition to capitalism in that time and place.

154 Rosemary E. Ommer, "Introduction," in *Merchant Credit and Labour Strategies in Historical Perspective*, ed. Rosemary E. Ommer (Fredericton: Acadiensis Press, 1990), 10.

155 George W. Hilton, "The British Truck System in the Nineteenth Century," *Journal of Political Economy* 65, no. 3 (1957): 237.

156 Brian Gettler, "Money and the Changing Nature of Colonial Space in Northern Quebec: Fur Trade Monopolies, the State, and Aboriginal Peoples during the Nineteenth Century," *Histoire sociale/Social History* 46, no. 92 (2013): 275.

157 Hilton, "The British Truck System in the Nineteenth Century," 241.

158 Hilton, "The British Truck System in the Nineteenth Century," 241.

159 Gettler, "Money and the Changing Nature of Colonial Space in Northern Quebec," 275.

160 Hilton, "The British Truck System in the Nineteenth Century," 239, identifies two versions in different sectors: first, employment was conditional on accepting company goods in lieu of wages, an arrangement common to weavers in the Midlands; second, the system served as a stopgap for wages expected but yet unpaid, an arrangement more prevalent in the coal-mining sector.

161 Hilton, "The British Truck System in the Nineteenth Century," 247.

162 Hilton, "The British Truck System in the Nineteenth Century," 246.

163 Hilton, "The British Truck System in the Nineteenth Century," 250.

164 Hilton, "The British Truck System in the Nineteenth Century," 252.

165 Hilton, "The British Truck System in the Nineteenth Century," 250.

166 Marx and Engels, *Collected Works of Marx and Engels*, 4: 171. This observation also demonstrates that the variable enforcement of existing statutes likewise contributes to the uneven and combined nature of legal transformation.

167 Marx and Engels, *Collected Works of Marx and Engels*, 25: 97.

168 Marx and Engels, *Collected Works of Marx and Engels*, 25: 152; Maurice Dobb, *Studies in the Development of Capitalism* (London: Routledge and Sons, 1946), 7, 35; Rodney Hilton, "Introduction," in *The Transition from Feudalism to Capitalism* (London: Verso, 1978), 14, 25; Paul M. Sweezy, "A Critique," in *The Transition from Feudalism to Capitalism* (London: Verso, 1978), 47, 49; Robert Brenner, "The Agrarian Roots of European Capitalism," in *The Brenner Debate: Agrarian Class Structure and Economic Development in Pre-Industrial Europe*, ed. T.H. Aston and C.H.E. Philpin (Cambridge: Cambridge University Press, 1985), 239.

206 Notes to pages 35–37

169 Michael Anderson, "India, 1858–1930: The Illusion of Free Labor," in *Masters, Servants, and Magistrates in Britain and the Empire, 1562–1955*, ed. Douglas Hay and Paul Craven (Chapel Hill: University of North Carolina Press, 2005), 443.

170 Robert Campbell, "The Truck System in the Cape Breton Fishery: Philip Robin and Company in Chéticamp, 1843–1852," *Labour/Le travail* 75 (2015): 75, http://www.lltjournal.ca/index.php/llt/article/view/5743.

171 Jerry Bannister, "Law and Labor in Eighteenth-Century Newfoundland," in *Masters, Servants, and Magistrates in Britain and the Empire, 1562–1955*, ed. Douglas Hay and Paul Craven (Chapel Hill: University of North Carolina Press, 2005), 155.

172 James K. Hiller, "The Newfoundland Credit System: An Interpretation," in *Merchant Credit and Labour Strategies in Historical Perspective*, ed. Rosemary E. Ommer (Fredericton: Acadiensis Press, 1990), 89.

173 Bannister, "Law and Labor in Eighteenth-Century Newfoundland," 156.

174 Mamdani, *Citizen and Subject*, 23. Mamdani develops his understanding of "decentralized administration" by comparing colonial governance relations in Cape and Natal. Here I use the term to describe colonial governance relations between far-flung jurisdictions, but later in the book I show that this term also applies to governance relations within the Red River Colony in a manner that coheres better with Mamdani's original formulation.

175 Deidre Simmons, *Keepers of the Record: The History of the Hudson's Bay Company Archives* (Montreal and Kingston: McGill-Queen's University Press, 2007), 155.

176 Luxemburg, *The Accumulation of Capital*, 389–91.

177 Colonial Office, "Hudson's Bay Company: Papers Presented by Command of Her Majesty to the House of Commons, in Pursuance of an Address Praying that Her Majesty Would Be Graciously Pleased to Direct that Such Means as to Her Majesty Shall Seem Most Fitting and Effectual, to Be Taken to Ascertain the Legality of the Powers in Respect to Territory, Trade, Taxation and Government, which Are, or Recently Have Been, Claimed or Exercised by the Hudson's Bay Company, on the Continent of North America, under the Charter of His Majesty King Charles the Second, Issued in the Year 1670, or in Virtue of Any Other Right or Title," House of Commons, 1850, 4.

178 Ann M. Carlos and Frank D. Lewis, *Commerce by a Frozen Sea: Native Americans and the European Fur Trade* (Philadelphia: University of Pennsylvania Press, 2011), 2; John G.T. Anderson, *Deep Things out of Darkness: A History of Natural History* (Berkeley: University of California Press, 2013), 175.

179 Glyndwr Williams, "The Hudson's Bay Company and Its Critics in the Eighteenth Century," *Transactions of the Royal Historical Society* 20 (1970): 149.

180 Mancke and Rupert's Land Research Centre, *A Company of Businessmen*, 16.

181 Stephen, *Masters and Servants*, 18. Instead, it appears that France had a more overtly expansionist objective earlier in the eighteenth century, particularly around Hudson Bay. See Scott Berthelette, "New France and the Hudson Bay Watershed: Transatlantic Networks, Backcountry Specialists, and French Imperial Projects in Post-Utrecht North America, 1713–29," *Canadian Historical Review* 101, no. 1 (2019): 24–25.

182 *Hudson's Bay Company. The Royal Charter for Incorporating the Hudson's Bay Company: Granted by His Majesty King Charles the Second, in the Twenty-Second Year of His Reign, A.D. 1670* (London: K.K. Causton, 1865), 14.

183 Burley, *Servants of the Honourable Company*, 1.

184 Stephen, *Masters and Servants*, 50.

185 Ann M. Carlos and Stephen Nicholas, "Managing the Manager: An Application of the Principal Agent Model to the Hudson's Bay Company," *Oxford Economic Papers* 45, no. 2 (1993): 244. Although the Hudson's Bay Company was organized during the so-called

Notes to pages 37–39 207

feudal era in England, and includes the hierarchical hallmark of a nominally servant class, I do not entertain the discussion of what constitutes a "real" feudalist relation. What matters for the purposes of my analysis is the relation between the notion of "servant" as a formal legal designation and the actual conditions, practices, and contexts of labour compulsion.

186 Jennifer S.H. Brown, *Strangers in Blood: Fur Trade Company Families in Indian Country* (Vancouver: UBC Press, 1996), xi. This was especially true as of the 1720s; see Stephen, *Masters and Servants*, 150.

187 Ford, *Settler Sovereignty*, 17.

188 Dale Gibson, *Law, Life, and Government at Red River, Volume 1: Settlement and Governance, 1812–1872* (Montreal and Kingston: McGill-Queen's University Press, 2015), 4.

189 Quoted in A.K. (Alexander Kennedy) Isbister, *A Few Words on the Hudson's Bay Company: With a Statement of the Grievances of the Native and Half-Caste Indians, Addressed to the British Government through Their Delegates Now in London* (London: C. Gilpin, 1846), 22.

190 Paul C. Nigol, "Discipline and Discretion in the Mid-Eighteenth-Century Hudson's Bay Company Private Justice System," in *Laws and Societies in the Canadian Prairie West, 1670–1940*, ed. Louis A. Knafla and Jonathan Swainger (Vancouver: UBC Press, 2005), 151.

191 Great Britain, House of Commons, *Journals of the House of Commons* (London: H.M. Stationery Office, 1742), 392, 412. For more context on the role of London felters in relation to the HBC charter, see Mancke, *A Company of Businessmen*, 30–31.

192 Ford, *Settler Sovereignty*, 20.

193 Richard S. Mackie, *Trading beyond the Mountains: The British Fur Trade on the Pacific, 1793–1843* (Vancouver: UBC Press, 2011), 4. The Northwest Passage refers to the route that connects three oceans: the Atlantic and the Pacific via the Arctic.

194 An Act for Giving a Publick Reward to Such Person or Persons ... as Shall Discover a North West Passage, 1745, in *Statutes at Large, from the 15th to the 20th Year of King George II*, vol. 18 (Cambridge: Cambridge University Press, 1765), 329.

195 H. Clare Pentland, *Labour and Capital in Canada 1650–1860* (Toronto: James Lorimer, 1981), 30.

196 Nicholas Rogers, "From Vernon to Wolfe: Empire and Identity in the British Atlantic World of the Mid-Eighteenth Century," in *The Culture of the Seven Years' War: Empire, Identity, and the Arts in the Eighteenth-Century Atlantic World*, ed. Frans De Bruyn and Shaun Regan (Toronto: University of Toronto Press, 2014), 37.

197 W.A. Mackintosh, "Economic Factors in Canadian History," *Canadian Historical Review* 4, no. 1 (1923): 14; Barman, *French Canadians, Furs, and Indigenous Women*, 17.

198 Rogers, "From Vernon to Wolfe," 38.

199 Gibson, *Law, Life, and Government at Red River, Volume 1*, 4.

200 Gallagher, "A Re-Examination of Race, Class and Society in Red River," 54.

201 Burley, *Servants of the Honourable Company*, 2; Stephen, *Masters and Servants*, 20.

202 Carolyn Podruchny, *Making the Voyageur World: Travelers and Traders in the North American Fur Trade* (Lincoln: University of Nebraska Press, 2006), 3. Insofar as these labourers were contracted servants from less well-off families, the term "indenture" is an apt but imperfect descriptor. In the case of the Orcadians, their labour was not contracted to a third party, they could negotiate some of the terms of the contract, and they received some compensation in the form of cash wages (in the decades after 1670, the annual payment was six pounds). See Burley, *Servants of the Honourable Company*, 71, 68. A more pronounced relation of indentured servitude was practised with the children of the poor (some as young as five and bound until the age of twenty-four), consigned

208 *Notes to pages 39–42*

to the Hudson's Bay Company as apprentices and trained in "navigation, surveying, and mathematics" (65–66).

203 Burley, *Servants of the Honourable Company*, 2.

204 Scott Stephen, "'Covenant Servants': Contract, Negotiation, and Accommodation in Hudson Bay, 1670–1782," *Manitoba History* 60 (2009): 24–25.

205 Burley, *Servants of the Honourable Company*, 3.

206 Pentland, *Labour and Capital in Canada*, 31–32; Stephen, *Masters and Servants*, 16. Stephen articulates the master-servant relationship as founded on reciprocity with obligations arising from a patriarchal understanding of duty within the household. This is notable because this organizational feature of the Hudson's Bay Company represents another facet of the disciplinary strategies integral to the truck economy (22).

207 Arthur J. Ray, "The Decline of Paternalism in the Hudson's Bay Company Fur Trade, 1870–1945," in *Merchant Credit and Labour Strategies in Historical Perspective*, ed. Rosemary E. Ommer (Fredericton: Acadiensis Press, 1990), 189–90.

208 Stephen, *Masters and Servants*, 12.

209 Carol M. Judd, "Native Labour and Social Stratification in the Hudson's Bay Company's Northern Department, 1770–1870," *Canadian Review of Sociology/Revue canadienne de sociologie* 17, no. 4 (1980): 306.

210 Judd, "Native Labour and Social Stratification," 306.

211 Burley, *Servants of the Honourable Company*, 79.

212 Judd, "Native Labour and Social Stratification," 306.

213 Thomas Thomas, "Letter to Governor of HBC, 15 September 1815," LAC – Selkirk Collection, 1427, http://heritage.canadiana.ca/view/oocihm.lac_reel_c2/385?r=0&s=3. Here a high-ranking officer describes offering a "keg of rum" to calm workers upset at not receiving what they believed they were owed – a notable passage not only because he reports to the head of the company but also because he refers to the workers as "thoughtless people." See also Burley, *Servants of the Honourable Company*, 35.

214 In his study of the master-servant relationship in the Hudson's Bay Company, Stephen lists the various means of labour compulsion that I detail throughout: "enforcing the legal and moral authority of the service contract; promising both monetary and nonmonetary rewards; threatening punishment for misbehaviour; emphasizing reciprocal obligations; and ultimately appealing to the employer as a client appeals to a patron or as a child to a father." See Stephen, *Masters and Servants*, 218.

215 Arthur J. Ray, *Indians in the Fur Trade: Their Role as Trappers, Hunters, and Middlemen in the Lands Southwest of Hudson Bay, 1660–1870*, 2nd ed., ACLS Humanities E-Book (Toronto: University of Toronto Press, 1998), 63.

216 Toby Morantz, "'So Evil a Practice': A Look at the Debt System in the James Bay Fur Trade," in *Merchant Credit and Labour Strategies in Historical Perspective*, ed. Rosemary E. Ommer (Fredericton: Acadiensis Press, 1990), 204.

217 James Dodds, *The Hudson's Bay Company, Its Position and Prospects: The Substance of an Address, Delivered at a Meeting of the Shareholders, in the London Tavern, on the 24th January, 1866* (London: Edward Stanford and A.H. Baily and Company, 1866), 47.

218 Dodds, *The Hudson's Bay Company, Its Position and Prospects*, 47.

219 Dodds, *The Hudson's Bay Company, Its Position and Prospects*, 47.

220 Louis Bird, *Telling Our Stories: Omushkego Legends and Histories from Hudson Bay* (Toronto: University of Toronto Press, 2005), 49–50.

221 Janna Promislow, "'Thou Wilt Not Die of Hunger ... for I Bring Thee Merchandise': Consent, Intersocietal Normativity, and the Exchange of Food at York Factory, 1682–1763," in *Between Consenting Peoples: Political Community and the Meaning of Consent*, ed. Jeremy Webber and Colin M. Macleod (Vancouver: UBC Press, 2010), 99.

222 Burley, *Servants of the Honourable Company,* 2.

223 William Barr, "The Eighteenth Century Trade between the Ships of the Hudson's Bay Company and the Hudson Strait Inuit," *Arctic* 47, no. 3 (1994): 236.

224 Ann M. Carlos and Frank D. Lewis, "Trade, Consumption, and the Native Economy: Lessons from York Factory, Hudson Bay," *Journal of Economic History* 61, no. 4 (2001): 1044–46.

225 Leanna Parker's dissertation explores the connection between culture and political economy among specific Indigenous societies in detail. I support her appeal for a better understanding of how "both external structures and cultural perspectives influenc[e] behaviour." See Leanna Parker, "Re-Conceptualizing the Traditional Economy: Indigenous Peoples' Participation in the Nineteenth Century Fur Trade in Canada and Whaling Industry in New Zealand" (PhD diss., University of Alberta, 2011), 30. My modified dialectical materialist approach builds upon this type of study by providing a robust frame of analysis that better balances cultural and economic considerations.

226 Carlos and Lewis, "Trade, Consumption, and the Native Economy," 1047.

227 Ray, *Indians in the Fur Trade,* 65.

228 Carlos and Lewis, "Trade, Consumption, and the Native Economy," 1048.

229 J.R. Miller, "Compact, Contract, Covenant: The Evolution of Indian Treaty-Making," in *New Histories for Old: Changing Perspectives on Canada's Native Pasts,* ed. Theodore Binnema and Susan Neylan (Vancouver: UBC Press, 2007), 68.

230 Miller, "Compact, Contract, Covenant," 68–69. For more details regarding these ceremonies, especially farther north among the Dene, see Janna Promislow, "'It Would Only Be Just': A Study of Territoriality and Trading Posts along the Mackenzie River 1800-27," in *Between Indigenous and Settler Governance,* ed. Lisa Ford and Tim Rowse (London: Routledge, 2012), 37–39.

231 Lisa Ford and P.G. McHugh, "Settler Sovereignty and the Shapeshifting Crown," in *Between Indigenous and Settler Governance,* ed. Lisa Ford and Tim Rowse (London: Routledge, 2012), 29.

232 Promislow, "'It Would Only Be Just,'" 39.

233 On the politics of gift-giving among Algonquian-speaking societies in the seventeenth century, which echoes some of what I state here, see White, *The Middle Ground,* 15.

234 Lutz, *Makúk,* 23; Parker, "Re-Conceptualizing the Traditional Economy," 7.

235 Ray, "The Decline of Paternalism in the Hudson's Bay Company Fur Trade," 189.

236 Ray and Freeman, *"Give Us Good Measure,"* 236.

237 Miller, "Gifts as Treaties," 222.

238 Colin G. Calloway, "Foundations of Sand: The Fur Trade and the British-Indian Relations, 1783–1815," in *"Le castor fait tout": Selected Papers of the Fifth North American Fur Trade Conference, 1985,* ed. Bruce G. Trigger, Toby Morantz, and Louise Dechêne (Montreal: Lake St. Louis Historical Society, 1987), 147.

239 Chris A. Gregory, *Gifts and Commodities* (London: Academic Press, 1982), 19; David Murray, *Indian Giving: Economies of Power in Indian-White Exchanges* (Amherst: University of Massachusetts Press, 2000), 39.

240 Morantz, "Foreword," 14, notes that the last recorded appointment was in 1815 around James Bay.

241 Charles A. Bishop, "The First Century: Adaptive Changes among the Western James Bay Cree between the Early Seventeenth and Early Eighteenth Centuries," in *The Subarctic Fur Trade: Native Social and Economic Adaptations,* ed. Shepard Krech III (Vancouver: UBC Press, 1984), 39. There is some disparity between the usage of the terms "middleman" and "captain" in fur trade studies. Some historians suggest that there was a temporal difference between the middleman, who travelled to the bayside posts from the

210   Notes to pages 44–45

interior prior to 1774, and the captain, an appointed leader in the exchange. See Harris, "Arthur J. Ray and the Empirical Opportunity," 254. I use the term "trade captain" as a way of underscoring the social and political dimensions of this position and because of the extensive evidence that such appointments of leaders predated the company's inland shift in business.

242 Promislow, "One Chief, Two Chiefs, Red Chiefs, Blue Chiefs," 70; Mancke and Rupert's Land Research Centre, *A Company of Businessmen*, 79.

243 Ray and Freeman, *"Give Us Good Measure,"* 74.

244 Stephen, *Masters and Servants;* Yerbury, "Protohistoric Canadian Athapaskan Populations," 22. Throughout this book, I use "agents" as a general term for Hudson's Bay Company employees, and I use "officers" or "officials" when referring to high-ranking men, which includes factors/masters and superintendents; see Burley, *Servants of the Honourable Company.* With respect to the Nēhiyawok and Stone Sioux (Assiniboine) supplying the Blackfoot, see Milloy, *The Plains Cree,* 10.

245 Promislow, "One Chief, Two Chiefs, Red Chiefs, Blue Chiefs," 70. On the eastern bay-side, a similar practice was reported as early as 1744; see Francis and Morantz, *Partners in Furs,* 43–44.

246 Promislow, "One Chief, Two Chiefs, Red Chiefs, Blue Chiefs," 69, 66.

247 Promislow, "One Chief, Two Chiefs, Red Chiefs, Blue Chiefs," 72.

248 Tough, "From the 'Original Affluent Society' to the 'Unjust Society,'" 34.

249 Peter Linebaugh, *The Magna Carta Manifesto: Liberties and Commons for All* (Berkeley: University of California Press, 2009), 275.

250 Ford, *Settler Sovereignty,* 18.

251 Promislow, "One Chief, Two Chiefs, Red Chiefs, Blue Chiefs," 70–71.

252 Brown, *Strangers in Blood,* xvii.

253 Ann M. Carlos, "Agent Opportunism and the Role of Company Culture: The Hudson's Bay and Royal African Companies Compared," *Business and Economic History* 20 (1991): 148.

254 Carlos, "Agent Opportunism and the Role of Company Culture," 144.

255 Mamdani's notion of "decentralized despotism" is a phenomenon that occurs along with and following more extensive colonial measures (e.g., settlement), and is in some instances typified by the prevalence of extra-economic force; see, for example, Mamdani, *Citizen and Subject,* 23. However, I focus on a period just prior to full-scale settlement, when extra-economic force was rampant but checked by prevailing autonomy of Indigenous populations at this locale. Mamdani's account of the gradual institutionalization of exploitation is revealing and apt, and although the particulars of his version of "decentralized despotism" do not apply exactly to the case of the Red River Colony, I find aspects of his account useful when it comes to dissecting discrete processes of dispossession, which I detail in later chapters.

256 Carlos and Lewis, "Trade, Consumption, and the Native Economy," 1047.

257 Ray, *Indians in the Fur Trade,* xvii.

258 Karl Marx and Friedrich Engels, *Collected Works of Marx and Engels: 1845–1848,* vol. 6 (New York: International Publishers, 1976), 425.

259 E.E. Rich, "Trade Habits and Economic Motivation among the Indians of North America," *Canadian Journal of Economics and Political Science/Revue canadienne d'economique et de science politique* 26, no. 1 (1960): 47.

260 Laura da Graca and Andrea Zingarelli, "Introduction to Studies on Pre-Capitalist Modes of Production," in *Studies on Pre-Capitalist Modes of Production,* ed. Laura da Graca and Andrea Zingarelli (Leiden: Brill, 2015), 12.

261 Carlos and Lewis, "Trade, Consumption, and the Native Economy," 1039.

Notes to pages 46–50   211

262 Murray, *Indian Giving*, 39.
263 Ray, *Indians in the Fur Trade*, 68.
264 Rich, "Trade Habits and Economic Motivation among the Indians of North America," 53.
265 Parker, "Re-Conceptualizing the Traditional Economy," 30.
266 Carlos and Lewis, "Trade, Consumption, and the Native Economy," 1038.
267 Carlos and Lewis, "Trade, Consumption, and the Native Economy," 1040.
268 Carlos and Lewis, "Trade, Consumption, and the Native Economy," 1039.
269 Carlos and Lewis, "Trade, Consumption, and the Native Economy," 1049.
270 Carlos and Lewis, "Trade, Consumption, and the Native Economy," 1053.
271 Edward Palmer Thompson, *Whigs and Hunters: The Origin of the Black Act* (London: Penguin Books, 1990), 54. He is speaking of those who resisted the violent excesses of forest laws in Windsor and Hampshire in the early eighteenth century.
272 Luxemburg, *The Accumulation of Capital*, 338.
273 Tough, "From the 'Original Affluent Society' to the 'Unjust Society,'" 33.
274 Harris, "Arthur J. Ray and the Empirical Opportunity," 257.
275 Morantz, "'So Evil a Practice,'" 209.
276 Lutz, *Makúk*, 11.
277 Carlos and Lewis, "Trade, Consumption, and the Native Economy," 1052–53.
278 Some wage labour was available in the summer for Indigenous traders and trappers who had paid their debts to the Hudson's Bay Company; see Harris, "Arthur J. Ray and the Empirical Opportunity," 258.
279 Marx, *Capital*, 1: 205.
280 Ray and Freeman, *"Give Us Good Measure,"* 97.
281 Carlos and Lewis, "Trade, Consumption, and the Native Economy," 1043.
282 Carlos and Lewis, "Trade, Consumption, and the Native Economy," 1044–45.
283 Carlos and Lewis, "Trade, Consumption, and the Native Economy," 1043.
284 Ray, *Indians in the Fur Trade*, 61.
285 Ray, *Indians in the Fur Trade*, 63; Carlos and Lewis, "Trade, Consumption, and the Native Economy," 1047.
286 Ray, *Indians in the Fur Trade*, 65.
287 Anievas and Nişancıoğlu, *How the West Came to Rule*, 169.
288 Luxemburg, *The Accumulation of Capital*, 365. I object to Luxemburg's use of the term "natural economy" to describe an extant mode of production since it could lead to an unhelpful dichotomy for the purposes of this book.
289 Luxemburg, *The Accumulation of Capital*, 382.
290 White, *The Middle Ground*, xxi. In his study of the French incursions around the Great Lakes, the concept of "the middle ground" is as much about the combination of mutual misunderstandings and shared understandings as it is about the uneven-ness of the outcomes arising from these encounters (xiii). I reference the concept here to acknowledge that I share his view that such colonial encounters were not beset by annihilating violence but often involved more complex transformations and exchanges. Instead of attempting to explain these encounters as miscommunica-tions – using a "behavioral model for understanding human interaction" (see Susan Sleeper-Smith, "Introduction," *William and Mary Quarterly* 63, no. 1 [2006]: 4) – I focus on the legal and economic contexts of transformation. In the region and the era that I assess, I note not miscommunication but relative autonomy and inten-tional distortion.
291 Mamdani, *Citizen and Subject*, 40.
292 Mancke and Rupert's Land Research Centre, *A Company of Businessmen*, 55.
293 McCormack, *Fort Chipewyan and the Shaping of Canadian History*, 33.

294 Mamdani, *Citizen and Subject*, 38–39.
295 Marx, *Capital*, 2: 190.
296 Marx, *Capital*, 2: 190.
297 Ray, *Indians in the Fur Trade*, 78.
298 Quoted in Morantz, "'So Evil a Practice,'" 206.
299 Ray, *Indians in the Fur Trade*, 63.
300 Ray, *Indians in the Fur Trade*, 65.
301 Roxanne Dunbar-Ortiz, *An Indigenous Peoples' History of the United States* (2014; reprinted, Boston: Beacon Press, 2015), 79.
302 Benton, *Law and Colonial Cultures*, 17.
303 Mamdani, *Citizen and Subject*, 50.
304 Mamdani, *Citizen and Subject*, 11.
305 This followed French forays into the fur trade centuries earlier; see Berthelette, "New France and the Hudson Bay Watershed"; and Ray and Freeman, *"Give Us Good Measure,"* 23.
306 Brian Slattery, "The Royal Proclamation of 1763 and the Aboriginal Constitution," in *Keeping Promises: The Royal Proclamation of 1763, Aboriginal Rights, and Treaties in Canada*, ed. Jim Aldridge and Terry Fenge, McGill-Queen's Native and Northern Series 78 (Montreal and Kingston: McGill-Queen's University Press, 2015), 22.
307 Audra Simpson, *Mohawk Interruptus: Political Life across the Borders of Settler States* (Durham, NC: Duke University Press, 2014), 2.
308 Slattery, "The Royal Proclamation of 1763 and the Aboriginal Constitution," 22.

Chapter 2: Monopoly and Competition

1 Jodi A. Byrd, *The Transit of Empire: Indigenous Critiques of Colonialism* (Minneapolis: University of Minnesota Press, 2011), xxi.
2 Audra Simpson, *Mohawk Interruptus: Political Life across the Borders of Settler States* (Durham, NC: Duke University Press, 2014), 2.
3 Emma LaRocque, *When the Other Is Me: Native Resistance Discourse, 1850–1990* (Winnipeg: University of Manitoba Press, 2010), 22.
4 Jill Doerfler, "A Philosophy for Living: Ignatia Broker and Constitutional Reform among the White Earth Anishinaabeg," in *Centering Anishinaabeg Studies: Understanding the World through Stories*, ed. Jill Doerfler, Niigaanwewidam James Sinclair, and Heidi Kiiwetinepinesiik Stark, American Indian Studies Series (East Lansing: Michigan State University Press; Winnipeg: University of Manitoba Press, 2013), 176.
5 For example, Alexander Mackenzie, *Voyages from Montreal through the Continent of North America to the Frozen and Pacific Oceans in 1789 and 1793*, vol. 1 (New York: A.S. Barnes and Company, 1801); George Bryce, *The Remarkable History of the Hudson's Bay Company, Including That of the French Traders of North-Western Canada and of the North-West, XY, and Astor Fur Companies*, 3rd ed. (New York: Charles Scribner's Sons, 1910); and W.L. Morton, "The North West Company: Pedlars Extraordinary," *Minnesota History* 40, no. 4 (1966): 157–65.
6 Commercial value is the value of the item at the point of exchange with a commercial agent.
7 Wayne E. Stevens, "The Organization of the British Fur Trade, 1760–1800," *Mississippi Valley Historical Review* 3, no. 2 (1916): 176–77, https://doi.org/10.2307/1886434.
8 Stevens, "The Organization of the British Fur Trade," 177.
9 Stevens, "The Organization of the British Fur Trade," 180.
10 Stevens, "The Organization of the British Fur Trade," 181.
11 The louis, in both gold and silver coinage, was likely among "the first coins to appear in the colony in quantity." A.B. McCullough, *Money and Exchange in Canada to 1900* (Toronto: Dundurn, 1996), 30.

Notes to pages 54–58 213

12 Gordon Charles Davidson, *The North West Company* (Berkeley: University of California Press, 1918), 78.
13 Harold Adams Innis, *The Fur Trade in Canada: An Introduction to Canadian Economic History* (Toronto: University of Toronto Press, 1999), 178–79.
14 Innis, *The Fur Trade in Canada*, 185.
15 John D. Haeger, "Business Strategy and Practice in the Early Republic: John Jacob Astor and the American Fur Trade," *Western Historical Quarterly* 19, no. 2 (1988): 184.
16 Haeger, "Business Strategy and Practice in the Early Republic," 184–85.
17 Innis, *The Fur Trade in Canada*, 180.
18 Innis, *The Fur Trade in Canada*, 181.
19 Haeger, "Business Strategy and Practice in the Early Republic," 185.
20 Davidson, *The North West Company*, 29.
21 Innis, *The Fur Trade in Canada*, 182.
22 Innis, *The Fur Trade in Canada*, 228–29. Grand Portage, and later Fort William, were where the "wintering" partners resided.
23 Samuel Flagg Bemis, *Jay's Treaty: A Study in Commerce and Diplomacy* (New York: Macmillan, 1923), 10.
24 Bemis, *Jay's Treaty*, 16.
25 Bemis, *Jay's Treaty*, 18–19.
26 Bemis, *Jay's Treaty*, 165; Anthony Hall, *Earth into Property: Colonization, Decolonization, and Capitalism*, McGill-Queen's Native and Northern Series 62 (Montreal and Kingston: McGill-Queen's University Press, 2010), 284–85.
27 Roxanne Dunbar-Ortiz, *An Indigenous Peoples' History of the United States* (2014; reprinted, Boston: Beacon Press, 2015), 78, 79.
28 Colin G. Calloway, *The Indian World of George Washington: The First President, the First Americans, and the Birth of the Nation* (Oxford: Oxford University Press, 2018), 396.
29 Bemis, *Jay's Treaty*, 169.
30 Dunbar-Ortiz, *An Indigenous Peoples' History of the United States*, 82.
31 Calloway, *The Indian World of George Washington*, 391.
32 Davidson, *The North West Company*, 6–7.
33 Lisa Ford and P.G. McHugh, "Settler Sovereignty and the Shapeshifting Crown," in *Between Indigenous and Settler Governance*, ed. Lisa Ford and Tim Rowse (London: Routledge, 2012), 25.
34 Bemis, *Jay's Treaty*, 189.
35 Dunbar-Ortiz, *An Indigenous Peoples' History of the United States*, 82–83.
36 "A Century of Lawmaking for a New Nation: U.S. Congressional Documents and Debates, 1774–1875 – Execution of British Treaty," Library of Congress 1796, 971, http://memory.loc.gov/cgi-bin/ampage?collId=llac&fileName=005/llac005.db&recNum=481.
37 Lawrence B.A. Hatter, "The Jay Charter: Rethinking the American National State in the West, 1796–1819," *Diplomatic History* 37, no. 4 (2013): 693.
38 "A Century of Lawmaking for a New Nation: U.S. Congressional Documents and Debates, 1774–1875 – Treaty with Great Britain, 1794," Library of Congress, 1794, 117, http://memory.loc.gov/cgi-bin/ampage?collId=llsl&fileName=008/llsl008.db&recNum=130.
39 Hatter, "The Jay Charter," 695–96.
40 Innis, *The Fur Trade in Canada*, 179–80.
41 Davidson, *The North West Company*, 15.
42 W.L. Morton, "The North West Company: Pedlars Extraordinary," *Minnesota History* 40, no. 4 (1966): 157.

214 Notes to pages 58–60

43 Morton, "The North West Company," 158.
44 Bryce, *The Remarkable History of the Hudson's Bay Company*, 112.
45 Bryce, *The Remarkable History of the Hudson's Bay Company*, 113.
46 Jennifer S.H. Brown, *Strangers in Blood: Fur Trade Company Families in Indian Country*, Canadian Electronic Library (Vancouver: UBC Press, 1980), 35.
47 Brown, *Strangers in Blood*, 36, 38.
48 Bryce, *The Remarkable History of the Hudson's Bay Company*, 117–20.
49 Davidson, *The North West Company*, 77.
50 Thomas Douglas Selkirk, *A Sketch of the British Fur Trade in North America with Observations Relative to the North-West Company of Montreal* (London: Printed for James Ridgway, 1816), 86; Innis, *The Fur Trade in Canada*, 237.
51 Innis, *The Fur Trade in Canada*, 232–33.
52 Bryce, *The Remarkable History of the Hudson's Bay Company*, 122.
53 Innis, *The Fur Trade in Canada*, 206, 210–11.
54 Karl Marx, *Capital: A Critique of Political Economy*, trans. Ben Fowkes, vol. 1 (New York: Vintage Books, 1977), 741.
55 Sylvia Van Kirk, *Many Tender Ties: Women in Fur-Trade Society, 1670–1870* (Winnipeg: Watson and Dwyer, 1996), 22.
56 Jean Barman, *French Canadians, Furs, and Indigenous Women in the Making of the Pacific Northwest* (Vancouver: UBC Press, 2014), 59–60; Morton, "The North West Company," 162.
57 Scott Berthelette, "New France and the Hudson Bay Watershed: Transatlantic Networks, Backcountry Specialists, and French Imperial Projects in Post-Utrecht North America, 1713–29," *Canadian Historical Review* 101, no. 1 (2019): 19–20; Innis, *The Fur Trade in Canada*, 167.
58 Morton, "The North West Company," 158. This is a point buttressed by more recent scholarship; see Scott P. Stephen, *Masters and Servants: The Hudson's Bay Company and Its North American Workforce, 1668–1786* (Edmonton: University of Alberta Press, 2019), 171; and Berthelette, "New France and the Hudson Bay Watershed," 4.
59 Carolyn Podruchny, "Unfair Masters and Rascally Servants? Labour Relations among Bourgeois, Clerks and Voyageurs in the Montreal Fur Trade, 1780–1821," *Labour/Le travail* 43 (1999): 48.
60 Kirk, *Many Tender Ties*, 22.
61 Stephen, *Masters and Servants*, 225.
62 Kirk, *Many Tender Ties*, 23.
63 "The Royal Charter," HBC History Foundation, http://www.hbcheritage.ca/things/artifacts/the-royal-charter.
64 Innis, *The Fur Trade in Canada*, 239.
65 Podruchny, "Unfair Masters and Rascally Servants?," 44.
66 Carolyn Podruchny, *Making the Voyageur World: Travelers and Traders in the North American Fur Trade* (Lincoln: University of Nebraska Press, 2006), 6.
67 Podruchny, "Unfair Masters and Rascally Servants?," 47. Allan Greer asks a comparable question regarding the increasing "ratcheting up of feudal exactions" from the habitants of the previous century: "Why did the habitant tolerate these escalating exactions?" Similar to Podruchny, Greer traces the vulnerability of this group to their illiteracy and relative disempowerment in the face of formal legal levers, but he also emphasizes that they "sometimes openly refused excessive charges and, more commonly, they evaded, avoided and delayed payment." See Allan Greer, *Property and Dispossession: Natives, Empires and Land in Early Modern North America* (Cambridge: Cambridge University Press, 2018), 174–75.

68 Podruchny, "Unfair Masters and Rascally Servants?," 51.
69 Edith I. Burley, *Servants of the Honourable Company: Work, Discipline, and Conflict in the Hudson's Bay Company, 1770–1879* (Toronto: Oxford University Press, 1997), 29.
70 Podruchny, "Unfair Masters and Rascally Servants?," 49.
71 Podruchny, "Unfair Masters and Rascally Servants?," 52.
72 Podruchny, "Unfair Masters and Rascally Servants?," 52–53.
73 Podruchny, "Unfair Masters and Rascally Servants?," 65.
74 Innis, *The Fur Trade in Canada*, 186–87.
75 Hatter, "The Jay Charter," 708.
76 Innis, *The Fur Trade in Canada*, 259; Podruchny, "Unfair Masters and Rascally Servants?," 67.
77 Davidson, *The North West Company*, 81.
78 Podruchny, "Unfair Masters and Rascally Servants?," 67.
79 Podruchny, "Unfair Masters and Rascally Servants?," 67.
80 Hiram Martin Chittenden, *The American Fur Trade of the Far West*, vol. 1 (Lincoln: University of Nebraska Press, 1986), 83.
81 Innis, *The Fur Trade in Canada*, 190, 228n192.
82 Donald B. Freeman and Frances L. Dungey, "A Spatial Duopoly: Competition in the Western Canadian Fur Trade, 1770–1835," *Journal of Historical Geography* 7, no. 3 (1981): 263–64.
83 Davidson, *The North West Company*, 69.
84 Wayne Moodie, "The Trading Post Settlement of the Canadian Northwest, 1774–1821," *Journal of Historical Geography* 13, no. 4 (1987): 367.
85 Innis, *The Fur Trade in Canada*, 201.
86 Bryce, *The Remarkable History of the Hudson's Bay Company*, 129.
87 Hudson's Bay Company, *HBC History Foundation – The Country of Adventurers: Dr. John Rae Narrated by Les Stroud*, 2015, https://www.youtube.com/watch?v=n-b_MaltYD4; Hudson's Bay Company, *HBC History Foundation – The Country of Adventurers: David Thompson Narrated by Rick Hansen*, 2015, https://www.youtube.com/watch?v=m_vzybpOiIM. See Barman, *French Canadians, Furs, and Indigenous Women*, 24–29, for an account of the French Canadians' role in Mackenzie's expeditions.
88 This erasure is even more widespread when it comes to records and recollections of and by Indigenous women; see Barman, *French Canadians, Furs, and Indigenous Women*, 116.
89 Davidson, *The North West Company*, 65.
90 Davidson, *The North West Company*, 58.
91 Davidson, *The North West Company*, 66.
92 Innis, *The Fur Trade in Canada*, 202.
93 Innis, *The Fur Trade in Canada*, 203.
94 Innis, *The Fur Trade in Canada*, 202.
95 Janna Promislow, "'It Would Only Be Just': A Study of Territoriality and Trading Posts along the Mackenzie River 1800–27," in *Between Indigenous and Settler Governance*, ed. Lisa Ford and Tim Rowse (London: Routledge, 2012), 35–36.
96 Bryce, *The Remarkable History of the Hudson's Bay Company*, 187.
97 Morton, "The North West Company," 159.
98 Ellen Meiksins Wood, *The Origin of Capitalism: A Longer View*, rev. ed. (London: Verso, 2002), 110.
99 Morton, "The North West Company," 161–62.
100 Marx, *Capital*, 1: 672.
101 Hudson's Bay Company, *HBC History Foundation – The Country of Adventurers: Dr. John Rae Narrated by Les Stroud*, 2015, https://www.youtube.com/watch?v=n-b_MaltYD4;

216 *Notes to pages 64–67*

Hudson's Bay Company, *HBC History Foundation – The Country of Adventurers: David Thompson Narrated by Rick Hansen*, 2015, https://www.youtube.com/watch?v=m_vzybpOiIM.

102 Davidson, *The North West Company*, 67.

103 Innis, *The Fur Trade in Canada*, 258–59.

104 Innis, *The Fur Trade in Canada*, 263.

105 Moodie, "The Trading Post Settlement of the Canadian Northwest," 369. More freemen also resulted from this consolidation.

106 Duncan M'Gillivray, *The Journal of Duncan M'Gillivray of the North West Company at Fort George on the Saskatchewan, 1794–5* (Toronto: Macmillan, 1929), 14. This quotation was sourced by Arthur S. Morton from McGillivray's essay, written shortly before his death in 1808, titled "Some Account of the Trade Carried on by the North West Company." Additions and edits were made by William McGillivray, who retitled it "Sketch of the Fur Trade, 1809." A subsequent revision to and an anonymous publication of the essay appeared in 1811, this time as "On the Origin and Progress of the North-West Company of Canada." In their biographical entry on Duncan McGillivray, Sylvia Van Kirk and Jennifer Brown suggest that this 1811 publication was likely the work of John Henry, though sometimes it is attributed to Nathaniel Atcheson. See Nathaniel Atcheson [attributed] and John Henry [attributed], *On the Origin and Progress of the North-West Company of Canada*, CIHM/ICMH Digital Series – CIHM/ICMH Collection Numérisée No. 27875 (London: Printed by Cox, Son and Baylis, 1811), http://www.library.yorku.ca/e/resolver/id/2012672; and Sylvia Van Kirk and Jennifer S.H. Brown, "McGillivray, Duncan (1770–1808)," in *Dictionary of Canadian Biography*, vol. 5 (Toronto: University of Toronto; Laval: Université Laval, 1983), http://www.biographi.ca/en/bio/mcgillivray_duncan_5E.html. However, the specific quotation with reference to Duncan McGillivray does not appear in the 1811 publication, though the former statement complements the views expressed in the latter.

107 Marx, *Capital*, 1: 739.

108 Elizabeth Mancke and Rupert's Land Research Centre, *A Company of Businessmen: The Hudson's Bay Company and Long-Distance Trade, 1670–1730* (Winnipeg: Rupert's Land Research Centre, 1988), 67, 55.

109 Mancke and Rupert's Land Research Centre, *A Company of Businessmen*, 80.

110 Mancke and Rupert's Land Research Centre, *A Company of Businessmen*, 68.

111 Ann M. Carlos and Elizabeth Hoffman, "The North American Fur Trade: Bargaining to a Joint Profit Maximum under Incomplete Information, 1804–1821," *Journal of Economic History* 46, no. 4 (1986): 968.

112 Carlos and Hoffman, "The North American Fur Trade," 969.

113 Marx, *Capital*, 1: 739.

114 John Smail, "Credit, Risk, and Honor in Eighteenth-Century Commerce," *Journal of British Studies* 44, no. 3 (2005): 446.

115 Karl Marx, *Capital*, vol. 3, trans. David Fernbach (London: Penguin Classics, 2006), 428.

116 Douglas MacKay, *The Honourable Company: A History of the Hudson's Bay Company* (Indianapolis: Bobbs-Merrill, 1936), iii.

117 Morton, "The North West Company," 163.

118 George Colpitts, *Pemmican Empire: Food, Trade, and the Last Bison Hunts in the North American Plains, 1780–1882* (Cambridge: Cambridge University Press, 2014); Van Kirk, "The Role of Native Women in the Fur Trade Society of Western Canada."

119 James Daschuk, *Clearing the Plains: Disease, Politics of Starvation, and the Loss of Aboriginal Life* (Regina: University of Regina Press, 2013), 31.

120 Beavers in particular, but other game such as martens, were in decline by the late eighteenth century; see Richard S. Mackie, *Trading beyond the Mountains: The British Fur Trade on the Pacific, 1793-1843* (Vancouver: UBC Press, 2011), 245; and Ann Carlos, "The Birth and Death of Predatory Competition in the North American Fur Trade: 1810-1821," *Explorations in Economic History* 19, no. 2 (1982): 166. Carlos in particular underscores competition between the rival companies as a contributing factor.

121 Ray, *Indians in the Fur Trade,* 140.

122 Ray, *Indians in the Fur Trade,* 141.

123 Rosa Luxemburg, *The Accumulation of Capital,* 2nd ed. (London: Routledge, 2003), 351.

124 Heidi Kiiwetinepinesiik Stark and Gina Starblanket, "Towards a Relational Paradigm – Four Points for Consideration: Knowledge, Gender, Land, and Modernity," in *Resurgence and Reconciliation: Indigenous-Settler Relations and Earth Teachings,* ed. Michael I. Asch, John Borrows, and James Tully (Toronto: University of Toronto Press, 2018), 191.

125 Toby Morantz, "'So Evil a Practice': A Look at the Debt System in the James Bay Fur Trade," in *Merchant Credit and Labour Strategies in Historical Perspective,* ed. Rosemary E. Ommer (Fredericton: Acadiensis Press, 1990), 208.

126 Morantz, "'So Evil a Practice,'" 208-9.

127 Morantz, "'So Evil a Practice,'" 207.

128 Morantz, "'So Evil a Practice,'" 206.

129 Morantz, "'So Evil a Practice,'" 221.

130 Morantz, "'So Evil a Practice,'" 221.

131 Ray, *Indians in the Fur Trade.*

132 In 1795, the factor that replaced McKay at Brandon House, Robert Godwin, reported that there were "upwards of 20 Houses on this river only"; see Robert Godwin, "1794-1795: 5 January 1795," Archives of Manitoba, Brandon House Post Journal, 12.

133 Donald McKay, "1793-1794: 22 December 1793," Archives of Manitoba, Brandon House Post Journal, 14.

134 Donald McKay, "1793-1794: 22 March 1794," Archives of Manitoba, Brandon House Post Journal, 22.

135 Laura L. Peers, *The Ojibwa of Western Canada, 1780 to 1870* (Winnipeg: University of Manitoba Press, 1984), 76.

136 Peers, *The Ojibwa of Western Canada,* 77.

137 Karl Marx, *Capital: A Critique of Political Economy,* trans. Ben Fowkes, vol. 1 (New York: Vintage Books, 1977), 876.

138 Daniel Francis and Toby Elaine Morantz, *Partners in Furs: A History of the Fur Trade in Eastern James Bay, 1600-1870* (Montreal and Kingston: McGill-Queen's University Press, 1983), 167, 169.

139 Nicole St-Onge highlights the terms of labour agreed to in contractual form by Kahnawake Mohawks, some of whom were offered money (livre from Lower Canada), as well as clothing and a firearm, as part of the terms of their employment. In other words, the labour of some Indigenous peoples was done for money, but such agreements were not widespread and tended to be offered for more specialized tasks. See Nicole St-Onge, "'He Was neither a Soldier nor a Slave: He Was under the Control of No Man': Kahnawake Mohawks in the Northwest Fur Trade, 1790-1850," *Canadian Journal of History* 51, no. 1 (2016): 6. Specifically, when the fur trade company rivalries were intensifying, St-Onge notes, there was an increase in the number of contracts issued to Mohawks, many of whom were recruited because they were "aggressive and fast" (10-11). See also Jean Barman, *Iroquois in the West,* McGill-Queen's Native and Northern Series 93 (Montreal and Kingston: McGill-Queen's University Press, 2019), 29-30.

218 *Notes to pages 69–72*

140 Ray, "Periodic Shortages, Native Welfare, and the Hudson's Bay Company," 4.
141 For an account of the role of honour in the master-officer relationship within the HBC hierarchy, see Stephen, *Masters and Servants*, 249.
142 Morantz, "'So Evil a Practice,'" 205.
143 As HBC trade activity moved inland more contact with producers (trappers and hunters alike) meant that there was less reliance on trade captains, and the debt obligation could be established more directly.
144 Arthur J. Ray, "The Decline of Paternalism in the Hudson's Bay Company Fur Trade, 1870–1945," in *Merchant Credit and Labour Strategies in Historical Perspective*, ed. Rosemary E. Ommer (Fredericton: Acadiensis Press, 1990), 189.
145 Smail, "Credit, Risk, and Honor in Eighteenth-Century Commerce," 439.
146 Freeman and Dungey, "A Spatial Duopoly," 264.
147 Jeffery Taylor, "Capitalist Development, Forms of Labour, and Class Formation in Prairie Canada," in *The West and Beyond: New Perspectives on an Imagined Region*, ed. Sarah Carter, Alvin Finkel, and Peter Fortna (Edmonton: Athabasca University Press, 2010), 169.
148 Daschuk, *Clearing the Plains*, 31.
149 John Milloy, "'Our Country': The Significance of the Buffalo Resource for a Plains Cree Sense of Territory," in *Aboriginal Resource Use in Canada: Historical and Legal Aspects*, ed. Kerry Abel and Jean Friesen, Manitoba Studies in Native History 6 (Winnipeg: University of Manitoba Press, 1991), 55.
150 Innis, *The Fur Trade in Canada*, 235.
151 Daschuk, *Clearing the Plains*, 31.
152 A.A. den Otter, *Civilizing the Wilderness: Culture and Nature in Pre-Confederation Canada and Rupert's Land* (Edmonton: University of Alberta Press, 2012), 188.
153 Donald McKay, "1793–1794: 23 April 1794," Archives of Manitoba, Brandon House Post Journal, 24.
154 Donald McKay, "1793–1794: 12 March 1794," Archives of Manitoba, Brandon House Post Journal, 20.
155 This diffuse web of obligations fuelled worries about productivity, addressed through sumptuary discipline when debt-based discipline fell short. Alcohol consumption became a concern, and some company traders attempted to curtail it at various points by refusing to trade in spirits. See den Otter, *Civilizing the Wilderness*, 45.
156 David Smyth, "The Niitsitapi Trade: Euroamericans and the Blackfoot-Speaking Peoples, to the Mid-1830s" (PhD diss., Carleton University, 2001), 169.
157 Donald McKay, "1793–1794: 7 February 1794," Archives of Manitoba, Brandon House Post Journal, 18.
158 Donald McKay, "1793–1794: 26 February 1794," Archives of Manitoba, Brandon House Post Journal, 19.
159 Peers, *The Ojibwa of Western Canada*, 73.
160 Daschuk, *Clearing the Plains*, 27; Michel Hogue, *Metis and the Medicine Line: Creating a Border and Dividing a People* (Chapel Hill: University of North Carolina Press, 2015), 19.
161 Smyth, "The Niitsitapi Trade," 170.
162 Daschuk, *Clearing the Plains*, 51.
163 Daschuk, *Clearing the Plains*, 50, 53.
164 Dale R. Russell, *Eighteenth Century Western Cree and Their Neighbours* (Hull, QC: Canadian Museum of Civilization, 1991), 217; Smyth, "The Niitsitapi Trade," 171.
165 John L. Tobias, "Protection, Civilization, Assimilation: An Outline History of Canada's Indian Policy," in *As Long as the Sun Shines and Water Flows: A Reader in Canadian Native Studies*, ed. Ian A.L. Getty and Antoine S. Lussier, Nakoda Institute Occasional Paper 1 (Vancouver: UBC Press, 1983), 40.

Chapter 3: Honour and Duplicity

1 Robert C.H. Sweeny, "Understanding Work Historically: A Reflection Prompted by Two Recent Studies of the Fur Trade," *Labour/Le travail* 41 (1998): 245.

2 John S. Galbraith, *Hudson's Bay Company, 1821–1869* (Berkeley: University of California Press, 1957), 119.

3 Glyndwr Williams, "The Hudson's Bay Company and Its Critics in the Eighteenth Century," *Transactions of the Royal Historical Society* 20 (1970): 150.

4 H.A. Innis, "Significant Factors in Canadian Economic Development," *Canadian Historical Review* 18, no. 4 (1937): 377.

5 Ann Carlos, "The Causes and Origins of the North American Fur Trade Rivalry: 1804–1810," *Journal of Economic History* 41, no. 4 (1981): 786.

6 Carlos, "The Causes and Origins of the North American Fur Trade Rivalry," 782–83.

7 Carlos, "The Causes and Origins of the North American Fur Trade Rivalry," 784–85.

8 Ann Carlos, "The Birth and Death of Predatory Competition in the North American Fur Trade: 1810–1821," *Explorations in Economic History* 19, no. 2 (1982): 166.

9 Arthur J. Ray, *Indians in the Fur Trade: Their Role as Trappers, Hunters, and Middlemen in the Lands Southwest of Hudson Bay, 1660–1870*, 2nd ed., ACLS Humanities E-Book (Toronto: University of Toronto Press, 1998), 117.

10 The scarcity of resources and accompanying displacement made for new alliances with company officials, providing commercial operators with some opportunity to exercise greater control over the people, land, and resource. However, this does not portend the erasure of Indigenous peoples' autonomy.

11 James Daschuk, *Clearing the Plains: Disease, Politics of Starvation, and the Loss of Aboriginal Life* (Regina: University of Regina Press, 2013), xi.

12 J.M. Bumsted, "Douglas, Thomas, Fifth Earl of Selkirk (1771–1820)," in *The Oxford Dictionary of National Biography*, ed. H.C.G. Matthew, B. Harrison, and David Cannadine (Oxford: Oxford University Press, 2004), 11, http://www.oxforddnb.com/view/article/7920.

13 Lauren Benton, *Law and Colonial Cultures: Legal Regimes in World History, 1400–1900* (Cambridge: Cambridge University Press, 2002), 13.

14 Paul C. Nigol, "Discipline and Discretion in the Mid-Eighteenth-Century Hudson's Bay Company Private Justice System," in *Laws and Societies in the Canadian Prairie West, 1670–1940*, ed. Louis A. Knafla and Jonathan Swainger (Vancouver: UBC Press, 2005), 152–53. For more on the measures that the HBC committee went to in an attempt to curb private trade in the late eighteenth century, see Scott P. Stephen, *Masters and Servants: The Hudson's Bay Company and Its North American Workforce, 1668–1786* (Edmonton: University of Alberta Press, 2019), 290–91.

15 Nigol, "Discipline and Discretion," 159.

16 Nigol, "Discipline and Discretion," 154.

17 Russell Smandych, "Colonialism, Settler Colonialism, and Law: Settler Revolutions and the Dispossession of Indigenous Peoples through Law in the Long Nineteenth Century," *Settler Colonial Studies* 3, no. 1 (2013): 90.

18 Hamar Foster, "Long-Distance Justice: The Criminal Jurisdiction of Canadian Courts West of the Canadas, 1763–1859," *American Journal of Legal History* 34, no. 1 (1990): 7.

19 Foster, "Long-Distance Justice," 7.

20 Foster, "Long-Distance Justice," 8.

21 Foster, "Long-Distance Justice," 8.

22 Foster, "Long-Distance Justice," 10.

23 Dale Brawn, *The Court of Queen's Bench of Manitoba, 1870–1950: A Biographical History* (Toronto: University of Toronto Press, 2006), 9.

24 Brawn, *The Court of Queen's Bench of Manitoba*, 9.

220 Notes to pages 75–78

25 Brawn, *The Court of Queen's Bench of Manitoba*, 10.
26 Duncan M'Gillivray, *The Journal of Duncan M'Gillivray of the North West Company at Fort George on the Saskatchewan, 1794–5* (Toronto: Macmillan, 1929), 21.
27 Thomas Douglas Selkirk, *A Sketch of the British Fur Trade in North America with Observations Relative to the North-West Company of Montreal* (London: Printed for James Ridgway, 1816), 56.
28 Selkirk, *A Sketch of the British Fur Trade*, 57–58.
29 Selkirk, *A Sketch of the British Fur Trade*, 58.
30 Carolyn Podruchny, "Unfair Masters and Rascally Servants? Labour Relations among Bourgeois, Clerks and Voyageurs in the Montreal Fur Trade, 1780–1821," *Labour/Le travail* 43 (1999): 52.
31 Lloyd Keith, *North of Athabasca: Slave Lake and Mackenzie River Documents of the North West Company, 1800–1821*, Rupert's Land Record Society Series (Montreal and Kingston: McGill-Queen's University Press, 2001), 38.
32 Keith, *North of Athabasca*, 37.
33 Keith, *North of Athabasca*, 37. Keith offers a few caveats regarding this incident. Although there is evidence of the murder, historical records suggest a lingering confusion between the names McDonald and McDonell. Keith cross-referenced depositions given to the Court of King's Bench at Montreal in March 1807 with other journal entries of the era and surmised that it was McDonald and not McDonell.
34 Wayne Moodie, "The Trading Post Settlement of the Canadian Northwest, 1774–1821," *Journal of Historical Geography* 13, no. 4 (1987): 368.
35 Keith, *North of Athabasca*, 29.
36 Keith, *North of Athabasca*, 28.
37 Keith, *North of Athabasca*, 30.
38 Jennifer S.H. Brown, "Rupert's Land, Nituskeenan, Our Land: Cree and English Naming and Claiming around the Dirty Sea," in *New Histories for Old: Changing Perspectives on Canada's Native Pasts*, ed. Theodore Binnema and Susan Neylan (Vancouver: UBC Press, 2007), 20.
39 Hamar Foster, "Law and Necessity in Western Rupert's Land and Beyond, 1670–1870," in *Laws and Societies in the Canadian Prairie West, 1670–1940*, ed. Louis A. Knafla and Jonathan Swainger (Vancouver: UBC Press, 2005), 73.
40 Foster, "Law and Necessity in Western Rupert's Land and Beyond," 74.
41 Gordon Charles Davidson, *The North West Company* (Berkeley: University of California Press, 1918), 79.
42 Scott Stephen, "The Fork in the Road: Red River, Retrenchment and the Struggle for the Future of the Hudson's Bay Company," *Manitoba History* 71 (2013): 41.
43 Davidson, *The North West Company*, 85.
44 Stephen, "The Fork in the Road," 40.
45 Ann M. Carlos and Elizabeth Hoffman, "The North American Fur Trade: Bargaining to a Joint Profit Maximum under Incomplete Information, 1804–1821," *Journal of Economic History* 46, no. 4 (1986): 972–73.
46 Carlos, "The Causes and Origins of the North American Fur Trade Rivalry," 781.
47 Carlos and Hoffman, "The North American Fur Trade," 972–73.
48 George Bryce, *The Remarkable History of the Hudson's Bay Company, Including That of the French Traders of North-Western Canada and of the North-West, XY, and Astor Fur Companies*, 3rd ed. (New York: Charles Scribner's Sons, 1910), 88.
49 Harold Adams Innis, *The Fur Trade in Canada: An Introduction to Canadian Economic History* (Toronto: University of Toronto Press, 1999), 241.
50 Podruchny, "Unfair Masters and Rascally Servants?," 59.

Notes to pages 78–81   221

51 Podruchny, "Unfair Masters and Rascally Servants?," 62.
52 Podruchny, "Unfair Masters and Rascally Servants?," 62.
53 Carlos, "The Causes and Origins of the North American Fur Trade Rivalry," 778.
54 Carlos, "The Causes and Origins of the North American Fur Trade Rivalry," 779–80.
55 M'Gillivray, *The Journal of Duncan M'Gillivray*, 21.
56 Nathaniel Atcheson [attributed] and John Henry [attributed], *On the Origin and Progress of the North-West Company of Canada*, CIHM/ICMH Digital Series – CIHM/ICMH Collection Numérisée No. 27875 (London: Printed by Cox, Son and Baylis, 1811), 21, http://www.library.yorku.ca/e/resolver/id/2012672.
57 Selkirk, *A Sketch of the British Fur Trade*, 68.
58 Selkirk, *A Sketch of the British Fur Trade*, 68.
59 Selkirk, *A Sketch of the British Fur Trade*, 69.
60 Selkirk, *A Sketch of the British Fur Trade*, 70–71.
61 Keith, *North of Athabasca*, 99n47.
62 Jean Morrison, "McKenzie, James (c. 1777–1849)," in *Dictionary of Canadian Biography*, vol. 7 (Toronto: University of Toronto; Laval: Université Laval, 1988), http://www.biographi.ca/en/bio/mckenzie_james_1849_7E.html.
63 Keith, *North of Athabasca*, 99n47.
64 Morrison, "McKenzie, James."
65 Davidson, *The North West Company*, 225.
66 Selkirk, *A Sketch of the British Fur Trade*, 50.
67 Selkirk, *A Sketch of the British Fur Trade*, 73. Selkirk states 1809, whereas Robert Allen suggests that this started in 1810; Robert S. Allen, "Fidler, Peter (1769–1821)," in *Dictionary of Canadian Biography*, vol. 6 (Toronto: University of Toronto; Laval: Université Laval, 1987), http://www.biographi.ca/en/bio/fidler_peter_6E.html.
68 Selkirk, *A Sketch of the British Fur Trade*, 75. As additional context, that Selkirk focused so much on this particular member of the company was important to the narrative that he attempted to construct at the time, since in 1816 Fidler was at the centre of the events at Seven Oaks, one of the gravest clashes between the Hudson's Bay Company and the North West Company, which resulted in over twenty deaths.
69 Edith I. Burley, *Servants of the Honourable Company: Work, Discipline, and Conflict in the Hudson's Bay Company, 1770–1879* (Toronto: Oxford University Press, 1997), 35.
70 Burley, *Servants of the Honourable Company*, 35.
71 Selkirk, *A Sketch of the British Fur Trade*, 93–94.
72 Selkirk, *A Sketch of the British Fur Trade*, 94.
73 Selkirk, *A Sketch of the British Fur Trade*, 96.
74 Selkirk, *A Sketch of the British Fur Trade*, 97–99.
75 Selkirk, *A Sketch of the British Fur Trade*, 99.
76 Selkirk, *A Sketch of the British Fur Trade*, 102.
77 Selkirk, *A Sketch of the British Fur Trade*, 103.
78 Foster, "Long-Distance Justice," 22.
79 Foster, "Long-Distance Justice," 22.
80 Frank Tough, "From the 'Original Affluent Society' to the 'Unjust Society': A Review Essay on Native Economic History in Canada," *Journal of Aboriginal Economic Development* 4, no. 2 (2005): 37.
81 Heidi Kiiwetinepinesiik Stark and Gina Starblanket, "Towards a Relational Paradigm – Four Points for Consideration: Knowledge, Gender, Land, and Modernity," in *Resurgence and Reconciliation: Indigenous-Settler Relations and Earth Teachings*, ed. Michael I. Asch, John Borrows, and James Tully (Toronto: University of Toronto Press, 2018), 191.

222 Notes to pages 82–86

82 Carlos, "The Causes and Origins of the North American Fur Trade Rivalry," 778.
83 Carlos, "The Causes and Origins of the North American Fur Trade Rivalry," 779.
84 Laura L. Peers, *The Ojibwa of Western Canada, 1780 to 1870* (Winnipeg: University of Manitoba Press, 1984), 66.
85 John Milloy, "'Our Country': The Significance of the Buffalo Resource for a Plains Cree Sense of Territory," in *Aboriginal Resource Use in Canada: Historical and Legal Aspects*, ed. Kerry Abel and Jean Friesen, Manitoba Studies in Native History 6 (Winnipeg: University of Manitoba Press, 1991), 66.
86 Robert Alexander Innes, "Challenging a Racist Fiction: A Closer Look at Métis–First Nations Relations," in *A People and a Nation: New Directions in Contemporary Métis Studies*, ed. Chris Andersen and Jennifer Adese (Vancouver: UBC Press, 2021), 95, 97.
87 Burley, *Servants of the Honourable Company*, 34.
88 Deidre Simmons, *Keepers of the Record: The History of the Hudson's Bay Company Archives* (Montreal and Kingston: McGill-Queen's University Press, 2007), 92.
89 Barry Kaye, "The Red River Settlement: Lord Selkirk's Isolated Colony in the Wilderness," in *The Early Northwest*, ed. Gregory P. Marchildon (Regina: University of Regina Press, 2008), 219.
90 Gary Spraakman, *Management Accounting at the Hudson's Bay Company: From Quill Pen to Digitization* (Bingley, UK: Emerald Group Publishing, 2015), 41.
91 Karl Marx, *Capital*, vol. 2 (New York: Penguin Group US, 1993), 329.
92 Spraakman, *Management Accounting at the Hudson's Bay Company*, 41.
93 Simmons, *Keepers of the Record*, 92, 94.
94 Burley, *Servants of the Honourable Company*, 43.
95 Burley, *Servants of the Honourable Company*, 43.
96 Burley, *Servants of the Honourable Company*, 45.
97 Simmons, *Keepers of the Record*, 94.
98 Burley, *Servants of the Honourable Company*, 36.
99 Simmons, *Keepers of the Record*, 94.
100 Burley, *Servants of the Honourable Company*, 40.
101 Burley, *Servants of the Honourable Company*, 35–36.
102 Burley, *Servants of the Honourable Company*, 40.
103 J.E. Foster, "Auld, William (c. 1770–c. 1830)," in *Dictionary of Canadian Biography*, vol. 6 (Toronto: University of Toronto; Laval: Université Laval, 1987), http://www.biographi.ca/en/bio/auld_william_6E.html.
104 Peers, *The Ojibwa of Western Canada*, 66.
105 Burley, *Servants of the Honourable Company*, 41.
106 Nigol, "Discipline and Discretion," 155.
107 Burley, *Servants of the Honourable Company*, 41.
108 Burley, *Servants of the Honourable Company*, 5.
109 Paul McHugh, *Aboriginal Societies and the Common Law: A History of Sovereignty, Status, and Self-Determination* (Oxford: Oxford University Press, 2004), 108, 104.
110 McHugh, *Aboriginal Societies and the Common Law*, 110.
111 It is in this sense that Mamdani's observation about "decentralized despotism" applies to this study; see Mahmood Mamdani, *Citizen and Subject: Contemporary Africa and the Legacy of Late Colonialism* (Princeton, NJ: Princeton University Press, 1996), 23. As I show in the pages ahead, the strategies of control (originating from the British Parliament or the HBC committee) had increasingly despotic aims, yet for a period of time, the execution of these strategies was decentralized in ways that reflect the specific processes of transformation underway around the Red River site.

Notes to pages 86–90   223

112 Hudson's Bay Company. *The Royal Charter for Incorporating the Hudson's Bay Company: Granted by His Majesty King Charles the Second, in the Twenty-Second Year of His Reign,* A.D. 1670 (London: H.K. Causton, 1865), 14.
113 Hudson's Bay Company. *The Royal Charter,* 15.
114 Hudson's Bay Company. *The Royal Charter,* 22.
115 Karl Marx, *Capital: A Critique of Political Economy,* trans. Ben Fowkes, vol. 1 (New York: Vintage Books, 1977), 918.
116 Arthur Dobbs, *An Account of the Countries Adjoining to Hudson's Bay, in the North-West Part of America* (London: J. Robinson, 1744), ii, http://archive.org/details/cihm_35075.
117 Dobbs, *An Account of the Countries Adjoining to Hudson's Bay,* 57.
118 Dobbs, *An Account of the Countries Adjoining to Hudson's Bay,* 168.
119 Dobbs, *An Account of the Countries Adjoining to Hudson's Bay,* 58.
120 Dobbs, *An Account of the Countries Adjoining to Hudson's Bay,* 168.
121 Jennifer S.H. Brown, *Strangers in Blood: Fur Trade Company Families in Indian Country* (Vancouver: UBC Press, 1996), xi.
122 Brown, *Strangers in Blood,* xi.
123 Brown, *Strangers in Blood,* 6.
124 Nicholas Rogers, "From Vernon to Wolfe: Empire and Identity in the British Atlantic World of the Mid-Eighteenth Century," in *The Culture of the Seven Years' War: Empire, Identity, and the Arts in the Eighteenth-Century Atlantic World,* ed. Frans De Bruyn and Shaun Regan (Toronto: University of Toronto Press, 2014), 42.
125 Smandych, "Colonialism, Settler Colonialism, and Law," 92.
126 Marx, *Capital,* 1: 423.
127 Karl Marx and Friedrich Engels, *Collected Works of Marx and Engels – Engels: Anti-Dühring; Dialectics of Nature,* vol. 25 (New York: International Publishers, 1987), 117.
128 Mahmood Mamdani, *Citizen and Subject: Contemporary Africa and the Legacy of Late Colonialism* (Princeton, NJ: Princeton University Press, 1996), 23.
129 Mamdani, *Citizen and Subject,* 73.
130 Mamdani, *Citizen and Subject,* 17.
131 J.M. Bumsted, "Editorial Introduction," in *The Collected Writings of Lord Selkirk 1799–1809,* ed. J.M. Bumsted (Winnipeg: Manitoba Record Society, 1984), 2.
132 Bumsted, "Editorial Introduction" (1984), 3.
133 Bumsted, "Douglas, Thomas, Fifth Earl of Selkirk."
134 George E. Carter, "Lord Selkirk and the Red River Colony," *Montana: The Magazine of Western History* 18, no. 1 (1968): 61; Eric Richards, *Debating the Highland Clearances,* Debates and Documents in Scottish History (Edinburgh: Edinburgh University Press, 2007), 39.
135 Bumsted, "Editorial Introduction" (1984), 2.
136 Bumsted, "Douglas, Thomas, Fifth Earl of Selkirk."
137 Bumsted, "Editorial Introduction" (1984), 23–25.
138 Richards, *Debating the Highland Clearances,* 36; Thomas Douglas Selkirk, "Lord Selkirk's Advertisement and Prospectus of the New Colony," in *A Narrative of Occurrences in the Indian Countries of North America since the Connexion of the Right Hon. the Earl of Selkirk with the Hudson's Bay Company, and His Attempt to Establish a Colony on the Red River,* ed. Samuel Hull Wilcocke, Simon McGillivray, and Edward Ellice (Covent-Garden, UK: B. McMillan, 1817), Appendix II, 5.
139 T.R. [Thomas Robert] Malthus, *An Essay on the Principle of Population, as It Affects the Future Improvement of Society* (London: J. Johnson, 1798), 13.
140 Malthus, *An Essay on the Principle of Population,* 120.
141 Malthus, *An Essay on the Principle of Population,* 126.

224 *Notes to pages 90–92*

142 Marx, *Capital,* 1: 666n7.
143 Marx, *Capital,* 1: 766n6.
144 Richards, *Debating the Highland Clearances,* 39.
145 Richards, *Debating the Highland Clearances,* 29–30.
146 T.M. Devine, "Highland Migration to Lowland Scotland, 1760–1860," *Scottish Historical Review* 62, no. 174 (1983): 141.
147 Thomas Martin Devine, *Clanship to Crofter's War: The Social Transformation of the Scottish Highlands* (Manchester: Manchester University Press, 1994), 78.
148 Marx, *Capital,* 1: 867.
149 Bumsted, "Editorial Introduction" (1984), 29; Carter, "Lord Selkirk and the Red River Colony," 61.
150 Thomas Douglas Selkirk, "A Proposal Tending to the Permanent Security of Ireland in a Memorial Addressed to H.M. Secretary of State," 1802, LAC – Selkirk Collection, 13911, http://heritage.canadiana.ca/view/oocihm.lac_reel_c13/740?r=0&s=4.
151 Selkirk, "A Proposal Tending to the Permanent Security of Ireland," 13911.
152 Selkirk, "A Proposal Tending to the Permanent Security of Ireland," 13912.
153 Thomas Douglas Selkirk, "Observations Supplementary to a Memorial Relative to the Security of Ireland," 1802, LAC – Selkirk Collection, 13913, http://heritage.canadiana.ca/view/oocihm.lac_reel_c13/740?r=0&s=4.
154 Selkirk, "Observations Supplementary to a Memorial Relative to the Security of Ireland," 13914.
155 Bumsted, "Editorial Introduction" (1984), 38, 42. Selkirk likely gained some knowledge from the experiences of these earlier settlements, especially Baldoon in Upper Canada, which may have shaped his thinking about title and land conveyances later at Red River; see Nathan Hasselstrom, "An Exploration of the Selkirk Treaty" (master's thesis, University of Ottawa, 2019), 45–46, 49.
156 John Morgan Gray, "Douglas, Thomas, Baron Daer and Shortcleuch, 5th Earl of Selkirk (1771–1820)," in *Dictionary of Canadian Biography,* vol. 5 (Toronto: University of Toronto; Laval: Université Laval, 1983), http://www.biographi.ca/en/bio/douglas_thomas_5E.html.
157 Thomas Douglas Selkirk, "Observations on the Present State of the Highlands of Scotland, with a View of the Causes and Probable Consequences of Emigration," in *The Collected Writings of Lord Selkirk 1799–1809,* ed. J.M. Bumsted (Winnipeg: Manitoba Record Society, 1984), 103.
158 Bumsted, "Editorial Introduction" (1984), 44.
159 Bumsted, "Editorial Introduction" (1984), 50, 53.
160 Here I have in mind the usage of "grant" as meaning "concession." See Allan Greer, *Property and Dispossession: Natives, Empires and Land in Early Modern North America* (Cambridge: Cambridge University Press, 2018), 172.
161 Selkirk, "Observations on the Present State of the Highlands of Scotland," 103.
162 *A Narrative of Occurrences,* 5, Appendix II.
163 John Halkett, *The Earl of Selkirk's Settlement* (Carlisle, MA: Applewood Books, 2006), 118.
164 *A Narrative of Occurrences,* 8, Appendix II.
165 *A Narrative of Occurrences,* 8, Appendix II.
166 J.M. Bumsted, "Editorial Introduction," in *The Collected Writings of Lord Selkirk 1810–1820,* ed. J.M. Bumsted (Winnipeg: Manitoba Record Society, 1988), xiv.
167 Alexander Mackenzie, *Voyages from Montreal through the Continent of North America to the Frozen and Pacific Oceans in 1789 and 1793,* vol. 1 (New York: A.S. Barnes and Company, 1801), 49.

Notes to pages 92–94 225

168 W. Kaye Lamb, "Mackenzie, Sir Alexander (1764–1820)," in *Dictionary of Canadian Biography*, vol. 5 (Toronto: University of Toronto; Laval: Université Laval, 1983), http://www.biographi.ca/en/bio/mackenzie_alexander_5E.html.
169 Kaye, "The Red River Settlement," 213.
170 Kaye, "The Red River Settlement," 215.
171 Kaye, "The Red River Settlement," 216.
172 Carter, "Lord Selkirk and the Red River Colony," 62.
173 Kaye, "The Red River Settlement," 218.
174 Kaye, "The Red River Settlement," 218.
175 Lamb, "Mackenzie, Sir Alexander."
176 Bumsted, "Editorial Introduction," xiv.
177 Wilcocke, *A Narrative of Occurrences*, 3.
178 Lamb, "Mackenzie, Sir Alexander."
179 Atcheson and Henry, *On the Origin and Progress of the North-West Company of Canada*, 28.
180 Richard S. Mackie, *Trading beyond the Mountains: The British Fur Trade on the Pacific, 1793–1843* (Vancouver: UBC Press, 2011), xvii.
181 Atcheson and Henry, *On the Origin and Progress of the North-West Company of Canada*, 22.
182 Atcheson and Henry, *On the Origin and Progress of the North-West Company of Canada*, 22.
183 Atcheson and Henry, *On the Origin and Progress of the North-West Company of Canada*, 26.
184 Note that the included copy of the letter refers to "McDonald," and the HBC reply refers to "McDonell"; both letters discuss the events that occurred at Eagle Lake in 1809.
185 McTavish, Fraser and Company, Inglis, Ellice and Company, and Alexander Mackenzie, "Letter to Mainwaring, 3 June 1811," LAC – Selkirk Collection, C-1, 199, http://heritage.canadiana.ca/view/oocihm.lac_reel_c1/206?r=0&s=1.
186 McTavish, Fraser and Company, Inglis, Ellice and Company, and Mackenzie, "Letter to Mainwaring," 200.
187 McTavish, Fraser and Company, Inglis, Ellice and Company, and Mackenzie, "Letter to Mainwaring," 201.
188 Hudson's Bay Company Committee, "Letter to McTavish, Fraser and Co., Inglis, Ellice and Co., and Alexander Mackenzie, 24 July 1811," LAC – Selkirk Collection, C-1, 210, http://heritage.canadiana.ca/view/oocihm.lac_reel_c1/216?r=0&s=2.
189 Hudson's Bay Company Committee, "Letter to McTavish, Fraser and Co., Inglis, Ellice and Co., and Alexander Mackenzie, 28 August 1811," LAC – Selkirk Collection, C-1, 216, http://heritage.canadiana.ca/view/oocihm.lac_reel_c1/222?r=0&s=2.
190 Lamb, "Mackenzie, Sir Alexander."
191 Thomas Douglas [Fifth Earl of Selkirk] and John Halkett, *A Letter to the Earl of Liverpool [Relating to the North-West Company's Attack upon the Red River Settlement]* (London: J. Brettell, 1819), 14.
192 "Grant of the District of Assiniboia by the Hudson's Bay Company to Lord Selkirk," in *The Canadian North-West, Its Early Development and Legislative Records: Minutes of the Councils of the Red River Colony and the Northern Department of Rupert's Land*, ed. Edmund Henry Oliver, vol. 1 (Ottawa: Government Printing Bureau, 1914), 159.
193 "Grant of the District of Assiniboia," 159–60.
194 "Grant of the District of Assiniboia," 163.
195 "Grant of the District of Assiniboia," 167.
196 John Halkett, *Statement Respecting the Earl of Selkirk's Settlement upon the Red River, in North America: Its Destruction in the Years 1815 and 1816; and the Massacre of Governor Semple and His Party; with Observations upon a Recent Publication, Entitled "A Narrative of Occurrances [sic] in the Indian Countries," &c* (London: John Murray, 1817), 8.

226 *Notes to pages 95–98*

197 William Thwaits, et al., "Protest of Proprietors of the Hudson's Bay Company, against the Grant to Lord Selkirk," in *A Narrative of Occurrences in the Indian Countries of North America*, ed. Samuel Hull Wilcocke, Simon McGillivray, and Edward Ellice (Covent-Garden, UK: B. McMillan, 1817), Appendix I, 1–4.

198 Dale Gibson, *Law, Life, and Government at Red River, Volume 1: Settlement and Governance, 1812–1872* (Montreal and Kingston: McGill-Queen's University Press, 2015), 5.

199 Gibson, *Law, Life, and Government at Red River, Volume 1*, 5.

200 Archer Martin, *The Hudson's Bay Company's Land Tenures and the Occupation of Assiniboia by Lord Selkirk's Settlers* (London: William Clowes and Sons, 1898), 1.

201 Gibson, *Law, Life, and Government at Red River, Volume 1*, 5.

202 Gibson, *Law, Life, and Government at Red River, Volume 1*, 5–6.

203 Martin, *The Hudson's Bay Company's Land Tenures*, 7. In 1796, Macdonell rose to the rank of captain of the Royal Canadian Volunteer Regiment while in Upper Canada, having previously served in New York with the King's Royal Regiment. See Herbert J. Mays, "Macdonell, Miles (1767–1828)," in *Dictionary of Canadian Biography*, vol. 6 (Toronto: University of Toronto; Laval: Université Laval, 1987), http://www.biographi.ca/en/bio/macdonell_miles_6E.html.

204 Mamdani, *Citizen and Subject*, 74.

205 Miles Macdonell, "Journal: 6 July 1812 to 22 April 1813," LAC – Selkirk Collection, 16735, http://heritage.canadiana.ca/view/oocihm.lac_reel_c16/207?r=0&s=1.

206 Thomas Douglas Selkirk, "Instructions to Miles McDonell," 1811, LAC – Selkirk Collection, 168–69, https://heritage.canadiana.ca/view/oocihm.lac_reel_c1/174?r=0&s=1.

207 Selkirk, "Instructions to Miles McDonell," 170.

208 Selkirk, "Instructions to Miles McDonell," 169.

209 Selkirk, "Instructions to Miles McDonell," 169.

210 Selkirk, "Instructions to Miles McDonell," 177.

211 Selkirk, "Instructions to Miles McDonell," 177.

212 Selkirk, "Instructions to Miles McDonell," 177.

213 Selkirk, "Instructions to Miles McDonell," 178. Forts with a more defensive purpose were first established bayside in the early eighteenth century. See Stephen, *Masters and Servants*, 90.

214 Paul Hackett, "Averting Disaster: The Hudson's Bay Company and Smallpox in Western Canada during the Late Eighteenth and Early Nineteenth Centuries," *Bulletin of the History of Medicine* 78, no. 3 (2004): 593.

215 Hackett, "Averting Disaster," 581; John W.R. McIntyre and C. Stuart Houston, "Smallpox and Its Control in Canada," *Canadian Medical Association Journal* 161 (1999): 1546.

216 Daschuk, *Clearing the Plains*, 37.

217 Selkirk, "Instructions to Miles McDonell," 178.

218 Selkirk, "Instructions to Miles McDonell," 178.

219 Hackett, "Averting Disaster," 592.

220 Ian Frazier, *Great Plains* (New York: Picador, 2001), 31; McIntyre and Houston, "Smallpox and Its Control in Canada"; Hackett, "Averting Disaster."

221 Hackett, "Averting Disaster," 594.

222 Selkirk, "Instructions to Miles McDonell," 177.

223 Thomas Douglas Selkirk, "Letter from Selkirk to Miles MacDonell, 1811," in *The Canadian North-West, Its Early Development and Legislative Records: Minutes of the Councils of the Red River Colony and the Northern Department of Rupert's Land*, ed. Edmund Henry Oliver, vol. 1 (Ottawa: Government Printing Bureau, 1914), 175.

224 "Notice Published in the *Quebec Gazette*, Dec 12, 1811," in *The Canadian North-West, Its Early Development and Legislative Records: Minutes of the Councils of the Red River*

Colony and the Northern Department of Rupert's Land, ed. Edmund Henry Oliver, vol. 1 (Ottawa: Government Printing Bureau, 1914), 176–77.

225 This was mirrored forty years later by the situation of James Douglas, appointed by the Hudson's Bay Company as chief factor in 1839 and made governor of Vancouver Island in 1851, notably without relinquishing his company title. See Margaret A. Ormsby, "Douglas, Sir James (1803–1877)," in *Dictionary of Canadian Biography*, vol. 10 (Toronto: University of Toronto; Laval: Université Laval, 1972), http://www.biographi.ca/en/bio/douglas_james_10E.html. Like Macdonell, Douglas appears to have had a preference for displays of power, ranging from military ceremony to corporal punishment. See Cole Harris, "The Native Land Policies of Governor James Douglas," *BC Studies* 174 (2012): 102–3.

226 Miles Macdonell, "Extract of Letter from Miles Macdonell to Selkirk, May 31, 1812," in *The Canadian North-West, Its Early Development and Legislative Records: Minutes of the Councils of the Red River Colony and the Northern Department of Rupert's Land,* ed. Edmund Henry Oliver, vol. 1 (Ottawa: Government Printing Bureau, 1914), 177.

227 Thomas Douglas Selkirk, "Letter from Selkirk to Miles Macdonell, June 12, 1813," in *The Canadian North-West, Its Early Development and Legislative Records: Minutes of the Councils of the Red River Colony and the Northern Department of Rupert's Land,* ed. Edmund Henry Oliver, vol. 1 (Ottawa: Government Printing Bureau, 1914), 178.

228 Selkirk, "Letter from Selkirk to Miles Macdonell, June 12, 1813," 179.

229 Selkirk, "Letter from Selkirk to Miles Macdonell, June 12, 1813," 180.

230 C.L.R. James, *The Black Jacobins: Toussaint L'Ouverture and the San Domingo Revolution,* 2nd ed. (New York: Vintage Books, 1989), 95.

231 Domenico Losurdo, *Liberalism: A Counter-History,* trans. Gregory Elliott (London: Verso Books, 2011), 9–10.

232 Losurdo, *Liberalism,* 17.

233 Losurdo, *Liberalism,* 18.

234 Jodi A. Byrd, *The Transit of Empire: Indigenous Critiques of Colonialism* (Minneapolis: University of Minnesota Press, 2011), xxi.

235 Quoted in Losurdo, *Liberalism,* 19.

236 Losurdo, *Liberalism,* 17, 22–23.

237 John Pritchard, Pierre Chrysologue Pambrun, and Frederick Damien Heurter, *Narratives of John Pritchard, Pierre Chrysologue Pambrun, and Frederick Damien Heurter, Respecting the Aggressions of the North-West Company, against the Earl of Selkirk's Settlement upon Red River* (London: John Murray, 1819), 3.

238 Glen Sean Coulthard, *Red Skin, White Masks: Rejecting the Colonial Politics of Recognition,* Indigenous Americas (Minneapolis: University of Minnesota Press, 2014), 125.

239 William A. Dobak, "Killing the Canadian Buffalo, 1821–1881," *Western Historical Quarterly* 27, no. 1 (1996): 33.

240 Douglas MacKay, *The Honourable Company: A History of the Hudson's Bay Company* (Indianapolis: Bobbs-Merrill, 1936), 48, 86.

Chapter 4: Servitude and Independence

1 Barry Kaye, "The Trade in Livestock between the Red River Settlement and the American Frontier, 1812–1870," in *Business and Industry,* ed. Gregory P. Marchildon, History of the Prairie West Series 4 (Regina: University of Regina Press, 2011), 4.

2 George Colpitts, *Pemmican Empire: Food, Trade, and the Last Bison Hunts in the North American Plains, 1780–1882* (Cambridge: Cambridge University Press, 2014), 129.

3 Lauren Benton, *Law and Colonial Cultures: Legal Regimes in World History, 1400–1900* (Cambridge: Cambridge University Press, 2002), 6.

228 *Notes to pages 103–6*

4 Benton, *Law and Colonial Cultures*, 10.
5 Benton, *Law and Colonial Cultures*, 23.
6 Benton, *Law and Colonial Cultures*, 12.
7 Mahmood Mamdani, *Citizen and Subject: Contemporary Africa and the Legacy of Late Colonialism* (Princeton, NJ: Princeton University Press, 1996).
8 Laura L. Peers, *The Ojibwa of Western Canada, 1780 to 1870* (Winnipeg: University of Manitoba Press, 1984), 63.
9 Rosa Luxemburg, *The Accumulation of Capital*, 2nd ed. (London: Routledge, 2003), 349.
10 Glen Sean Coulthard, *Red Skin, White Masks: Rejecting the Colonial Politics of Recognition*, Indigenous Americas (Minneapolis: University of Minnesota Press, 2014), 100.
11 Coulthard, *Red Skin, White Masks*, 100.
12 Marcus Rediker, *The Slave Ship: A Human History* (London: Penguin, 2007), 43.
13 Alexander Anievas and Kerem Nişancıoğlu, *How the West Came to Rule: The Geopolitical Origins of Capitalism* (London: Pluto Press, 2015), 161.
14 Anievas and Nişancıoğlu, *How the West Came to Rule*, 165.
15 Rediker, *The Slave Ship*, 32.
16 Rediker, *The Slave Ship*, 32.
17 Peter Burroughs, "Prevost, Sir George (1767–1816)," in *Dictionary of Canadian Biography*, vol. 5 (Toronto: University of Toronto; Laval: Université Laval, 1983), http://www.biographi.ca/en/bio/prevost_george_5E.html.
18 George Prevost, "Instructions for the Good Government of the Indian Department, 1812," in *Collections and Researches Made by the Michigan Pioneer and Historical Society*, vol. 23 (Lansing: Robert Smith and Company, State Printers and Binders, 1895), 86–87.
19 Prevost, "Instructions for the Good Government of the Indian Department," 87.
20 W.L. Morton, "The North West Company: Pedlars Extraordinary," *Minnesota History* 40, no. 4 (1966): 160.
21 Paul Hackett, "Historical Mourning Practices Observed among the Cree and Ojibway Indians of the Central Subarctic," *Ethnohistory* 52, no. 3 (2005): 506.
22 Peers, *The Ojibwa of Western Canada*, 13; Victor P. Lytwyn, *Muskekowuck Athinuwick: Original People of the Great Swampy Land* (Winnipeg: University of Manitoba Press, 2002), 174.
23 Heidi Kiiwetinepinesiik Stark and Gina Starblanket, "Towards a Relational Paradigm – Four Points for Consideration: Knowledge, Gender, Land, and Modernity," in *Resurgence and Reconciliation: Indigenous-Settler Relations and Earth Teachings*, ed. Michael I. Asch, John Borrows, and James Tully (Toronto: University of Toronto Press, 2018), 190.
24 Gerald Friesen, *River Road: Essays on Manitoba and Prairie History* (Winnipeg: University of Manitoba Press, 1996), 55.
25 Hamar Foster, "'The Queen's Law Is Better than Yours': International Homicide in Early British Columbia," in *Essays in the History of Canadian Law: Crime and Criminal Justice in Canadian History*, ed. Susan Lewthwaite, Tina Loo, and Jim Phillips, vol. 5 (Toronto: University of Toronto Press, 1994), 48; John Phillip Reid, *Patterns of Vengeance: Crosscultural Homicide in the North American Fur Trade* (Pasadena, CA: Ninth Judicial Circuit Historical Society, 1999), 27–28.
26 Edith I. Burley, *Servants of the Honourable Company: Work, Discipline, and Conflict in the Hudson's Bay Company, 1770–1879* (Toronto: Oxford University Press, 1997), 30–31. Henley House was one of the early attempts at an inland post, situated along the Albany River (near present-day Kenora, ON). In 1755, six Maškēkowak individuals (Wappesiss, his two sons, and three others) were sentenced to death for killing William Lamb and his four servants. Lamb kept the daughter and daughter-in-law of Wappesiss in his house but refused entry or supplements to Wappesiss. A trial at bayside Fort Albany was

overseen by Joseph Isbister, but after the execution the HBC committee recalled Isbister and expressed regret that so many deaths had resulted from Lamb's failure to uphold his social obligations. See Scott P. Stephen, *Masters and Servants: The Hudson's Bay Company and Its North American Workforce, 1668-1786* (Edmonton: University of Alberta Press, 2019), 96-97.

27 John Phillip Reid, "Principles of Vengeance: Fur Trappers, Indians, and Retaliation for Homicide in the Transboundary North American West," *Western Historical Quarterly* 24, no. 1 (1993): 26.

28 Foster, "'The Queen's Law Is Better than Yours,'" 52. Perhaps the early tendency of commercial traders to pursue less formal and more customary means of control shows the extent to which traders were influenced by Indigenous peoples' practices. See Hamar Foster, "Conflict Resolution during the Fur Trade in the Canadian North West, 1803-1859," *Cambrian Law Review* 25 (1994): 132-33; and Reid, "Principles of Vengeance," 23. On the selectivity of Indigenous peoples' vengeance, see Reid, *Patterns of Vengeance*, 34. For a more recent account of the customary principles that informed how select Indigenous societies negotiated the occurrence of violent acts, see John Borrows, "Heroes, Tricksters, Monsters, and Caretakers: Indigenous Law and Legal Education Special Issue – Indigenous Law and Legal Pluralism," *McGill Law Journal* 61 (2016): 795-846.

29 Douglas MacKay, *The Honourable Company: A History of the Hudson's Bay Company* (Indianapolis: Bobbs-Merrill, 1936), 48. Recorded instances of violence tended to occur in the context of warfare between Indigenous groups. See Arthur J. Ray and Donald B. Freeman, *"Give Us Good Measure": An Economic Analysis of Relations between the Indians and the Hudson's Bay Company before 1763* (Toronto: University of Toronto Press, 1978), 42-44; and Louis Bird, *The Spirit Lives in the Mind: Omushkego Stories, Lives and Dreams,* ed. Susan Elaine Gray (Montreal and Kingston: McGill-Queen's University Press, 2007), 40-45. Other instances were linked to drunken behaviour, as MacKay recounts: "'The beating of a servant for breaking fort rules, or of an Indian for drunkenness, gave the parliamentary committee no concern. Harsh treatment for petty offenses was commonplace." MacKay, *The Honourable Company,* 82.

30 Foster, "'The Queen's Law Is Better than Yours,'" 51; Reid, "Principles of Vengeance," 31.

31 David Fagundes, "What We Talk about When We Talk about Persons: The Language of a Legal Fiction," *Harvard Law Review* 114, no. 6 (2001): 1745-68.

32 Foster, "'The Queen's Law Is Better than Yours,'" 72-73, writes about a similar legal landscape in British Columbia in the 1860s-70s.

33 Macdonell, "Journal: 6 July 1812 to 22 April 1813," 16771.

34 Macdonell, "Journal: 6 July 1812 to 22 April 1813," 16802.

35 Reid, "Principles of Vengeance," 27; Reid, *Patterns of Vengeance,* 42.

36 Reid, "Principles of Vengeance," 33-34, mentions an example from 1826 when HBC Chief Factor Peter Skene Ogden came upon a group of Indigenous men known for having killed and appropriated items from company men in the area of present-day British Columbia. In this instance, Ogden distorted Indigenous principles of vengeance by invoking a biblically inspired notion of "preventative vengeance," which served his aim of making an example of the Indigenous group.

37 Foster, "Conflict Resolution during the Fur Trade in the Canadian North West," 129.

38 Luxemburg, *The Accumulation of Capital,* 350.

39 Luxemburg, *The Accumulation of Capital,* 351.

40 Mamdani, *Citizen and Subject,* 63.

41 Neville Thompson, "Bathurst, Henry, Third Earl Bathurst (1762-1834)," in *The Oxford Dictionary of National Biography,* ed. H.C.G. Matthew and B. Harrison (Oxford: Oxford University Press, 2004), http://www.oxforddnb.com/view/article/1696.

230 *Notes to pages 108–11*

42 HBC Committee, "Statement by HBC, Enclosed in Bathurst Letter, 18 March 1815," in *Papers Relating to the Red River Settlement: 1815–1819* (London: Colonial Department, 1819), 4.

43 HBC Committee, "Statement by HBC," 4.

44 William Cruise, "Law Opinions on Red River," 1813, LAC – Selkirk Collection, 12008, http://heritage.canadiana.ca/view/oocihm.lac_reel_c11/894?r=0&s=3; William Cruise, "Copy Queries and Opinions of Mr. Cruise," in *Appendix to the Journals of the House of Commons of Canada*, 14, I (Ottawa: Hunter Rose, 1880), 70.

45 Cruise, "Copy Queries and Opinions of Mr. Cruise," 14, I: 72.

46 Thomas Poole, *Reason of State: Law, Prerogative and Empire* (Cambridge: Cambridge University Press, 2015), 135.

47 Poole, *Reason of State*, 137.

48 Cruise, "Copy Queries and Opinions of Mr. Cruise," 14, I: 71; Cruise, "Law Opinions on Red River," 12008.

49 Cruise, "Copy Queries and Opinions of Mr. Cruise," 14, I: 71; Cruise, "Law Opinions on Red River," 12009.

50 Hamar Foster, "Law and Necessity in Western Rupert's Land and Beyond, 1670–1870," in *Laws and Societies in the Canadian Prairie West, 1670–1940*, ed. Louis A. Knafla and Jonathan Swainger (Vancouver: UBC Press, 2005), 69n70.

51 Joseph Berens, "Observations on Judicial Instructions Proposed, 1814," LAC – Selkirk Collection, http://heritage.canadiana.ca/view/oocihm.lac_reel_c11/904?r=0&s=3.

52 J.M. Bumsted, "Editorial Introduction," in *The Collected Writings of Lord Selkirk 1810–1820*, ed. J.M. Bumsted (Winnipeg: Manitoba Record Society, 1988), xxxii.

53 Cruise, "Copy Queries and Opinions of Mr. Cruise," 14, I: 72; Cruise, "Law Opinions on Red River," 12009.

54 Cruise, "Copy Queries and Opinions of Mr. Cruise," 14, I: 72; Cruise, "Law Opinions on Red River," 12010.

55 Government of Manitoba, Public Information Branch, "Features Service: This Week in History," June 14, 1968, http://news.gov.mb.ca/news/archives/1968/06/1968-06-14 -this_week_in_history.pdf.

56 Thomas Douglas Selkirk, "Letter to Macdonell, 13 June 1813," LAC – Selkirk Collection, 673, http://heritage.canadiana.ca/view/oocihm.lac_reel_c1/679?r=0&s=4. See also Edmund Henry Oliver, *The Canadian North-West, Its Early Development and Legislative Records: Minutes of the Councils of the Red River Colony and the Northern Department of Rupert's Land*, vol. 1 (Ottawa: Government Printing Bureau, 1914), 76.

57 Oliver, *The Canadian North-West*, 1: 76.

58 J.M. Bumsted, *Lord Selkirk: A Life* (Winnipeg: University of Manitoba Press, 2008), 309.

59 Richard Burn, *The Justice of the Peace, and Parish Officer*, ed. George Chetwynd, 23rd ed., vol. 1 (London: A. Strahan and W. Woodfall, 1820), 186–87.

60 J.S. Cockburn, *A History of English Assizes 1558–1714* (Cambridge: Cambridge University Press, 1972), ix.

61 Selkirk, "Letter to Macdonell, 13 June 1813," 680–81.

62 Oliver, *The Canadian North-West*, 1: 55.

63 Oliver, *The Canadian North-West*, 1: 34.

64 Joseph Howse, "Letter to Selkirk, 24 September 1813," LAC – Selkirk Collection, 871, http://heritage.canadiana.ca/view/oocihm.lac_reel_c1/882?r=0&s=4.

65 Oliver, *The Canadian North-West*, 1: 76.

66 Selkirk, "Letter to Macdonell, 13 June 1813," 676.

67 Selkirk, "Letter to Macdonell, 13 June 1813," 675.

68 Selkirk, "Letter to Macdonell, 13 June 1813," 677.

Notes to pages 112–17 231

69 Benton, *Law and Colonial Cultures*, 256.

70 Selkirk, "Letter to Macdonell, 13 June 1813," 676.

71 Selkirk, "Letter to Macdonell, 13 June 1813," 676.

72 Gibson, *Law, Life, and Government at Red River, Volume 1*, 15.

73 Bumsted, "Editorial Introduction" (1988), xix.

74 Bumsted, "Editorial Introduction" (1988), xix.

75 I hyphenate the status of the newcomers to underscore the complexity of their circumstances. Sometimes they are identified less ambiguously in historical records as "Emigrants" or "Settlers": see Peter Fidler, "1815–1816, 26 August 1815," Archives of Manitoba, Brandon House Post Journal, 5; "1815–1816, 26 January 1816," Archives of Manitoba, Brandon House Post Journal, 16. Other times there is evidence of this complex relation when they are identified as "Colony servants"; see Peter Fidler, "1817–1818, 25 August 1817," Archives of Manitoba, Brandon House Post Journal, 12.

76 Bumsted, "Editorial Introduction" (1988), xx.

77 Burley, *Servants of the Honourable Company*, 82.

78 Bumsted, "Editorial Introduction" (1988), xx.

79 Burley, *Servants of the Honourable Company*, 82.

80 William Auld, "Letter to Wedderburn, 16 September 1813," LAC – Selkirk Collection, 850, http://heritage.canadiana.ca/view/oocihm.lac_reel_c1/854?r=0&s=4.

81 Burley, *Servants of the Honourable Company*, 82–83.

82 Charles N. Bell, *The Selkirk Settlement and the Settlers: A Concise History of the Red River Country from Its Discovery, Including Information Extracted from Original Documents Lately Discovered, and Notes Obtained from Selkirk Settlement Colonists* (Winnipeg: Commercial, 1887), 9.

83 Burley, *Servants of the Honourable Company*, 82.

84 Bumsted, "Editorial Introduction" (1988), xxii.

85 Bell, *The Selkirk Settlement and the Settlers*, 9.

86 Burley, *Servants of the Honourable Company*, 82.

87 William Auld, "Notification to the Insurgents," May 1812, LAC – Selkirk Collection, 342, http://heritage.canadiana.ca/view/oocihm.lac_reel_c1/349?r=0&s=3.

88 Burley, *Servants of the Honourable Company*, 83.

89 Auld, "Notification to the Insurgents," 342.

90 Bell, *The Selkirk Settlement and the Settlers*, 10.

91 Macdonell, "Extract of Letter from Miles Macdonell to Selkirk, May 31, 1812," 177.

92 Thomas Douglas Selkirk, "Letter to Auld, 15 June 1813," LAC – Selkirk Collection, 689–90, http://heritage.canadiana.ca/view/oocihm.lac_reel_c1/698?r=0&s=4.

93 Selkirk, "Letter to Auld, 15 June 1813," 690.

94 Selkirk, "Letter from Selkirk to Miles Macdonell, June 12, 1813," 178.

95 Alexander Ross, *The Red River Settlement: Its Rise, Progress, and Present State: With Some Account of the Native* ... (London: Smith, Elder and Company, 1856), 20.

96 Macdonell, "Journal: 6 July 1812 to 22 April 1813," 16740.

97 Macdonell, "Journal: 6 July 1812 to 22 April 1813," 16744.

98 Macdonell, "Journal: 6 July 1812 to 22 April 1813," 16744.

99 Archer Martin, *The Hudson's Bay Company's Land Tenures and the Occupation of Assiniboia by Lord Selkirk's Settlers* (London: William Clowes and Sons, 1898), 182.

100 Bell, *The Selkirk Settlement and the Settlers*, 10.

101 Bell, *The Selkirk Settlement and the Settlers*, 10.

102 Macdonell, "Extract of Letter from Miles Macdonell to Selkirk, May 31, 1812," 177.

103 J.M. Bumsted, *Trials and Tribulations: The Red River Settlement and the Emergence of Manitoba, 1811–1870* (Winnipeg: Great Plains Publications, 2003), 14.

232 Notes to pages 117–19

104 Macdonell, "Journal: 6 July 1812 to 22 April 1813," 16760.
105 Bumsted, "Editorial Introduction" (1988), xxii.
106 One consideration to keep in mind regarding Macdonell's friendliness toward the North West Company was that Alexander Macdonell, his cousin and brother-in-law, was the head of Fort Gibraltar (at present-day Winnipeg). See Herbert J. Mays, "Macdonell, Miles (1767–1828)," in *Dictionary of Canadian Biography*, vol. 6 (Toronto: University of Toronto; Laval: Université Laval, 1987), http://www.biographi.ca/en/bio/macdonell_miles_6E.html.
107 Macdonell, "Journal: 6 July 1812 to 22 April 1813," 16755.
108 Macdonell, "Journal: 6 July 1812 to 22 April 1813," 16743.
109 Myrna Kostash, *The Seven Oaks Reader*, UK ed. (Edmonton: NeWest Press, 2016), 83.
110 Macdonell, "Journal: 6 July 1812 to 22 April 1813," 16762.
111 Sarah Carter, *Aboriginal People and Colonizers of Western Canada to 1900*, Themes in Canadian Social History (Toronto: University of Toronto Press, 1999), 65.
112 Bryce claims in his book, originally published in 1900, that a "Nor'-Wester trader confess[ed] that he had manufactured the speech and 'Grandes Oreilles' had never spoken it." See George Bryce, *The Remarkable History of the Hudson's Bay Company, Including That of the French Traders of North-Western Canada and of the North-West, XY, and Astor Fur Companies*, 3rd ed. (New York: Charles Scribner's Sons, 1910), 247.
113 Peers, *The Ojibwa of Western Canada*, 238n146.
114 James Rodger Miller, *Compact, Contract, Covenant: Aboriginal Treaty-Making in Canada* (Toronto: University of Toronto Press, 2009), 131.
115 Saulteaux leader Canard Noir (Black Duck) was an ally of Métis leader Cuthbert Grant.
116 Macdonell, "Journal: 6 July 1812 to 22 April 1813," 16757.
117 Macdonell, "Journal: 6 July 1812 to 22 April 1813," 16758.
118 Macdonell, "Journal: 6 July 1812 to 22 April 1813," 16758.
119 Macdonell, "Journal: 6 July 1812 to 22 April 1813," 16803–4.
120 Macdonell, "Journal: 6 July 1812 to 22 April 1813," 16805.
121 Macdonell, "Journal: 6 July 1812 to 22 April 1813," 16806.
122 Mark D. Walters, "'Your Sovereign and Our Father': The Imperial Crown and the Idea of Legal-Ethnohistory," in *Law and Politics in British Colonial Thought: Transpositions and Empire*, ed. Shaunnagh Dorsett and Ian Hunter (New York: Springer, 2010), 96–97.
123 Walters, "'Your Sovereign and Our Father,'" 97, 99.
124 Stephen, *Masters and Servants*, 46.
125 Anne McClintock's well-known tome *Imperial Leather* dives deeper into the father figure in British settler colonialism, and although she writes about South Africa, I find that her observations provide a meaningful way to interpret Macdonell's reactions to being called "father," and place him in a broader historical context. Specifically, I have in mind her argument that "the reinvention of fathers and kings" by British agents of colonialism should be seen "as a central attempt to mediate a number of contradictions: between the imperial bureaucracy and the declining landed gentry in Britain; between the colonial ruling patriarchy and the indigenous patriarchies of precapitalist polities, and last but most significantly, between women and men of all races." Anne McClintock, *Imperial Leather: Race, Gender and Sexuality in the Colonial Context* (London: Routledge, 1995), 251.
126 Laura L. Peers, "Rich Man, Poor Man, Beggarman, Chief: Saulteaux in the Red River Settlement," in *Papers of the Eighteenth Algonquian Conference*, ed. William Cowan (Ottawa: Carleton University, 1987), 264.
127 Miles Macdonell, "Journal: 22 April 1813 to 7 April 1815," LAC – Selkirk Collection, 16836, https://heritage.canadiana.ca/view/oocihm.lac_reel_c16/333?r=0&s=1.

Notes to pages 119–23 233

128 Macdonell, "Journal: 22 April 1813 to 7 April 1815," 16836.
129 Macdonell, "Journal: 22 April 1813 to 7 April 1815," 16843.
130 Macdonell, "Journal: 22 April 1813 to 7 April 1815," 16861–62.
131 Macdonell, "Journal: 22 April 1813 to 7 April 1815," 16862.
132 Gibson, *Law, Life, and Government at Red River, Volume 1*, 5.
133 Peers, "Rich Man, Poor Man, Beggarman, Chief," 263.
134 Peers, "Rich Man, Poor Man, Beggarman, Chief," 261.
135 Peers, "Rich Man, Poor Man, Beggarman, Chief," 262.
136 Macdonell, "Journal: 6 July 1812 to 22 April 1813," 16759. Peguis had many names; one was the Cut-Nosed Chief because of an injury to his nose sustained a decade earlier; another was William King, the name that he was given when baptized in 1840. See Hugh A. Dempsey, "Peguis (c. 1774–1864)," in *Dictionary of Canadian Biography*, vol. 9 (Toronto: University of Toronto; Laval: Université Laval, 1976), http://www.biographi.ca/en/bio/peguis_9E.html; and Donna Sutherland, "Peguis, Woodpeckers, and Myths: What Do We Really Know?," *Manitoba History* 71 (2013): 50.
137 Peers, "Rich Man, Poor Man, Beggarman, Chief," 262.
138 Colin G. Calloway, "Foundations of Sand: The Fur Trade and the British-Indian Relations, 1783–1815," in *"Le castor fait tout": Selected Papers of the Fifth North American Fur Trade Conference, 1985*, ed. Bruce G. Trigger, Toby Morantz, and Louise Dechêne (Montreal: Lake St. Louis Historical Society, 1987), 156.
139 Lisa Lowe, *The Intimacies of Four Continents* (Durham, NC: Duke University Press, 2015), 15.
140 Peers, "Rich Man, Poor Man, Beggarman, Chief," 263.
141 Walters, "'Your Sovereign and Our Father,'" 94.
142 Macdonell, "Journal: 6 July 1812 to 22 April 1813," 16758–59.
143 Peers, "Rich Man, Poor Man, Beggarman, Chief," 264.
144 Macdonell, "Journal: 6 July 1812 to 22 April 1813," 16768.
145 Bumsted, "Editorial Introduction" (1988), xxvi.
146 Thomas Douglas Selkirk, "Irish Catholics Proposition to Lord Liverpool, 2 July 1812," LAC – Selkirk Collection, 13983, http://heritage.canadiana.ca/view/oocihm.lac_reel_c13/740?r=0&s=4.
147 Selkirk, "Irish Catholics Proposition to Lord Liverpool," 13985. The act set a ratio of one passenger for every two tons of cargo, required that a surgeon be included if there were more than fifty passengers, and granted the right of passengers to disembark on request; for more details, see J.M. Bumsted, *The People's Clearance: Highland Emigration to British North America, 1770–1815* (Winnipeg: University of Manitoba Press, 1982), 143.
148 Selkirk, "Irish Catholics Proposition to Lord Liverpool," 13986.
149 Bumsted, "Editorial Introduction" (1988), xxi.
150 Selkirk, "Irish Catholics Proposition to Lord Liverpool," 13984.
151 Thomas Douglas Selkirk, "Instructions to Miles McDonell," 1811, LAC – Selkirk Collection, 179, https://heritage.canadiana.ca/view/oocihm.lac_reel_c16/333?r=0&s=1.
152 Selkirk, "Instructions to Miles McDonell," 168.
153 Selkirk, "Instructions to Miles McDonell," 179.
154 Stephen, *Masters and Servants*, 164.
155 Selkirk, "Instructions to Miles McDonell," 180.
156 Selkirk, "Instructions to Miles McDonell," 180.
157 Mamdani, *Citizen and Subject*, 66.
158 Thomas Douglas Selkirk, "Irish Catholic Church Arrangement Proposed to N. Vansittart, August 1812," LAC – Selkirk Collection, 13991, http://heritage.canadiana.ca/view/oocihm.lac_reel_c13/740?r=0&s=4.

234 Notes to pages 123–27

159 Bumsted, "Editorial Introduction" (1988), xxx–xxxi.
160 E.P. Thompson, *The Making of the English Working Class* (New York: Vintage, 1966), 13.
161 Susan Dianne Brophy, "Freedom, Law, and the Colonial Project," *Law and Critique* 24, no. 1 (2013): 39–61.
162 Lowe, *The Intimacies of Four Continents*, 16.
163 Miles Macdonell, "Letter to Selkirk, 17 July 1813," LAC – Selkirk Collection, 792, https://heritage.canadiana.ca/view/oocihm.lac_reel_c1/775?r=0&s=1.
164 Macdonell, "Letter to Selkirk, 17 July 1813," 792.
165 Burley, *Servants of the Honourable Company*, 84.
166 Bell, *The Selkirk Settlement and the Settlers*, 10.
167 Bell, *The Selkirk Settlement and the Settlers*, 10.
168 Macdonell, "Journal: 6 July 1812 to 22 April 1813," 16760.
169 Macdonell, "Journal: 6 July 1812 to 22 April 1813," 16774.
170 Macdonell, "Journal: 6 July 1812 to 22 April 1813," 16778.
171 Macdonell, "Letter to Selkirk, 17 July 1813," 787.
172 Macdonell, "Journal: 6 July 1812 to 22 April 1813," 16779.
173 Macdonell, "Journal: 6 July 1812 to 22 April 1813," 16791.
174 Macdonell, "Journal: 6 July 1812 to 22 April 1813," 16792–93.
175 Macdonell, "Journal: 6 July 1812 to 22 April 1813," 16793.
176 Macdonell, "Journal: 6 July 1812 to 22 April 1813," 16799.
177 Foster, "Law and Necessity in Western Rupert's Land and Beyond," 63.
178 Herbert L. Osgood, "The Proprietary Province as a Form of Colonial Government," *American Historical Review* 2, no. 4 (1897): 647.
179 Herbert L. Osgood, "The Proprietary Province as a Form of Colonial Government, II," *American Historical Review* 3, no. 1 (1897): 31–32.
180 Lisa Ford, *Settler Sovereignty: Jurisdiction and Indigenous People in America and Australia, 1788-1836* (Cambridge, MA: Harvard University Press, 2010), 17.
181 In terms of a proprietary colony established through a specific charter for that purpose, we can look at the colony founded on Vancouver Island on January 13, 1849. According to Barry Gough, the colony was established "to stay the tide of nascent American 'manifest destiny.'" See Barry M. Gough, "Crown, Company, and Charter: Founding Vancouver Island Colony – A Chapter in Victorian Empire Making," *BC Studies* 176 (Winter 2012–13): 11.
182 Michael J. Braddick, "The English Government, War, Trade, and Settlement, 1625–1688," in *The Origins of Empire: British Overseas Enterprise to the Close of the Seventeenth Century*, ed. Nicholas Canny, vol. 1 (Oxford: Oxford University Press, 1998), 295.
183 Philip Girard, "Imperial Legacies: Chartered Enterprises in Northern British America," in *Legal Histories of the British Empire: Laws, Engagements and Legacies*, ed. Shaunnagh Dorsett and John McLaren (New York: Routledge, 2014), 136.
184 Oliver, *The Canadian North-West*, 1: 72–73.
185 Julio César Rivera, "The Scope and Structure of Civil Codes, Relations with Commercial Law, Family Law, Consumer Law and Private International Law, a Comparative Approach," in *The Scope and Structure of Civil Codes*, ed. Julio César Rivera (Dordrecht: Springer, 2013), 7–8.
186 "The Hudson's Bay Company's Code of Penal Laws, Published at Moose Factory, 1 September 1815," in *The Canadian North-West, Its Early Development and Legislative Records: Minutes of the Councils of the Red River Colony and the Northern Department of Rupert's Land*, ed. Edmund Henry Oliver, vol. 2 (Ottawa: Government Printing Bureau, 1914), 1285–87; Gibson, *Law, Life, and Government at Red River, Volume 1*, 15.
187 Brophy, "Freedom, Law, and the Colonial Project."

Notes to pages 127–32 235

188 Macdonell, "Letter to Selkirk, 17 July 1813," 790.
189 Macdonell, "Letter to Selkirk, 17 July 1813," 790.
190 Macdonell, "Letter to Selkirk, 17 July 1813," 791.
191 William Auld, "Letter to Hillier, 8 April 1814," LAC – Selkirk Collection, 999, http://heritage.canadiana.ca/view/oocihm.lac_reel_c1/1002?r=0&s=4.
192 Although there was no identified factor at the settlement, there was one in the vicinity and westward along the Assiniboine River. Nearby, John McLeod, an experienced trader, was installed in the district and played a leading role in setting up posts at Turtle River and Portage la Prairie. See Sylvia Van Kirk, "McLeod, John (1788–1849)," in *Dictionary of Canadian Biography*, vol. 7 (Toronto: University of Toronto; Laval: Université Laval, 1988), http://www.biographi.ca/en/bio/mcleod_john_7E.html. Despite Macdonell's concerns about the lack of a trader at the settlement, McLeod was on hand at Turtle River in February 1815 when a large load of furs intended for the North West Company made its way to the HBC post. See Macdonell, "Journal: 22 April 1813 to 7 April 1815," 16955. For a reference to Macdonell engaging in fur trade exchange, see Macdonell, "Journal: 22 April 1813 to 7 April 1815," 16870.
193 Miles Macdonell, "Letter to Auld, 12 April 1814," LAC – Selkirk Collection, 1003, http://heritage.canadiana.ca/view/oocihm.lac_reel_c1/1013?r=0&s=4.
194 Colpitts, *Pemmican Empire*, 135.
195 Colpitts, *Pemmican Empire*, 136.

Chapter 5: Menace and Ally
1 Edith I. Burley, *Servants of the Honourable Company: Work, Discipline, and Conflict in the Hudson's Bay Company, 1770–1879* (Toronto: Oxford University Press, 1997), 41.
2 George Colpitts, *Pemmican Empire: Food, Trade, and the Last Bison Hunts in the North American Plains, 1780–1882* (Cambridge: Cambridge University Press, 2014), 135.
3 Ian Hunter, "Vattel in Revolutionary America: From the Rules of War to the Rule of Law," in *Between Indigenous and Settler Governance*, ed. Lisa Ford and Tim Rowse (London: Routledge, 2012), 18.
4 Samuel Hull Wilcocke, *A Narrative of Occurrences in the Indian Countries of North America* (Covent-Garden, UK: B. McMillan, 1817), 106. For the Hudson's Bay Company, there was a long history of overlap between loyalty to the company and loyalty to England, which became more pronounced during times of conflict with France. See Scott P. Stephen, *Masters and Servants: The Hudson's Bay Company and Its North American Workforce, 1668–1786* (Edmonton: University of Alberta Press, 2019), 202.
5 Glen Sean Coulthard, *Red Skin, White Masks: Rejecting the Colonial Politics of Recognition*, Indigenous Americas (Minneapolis: University of Minnesota Press, 2014), 95.
6 W. McGillivray, A.N. McLeod, and A. McKenzie, "Letter to Macdonell, 22 July 1813," LAC – Selkirk Collection, 798, https://heritage.canadiana.ca/view/oocihm.lac_reel_c1/807?r=0&s=3.
7 McGillivray, McLeod, and McKenzie, "Letter to Macdonell, 22 July 1813," 798.
8 Miles Macdonell, "Letter to Selkirk, 17 July 1813," LAC – Selkirk Collection, 764, https://heritage.canadiana.ca/view/oocihm.lac_reel_c1/775?r=0&s=1.
9 Macdonell, "Letter to Selkirk, 17 July 1813," 768, 771, 774.
10 Macdonell, "Letter to Selkirk, 17 July 1813," 792.
11 Thomas Douglas Selkirk, "Letter to Macdonell, 13 June 1813," LAC – Selkirk Collection, 670, http://heritage.canadiana.ca/view/oocihm.lac_reel_c1/679?r=0&s=4.
12 J.M. Bumsted, "Editorial Introduction," in *The Collected Writings of Lord Selkirk 1810–1820*, ed. J.M. Bumsted (Winnipeg: Manitoba Record Society, 1988), xxix.
13 Colpitts, *Pemmican Empire*, 128.
14 Colpitts, *Pemmican Empire*, 128.

236 Notes to pages 132–34

15 Colpitts, *Pemmican Empire*, 129.
16 Michel Hogue, *Metis and the Medicine Line: Creating a Border and Dividing a People* (Chapel Hill: University of North Carolina Press, 2015), 30.
17 Colpitts, *Pemmican Empire*, 132.
18 Colpitts, *Pemmican Empire*, 134.
19 Colpitts, *Pemmican Empire*, 134.
20 Richard Burn, *The Justice of the Peace, and Parish Officer*, ed. George Chetwynd, 23rd ed., vol. 1 (London: A. Strahan and W. Woodfall, 1820), xix–xx.
21 Burn, *The Justice of the Peace, and Parish Officer*, 1: 27.
22 Bumsted, "Editorial Introduction" (1988), xxx.
23 Miles Macdonell, "Proclamation, 8 January 1814," LAC – Selkirk Collection, 916, http://heritage.canadiana.ca/view/oocihm.lac_reel_c1/927?r=0&s=4.
24 Miles Macdonell, "Journal: 22 April 1813 to 7 April 1815," LAC – Selkirk Collection, 16872, http://heritage.canadiana.ca/view/oocihm.lac_reel_c16/207?r=0&s=1.
25 Bumsted, "Editorial Introduction" (1988), xix.
26 Macdonell, "Proclamation, 8 January 1814," 918.
27 Colpitts, *Pemmican Empire*, 140.
28 William Auld, "Letter to Hillier, 8 April 1814," LAC – Selkirk Collection, 998, http://heritage.canadiana.ca/view/oocihm.lac_reel_c1/1002?r=0&s=4.
29 Colpitts, *Pemmican Empire*, 136.
30 J.M. Bumsted, *Lord Selkirk: A Life* (Winnipeg: University of Manitoba Press, 2008), 68.
31 Alexander Ross, *The Red River Settlement: Its Rise, Progress, and Present State: With Some Account of the Native* ... (London: Smith, Elder and Company, 1856), 25.
32 Bumsted, "Editorial Introduction" (1988), xxxii.
33 Gerhard J. Ens and Joe Sawchuk, *From New Peoples to New Nations: Aspects of Metis History and Identity from the Eighteenth to the Twenty-First Centuries* (Toronto: University of Toronto Press, 2015), 74.
34 Macdonell, "Journal: 22 April 1813 to 7 April 1815," 16881; Ross Mitchell, "Early Doctors of Red River and Manitoba," *Transactions* (Manitoba Historical Society), Series 3 (1947–1948), http://www.mhs.mb.ca/docs/transactions/3/earlydoctors.shtml.
35 Macdonell, "Journal: 22 April 1813 to 7 April 1815," 16899–900.
36 Macdonell, "Journal: 22 April 1813 to 7 April 1815," 16901.
37 Macdonell, "Journal: 22 April 1813 to 7 April 1815," 16902.
38 Miles Macdonell, "Letter Respecting the Arrest of Mr. Howse, 15 June 1814," LAC – Selkirk Collection, 938, http://heritage.canadiana.ca/view/oocihm.lac_reel_c1/949?r=0&s=4.
39 Bumsted, "Editorial Introduction" (1988), xxiv.
40 Duncan Cameron, John McDonald, John Wills, and J.D. Cameron, "From Proprietors of NWC, 16 June 1814," LAC – Selkirk Collection, 942, http://heritage.canadiana.ca/view/oocihm.lac_reel_c1/953?r=0&s=4.
41 Bumsted, "Editorial Introduction" (1988), xxxiv.
42 Gerhard John Ens, *Homeland to Hinterland: The Changing Worlds of the Red River Metis in the Nineteenth Century* (Toronto: University of Toronto Press, 1996), 15.
43 Ens, *Homeland to Hinterland*, 17.
44 Carolyn Podruchny and Nicole St-Onge, "Scuttling along a Spider's Web: Mobility and Kinship in Metis Ethnogenesis," in *Contours of a People: Metis Family, Mobility, and History*, ed. Nicole St-Onge, Carolyn Podruchny, and Brenda Macdougall (Norman: University of Oklahoma Press, 2012), 69.
45 Colpitts, *Pemmican Empire*, 138.
46 Colpitts, *Pemmican Empire*, 138.
47 Colpitts, *Pemmican Empire*, 137.

Notes to pages 134–37   237

48 Colpitts, *Pemmican Empire*, 136.
49 Miles Macdonell, "Journal: 6 July 1812 to 22 April 1813," LAC – Selkirk Collection, 16754, 16778, http://heritage.canadiana.ca/view/oocihm.lac_reel_c16/207?r=0&s=1. Notably, he was the grandfather of Louis Riel, the famed leader of the Métis in the mid- to late nineteenth century.
50 Colpitts, *Pemmican Empire*, 136.
51 Macdonell, "Journal: 6 July 1812 to 22 April 1813," 16763. Macdonell actually mentioned two people by the name of Francois De Lorme, a father and his son; the former was the French Canadian freeman in question, and the latter was one of the Métis children from the marriage of Francois Sr. and Madeleine Sauteuse, a Saulteaux woman. See Doris Jeanne MacKinnon, *The Identities of Marie Rose Delorme Smith: Portrait of a Metis Woman, 1861–1960* (Regina: University of Regina Press, 2012), 13.
52 Colpitts, *Pemmican Empire*, 137; Macdonell, "Journal: 6 July 1812 to 22 April 1813," 16763.
53 Ens, *Homeland to Hinterland*, 17, clarifies that those usually deemed "halfbreeds" were descendants of British men who worked for the Hudson's Bay Company, whereas "Métis" referred to those who were likely French in origin and had some connection to the North West Company.
54 Macdonell, "Journal: 6 July 1812 to 22 April 1813," 16777, 16787. See also Colpitts, *Pemmican Empire*, 135.
55 Macdonell, "Journal: 6 July 1812 to 22 April 1813," 16765–66.
56 Ens and Sawchuk, *From New Peoples to New Nations*, 74.
57 Sarah Carter, *Aboriginal People and Colonizers of Western Canada to 1900*, Themes in Canadian Social History (Toronto: University of Toronto Press, 1999), 66.
58 Bumsted, "Editorial Introduction" (1988), xxxv; Macdonell, "Letter to Selkirk, 17 July 1813," 793.
59 See, for example, Macdonell, "Journal: 22 April 1813 to 7 April 1815," 16914.
60 Bumsted, "Editorial Introduction" (1988), xxxv.
61 Carter, *Aboriginal People and Colonizers of Western Canada to 1900*, 68.
62 Michael Hughes, "Within the Grasp of Company Law: Land, Legitimacy, and the Racialization of the Métis, 1815–1821," *Ethnohistory* 63, no. 3 (2016): 522, https://doi.org/10.1215/00141801-3496811; Lyle Dick, "The Seven Oaks Incident and the Construction of a Historical Tradition, 1816 to 1970," *Journal of the Canadian Historical Association* 2, no. 1 (1991): 98–99; Ens and Sawchuk, *From New Peoples to New Nations*, 81–82.
63 Miles Macdonell, "Letter to William Auld, 4 February 1814," LAC – Selkirk Collection, 959, http://heritage.canadiana.ca/view/oocihm.lac_reel_c1/962?r=0&s=4.
64 Bumsted, "Editorial Introduction" (1988), xxxiv.
65 Ens and Sawchuk, *From New Peoples to New Nations*, 77.
66 Ens and Sawchuk, *From New Peoples to New Nations*, 77.
67 Bumsted, "Editorial Introduction" (1988), xxxiv.
68 J.M. Bumsted, *Trials and Tribulations: The Red River Settlement and the Emergence of Manitoba, 1811–1870* (Winnipeg: Great Plains Publications, 2003), 13.
69 Jean Morrison, *Superior Rendezvous-Place: Fort William in the Canadian Fur Trade*, 2nd ed. (Toronto: Natural Heritage, 2007), 81.
70 Morrison, *Superior Rendezvous-Place*, 81, 83.
71 William Auld, "Letter to Macdonell, 13 March 1814," LAC – Selkirk Collection, 977, http://heritage.canadiana.ca/view/oocihm.lac_reel_c1/983?r=0&s=3.
72 Auld, "Letter to Hillier, 8 April 1814," 992–93.
73 Macdonell, "Journal: 22 April 1813 to 7 April 1815," 16915.
74 Ens and Sawchuk, *From New Peoples to New Nations*, 77.

238 *Notes to pages 137–40*

75 Ens and Sawchuk, *From New Peoples to New Nations*, 77.
76 Alice E. Brown, "A Brief Chronology of Events Relative to Lord Selkirk's Settlement at Red River: 1811 to 1815," *Manitoba Pageant* 7, no. 3 (1962), http://www.mhs.mb.ca/docs/pageant/07/selkirkchronology.shtml.
77 Macdonell, "Journal: 22 April 1813 to 7 April 1815," 16906.
78 Macdonell, "Journal: 22 April 1813 to 7 April 1815," 16910. By this time, the Premier and his group had been farming in the area along the Red River. See Peter Fidler, "1815–1816: 29 May 1816," Archives of Manitoba, Brandon House Post Journal, 36, http://pam.minisisinc.com/DIGITALOBJECTS/Access/HBCA%20Microfilm/1M17/B22-A-19.pdf.
79 Macdonell, "Journal: 22 April 1813 to 7 April 1815," 16911.
80 Macdonell, "Journal: 22 April 1813 to 7 April 1815," 16910.
81 Macdonell, "Journal: 22 April 1813 to 7 April 1815," 16915.
82 John MacIntyre, "MacIntyre Complaint to Selkirk, 25 July 1814," LAC – Selkirk Collection, 1182, http://heritage.canadiana.ca/view/oocihm.lac_reel_c2/133?r=0&s=3.
83 J.E. Foster, "Auld, William (c. 1770–c. 1830)," in *Dictionary of Canadian Biography*, vol. 6 (Toronto: University of Toronto; Laval: Université Laval, 1987), http://www.biographi.ca/en/bio/auld_william_6E.html.
84 Macdonell, "Journal: 22 April 1813 to 7 April 1815," 16912.
85 Macdonell, "Journal: 22 April 1813 to 7 April 1815," 16914.
86 Macdonell, "Journal: 22 April 1813 to 7 April 1815," 16913.
87 Miles Macdonell, "Letter to Selkirk, 25 July 1814," LAC – Selkirk Collection, 1193, https://heritage.canadiana.ca/view/oocihm.lac_reel_c2/279?r=0&s=1.
88 Macdonell, "Letter to Selkirk, 25 July 1814," 1197.
89 Herbert J. Mays, "Macdonell, Miles (1767–1828)," in *Dictionary of Canadian Biography*, vol. 6 (Toronto: University of Toronto; Laval: Université Laval, 1987), http://www.biographi.ca/en/bio/macdonell_miles_6E.html.
90 Bumsted, "Editorial Introduction" (1988), xxxv.
91 Thomas Douglas Selkirk, "General Instructions and Observations, 12 April 1814," LAC – Selkirk Collection, 1009–10, http://heritage.canadiana.ca/view/oocihm.lac_reel_c1/1017?r=0&s=4.
92 Macdonell, "Journal: 22 April 1813 to 7 April 1815," 16919–20.
93 Macdonell, "Journal: 22 April 1813 to 7 April 1815," 16921.
94 Abel Edwards, "Report on the State of M. Macdonell Aug–Sept 1814," LAC – Selkirk Collection, 1207–9, http://heritage.canadiana.ca/view/oocihm.lac_reel_c2/158?r=0&s=3.
95 Miles Macdonell, "Resignation Letter from Macdonell, 2 September 1814," LAC – Selkirk Collection, 1213–14, http://heritage.canadiana.ca/view/oocihm.lac_reel_c2/164?r=0&s=3.
96 Macdonell, "Journal: 22 April 1813 to 7 April 1815," 16925.
97 Irene Ternier Gordon, *The Laird of Fort William: William McGillivray and the North West Company* (Victoria: Heritage House, 2013), 114.
98 Gordon, *The Laird of Fort William*, 113.
99 Barry Gough, *Through Water, Ice and Fire: The HMS Nancy and the War of 1812* (Toronto: Dundurn, 2006), 41.
100 Gough, *Through Water, Ice and Fire*, 41.
101 Gough, *Through Water, Ice and Fire*, 45.
102 Gough, *Through Water, Ice and Fire*, 51.
103 Gough, *Through Water, Ice and Fire*, 55.
104 Gough, *Through Water, Ice and Fire*, 113.
105 Gough, *Through Water, Ice and Fire*, 117.
106 Macdonell, "Journal: 22 April 1813 to 7 April 1815," 16932.
107 Macdonell, "Journal: 22 April 1813 to 7 April 1815," 16933.

Notes to pages 140–44 239

108 Joseph Berens, "Observations on Judicial Instructions Proposed, 1814," LAC – Selkirk Collection, 12016, http://heritage.canadiana.ca/view/oocihm.lac_reel_c11/904?r=0&s=3.
109 John Spencer, "Letter to Selkirk, 8 December 1814," LAC – Selkirk Collection, 1139, http://heritage.canadiana.ca/view/oocihm.lac_reel_c2/84?r=0&s=3.
110 Miles Macdonell, "Notice to Allan McDonnell," 1814, LAC – Selkirk Collection, 11978, http://heritage.canadiana.ca/view/oocihm.lac_reel_c11/865?r=0&s=3; Miles Macdonell, "Notice to Andrew Poitras," 1814, LAC – Selkirk Collection, 11979, http://heritage.canadiana.ca/view/oocihm.lac_reel_c11/866?r=0&s=3; Miles Macdonell, "Notice to Duncan Cameron," 1814, LAC – Selkirk Collection, 1250, http://heritage.canadiana.ca/view/oocihm.lac_reel_c2/201?r=0&s=3; Miles Macdonell, "Notice to John Dugal Cameron," 1814, LAC – Selkirk Collection, 1251, http://heritage.canadiana.ca/view/oocihm.lac_reel_c2/202?r=0&s=3; Miles Macdonell, "Notice to Alexander Kennedy," 1814, LAC – Selkirk Collection, 1460, http://heritage.canadiana.ca/view/oocihm.lac_reel_c2/418?r=0&s=3; Miles Macdonell, "Notice to Joseph McAngus McGilles," 1814, LAC – Selkirk Collection, 1491, http://heritage.canadiana.ca/view/oocihm.lac_reel_c2/449?r=0&s=3; Macdonell, "Letter to Selkirk, 25 July 1814," 1200.
111 Macdonell, "Letter to Selkirk, 25 July 1814," 1200.
112 Macdonell, "Letter to Selkirk, 25 July 1814," 1200.
113 Macdonell, "Letter to Selkirk, 25 July 1814," 1201.
114 Thomas Douglas Selkirk, "Letter to Macdonell, 21 December 1814," LAC – Selkirk Collection, 1288, http://heritage.canadiana.ca/view/oocihm.lac_reel_c2/238?r=0&s=3.
115 Selkirk, "Letter to Macdonell, 21 December 1814," 1289.
116 HBC Committee, "Letter to Thomas, April 1814," LAC – Selkirk Collection, 1369, https://heritage.canadiana.ca/view/oocihm.lac_reel_c2/279?r=0&s=1.
117 HBC Committee, "Letter to Thomas, April 1814," 1371.
118 William Auld, "Letter to Thomas, 29 March 1815," LAC – Selkirk Collection, 1512, http://heritage.canadiana.ca/view/oocihm.lac_reel_c2/466?r=0&s=3.
119 Bumsted, "Editorial Introduction" (1988), xxxii.
120 HBC Committee, "Instructions to Thomas, May 1814," LAC – Selkirk Collection, 1308–9, https://heritage.canadiana.ca/view/oocihm.lac_reel_c2/260?r=0&s=2.
121 Bumsted, "Editorial Introduction" (1988), xxxii.
122 Macdonell, "Journal: 22 April 1813 to 7 April 1815," 16953.
123 Laura L. Peers, "The Ojibwa, Red River and the Forks, 1770–1870," in *The Forks and the Battle of Seven Oaks in Manitoba History,* ed. Robert Coutts and Richard Stuart (Winnipeg: Manitoba Historical Society, 1994), http://www.mhs.mb.ca/docs/forkssevenoaks/ojibwa.shtml.
124 Macdonell, "Journal: 22 April 1813 to 7 April 1815," 16948.
125 Macdonell, "Journal: 22 April 1813 to 7 April 1815," 16956.
126 Macdonell, "Journal: 22 April 1813 to 7 April 1815," 16957.
127 A lack of willingness among servants to adopt military positions in defence of the Hudson's Bay Company was not a new phenomenon but dated back to the late 1600s; see Stephen, *Masters and Servants,* 41.
128 Bumsted, "Editorial Introduction" (1988), xxxviii.
129 Bumsted, "Editorial Introduction" (1988), xxxix.
130 Thomas Douglas Selkirk, "Letter to Bathurst, 3 March 1815," LAC – Selkirk Collection, 1476, http://heritage.canadiana.ca/view/oocihm.lac_reel_c2/434?r=0&s=3.
131 Selkirk, "Letter to Bathurst, 3 March 1815," 1476.
132 Selkirk, "Letter to Bathurst, 3 March 1815," 1476.
133 Selkirk, "Letter to Bathurst, 3 March 1815," 1479.
134 Selkirk, "Letter to Bathurst, 3 March 1815," 1482.

240   Notes to pages 144–48

135   Lord Bathurst, "Memo to Selkirk, 11 March 1815," LAC – Selkirk Collection, 1487, http://heritage.canadiana.ca/view/oocihm.lac_reel_c2/445?r=0&s=3.
136   Bumsted, "Editorial Introduction" (1988), xl.
137   Thomas Douglas Selkirk, "Letter to Macdonell, 23 March 1815," LAC – Selkirk Collection, 1498, http://heritage.canadiana.ca/view/oocihm.lac_reel_c2/450?r=0&s=3.
138   Selkirk, "Letter to Macdonell, 23 March 1815," 1492.
139   Bumsted, "Editorial Introduction" (1988), xli.
140   Selkirk, "Letter to Macdonell, 23 March 1815," 1493.
141   Selkirk, "Letter to Macdonell, 23 March 1815," 1493.
142   Selkirk, "Letter to Macdonell, 23 March 1815," 1494.
143   Selkirk, "Letter to Macdonell, 23 March 1815," 1494.
144   Selkirk, "Letter to Macdonell, 23 March 1815," 1502.
145   Selkirk, "Letter to Macdonell, 23 March 1815," 1503.
146   Macdonell, "Journal: 22 April 1813 to 7 April 1815," 16960.
147   John McLeod, "Letter to Selkirk, 5 August 1815," LAC – Selkirk Collection, 1593, http://heritage.canadiana.ca/view/oocihm.lac_reel_c2/551?r=0&s=3.
148   Bumsted, *Trials and Tribulations*, 14.
149   Macdonell, "Journal: 22 April 1813 to 7 April 1815," 16964.
150   Macdonell, "Journal: 22 April 1813 to 7 April 1815," 16970.
151   Macdonell, "Journal: 22 April 1813 to 7 April 1815," 16972.
152   Macdonell, "Journal: 22 April 1813 to 7 April 1815," 16976–77.
153   Macdonell, "Journal: 22 April 1813 to 7 April 1815," 16980–81.
154   Miles Macdonell, "Letter to Selkirk, 20 June 1815," LAC – Selkirk Collection, 1563, http://heritage.canadiana.ca/view/oocihm.lac_reel_c2/519?r=0&s=3.
155   Miles Macdonell, "Journal: 7 April 1815 to 17 June 1815," LAC – Selkirk Collection, 16984, http://heritage.canadiana.ca/view/oocihm.lac_reel_c16/497?r=0&s=4.
156   Macdonell, "Journal: 7 April 1815 to 17 June 1815," 16989.
157   Macdonell, "Journal: 7 April 1815 to 17 June 1815," 17001.
158   Ross, *The Red River Settlement*, 28.
159   Hartwell Bowsfield, "Semple, Robert (1777–1816)," in *Dictionary of Canadian Biography*, vol. 5 (Toronto: University of Toronto; Laval: Université Laval, 1983), http://www.biographi.ca/en/bio/semple_robert_5E.html.
160   Bumsted, "Editorial Introduction" (1988), xli.
161   Samuel Hull Wilcocke, Simon McGillivray, and Edward Ellice, *A Narrative of Occurrences in the Indian Countries of North America, since the Connexion of the Right Hon. the Earl of Selkirk with the Hudson's Bay Company, and His Attempt to Establish a Colony on the Red River: With a Detailed Account of His Lordship's Military Expedition To, and Subsequent Proceedings at Fort William, in Upper Canada* (Covent-Garden, UK: B. McMillan, 1817), 41.
162   Bumsted, "Editorial Introduction" (1988), xlii.
163   James Daschuk, *Clearing the Plains: Disease, Politics of Starvation, and the Loss of Aboriginal Life* (Regina: University of Regina Press, 2013), 54.
164   George Woodcock, "Robertson, Colin (1783–1842)," in *Dictionary of Canadian Biography*, vol. 7 (Toronto: University of Toronto; Laval: Université Laval, 1988), http://www.biographi.ca/en/bio/robertson_colin_7E.html.
165   Bumsted, *Trials and Tribulations*, 15.
166   Macdonell, "Journal: 7 April 1815 to 17 June 1815," 17008–10.
167   Macdonell, "Journal: 7 April 1815 to 17 June 1815," 17011.
168   Macdonell, "Journal: 7 April 1815 to 17 June 1815," 17013.
169   Macdonell, "Journal: 7 April 1815 to 17 June 1815," 17014–15.

Notes to pages 148–51 241

170 Macdonell, "Journal: 7 April 1815 to 17 June 1815," 17017–18.
171 Macdonell, "Journal: 7 April 1815 to 17 June 1815," 17021.
172 Macdonell, "Journal: 7 April 1815 to 17 June 1815," 17023.
173 Duncan Cameron, "To the Servants of HBC, 7 June 1815," LAC – Selkirk Collection, 1534, http://heritage.canadiana.ca/view/oocihm.lac_reel_c2/492?r=0&s=3.
174 James White, Archibald McDonald, Joseph Sutherland, and Peter Fidler, "To Duncan Cameron, 12 June 1815," LAC – Selkirk Collection, 1535, http://heritage.canadiana.ca/view/oocihm.lac_reel_c2/494?r=0&s=3.
175 White et al., "To Duncan Cameron, 12 June 1815," 1535.
176 Miles Macdonell, "Letter to Selkirk, 25 June 1815," LAC – Selkirk Collection, 1580, C-2, http://heritage.canadiana.ca/view/oocihm.lac_reel_c2/537?r=0&s=3.

Chapter 6: Consciousness and Ignorance

1 Louis Aubrey Wood, *The Red River Colony: A Chronicle of the Beginnings of Manitoba* (Glasgow: Brook, 1915), 67.
2 Laura L. Peers, "Rich Man, Poor Man, Beggarman, Chief: Saulteaux in the Red River Settlement," in *Papers of the Eighteenth Algonquian Conference*, ed. William Cowan (Ottawa: Carleton University, 1987), 263.
3 John Halkett, *Statement Respecting the Earl of Selkirk's Settlement upon the Red River, in North America: Its Destruction in the Years 1815 and 1816; and the Massacre of Governor Semple and His Party; with Observations upon a Recent Publication, Entitled "A Narrative of Occurrances [sic] in the Indian Countries," &c* (London: John Murray, 1817), xxxi.
4 Miles Macdonell, "Journal: 22 April 1813 to 7 April 1815," LAC – Selkirk Collection, 16954, https://heritage.canadiana.ca/view/oocihm.lac_reel_c16/333?r=0&s=2.
5 Macdonell's entry names the leader as "Cayach Cobion, i.e. strong painting," but this might be an error in transcription since the handwriting is unclear; see Macdonell, "Journal: 22 April 1813 to 7 April 1815," 16954–55. The nearest phonetic, geographical, and temporal approximation of this name is "Kaygecaon"; see Alexander Henry and David Thompson, *New Light on the Early History of the Greater Northwest* (Cambridge: Cambridge University Press, 2015), 53.
6 Gerhard John Ens, "The Battle of Seven Oaks and the Articulation of a Metis National Tradition, 1811–1849," in *Contours of a People: Metis Family, Mobility, and History*, ed. Nicole St-Onge, Carolyn Podruchny, and Brenda Macdougall (Norman: University of Oklahoma Press, 2014), 99; J.M. Bumsted, *Trials and Tribulations: The Red River Settlement and the Emergence of Manitoba, 1811–1870* (Winnipeg: Great Plains Publications, 2003), 15.
7 J.M. Bumsted, "Editorial Introduction," in *The Collected Writings of Lord Selkirk 1810–1820*, ed. J.M. Bumsted (Winnipeg: Manitoba Record Society, 1988), xl.
8 Macdonell, "Journal: 7 April 1815 to 17 June 1815," 16985.
9 Bumsted, "Editorial Introduction" (1988), xliv.
10 Miles Macdonell, "Letter from Macdonell to Selkirk, 19 September 1815," LAC – Selkirk Collection, 1710, C-2, http://heritage.canadiana.ca/view/oocihm.lac_reel_c2/656?r=0&s=2.
11 Peers, "Rich Man, Poor Man, Beggarman, Chief," 264.
12 Peers, "Rich Man, Poor Man, Beggarman, Chief," 264.
13 Laura L. Peers, *The Ojibwa of Western Canada, 1780 to 1870* (Winnipeg: University of Manitoba Press, 1984), 75. Peguis was previously aligned with the North West Company until a disagreement occurred in 1812.
14 Peers, "Rich Man, Poor Man, Beggarman, Chief," 264.
15 Peers, *The Ojibwa of Western Canada*, 67.
16 Peers, *The Ojibwa of Western Canada*, 68.

242 Notes to pages 151–56

17 Peers, *The Ojibwa of Western Canada*, 70–71.
18 Peers, *The Ojibwa of Western Canada*, 73.
19 Jennifer S.H. Brown, *Strangers in Blood: Fur Trade Company Families in Indian Country* (Vancouver: UBC Press, 1996), 173.
20 Brown, *Strangers in Blood*, 173.
21 Margaret MacLeod and W.L. Morton, *Cuthbert Grant of Grantown* (Montreal and Kingston: McGill-Queen's University Press, 1963), 28.
22 MacLeod and Morton, *Cuthbert Grant of Grantown*, 29.
23 Carolyn Podruchny and Nicole St-Onge, "Scuttling along a Spider's Web: Mobility and Kinship in Metis Ethnogenesis," in *Contours of a People: Metis Family, Mobility, and History*, ed. Nicole St-Onge, Carolyn Podruchny, and Brenda Macdougall (Norman: University of Oklahoma Press, 2012), 61–62.
24 Quoted in Myrna Kostash, *The Seven Oaks Reader*, UK ed. (Edmonton: NeWest Press, 2016), 134.
25 For a recent analysis of "racial mixing as a tool" in the Canadian political and academic landscapes, see Daniel Voth, "The Race Question in Canada and the Politics of Racial Mixing," in *A People and a Nation: New Direction in Contemporary Métis Studies*, ed. Jennifer Adese amd Chris Andersen (Vancouver: UBC Press, 2021), 69. Voth traces the "tradition of operationalizing racial mixing in the service of settler Canadian state building" (86), arguing convincingly that this provided (and continues to provide) fodder for a multiculturalist ideal in a manner that "advances the violent, heteronormative, gendered disempowerment of the Métis and other Indigenous Peoples" (88).
26 MacLeod and Morton, *Cuthbert Grant of Grantown*, 29–30.
27 MacLeod and Morton, *Cuthbert Grant of Grantown*, 29–30.
28 Brown, *Strangers in Blood*, 173.
29 Bumsted, "Editorial Introduction" (1988), xlv.
30 Bumsted, "Editorial Introduction" (1988), xlv.
31 Macdonell, "Letter from Macdonell to Selkirk, 19 September 1815," 1699.
32 Macdonell, "Letter from Macdonell to Selkirk, 19 September 1815," 1709.
33 Macdonell, "Letter from Macdonell to Selkirk, 19 September 1815," 1700.
34 Macdonell, "Letter from Macdonell to Selkirk, 19 September 1815," 1705.
35 Wood, *The Red River Colony*, 78.
36 Gerhard J. Ens and Joe Sawchuk, *From New Peoples to New Nations: Aspects of Metis History and Identity from the Eighteenth to the Twenty-First Centuries* (Toronto: University of Toronto Press, 2015), 78.
37 Robert B. Hill, *Manitoba: History of Its Early Settlement, Development, and Resources* (Toronto: W. Briggs, 1890), 33.
38 Bumsted, "Editorial Introduction" (1988), xlvi.
39 Bumsted, "Editorial Introduction" (1988), xlvi.
40 Ens and Sawchuk, *From New Peoples to New Nations*, 78.
41 Wood, *The Red River Colony*, 83–84.
42 Peter Fidler, "1815–1816: 31 August 1815," Archives of Manitoba, Brandon House Post Journal, 5; Peter Fidler, "1815–1816: 11 September 1815," Archives of Manitoba, Brandon House Post Journal, 6.
43 Hill, *Manitoba*, 34.
44 Quoted in Wood, *The Red River Colony*, 86.
45 Macdonell, "Letter from Macdonell to Selkirk, 19 September 1815," 1707.
46 Wood, *The Red River Colony*, 84.
47 Colin Robertson, "Journal of Colin Robertson," 1815, LAC – Selkirk Collection, 1712, C-2, http://heritage.canadiana.ca/view/oocihm.lac_reel_c2/669?r=0&s=2.

Notes to pages 156–61   243

48 Robertson, "Journal of Colin Robertson," 1713.
49 Robertson, "Journal of Colin Robertson," 1712.
50 Chester Martin, *Lord Selkirk's Work in Canada*, vol. 7, Oxford Historical and Literary Studies (Oxford: Clarendon Press, 1916), 99, http://archive.org/details/lordselkirksworko7martuoft.
51 Henry ("Mercator") McKenzie, *The Communications of Mercator, upon the Contest between the Earl of Selkirk and the Hudson's Bay Company, on One Side, and the North West Company on the Other* (Montreal: W. Gray, 1817), 21, http://peel.library.ualberta.ca/bibliography/105.html.
52 Bumsted, "Editorial Introduction" (1988), l.
53 Samuel Hull Wilcocke, *A Narrative of Occurrences in the Indian Countries of North America* (Covent-Garden, UK: B. McMillan, 1817), 47.
54 Hill, *Manitoba*, 34.
55 Bumsted, "Editorial Introduction" (1988), l.
56 Martin, *Lord Selkirk's Work in Canada*, 7: 100.
57 William McGillivray, "Letter, 28 November 1815," in *Papers Relating to the Red River Settlement: 1815–1819* (London: Colonial Department, 1819), 36.
58 McGillivray, "Letter, 28 November 1815," 37.
59 See, for example, Martin, *Lord Selkirk's Work in Canada*, 7: 103.
60 Robert Semple, "Letter to Robertson, 5 September 1815," LAC – Selkirk Collection, 1653, C-2, http://heritage.canadiana.ca/view/oocihm.lac_reel_c2/610?r=0&s=2.
61 MacLeod and Morton, *Cuthbert Grant of Grantown*, 31.
62 Thomas Douglas Selkirk, "Deposition of Mitchell Chrain," January 1816, LAC – Selkirk Collection, 1862, C-2, http://heritage.canadiana.ca/view/oocihm.lac_reel_c2/822?r=0&s=2.
63 Dale Gibson, *Law, Life, and Government at Red River, Volume 1: Settlement and Governance, 1812–1872* (Montreal and Kingston: McGill-Queen's University Press, 2015), 7.
64 Bumsted, "Editorial Introduction" (1988), li.
65 Bumsted, "Editorial Introduction" (1988), li; Halkett, *Statement Respecting the Earl of Selkirk's Settlement upon the Red River, in North America*, lxxxiv.
66 Martin, *Lord Selkirk's Work in Canada*, 7: 106.
67 Duncan Cameron, "Letter to A. Macdonell, 24 February 1816," LAC – Selkirk Collection, 8862, C-8, http://heritage.canadiana.ca/view/oocihm.lac_reel_c8/1087?r=0&s=2.
68 Cameron, "Letter to A. Macdonell, 24 February 1816," 8864.
69 Cuthbert Grant, "Letter to J.D. Cameron, 13 March 1816," LAC – Selkirk Collection, 1881, C-2, http://heritage.canadiana.ca/view/oocihm.lac_reel_c2/841?r=0&s=2.
70 Martin, *Lord Selkirk's Work in Canada*, 7: 107–8.
71 Thomas Douglas Selkirk, "Letter to Robertson, 30 March 1816," LAC – Selkirk Collection, 1894, C-2, http://heritage.canadiana.ca/view/oocihm.lac_reel_c2/854?r=0&s=2.
72 Selkirk, "Letter to Robertson, 30 March 1816," 1897.
73 Selkirk, "Letter to Robertson, 30 March 1816," 1895–96.
74 James Sutherland, "Narrative of Joseph Sutherland Respecting Proceedings at Qu'Appelle in Winter of 1815–1816," 1816, LAC – Selkirk Collection, 1951, C-2, http://heritage.canadiana.ca/view/oocihm.lac_reel_c2/906?r=0&s=2. At various points, the Métis referred to the HBC men as the English; I keep those references intact where they occur, but I do recognize that many of the HBC men operating in the district were Scottish, though the company itself was chartered and headquartered in England.
75 Sutherland, "Narrative of Joseph Sutherland Respecting Proceedings at Qu'Appelle in Winter of 1815–1816," 1952.
76 James Sutherland, "Letter to Fidler, 2 April 1816," LAC – Selkirk Collection, 2161, C-3, http://heritage.canadiana.ca/view/oocihm.lac_reel_c3/62?r=0&s=2.

244 Notes to pages 161–64

77 Sutherland, "Narrative of Joseph Sutherland Respecting Proceedings at Qu'Appelle in Winter of 1815–1816," 1954.
78 Sutherland, "Narrative of Joseph Sutherland Respecting Proceedings at Qu'Appelle in Winter of 1815–1816," 1958.
79 Peter Fidler, "1815–1816, 12 May 1816," Archives of Manitoba, Brandon House Post Journal, 30; "1815–1816, 13 May 1816," Archives of Manitoba, Brandon House Post Journal, 31.
80 Meredith Bacola, "'Through the Intercession of the Apostle of Their Nation': The Context of St Boniface's Church Dedication in the Formation of the Archdioceses of St Boniface and Winnipeg," *Historical Studies* 84 (2018): 94.
81 Gordon Drummond, "Letter to Selkirk, 23 March 1816," LAC – Selkirk Collection, 2110, C-3, http://heritage.canadiana.ca/view/oocihm.lac_reel_c3/9?r=0&s=2.
82 Gordon Drummond, "Letter to Selkirk, 13 April 1816," LAC – Selkirk Collection, 2238, C-3, http://heritage.canadiana.ca/view/oocihm.lac_reel_c3/138?r=0&s=2.
83 Halkett, *Statement Respecting the Earl of Selkirk's Settlement upon the Red River, in North America*, lxxxv.
84 Bumsted, "Editorial Introduction" (1988), liv.
85 The Premier, "Premier (Chief) Speech to Governor Semple," May 10, 1816, LAC – Selkirk Collection, 9211, C-9, http://heritage.canadiana.ca/view/oocihm.lac_reel_c9/316?r=0&s=3.
86 Sutherland, "Narrative of Joseph Sutherland Respecting Proceedings at Qu'Appelle in Winter of 1815–1816," 1954.
87 Peter Fidler, "Letter to Semple, 2 June 1816," LAC – Selkirk Collection, 2315, C-3, http://heritage.canadiana.ca/view/oocihm.lac_reel_c3/217?r=0&s=2.
88 Fidler, "Letter to Semple, 2 June 1816," 2315.
89 Fidler, "Letter to Semple, 2 June 1816," 2316.
90 Kostash, *The Seven Oaks Reader*, 114.
91 W. McGillivray, "Letter to Johnstone, 18 July 1816," LAC – Selkirk Collection, 2455, C-3, http://heritage.canadiana.ca/view/oocihm.lac_reel_c3/363?r=0&s=2.
92 Martin, *Lord Selkirk's Work in Canada*, 7: 110.
93 Kostash, *The Seven Oaks Reader*, 2.
94 McGillivray, "Letter to Johnstone, 18 July 1816," 2457.
95 Wilcocke, McGillivray, and Ellice, *A Narrative of Occurrences in the Indian Countries*, 55.
96 Wilcocke, McGillivray, and Ellice, *A Narrative of Occurrences in the Indian Countries*, 56.
97 Kostash, *The Seven Oaks Reader*, 154.
98 Martin, *Lord Selkirk's Work in Canada*, 7: 110.
99 Kostash, *The Seven Oaks Reader*, 2.
100 Martin, *Lord Selkirk's Work in Canada*, 7: 111.
101 Martin, *Lord Selkirk's Work in Canada*, 7: 112.
102 Kostash, *The Seven Oaks Reader*, 155.
103 Peers, *The Ojibwa of Western Canada*, 91.
104 Peers, *The Ojibwa of Western Canada*, 92.
105 Kostash, *The Seven Oaks Reader*, 2.
106 Lyle Dick, "The Seven Oaks Incident and the Construction of a Historical Tradition, 1816 to 1970," *Journal of the Canadian Historical Association* 2, no. 1 (1991): 96.
107 Ens, "The Battle of Seven Oaks and the Articulation of a Metis National Tradition," 94.
108 Ens, "The Battle of Seven Oaks and the Articulation of a Metis National Tradition," 101.
109 Ens, "The Battle of Seven Oaks and the Articulation of a Metis National Tradition," 102–3.
110 Robin D.G. Kelley, *Freedom Dreams: The Black Radical Imagination* (Boston: Beacon Press, 2003).

Notes to pages 164–68   245

111 Dick, "The Seven Oaks Incident and the Construction of a Historical Tradition," 102.
112 Ens, "The Battle of Seven Oaks and the Articulation of a Metis National Tradition," 106.
113 George Woodcock, "Grant, Cuthbert (1793–1854)," in *Dictionary of Canadian Biography*, vol. 8 (Toronto: University of Toronto; Laval: Université Laval, 1985), http://www.biographi.ca/en/bio/grant_cuthbert_1854_8E.html.
114 Pierre Falcon, "Chanson des Bois Brûlés," 1816, LAC – Selkirk Collection, C-9, http://heritage.canadiana.ca/view/oocihm.lac_reel_c9/312?r=0&s=2; Pierre Falcon, "La Bataille des Sept Chênes," in *Songs of Old Manitoba: With Airs, French and English Words, and Introductions*, ed. Margaret MacLeod (Toronto: Ryerson Press, 1959), 1–9.
115 Falcon, "Chanson des Bois Brûlés," 9207.
116 Falcon, "Chanson des Bois Brûlés," 9207.
117 Falcon, "Chanson des Bois Brûlés," 9208.
118 Falcon also penned lyrics to a song titled "Li Lord Selkirk au Fort William," which depicts Selkirk hosting a ball to which a group of Métis was invited. Warren Cariou and Niigaanwewidam James Sinclair reflect on this song: "The men participate in the dance, but at the same time they undermine it by insisting on dancing and playing music in their own traditional ways ... The result is an ironic dialogue that shows the Métis asserting their own autonomy in the face of a colonizing presence." See Warren Cariou and Niigaanwewidam James Sinclair, "Pierre Falcon," in *Manitowapow: Aboriginal Writings from the Land of Water*, ed. Warren Cariou and Niigaanwewidam James Sinclair (Winnipeg: Portage and Main Press, 2011), 17.
119 Ens, "The Battle of Seven Oaks and the Articulation of a Metis National Tradition," 107.
120 Ens, "The Battle of Seven Oaks and the Articulation of a Metis National Tradition," 110–11.
121 Ens, "The Battle of Seven Oaks and the Articulation of a Metis National Tradition," 112.
122 Eric Hobsbawm, *Age of Revolution: 1789–1848* (New York: Vintage Books, 1996), 257.
123 Peter Fidler, "A Narrative of the Re-Establishment, Progress and Total Destruction of the Colony in Red River 1816," LAC – Selkirk Collection, 2530, C-3, http://heritage.canadiana.ca/view/oocihm.lac_reel_c3/413?r=0&s=2.
124 Colin Robertson, "Letter to Selkirk, 12 August 1816," LAC – Selkirk Collection, 2508, C-3, http://heritage.canadiana.ca/view/oocihm.lac_reel_c3/412?r=0&s=2.
125 Fidler, "A Narrative of the Re-Establishment, Progress and Total Destruction of the Colony in Red River 1816," 2531.
126 Halkett, *Statement Respecting the Earl of Selkirk's Settlement upon the Red River, in North America*, lxxxv.
127 Wilcocke, McGillivray, and Ellice, *A Narrative of Occurrences in the Indian Countries*, 67.
128 Wilcocke, McGillivray, and Ellice, *A Narrative of Occurrences in the Indian Countries*, 68.
129 Wilcocke, McGillivray, and Ellice, *A Narrative of Occurrences in the Indian Countries*, 74–75.
130 See, for example, Alexander Sutherland, "Loses [sic] Sustained by Alexander Sutherland, Summer 1815–16," 1816, LAC – Selkirk Collection, 2485, C-3, http://heritage.canadiana.ca/view/oocihm.lac_reel_c3/389?r=0&s=2. The records that follow also detail the number of buildings, dogs, provisions, and arms lost at other forts during the period in question.
131 Thomas Douglas Selkirk, "Letter to Lt. Governor Gore, 21 August 1816," LAC – Selkirk Collection, 2567, C-3, http://heritage.canadiana.ca/view/oocihm.lac_reel_c3/472?r=0&s=2.
132 Douglas MacKay, *The Honourable Company: A History of the Hudson's Bay Company* (Indianapolis: Bobbs-Merrill, 1936), 145.
133 John Perry Pritchett, *Red River Valley, 1811–1849* (New York: Russell and Russell, 1970), 189.

246 Notes to pages 168–69

134 "Agreement between Lord Selkirk and D. McKenzie," 1816, LAC – Selkirk Collection, 2811, C-3, http://heritage.canadiana.ca/view/oocihm.lac_reel_c3/718?r=0&s=2.
135 Daniel McKenzie, "Protest of Daniel McKenzie," November 11, 1816, LAC – Selkirk Collection, 2914, C-3, http://heritage.canadiana.ca/view/oocihm.lac_reel_c3/827?r=0&s=2.
136 MacKay, *The Honourable Company*, 145.
137 MacKay, *The Honourable Company*, 146.
138 Thomas Douglas Selkirk, "Letter to Lt. Governor Gore, 12 November 1816," LAC – Selkirk Collection, 2915, C-3, http://heritage.canadiana.ca/view/oocihm.lac_reel_c3/828?r=0&s=2.
139 Selkirk, "Letter to Lt. Governor Gore, 12 November 1816," 2916.
140 William Bachelor Coltman, "A General Statement and Report Relative to the Disturbances in the Indian Territories of British North America, 1818," in *Papers Relating to the Red River Settlement: 1815–1819* (London: Colonial Department, 1819), 214.
141 Selkirk, "Letter to Lt. Governor Gore, 21 August 1816," 2573.
142 Selkirk, "Letter to Lt. Governor Gore, 21 August 1816," 2570.
143 Pritchett, *Red River Valley, 1811–1849*, 188.
144 Selkirk, "Letter to Lt. Governor Gore, 21 August 1816," 2575.
145 Pritchett, *Red River Valley, 1811–1849*, 194.
146 Miles Macdonell, "Letter to Selkirk, 6 March 1817," LAC – Selkirk Collection, 3237, C-3, http://heritage.canadiana.ca/view/oocihm.lac_reel_c4/82?r=0&s=2.
147 Macdonell, "Letter to Selkirk, 6 March 1817," 3236.
148 Macdonell, "Letter to Selkirk, 6 March 1817," 3240.
149 Macdonell, "Letter to Selkirk, 6 March 1817," 3241.
150 Macdonell, "Letter to Selkirk, 6 March 1817," 3242.
151 Macdonell, "Letter to Selkirk, 6 March 1817," 3244.
152 Miles Macdonell, "Journal: 5 April 1817 to 30 August 1817," LAC – Selkirk Collection, 17248–49, https://heritage.canadiana.ca/view/oocihm.lac_reel_c16/753?r=0&s=3.
153 Macdonell, "Journal: 5 April 1817 to 30 August 1817," 17243.
154 When Peguis arrived with Le Sonnat, both received an official salute with a flag raising and gun firing; see Macdonell, "Journal: 5 April 1817 to 30 August 1817," 17251–52.
155 Pritchett, *Red River Valley, 1811–1849*, 195.
156 Pritchett, *Red River Valley, 1811–1849*, 195. For instance, as Selkirk and his travelling party drew nearer to the Forks, Macdonell was concerned they would be attacked, prompting him to station lookouts to "prevent the Brulés from meeting his Lordship," and sent Cuthbert Grant provisions to induce him to stay away. To avoid another clash, Peguis again attempted to broker peace between the colonists and local Indigenous groups. He argued that they should let the NWC men pass on their seasonal journey without disturbing them, despite their proximity to Selkirk's planned route; although this proposal was opposed by Indigenous allies and met with "censure" by Macdonell the next day, open conflict was averted. The specific reasons for this outcome are unclear, but judging from Macdonell's journal, there appear to have been many more settler colony/HBC allies in the region compared to the Métis/NWC at that time, suggesting that Peguis was deft at building these alliances and in expressing confidence of this advantage in numbers. See Macdonell, "Journal: 5 April 1817 to 30 August 1817," 17287–92.
157 Robert Alexander Innes, "Challenging a Racist Fiction: A Closer Look at Métis–First Nations Relations," in *A People and a Nation: New Directions in Contemporary Métis Studies*, ed. Jennifer Adese and Chris Andersen (Vancouver: UBC Press, 2021), 97.
158 Bumsted, "Editorial Introduction" (1988), lx–lxi.

Notes to pages 169–72 247

159 Kostash, *The Seven Oaks Reader,* 183. I have referred to some of the same narratives in the above account of the violence at Seven Oaks – note that John Halkett was Selkirk's brother-in-law, and it was believed that Samuel Wilcocke responded to his piece.

160 Lord Bathurst, "Extract Dispatches from Lord Bathurst," February 11, 1817, LAC – Selkirk Collection, 3117, C-3, http://heritage.canadiana.ca/view/oocihm.lac_reel_c3/1032?r=0&s=2.

161 Joseph Berens, "Letter to Lord Bathurst, 1 May, 1817," in *Papers Relating to the Red River Settlement: 1815–1819* (London: Colonial Department, 1819), 95.

162 John Sherbrooke, "Letter to Lord Bathurst, 5 May, 1817," in *Papers Relating to the Red River Settlement: 1815–1819* (London: Colonial Department, 1819), 94.

163 Thomas Douglas Selkirk, "Letter to Sherbrooke, 3 September 1816," LAC – Selkirk Collection, 2655, C-3, http://heritage.canadiana.ca/view/oocihm.lac_reel_c3/557?r=0&s=2.

164 Bumsted, "Editorial Introduction" (1988), lxiv.

165 J.M. Bumsted, *Fur Trade Wars: The Founding of Western Canada* (Winnipeg: Great Plains Publications, 1999), 178.

166 "Indian Territories – Proclamation of His Royal Highness the Prince Regent" (P.E. Desbarats, May 3, 1817), https://ia800209.us.archive.org/10/items/cihm_44939/cihm_44939.pdf.

167 Great Britain, Colonial Department, *Papers Relating to the Red River Settlement ... 1819,* 94.

168 Kostash, *The Seven Oaks Reader,* 195.

169 Bumsted, "Editorial Introduction" (1988), lxvi.

170 Bumsted, *Fur Trade Wars,* lxvii.

171 Donald McPherson, "Letter to Selkirk, 16 March 1817," LAC – Selkirk Collection, 3287, C-4, http://heritage.canadiana.ca/view/oocihm.lac_reel_c4/137?r=0&s=2.

172 Rosa Luxemburg, *The Accumulation of Capital,* 2nd ed. (London: Routledge, 2003), 365.

173 Gibson, *Law, Life, and Government at Red River, Volume 1,* 7.

174 Pritchett, *Red River Valley, 1811–1849,* 196.

175 MacKay, *The Honourable Company,* 147.

176 Gibson, *Law, Life, and Government at Red River, Volume 1,* 7.

177 Although Selkirk used the term "treaty" in his 1811 instructions to Macdonell when speculating about the land use agreement that might arise, the term does not appear to be coeval with the signing of the 1817 document itself; see Thomas Douglas Selkirk, "Instructions to Miles McDonell," 1811, LAC – Selkirk Collection, 177, http://heritage. canadiana.ca/view/oocihm.lac_reel_c1. Unless otherwise stated, my use of the term "treaty" throughout this section not only refers to the document signed in 1817, but also to "the entire council deliberations" as well as new and evolving practices associated with land use that were not stipulated in the signed agreement; see Heidi Kiiwetinepinesiik Stark, "Respect, Responsibility, and Renewal: The Foundations of Anishinaabe Treaty Making with the United States and Canada," *American Indian Culture and Research Journal* 34, no. 2 (2010): 149. For an argument about the value of clearly differentiating between "Treaty" and "Indenture," see Nathan Hasselstrom, "An Exploration of the Selkirk Treaty" (master's thesis, University of Ottawa, 2019), 37–39.

178 Bumsted, *Fur Trade Wars,* 175.

179 John Fletcher, "Letter to Sherbrooke," July 22, 1817, in *Papers Relating to the Red River Settlement: 1815–1819* (London: Colonial Department, 1819), 101.

180 John Fletcher, "Letter to Sherbrooke," 101.

181 Macdonell, "Journal: 5 April 1817 to 30 August 1817," 17294.

182 Macdonell, "Journal: 5 April 1817 to 30 August 1817," 17301-2. Bostonais was among the assembled Indigenous allied parties at the Premier's council, but based on Macdonell's journal, it is not known if Bostonais was invited to give a speech as other leaders were.

248 *Notes to pages 172–75*

183 William Bachelor Coltman, "Letter to Selkirk, 18 July 1817," LAC – Selkirk Collection, 3818, C-4, https://heritage.canadiana.ca/view/oocihm.lac_reel_c4/673?r=0&s=5. In the intervening period, Macdonell noted that he was leaving "for Canada" and "surrendered the superintendance of affairs"; see Macdonell, "Journal: 5 April 1817 to 30 August 1817," 17311.

184 Macdonell, "Journal: 5 April 1817 to 30 August 1817," 17316.

185 Macdonell, "Journal: 5 April 1817 to 30 August 1817," 17317. Peter Fidler's journals show that the document was signed at the "Commissioner's House" but that Coltman himself was absent; see Peter Fidler, "1817–1818: 18 July 1817," Archives of Manitoba, Brandon House Post Journal, 6. His journals also state that "Bostonais & the rest of the ½ breeds" left on July 14, so there does not appear to have been any Métis leaders in the vicinity during this signing; see Peter Fidler, "1817–1818: 14 July 1817," 5.

186 Macdonell, "Journal: 5 April 1817 to 30 August 1817," 17317.

187 Peter Fidler, "1817–1818: 29 July 1817," 7.

188 Thomas Douglas Selkirk, "Letter to Coltman, 17 July 1817," LAC – Selkirk Collection, 3810, C-4, https://heritage.canadiana.ca/view/oocihm.lac_reel_c4/664?r=0&s=5.

189 "Treaty of 18 July 1817," LAC – Selkirk Collection, 3825, C-4, http://heritage.canadiana.ca/view/oocihm.lac_reel_c4/679?r=0&s=2.

190 Peers, *The Ojibwa of Western Canada*, 63.

191 Leo Waisberg and Tim Holzkamm, "'We Have One Mind and One Mouth. It Is the Decision of All of Us': Traditional Anishinaabe Governance of Treaty #3," Grand Council Treaty #3 Draft Confidential Working Paper, October 2001, 6; Sara J. Mainville, "Manidoo Mazina'igan: An Anishinaabe Perspective of Treaty 3" (LLM, University of Toronto, 2007), 26.

192 Kostash, *The Seven Oaks Reader*, 187. When it came to negotiating the agreement for land, Coltman wrote to Selkirk and mentioned informing the Saulteaux of the importance of not "causing trouble with the Crees or driving the Metifs [sic] to despair either." William Bachelor Coltman, "Letter to Selkirk, 18 July 1817," 3818.

193 Selkirk may have been thinking about the 1763 Royal Proclamation when he mentioned an "acknowledgement of their right"; see Thomas Douglas Selkirk, "Letter to Coltman, 17 July 1817," 3810.

194 "Treaty of 18 July 1817," 3825.

195 Thomas Douglas Selkirk, "Instructions to Miles McDonell," 177.

196 Peers, *The Ojibwa of Western Canada*, 92.

197 Aimée Craft, *Breathing Life into the Stone Fort Treaty: An Anishnabe Understanding of Treaty One* (Saskatoon: Purich Publishing, 2013), 78.

198 Adam Gaudry, "Fantasies of Sovereignty: Deconstructing British and Canadian Claims to Ownership of the Historic North-West," *Native American and Indigenous Studies* 3, no. 1 (2016): 54.

199 Gaudry, "Fantasies of Sovereignty," 55.

200 Peers, *The Ojibwa of Western Canada*, 124.

201 Peers, *The Ojibwa of Western Canada*, 89.

202 Peers, *The Ojibwa of Western Canada*, 91.

203 Practices associated with the land changed significantly throughout these decades, and inform this eventual questioning. Changes included increased activity, including private trading, with American outfits down the Red River; from the HBC in 1845 (reminiscent of the Pemmican Proclamation), rules for new landholders preventing them from trading fur – restrictions that led to widespread discontent among private businessmen and Indigenous peoples alike, especially the many Métis in the district (see Pritchett, *Red*

River Valley, 410–11, 417–20); increasingly hierarchical and rigid layers of legal administration and enforcement (see Nelly Laudicina, "The Rules of Red River: The Council of Assiniboia and Its Impact on the Colony, 1820–1869," *Past Imperfect* 15 [2009]: 41, 49–50); and the arrival of missionaries and the eventual establishment of parishes (see Alexander Ross, *The Red River Settlement: Its Rise, Progress, and Present State: With Some Account of the Native ...* [London: Smith, Elder and Company, 1856], 48, 53).

204 Peguis, "An Open Letter to the Queen's Representatives," in *Manitowapow: Aboriginal Writings from the Land of Water,* ed. Warren Cariou and Niigaanwewidam James Sinclair (Winnipeg: Portage and Main Press, 2011), 14–15.

205 Peguis, "Native Title to Indian Lands," *Nor'Wester,* February 14, 1860, 3.

206 Peguis [a.k.a. William King], "Important Statement of Pegowis, the Indian Chief," *Nor'Wester,* October 14, 1863, 3.

207 Selkirk admitted that the agreement was incomplete in 1817, when he instructed his colonial governor to bring a "duplicate of the Indian Deed for the land in order to get the transaction completed on the part of the Crees & signed by as many of their chiefs as possible"; see Thomas Douglas Selkirk, "Letter to Alexander Macdonell, 14 September 1817," LAC – Selkirk Collection, 4054, C-4, https://heritage.canadiana.ca/view/oocihm. lac_reel_c4/910?r=0&s=1. Note that the recipient is a different Alexander Macdonell than the man with the same name from the NWC.

208 Peguis, "Important Statement of Pegowis, the Indian Chief," 3.

209 Barry E. Hyman, "McDermot, Andrew (1790–1881)," in *Dictionary of Canadian Biography,* vol. 11 (Toronto: University of Toronto; Laval: Université Laval, 1982), http://www. biographi.ca/en/bio/mcdermot_andrew_11E.html.

210 This is supported by a letter from Coltman to Selkirk from the day before the agreement was signed, wherein the former states that "the Cree Indians have agreed that the Saulteurns [sic] may treat for the lands as far as the River aux Champignons." William Bachelor Coltman, "Letter to Selkirk, 17 July 1817," LAC – Selkirk Collection, 3814, C-4, https://heritage.canadiana.ca/view/oocihm.lac_reel_c4/669?r=0&s=5.

211 Andrew McDermot, "The Peguis Land Controversy," *Nor'Wester,* May 14, 1860, 1.

212 Peguis, "A Reply to the Selkirk Settlers' Call for Help," in *Manitowapow: Aboriginal Writings from the Land of Water,* ed. Warren Cariou and Niigaanwewidam James Sinclair (Winnipeg: Portage and Main Press, 2011), 14.

213 Heidi Kiiwetinepinesiik Stark and Gina Starblanket, "Towards a Relational Paradigm – Four Points for Consideration: Knowledge, Gender, Land, and Modernity," in *Resurgence and Reconciliation: Indigenous-Settler Relations and Earth Teachings,* ed. Michael I. Asch, John Borrows, and James Tully (Toronto: University of Toronto Press, 2018), 190.

214 Stark, "Respect, Responsibility, and Renewal," 146.

215 Stark and Starblanket, "Towards a Relational Paradigm," 179.

216 "The Land Question: The Council and the Press," *Nor'Wester,* March 14, 1860, 2.

217 Mahmood Mamdani, *Citizen and Subject: Contemporary Africa and the Legacy of Late Colonialism* (Princeton, NJ: Princeton University Press, 1996), 140.

218 Ellen Meiksins Wood, "The Separation of the Economic and the Political in Capitalism," *New Left Review* 127 (1981): 89.

219 Wood, "The Separation of the Economic and the Political in Capitalism," 90–91.

220 Wood, "The Separation of the Economic and the Political in Capitalism," 91.

221 Mamdani, *Citizen and Subject,* 28.

222 Lisa Ford and P.G. McHugh, "Settler Sovereignty and the Shapeshifting Crown," in *Between Indigenous and Settler Governance,* ed. Lisa Ford and Tim Rowse (London: Routledge, 2012), 33.

Conclusion

1 Hamar Foster, "Forgotten Arguments: Aboriginal Title and Sovereignty in Canada Jurisdiction Act Cases," *Manitoba Law Journal* 21, no. 3 (1992): 347.

2 Henry Youle Hind, *Narrative of the Canadian Red River Exploring Expedition of 1857, and of the Assinniboine and Saskatchewan Exploring Expedition of 1858* (London: Longman, Green, Longman and Roberts, 1860), 177, http://archive.org/details/narrativeofcanado2hind.

3 Alexander Ross, *The Red River Settlement: Its Rise, Progress, and Present State: With Some Account of the Native ...* (London: Smith, Elder and Company, 1856), 160.

4 Laura L. Peers, *The Ojibwa of Western Canada, 1780 to 1870* (Winnipeg: University of Manitoba Press, 1984), 95.

5 Peers, *The Ojibwa of Western Canada*, 95.

6 James Bird, "Letter to Selkirk, 26 July 1817," LAC – Selkirk Collection, 3846, C-4, http://heritage.canadiana.ca/view/oocihm.lac_reel_c4/700?r=0&s=3.

7 Thomas Douglas Selkirk, "Letter to Coltman, 27 July 1817," LAC – Selkirk Collection, 3847, C-4, http://heritage.canadiana.ca/view/oocihm.lac_reel_c4/702?r=0&s=3; William Bachelor Coltman, "Letter to Selkirk, 27 July 1817," LAC – Selkirk Collection, 3855, C-4, http://heritage.canadiana.ca/view/oocihm.lac_reel_c4/712?r=0&s=3.

8 William Bachelor Coltman, "A General Statement and Report Relative to the Disturbances in the Indian Territories of British North America, 1818," in *Papers Relating to the Red River Settlement: 1815–1819* (London: Colonial Department, 1819), 152–53.

9 Coltman, "A General Statement and Report," 164.

10 Coltman, "A General Statement and Report," 250.

11 Coltman, "A General Statement and Report," 191.

12 Coltman, "A General Statement and Report," 190.

13 William Bachelor Coltman, "Letter to the NWC and the HBC, 27 July 1817," LAC – Selkirk Collection, 3865, C-4, http://heritage.canadiana.ca/view/oocihm.lac_reel_c4/721?r=0&s=3.

14 Charles N. Bell, *The Selkirk Settlement and the Settlers: A Concise History of the Red River Country from Its Discovery, Including Information Extracted from Original Documents Lately Discovered, and Notes Obtained from Selkirk Settlement Colonists* (Winnipeg: Commercial, 1887), 23.

15 J.M. Bumsted, "Editorial Introduction," in *The Collected Writings of Lord Selkirk 1810–1820*, ed. J.M. Bumsted (Winnipeg: Manitoba Record Society, 1988), lxviii.

16 William Bachelor Coltman, "Letter to Sherbrooke, 15 July 1817," in *Papers Relating to the Red River Settlement: 1815–1819* (London: Colonial Department, 1819), 105.

17 William Bachelor Coltman, "Letter to Sherbrooke, 15 July 1817," 105.

18 Hannis Taylor, *The Origin and Growth of the English Constitution*, vol. 2 (Boston: Houghton, Mifflin and Company, 1900), 196–97.

19 Tim Moreman, "'Watch and Ward': The Army in India and the North-West Frontier, 1920–1939," in *Guardians of Empire: The Armed Forces of the Colonial Powers c. 1700–1964*, ed. David Killingray and David E. Omissi (Manchester: Manchester University Press, 1999), 137–56; Edgar J. McManus, *Law and Liberty in Early New England: Criminal Justice and Due Process, 1620–1692* (Amherst: University of Massachusetts Press, 2009), 65.

20 Laura L. Peers, "Rich Man, Poor Man, Beggarman, Chief: Saulteaux in the Red River Settlement," in *Papers of the Eighteenth Algonquian Conference*, ed. William Cowan (Ottawa: Carleton University, 1987), 265.

21 John Perry Pritchett, *Red River Valley, 1811–1849* (New York: Russell and Russell, 1970), 209.

22 Bumsted, "Editorial Introduction" (1988), lxx.

23 Pritchett, *Red River Valley, 1811–1849*, 210–11.

Notes to pages 182–84 251

24 Myrna Kostash, *The Seven Oaks Reader*, UK ed. (Edmonton: NeWest Press, 2016), 201.
25 Bumsted, "Editorial Introduction" (1988), lxxi.
26 Bumsted, "Editorial Introduction" (1988), lxxi.
27 Bumsted, "Editorial Introduction" (1988), lxxiv–lxxv. Cuthbert Grant, as well as Joseph Cadotte, fled to Brandon House around the time of Selkirk's arrival at the Forks; Alexander Macdonell of the NWC appears to have also vacated the area "to avoid being taken Prisoner"; see Peter Fidler, "1817–1818: 25 June 1817," 3.
28 Ross, *The Red River Settlement*, 48–50, 56.
29 Ross, *The Red River Settlement*, 50.
30 Kostash, *The Seven Oaks Reader*, 206.
31 Kostash, *The Seven Oaks Reader*, 209.
32 John S. Galbraith, *Hudson's Bay Company, 1821–1869* (Berkeley: University of California Press, 1957), 6.
33 Galbraith, *Hudson's Bay Company*, 5. Galbraith quotes Coltman but does not explain why he held this view.
34 Edith I. Burley, *Servants of the Honourable Company: Work, Discipline, and Conflict in the Hudson's Bay Company, 1770–1879* (Toronto: Oxford University Press, 1997), 48; Gary Spraakman, *Management Accounting at the Hudson's Bay Company: From Quill Pen to Digitization* (Bingley, UK: Emerald Group Publishing, 2015), 60.
35 Cole Harris, "Arthur J. Ray and the Empirical Opportunity," in *New Histories for Old: Changing Perspectives on Canada's Native Pasts*, ed. Theodore Binnema and Susan Neylan (Vancouver: UBC Press, 2007), 254–55.
36 Burley, *Servants of the Honourable Company*, 52. Similar sentiments flowed among NWC partners; see Jean Barman, *French Canadians, Furs, and Indigenous Women in the Making of the Pacific Northwest* (Vancouver: UBC Press, 2014), 59.
37 Barman, *French Canadians, Furs, and Indigenous Women*, 61; Leanna Parker, "Labour Relations in the Rupertsland Fur Trade and the Formation of Métis Identity," in *Hidden in Plain Sight: Contributions of Aboriginal Peoples to Canadian Identity and Culture*, ed. Cora J. Voyageur, David Newhouse, and Dan Beavon (Toronto: University of Toronto Press, 2011), 91.
38 Frank Tough, "From the 'Original Affluent Society' to the 'Unjust Society': A Review Essay on Native Economic History in Canada," *Journal of Aboriginal Economic Development* 4, no. 2 (2005): 35–36.
39 George Simpson, "Letter to Colvile, 20 May 1822," LAC – Selkirk Collection, 7588, C-7, http://heritage.canadiana.ca/view/oocihm.lac_reel_c7/983?r=0&s=3; Parker, "Labour Relations in the Rupertsland Fur Trade," 93.
40 Harris, "Arthur J. Ray and the Empirical Opportunity," 255.
41 Simpson, "Letter to Colvile, 20 May 1822," 7588.
42 Simpson, "Letter to Colvile, 20 May 1822," 7588.
43 Arthur Lincoln Haydon, *The Riders of the Plains: A Record of the Royal North-West Mounted Police of Canada, 1873–1910* (London: Melrose, 1910), 7.
44 Andrew R. Graybill, *Policing the Great Plains: Rangers, Mounties, and the North American Frontier, 1875–1910* (Lincoln: University of Nebraska Press, 2007), 5.
45 Quoted in Andrew Graybill, "Rangers, Mounties, and the Subjugation of Indigenous Peoples, 1870–1885," *Great Plains Quarterly* 24, no. 2 (2004): 96.
46 The objective of the Royal North West Mounted Police was "to prevent Native populations from interfering with white migration and the establishment of Euro-American military and political authority." See Andrew Graybill, "Rangers, Mounties, and the Subjugation of Indigenous Peoples, 1870–1885," 96.

252 *Notes to pages 184–87*

47 National Inquiry into Missing and Murdered Indigenous Women and Girls (Canada), *Reclaiming Power and Place: Final Report of the National Inquiry into Missing and Murdered Indigenous Women and Girls* (Ottawa: Privy Council Office, 2019), 18–19, 54, http://epe.lac-bac.gc.ca/100/201/301/weekly_acquisitions_list-ef/2019/19-23/publications.gc.ca/collections/collection_2019/bcp-pco/CP32-163-2-1-2019-eng.pdf.

48 National Inquiry into Missing and Murdered Indigenous Women and Girls, *Reclaiming Power and Place*, 25.

49 National Inquiry into Missing and Murdered Indigenous Women and Girls, *Reclaiming Power and Place*, 28.

50 National Inquiry into Missing and Murdered Indigenous Women and Girls, *Reclaiming Power and Place*, 30.

51 As Allan Greer comments, "the fact that pure private property did not and could not exist did not prevent it becoming a potent ideal." See Allan Greer, *Property and Dispossession: Natives, Empires and Land in Early Modern North America* (Cambridge: Cambridge University Press, 2018), 397. Robert Gordon explains that, in reality, property rights were "fragmented and split among many holders" and that these rights were "surrounded by restriction on use and alienation." See Robert Gordon, "Paradoxical Property," in *Early Modern Conceptions of Property*, ed. John Brewer and Susan Staves (London: Routledge, 1996), 96. Although he goes on to chronicle a number of instances that illustrate the partiality of private property, the consequences of this reality for the purposes of a Marxist-informed commentary on the transition to capitalism in the settler colonial context are most salient. This gap between the idea and the practice of property supports the need to reject the simplistic notion of the transition to capitalism as involving a shift from violent, direct extra-economic force to economic compulsion, which I discuss throughout this book with reference to the relative yet unrelinquished autonomy of Indigenous peoples.

52 This measure, an amendment in 1884 to the Indian Act, forced Indigenous children into state-funded boarding schools, often run by religious organizations. Stripped from their families, many of the children suffered abuse and became severely alienated from their own cultures.

53 Starting about the 1950s, thousands of Indigenous children were taken from their families and placed in foster care or adopted by white families.

54 Nikhil Pal Singh, "On Race, Violence, and So-Called Primitive Accumulation," *Social Text* 34, no. 3 (2016): 43.

55 Ellen Meiksins Wood, "The Separation of the Economic and the Political in Capitalism," *New Left Review* 127 (1981): 66.

56 National Inquiry into Missing and Murdered Indigenous Women and Girls, *Reclaiming Power and Place*, 46–47.

Bibliography

Archival Sources

Library and Archives Canada
"Indian Territories – Proclamation of His Royal Highness the Prince Regent" (P.E. Desbarats, May 3, 1817). https://ia800209.us.archive.org/10/items/cihm_44939/cihm_44939.pdf.
Selkirk Collection, 1769–1870, 114525, C-1–C-19, Thomas Douglas, 5th Earl of Selkirk fonds.

Archives of Manitoba
Brandon House Post Journals, 1793–1830, B.22/a/1–B.22/a/23.

United States Library of Congress
Annals of Congress, 4th Cong., 1st sess., 969–70. http://memory.loc.gov/cgi-bin/ampage?collId=llac&fileName=005/llac005.db&recNum=481.

United States Statutes at Large
Treaty of November 19, 1794. https://memory.loc.gov/cgi-bin/ampage?collId=llsl&fileName=008/llsl008.db&recNum=129.

Other Sources

Adams, Howard. *Prison of Grass: Canada from a Native Point of View.* 2nd ed. Saskatoon: Fifth House, 1989.

Ahenakew, Edward. *Voices of the Plains Cree.* Edited by Ruth Matheson Buck. 2nd ed. Regina: Canadian Plains Research Center, 1995.

Amin, Samir. *Accumulation on a World Scale: A Critique of the Theory of Underdevelopment, Volume 1.* New York: Monthly Review Press, 1974.

An Act for Giving a Publick Reward to Such Person or Persons … as Shall Discover a North West Passage, 1745. In *Statutes at Large, from the 15th to the 20th Year of King George II,* vol. 18, 327–29. Cambridge: Cambridge University Press, 1765.

Andersen, Chris. *"Métis": Race, Recognition, and the Struggle for Indigenous Peoplehood.* Vancouver: UBC Press, 2014.

Anderson, Michael. "India, 1858–1930: The Illusion of Free Labor." In *Masters, Servants, and Magistrates in Britain and the Empire, 1562–1955,* edited by Douglas Hay and Paul Craven, 422–54. Chapel Hill: University of North Carolina Press, 2005.

Anievas, Alexander, and Kerem Nişancıoğlu. *How the West Came to Rule: The Geopolitical Origins of Capitalism.* London: Pluto Press, 2015.

Atcheson, Nathaniel [attributed], and John Henry [attributed]. *On the Origin and Progress of the North-West Company of Canada.* CIHM/ICMH Digital Series – CIHM/ICMH Collection Numérisée No. 27875. London: Printed by Cox, Son and Baylis, 1811.

Awashish, Philip. "A Brief Introduction to the Eeyou Traditional System of Governance of Hunting Territories (Traditional Eeyou Indoh-Hoh Istchee Governance)." *Anthropologica* 60, no. 1 (2018): 1–4.

Bacola, Meredith. "'Through the Intercession of the Apostle of Their Nation': The Context of St Boniface's Church Dedication in the Formation of the Archdioceses of St Boniface and Winnipeg." *Historical Studies* 84 (2018): 87–100.

Bakker, Isabella, and Rachel Silvey. "Introduction: Social Reproduction and Global Transformations – from the Everyday to the Global." In *Beyond States and Markets: The Challenges of Social Reproduction,* edited by Isabella Bakker and Rachel Silvey, 1–16. London: Routledge, 2012.

Banaji, Jairus. *Theory as History: Essays on Modes of Production and Exploitation.* 1st trade paper ed. Chicago: Haymarket Books, 2011.

Bannister, Jerry. "Law and Labor in Eighteenth-Century Newfoundland." In *Masters, Servants, and Magistrates in Britain and the Empire, 1562–1955,* edited by Douglas Hay and Paul Craven, 153–74. Chapel Hill: University of North Carolina Press, 2005.

Barman, Jean. *French Canadians, Furs, and Indigenous Women in the Making of the Pacific Northwest.* Vancouver: UBC Press, 2014.

–. *Iroquois in the West.* McGill-Queen's Native and Northern Series 93. Montreal and Kingston: McGill-Queen's University Press, 2019.

Barr, William. "The Eighteenth Century Trade between the Ships of the Hudson's Bay Company and the Hudson Strait Inuit." *Arctic* 47, no. 3 (1994): 236–46.

Bell, Charles N. *The Selkirk Settlement and the Settlers: A Concise History of the Red River Country from Its Discovery, Including Information Extracted from Original Documents Lately Discovered, and Notes Obtained from Selkirk Settlement Colonists.* Winnipeg: Commercial, 1887.

Bemis, Samuel Flagg. *Jay's Treaty: A Study in Commerce and Diplomacy.* New York: Macmillan, 1923.

Benton, Lauren. *Law and Colonial Cultures: Legal Regimes in World History, 1400–1900.* Cambridge: Cambridge University Press, 2002.

Benton, Lauren, and Richard J. Ross. "Empires and Legal Pluralism: Jurisdiction, Sovereignty, and Political Imagination in the Early Modern World." In *Legal Pluralism and Empires, 1500–1850,* edited by Lauren Benton and Richard J. Ross, 1–20. New York: New York University Press, 2013.

Benton, Lauren, and Benjamin Straumann. "Acquiring Empire by Law: From Roman Doctrine to Early Modern European Practice." *Law and History Review* 28, no. 1 (2010): 1–38.

Berthelette, Scott. "The Making of a Manitoban Hero: Commemorating La Verendrye in St. Boniface and Winnipeg, 1886–1938." *Manitoba History* 74 (2014): 15–26.

–. "New France and the Hudson Bay Watershed: Transatlantic Networks, Backcountry Specialists, and French Imperial Projects in Post-Utrecht North America, 1713–29." *Canadian Historical Review* 101, no. 1 (2019): 1–26. https://doi.org/10.3138/chr.2018-0094.

Bhandar, Brenna. *Colonial Lives of Property: Law, Land, and Racial Regimes of Ownership.* Durham, NC: Duke University Press, 2018.

Bird, Louis. *The Spirit Lives in the Mind: Omushkego Stories, Lives and Dreams.* Edited by Susan Elaine Gray. Montreal and Kingston: McGill-Queen's University Press, 2007.

–. *Telling Our Stories: Omushkego Legends and Histories from Hudson Bay*. Toronto: University of Toronto Press, 2005.

Bishop, Charles A. "The First Century: Adaptive Changes among the Western James Bay Cree between the Early Seventeenth and Early Eighteenth Centuries." In *The Subarctic Fur Trade: Native Social and Economic Adaptations*, edited by Shepard Krech III, 21–54. Vancouver: UBC Press, 1984.

Bonefeld, Werner. *Critical Theory and the Critique of Political Economy: On Subversion and Negative Reason*. New York: Bloomsbury, 2014.

Borrows, John. "Canada's Colonial Constitution." In *The Right Relationship: Reimagining the Implementation of Historical Treaties*, edited by Michael Coyle and John Borrows, 17–38. Toronto: University of Toronto Press, 2017.

–. "Constitutional Law from a First Nation Perspective: Self-Government and the Royal Proclamation." *UBC Law Review* 28, no. 1 (1994): 1–47.

–. "Heroes, Tricksters, Monsters, and Caretakers: Indigenous Law and Legal Education Special Issue – Indigenous Law and Legal Pluralism." *McGill Law Journal* 61 (2016): 795–846.

Bouchard, Michel, Sébastien Malette, and Guillaume Marcotte. *Bois-Brûlés: The Untold Story of the Métis of Western Quebec*. Vancouver: UBC Press, 2020.

Bourgeault, Ron G. "The Indian, the Métis and the Fur Trade: Class, Sexism and Racism in the Transition from 'Communism' to Capitalism." *Studies in Political Economy* 12, no. 1 (1983): 45–80.

Braddick, Michael J. "The English Government, War, Trade, and Settlement, 1625–1688." In *The Origins of Empire: British Overseas Enterprise to the Close of the Seventeenth Century*, edited by Nicholas Canny, vol. 1, 286–308. Oxford: Oxford University Press, 1998.

Brawn, Dale. *The Court of Queen's Bench of Manitoba, 1870–1950: A Biographical History*. Toronto: University of Toronto Press, 2006.

Brenner, Robert. "The Agrarian Roots of European Capitalism." In *The Brenner Debate: Agrarian Class Structure and Economic Development in Pre-Industrial Europe*, edited by T.H. Aston and C.H.E. Philpin, 213–327. Cambridge: Cambridge University Press, 1985.

–. *Merchants and Revolution: Commercial Change, Political Conflict, and London's Overseas Traders, 1550–1653*. London: Verso, 2003.

–. "The Origins of Capitalist Development: A Critique of Neo-Smithian Marxism." *New Left Review* I/104 (1977): 25–92.

Brophy, Susan Dianne. "The Emancipatory Praxis of Ukrainian Canadians (1891–1919) and the Necessity of a Situated Critique." *Labour/Le travail* 77 (2016): 151–79.

–. "The Explanatory Value of the Theory of Uneven and Combined Development." *Historical Materialism* (blog), 2018. http://www.historicalmaterialism.org/blog/explanatory-value-theory-uneven-and-combined-development.

–. "Freedom, Law, and the Colonial Project." *Law and Critique* 24, no. 1 (2013): 39–61.

–. "An Uneven and Combined Development Theory of Law: Initiation." *Law and Critique* 28, no. 2 (2017): 167–91.

Brown, Alice E. "A Brief Chronology of Events Relative to Lord Selkirk's Settlement at Red River: 1811 to 1815." *Manitoba Pageant* 7, no. 3 (1962). http://www.mhs.mb.ca/docs/pageant/07/selkirkchronology.shtm.

Brown, Jennifer S.H. "Rupert's Land, Nituskeenan, Our Land: Cree and English Naming and Claiming around the Dirty Sea." In *New Histories for Old: Changing Perspectives on Canada's Native Pasts*, edited by Theodore Binnema and Susan Neylan, 18–40. Vancouver: UBC Press, 2007.

–. *Strangers in Blood: Fur Trade Company Families in Indian Country.* Vancouver: UBC Press, 1996.

–. *Strangers in Blood: Fur Trade Company Families in Indian Country.* Canadian Electronic Library. Vancouver: UBC Press, 1980. http://ezproxy.library.yorku.ca/login?url=http://books.scholarsportal.info/viewdoc.html?id=/ebooks/ebookso/gibson_crkn/2009-12-01/3/404391.

Brownlie, Robin, and Mary-Ellen Kelm. "Desperately Seeking Absolution: Native Agency as Colonialist Alibi?" *Canadian Historical Review* 75, no. 4 (1994): 543–56.

Bryan, Bradley. "Property as Ontology: On Aboriginal and English Understandings of Ownership." *Canadian Journal of Law and Jurisprudence* 13 (2000): 3–32.

Bryce, George. *The Remarkable History of the Hudson's Bay Company, Including That of the French Traders of North-Western Canada and of the North-West, XY, and Astor Fur Companies.* 3rd ed. New York: Charles Scribner's Sons, 1910.

Bumsted, J.M. "Editorial Introduction." In *The Collected Writings of Lord Selkirk 1799–1809*, edited by J.M. Bumsted, 1–86. Winnipeg: Manitoba Record Society, 1984.

–. "Editorial Introduction." In *The Collected Writings of Lord Selkirk 1810–1820*, edited by J.M. Bumsted, xiii–xciv. Winnipeg: Manitoba Record Society, 1988.

–. *Fur Trade Wars: The Founding of Western Canada.* Winnipeg: Great Plains Publications, 1999.

–. *Lord Selkirk: A Life.* Winnipeg: University of Manitoba Press, 2008.

–. *The People's Clearance: Highland Emigration to British North America, 1770–1815.* Winnipeg: University of Manitoba Press, 1982.

–. *Trials and Tribulations: The Red River Settlement and the Emergence of Manitoba, 1811–1870.* Winnipeg: Great Plains Publications, 2003.

Burley, Edith I. *Servants of the Honourable Company: Work, Discipline, and Conflict in the Hudson's Bay Company, 1770–1879.* Toronto: Oxford University Press, 1997.

Burn, Richard. *The Justice of the Peace, and Parish Officer.* Edited by George Chetwynd. 23rd ed. Vol. 1. London: A. Strahan and W. Woodfall, 1820.

Byrd, Jodi A. *The Transit of Empire: Indigenous Critiques of Colonialism.* Minneapolis: University of Minnesota Press, 2011.

Calloway, Colin G. "Foundations of Sand: The Fur Trade and the British-Indian Relations, 1783–1815." In *"Le castor fait tout": Selected Papers of the Fifth North American Fur Trade Conference, 1985*, edited by Bruce G. Trigger, Toby Morantz, and Louise Dechêne, 144–63. Montreal: Lake St. Louis Historical Society, 1987.

–. *The Indian World of George Washington: The First President, the First Americans, and the Birth of the Nation.* Oxford: Oxford University Press, 2018.

Campbell, Robert. "The Truck System in the Cape Breton Fishery: Philip Robin and Company in Chéticamp, 1843–1852." *Labour/Le travail* 75 (2015). http://www.lltjournal.ca/index.php/llt/article/view/5743.

Cariou, Warren, and Niigaanwewidam James Sinclair. "Peguis." In *Manitowapow: Aboriginal Writings from the Land of Water*, edited by Warren Cariou and Niigaanwewidam James Sinclair, 13. Winnipeg: Portage and Main Press, 2011.

–. "Pierre Falcon." In *Manitowapow: Aboriginal Writings from the Land of Water*, edited by Warren Cariou and Niigaanwewidam James Sinclair, 17. Winnipeg: Portage and Main Press, 2011.

Carlos, Ann. "Agent Opportunism and the Role of Company Culture: The Hudson's Bay and Royal African Companies Compared." *Business and Economic History* 20 (1991): 142–51.

–. "The Birth and Death of Predatory Competition in the North American Fur Trade: 1810–1821." *Explorations in Economic History* 19, no. 2 (1982): 156–83. https://doi.org/10.1016/0014-4983(82)90016-X.

–. "The Causes and Origins of the North American Fur Trade Rivalry: 1804–1810." *Journal of Economic History* 41, no. 4 (1981): 777–94.

Carlos, Ann M., and Elizabeth Hoffman. "The North American Fur Trade: Bargaining to a Joint Profit Maximum under Incomplete Information, 1804–1821." *Journal of Economic History* 46, no. 4 (1986): 967–86.

Carlos, Ann M., and Frank D. Lewis. "Trade, Consumption, and the Native Economy: Lessons from York Factory, Hudson Bay." *Journal of Economic History* 61, no. 4 (2001): 1037–64. https://doi.org/10.1017/S0022050701042073.

Carlson, Hans M. *Home Is the Hunter: The James Bay Cree and Their Land*. Vancouver: UBC Press, 2009.

Carter, George E. "Lord Selkirk and the Red River Colony." *Montana: The Magazine of Western History* 18, no. 1 (1968): 60–69.

Carter, Sarah. *Aboriginal People and Colonizers of Western Canada to 1900*. Themes in Canadian Social History. Toronto: University of Toronto Press, 1999.

Chittenden, Hiram Martin. *The American Fur Trade of the Far West*. Vol. 1. Lincoln: University of Nebraska Press, 1986.

Christensen, Deanna. *Ahtahkakoop: The Epic Account of a Plains Cree Head Chief, His People, and Their Struggle for Survival, 1816–1896*. Shell Lake, SK: Ahtahkakoop Publishing, 2000.

Churchill, Ward, ed. *Marxism and Native Americans*. Boston: South End Press, 1983.

Cockburn, J.S. *A History of English Assizes 1558–1714*. Cambridge: Cambridge University Press, 1972.

Colpitts, George. *Pemmican Empire: Food, Trade, and the Last Bison Hunts in the North American Plains, 1780–1882*. Cambridge: Cambridge University Press, 2014.

Coltman, William Bachelor. "A General Statement and Report Relative to the Disturbances in the Indian Territories of British North America, 1818." In *Papers Relating to the Red River Settlement: 1815–1819*. London: Colonial Department, 1819.

–. "Letter to Sherbrooke, 15 July 1817." In *Papers Relating to the Red River Settlement: 1815–1819*. London: Colonial Department, 1819.

Coulthard, Glen Sean. *Red Skin, White Masks: Rejecting the Colonial Politics of Recognition*. Indigenous Americas. Minneapolis: University of Minnesota Press, 2014.

Craft, Aimée. *Breathing Life into the Stone Fort Treaty: An Anishnabe Understanding of Treaty One*. Saskatoon: Purich Publishing, 2013.

Cruise, William. "Copy Queries and Opinions of Mr. Cruise." In *Appendix to the Journals of the House of Commons of Canada*, 14, app. I. Ottawa: Hunter Rose, 1880.

The Current. "Injustice Is a Way of Indigenous Life, Say Advocates Dismayed at Verdict in Tina Fontaine Murder Trial." CBC Radio, February 23, 2018. https://www.cbc.ca/radio/thecurrent/the-current-for-february-23-2018-1.4547552/injustice-is-a-way-of-indigenous-life-say-advocates-dismayed-at-verdict-in-tina-fontaine-murder-trial-1.4548471.

Daschuk, James. *Clearing the Plains: Disease, Politics of Starvation, and the Loss of Aboriginal Life*. Regina: University of Regina Press, 2013.

–. "Who Killed the Prairie Beaver? An Environmental Case for Eighteenth Century Migration in Western Canada." *Prairie Forum* 37 (2012): 151–72.

Davidson, Gordon Charles. *The North West Company*. Berkeley: University of California Press, 1918.

den Otter, A.A. *Civilizing the Wilderness: Culture and Nature in Pre-Confederation Canada and Rupert's Land*. Edmonton: University of Alberta Press, 2012.

Devine, Thomas Martin. *Clanship to Crofter's War: The Social Transformation of the Scottish Highlands*. Manchester: Manchester University Press, 1994.

–. "Highland Migration to Lowland Scotland, 1760–1860." *Scottish Historical Review* 62, no. 174 (1983): 137–49.

Dick, Lyle. "The Seven Oaks Incident and the Construction of a Historical Tradition, 1816 to 1970." *Journal of the Canadian Historical Association* 2, no. 1 (1991): 91–113.

Dobak, William A. "Killing the Canadian Buffalo, 1821–1881." *Western Historical Quarterly* 27, no. 1 (1996): 33–52.

Dobb, Maurice. *Studies in the Development of Capitalism*. London: Routledge and Sons, 1946.

Dobbs, Arthur. *An Account of the Countries Adjoining to Hudson's Bay, in the North-West Part of America*. London: J. Robinson, 1744.

Dodds, James. *The Hudson's Bay Company, Its Position and Prospects: The Substance of an Address, Delivered at a Meeting of the Shareholders, in the London Tavern, on the 24th January, 1866*. London: Edward Stanford and A.H. Baily and Company, 1866.

Doerfler, Jill. "A Philosophy for Living: Ignatia Broker and Constitutional Reform among the White Earth Anishinaabeg." In *Centering Anishinaabeg Studies: Understanding the World through Stories*, edited by Jill Doerfler, Niigaanwewidam James Sinclair, and Heidi Kiiwetinepinesiik Stark, 173–90. American Indian Studies Series. East Lansing: Michigan State University Press; Winnipeg: University of Manitoba Press, 2013.

Dunbar-Ortiz, Roxanne. *An Indigenous Peoples' History of the United States*. 2014; reprinted, Boston: Beacon Press, 2015.

Ens, Gerhard J. "The Battle of Seven Oaks and the Articulation of a Metis National Tradition, 1811–1849." In *Contours of a People: Metis Family, Mobility, and History*, edited by Nicole St-Onge, Carolyn Podruchny, and Brenda Macdougall. Norman: University of Oklahoma Press, 2014.

–. *Homeland to Hinterland: The Changing Worlds of the Red River Metis in the Nineteenth Century*. Toronto: University of Toronto Press, 1996.

Ens, Gerhard J., and Joe Sawchuk. *From New Peoples to New Nations: Aspects of Metis History and Identity from the Eighteenth to the Twenty-First Centuries*. Toronto: University of Toronto Press, 2015.

Fagundes, David. "What We Talk about When We Talk about Persons: The Language of a Legal Fiction." *Harvard Law Review* 114, no. 6 (2001): 1745–68.

Falcon, Pierre. "La Bataille des Sept Chênes." In *Songs of Old Manitoba: With Airs, French and English Words, and Introductions*, edited by Margaret MacLeod, 1–9. Toronto: Ryerson Press, 1959.

Federici, Silvia. *Caliban and the Witch*. Brooklyn: Autonomedia, 2004.

Fitzpatrick, Peter. "Ultimate Plurality: International Law and the Possibility of Resistance." *Inter Gentes* 1, no. 1 (2016): 5–17.

Flanagan, Thomas, Christopher Alcantara, and André Le Dressay. *Beyond the Indian Act: Restoring Aboriginal Property Rights*. Montreal and Kingston: McGill-Queen's University Press, 2010.

Ford, Lisa. *Settler Sovereignty: Jurisdiction and Indigenous People in America and Australia, 1788–1836*. Cambridge, MA: Harvard University Press, 2010.

Ford, Lisa, and P.G. McHugh. "Settler Sovereignty and the Shapeshifting Crown." In *Between Indigenous and Settler Governance*, edited by Lisa Ford and Tim Rowse, 23–34. London: Routledge, 2012.

Foster, Hamar. "Conflict Resolution during the Fur Trade in the Canadian North West, 1803–1859." *Cambrian Law Review* 25 (1994): 127–36.

–. "Forgotten Arguments: Aboriginal Title and Sovereignty in Canada Jurisdiction Act Cases." *Manitoba Law Journal* 21, no. 3 (1992): 343–89.

–. "Law and Necessity in Western Rupert's Land and Beyond, 1670–1870." In *Laws and Societies in the Canadian Prairie West, 1670–1940*, edited by Louis A. Knafla and Jonathan Swainger, 57–91. Vancouver: UBC Press, 2005.

–. "Long-Distance Justice: The Criminal Jurisdiction of Canadian Courts West of the Canadas, 1763–1859." *American Journal of Legal History* 34, no. 1 (1990): 1–48.

–. "'The Queen's Law Is Better than Yours': International Homicide in Early British Columbia." In *Essays in the History of Canadian Law: Crime and Criminal Justice in Canadian History*, edited by Susan Lewthwaite, Tina Loo, and Jim Phillips, vol. 5, 41–111. Toronto: University of Toronto Press, 1994.

Francis, Daniel, and Toby Elaine Morantz. *Partners in Furs: A History of the Fur Trade in Eastern James Bay, 1600–1870*. Montreal and Kingston: McGill-Queen's University Press, 1983.

Frazier, Ian. *Great Plains*. New York: Picador, 2001.

Freeman, Donald B., and Frances L. Dungey. "A Spatial Duopoly: Competition in the Western Canadian Fur Trade, 1770–1835." *Journal of Historical Geography* 7, no. 3 (1981): 252–70.

Friesen, Gerald. *River Road: Essays on Manitoba and Prairie History*. Winnipeg: University of Manitoba Press, 1996.

Galbraith, John S. *Hudson's Bay Company, 1821–1869*. Berkeley: University of California Press, 1957.

Gallagher, Brian. "A Re-Examination of Race, Class and Society in Red River." *Native Studies Review* 4, nos. 1–2 (1988): 25–65.

Gaudry, Adam. "Fantasies of Sovereignty: Deconstructing British and Canadian Claims to Ownership of the Historic North-West." *Native American and Indigenous Studies* 3, no. 1 (2016): 46–74.

Gaudry, Adam, and Darryl Leroux. "White Settler Revisionism and Making Métis Everywhere: The Evocation of Métissage in Quebec and Nova Scotia." *Critical Ethnic Studies* 3, no. 1 (2017): 116–42.

Gettler, Brian. "Money and the Changing Nature of Colonial Space in Northern Quebec: Fur Trade Monopolies, the State, and Aboriginal Peoples during the Nineteenth Century." *Histoire sociale/Social History* 46; no. 92 (2013): 271–93.

Gibson, Dale. *Law, Life, and Government at Red River, Volume 1: Settlement and Governance, 1812–1872*. Montreal and Kingston: McGill-Queen's University Press, 2015.

Girard, Philip. "Imperial Legacies: Chartered Enterprises in Northern British America." In *Legal Histories of the British Empire: Laws, Engagements and Legacies*, edited by Shaunnagh Dorsett and John McLaren, 127–40. New York: Routledge, 2014.

Gordon, Irene Ternier. *The Laird of Fort William: William McGillivray and the North West Company*. Victoria: Heritage House, 2013.

Gordon, Robert. "Critical Legal Histories." *Faculty Scholarship Series*, January 1, 1984. http://digitalcommons.law.yale.edu/fss_papers/1368.

–. "Paradoxical Property." In *Early Modern Conceptions of Property*, edited by John Brewer and Susan Staves, 95–110. London: Routledge, 1996.

Gough, Barry. "Crown, Company, and Charter: Founding Vancouver Island Colony – A Chapter in Victorian Empire Making." *BC Studies* 176 (2012–13): 9–54.

–. *Through Water, Ice and Fire: The HMS Nancy and the War of 1812*. Toronto: Dundurn, 2006.

Graca, Laura da, and Andrea Zingarelli. "Introduction to Studies on Pre-Capitalist Modes of Production." In *Studies on Pre-Capitalist Modes of Production*, edited by Laura da Graca and Andrea Zingarelli, 1–26. Leiden: Brill, 2015.

"Grant of the District of Assiniboia by the Hudson's Bay Company to Lord Selkirk." In *The Canadian North-West, Its Early Development and Legislative Records: Minutes of the Councils of the Red River Colony and the Northern Department of Rupert's Land*, edited by Edmund Henry Oliver, vol. 1, 154–67. Ottawa: Government Printing Bureau, 1914.

Graybill, Andrew R. *Policing the Great Plains: Rangers, Mounties, and the North American Frontier, 1875–1910*. Lincoln: University of Nebraska Press, 2007.

–. "Rangers, Mounties, and the Subjugation of Indigenous Peoples, 1870–1885." *Great Plains Quarterly* 24, no. 2 (2004): 83–100.

Great Britain. House of Commons. *Journals of the House of Commons*. London: H.M. Stationery Office, 1742.

Greer, Allan. "Fur-Trade Labour and Lower Canadian Agrarian Structures." *Historical Papers* 16, no. 1 (1981): 197–214.

–. *Property and Dispossession: Natives, Empires and Land in Early Modern North America*. Cambridge: Cambridge University Press, 2018.

Gregory, Chris A. *Gifts and Commodities*. London: Academic Press, 1982.

Hackett, Paul. "Averting Disaster: The Hudson's Bay Company and Smallpox in Western Canada during the Late Eighteenth and Early Nineteenth Centuries." *Bulletin of the History of Medicine* 78, no. 3 (2004): 575–609.

–. "Historical Mourning Practices Observed among the Cree and Ojibway Indians of the Central Subarctic." *Ethnohistory* 52, no. 3 (2005): 503–32.

Haeger, John D. "Business Strategy and Practice in the Early Republic: John Jacob Astor and the American Fur Trade." *Western Historical Quarterly* 19, no. 2 (1988): 183–202.

Haldon, John. "Mode of Production, Social Action, and Historical Change: Some Questions and Issues." In *Studies on Pre-Capitalist Modes of Production*, edited by Laura da Graca and Andrea Zingarelli, 204–36. Leiden: Brill, 2015.

Halkett, John. *The Earl of Selkirk's Settlement*. Carlisle, MA: Applewood Books, 2006.

–. *Statement Respecting the Earl of Selkirk's Settlement upon the Red River, in North America: Its Destruction in the Years 1815 and 1816; and the Massacre of Governor Semple and His Party; with Observations upon a Recent Publication, Entitled "A Narrative of Occurrances [sic] in the Indian Countries," &c*. London: John Murray, 1817.

Hall, Anthony. *Earth into Property: Colonization, Decolonization, and Capitalism*. McGill-Queen's Native and Northern Series 62. Montreal and Kingston: McGill-Queen's University Press, 2010.

Harris, Cole. "Arthur J. Ray and the Empirical Opportunity." In *New Histories for Old: Changing Perspectives on Canada's Native Pasts*, edited by Theodore Binnema and Susan Neylan, 249–64. Vancouver: UBC Press, 2007.

–. "The Native Land Policies of Governor James Douglas." *BC Studies* 174 (2012): 101–22.

Harvey, David. *The New Imperialism*. Oxford: Oxford University Press, 2005.

–. "Notes towards a Theory of Uneven Geographical Development." In *Spaces of Neoliberalization: Towards a Theory of Uneven Geographical Development*, edited by David Harvey, vol. 8, 55–92. Hettner Lectures. Stuttgart: Franz Steiner Verlag, 2005.

Hasselstrom, Nathan. "An Exploration of the Selkirk Treaty." MA thesis, University of Ottawa, 2019.

Hatter, Lawrence B.A. "The Jay Charter: Rethinking the American National State in the West, 1796–1819." *Diplomatic History* 37, no. 4 (2013): 693–726.

Haydon, Arthur Lincoln. *The Riders of the Plains: A Record of the Royal North-West Mounted Police of Canada, 1873–1910.* London: Melrose, 1910.

Heller, Henry. *The Birth of Capitalism: A 21st Century Perspective.* London: Pluto Press, 2011.

Henry, Alexander, and David Thompson. *New Light on the Early History of the Greater Northwest.* Cambridge: Cambridge University Press, 2015.

Hickerson, Harold. *The Chippewa and Their Neighbors: A Study in Ethnohistory.* New York: Holt, Rinehart and Winston, 1970.

Hill, Robert B. *Manitoba: History of Its Early Settlement, Development, and Resources.* Toronto: W. Briggs, 1890.

Hiller, James K. "The Newfoundland Credit System: An Interpretation." In *Merchant Credit and Labour Strategies in Historical Perspective,* edited by Rosemary E. Ommer, 86–101. Fredericton: Acadiensis Press, 1990.

Hilton, George W. "The British Truck System in the Nineteenth Century." *Journal of Political Economy* 65, no. 3 (1957): 237–56.

Hilton, Rodney. "Introduction." In *The Transition from Feudalism to Capitalism,* 9–30. London: Verso, 1978.

Hind, Henry Youle. *Narrative of the Canadian Red River Exploring Expedition of 1857, and of the Assinniboine and Saskatchewan Exploring Expedition of 1858.* London: Longman, Green, Longman and Roberts, 1860. http://archive.org/details/narrativeofcanad02hind.

Hobsbawm, Eric. *Age of Revolution: 1789–1848.* New York: Vintage Books, 1996.

Hobson, Brittany. "'They're Stealing Our Identity': Métis National Council Calls Out Eastern Métis Groups." APTN News, November 26, 2018. https://www.aptnnews.ca/national-news/theyre-stealing-our-identity-metis-national-council-calls-out-eastern-metis-groups/.

Hoffman, Kelly M., Sophie Trawalter, Jordan R. Axt, and M. Norman Oliver. "Racial Bias in Pain Assessment and Treatment Recommendations, and False Beliefs about Biological Differences between Blacks and Whites." *Proceedings of the National Academy of Sciences* 113, no. 16 (2016): 4296–4301.

Hogue, Michel. *Metis and the Medicine Line: Creating a Border and Dividing a People.* Chapel Hill: University of North Carolina Press, 2015.

Horn-Miller, Kahente. "Distortion and Healing: Finding Balance and a 'Good Mind' through the Rearticulation of Sky Woman's Journey." In *Living on the Land: Indigenous Women's Understanding of Place,* edited by Nathalie Kermoal and Isabel Altamirano-Jiménez, 19–38. Edmonton: Athabasca University Press, 2016.

Hudson's Bay Company Committee. "Statement by HBC, Enclosed in Bathurst Letter, 18 March 1815." In *Papers Relating to the Red River Settlement: 1815–1819,* 4. London: House of Commons, 1819.

Hudson's Bay Company. *The Royal Charter for Incorporating the Hudson's Bay Company: Granted by His Majesty King Charles the Second, in the Twenty-Second Year of His Reign, A.D. 1670.* London: H.K. Causton, 1865.

"The Hudson's Bay Company's Code of Penal Laws, Published at Moose Factory, 1 September 1815." In *The Canadian North-West, Its Early Development and Legislative Records: Minutes of the Councils of the Red River Colony and the Northern Department of Rupert's Land,* edited by Edmund Henry Oliver, vol. 2, 1285–87. Ottawa: Government Printing Bureau, 1914.

262 Bibliography

Hughes, Michael. "Within the Grasp of Company Law: Land, Legitimacy, and the Racialization of the Métis, 1815–1821." *Ethnohistory* 63, no. 3 (2016): 519–40.

Hunt, Alan. "The Ideology of Law: Advances and Problems in Recent Applications of the Concept of Ideology to the Analysis of Law." *Law and Society Review* 19, no. 1 (1985): 11–37.

Hunter, Ian. "Global Justice and Regional Metaphysics: On the Critical History of the Law of Nature and Nations." In *Law and Politics in British Colonial Thought: Transpositions and Empire*, edited by Shaunnagh Dorsett and Ian Hunter, 11–30. New York: Springer, 2010.

–. "Vattel in Revolutionary America: From the Rules of War to the Rule of Law." In *Between Indigenous and Settler Governance*, edited by Lisa Ford and Tim Rowse, 12–22. London: Routledge, 2012.

Innes, Robert Alexander. "Challenging a Racist Fiction: A Closer Look at Métis–First Nations Relations." In *A People and a Nation: New Directions in Contemporary Métis Studies*, edited by Chris Andersen and Jennifer Adese, 92–114. Vancouver: UBC Press, 2021.

–. *Elder Brother and the Law of the People: Contemporary Kinship and Cowessess First Nation*. Winnipeg: University of Manitoba Press, 2013.

Innis, Harold Adams. *The Fur Trade in Canada: An Introduction to Canadian Economic History*. Toronto: University of Toronto Press, 1999.

–. "Significant Factors in Canadian Economic Development." *Canadian Historical Review* 18, no. 4 (1937): 374–84.

Isbister, A.K. (Alexander Kennedy). *A Few Words on the Hudson's Bay Company: With a Statement of the Grievances of the Native and Half-Caste Indians, Addressed to the British Government through Their Delegates Now in London*. London: C. Gilpin, 1846.

James, C.L.R. *The Black Jacobins: Toussaint L'Ouverture and the San Domingo Revolution*. 2nd ed. New York: Vintage Books, 1989.

Johnston, Basil. *Ojibway Heritage*. Toronto: McClelland and Stewart, 1987.

Judd, Carol M. "Native Labour and Social Stratification in the Hudson's Bay Company's Northern Department, 1770–1801." *Canadian Review of Sociology/Revue canadienne de sociologie* 17, no. 4 (1980): 305–14.

Kaye, Barry. "The Red River Settlement: Lord Selkirk's Isolated Colony in the Wilderness." In *The Early Northwest*, edited by Gregory P. Marchildon, 209–32. Regina: University of Regina Press, 2008.

–. "The Trade in Livestock between the Red River Settlement and the American Frontier, 1812–1870." In *Business and Industry*, edited by Gregory P. Marchildon, vol. 4, 3–26. History of the Prairie West Series. Regina: University of Regina Press, 2011.

Keith, Lloyd. *North of Athabasca: Slave Lake and Mackenzie River Documents of the North West Company, 1800–1821*. Rupert's Land Record Society Series. Montreal and Kingston: McGill-Queen's University Press, 2001.

Kelley, Robin D.G. *Freedom Dreams: The Black Radical Imagination*. Boston: Beacon Press, 2003.

Kostash, Myrna. *The Seven Oaks Reader*. UK ed. Edmonton: NeWest Press, 2016.

Kulchyski, Peter. *Like the Sound of a Drum: Aboriginal Cultural Politics in Denendeh and Nunavut*. Winnipeg: University of Manitoba Press, 2005.

Kuokkanen, Rauna. "Globalization as Racialized, Sexualized Violence: The Case of Indigenous Women." *International Feminist Journal of Politics* 10, no. 2 (2008): 216–33.

–. "The Politics of Form and Alternative Autonomies: Indigenous Women, Subsistence Economies and the Gift Paradigm." Working Paper Series – Globalization Working Papers, McMaster University, 2007.

–. *Reshaping the University: Responsibility, Indigenous Epistemes, and the Logic of the Gift.* Vancouver: UBC Press, 2007.

LaDuke, Winona. "Preface: Natural to Synthetic and Back." In *Marxism and Native Americans,* edited by Ward Churchill, i–iix. Boston: South End Press, 1983.

"The Land Question: The Council and the Press." *Nor'Wester,* March 14, 1860, 2.

LaRocque, Emma. *When the Other Is Me: Native Resistance Discourse, 1850–1990.* Winnipeg: University of Manitoba Press, 2010.

Laudicina, Nelly. "The Rules of Red River: The Council of Assiniboia and Its Impact on the Colony, 1820–1869." *Past Imperfect* 15 (2009): 36–75.

Lawrence, Bonita, and Enakshi Dua. "Decolonizing Antiracism." *Social Justice* 32, no. 4 (102) (2005): 120–43.

Leacock, Eleanor. "Relations of Production in Band Society." In *Politics and History in Band Societies,* edited by Eleanor Leacock and Richard Lee, 159–70. Cambridge: Cambridge University Press, 1982.

Le Dressay, André, Normand Lavallee, and Jason Reeves. "First Nations Trade, Specialization, and Market Institutions: A Historical Survey of First Nation Market Culture." London, ON: Aboriginal Policy Research Consortium International, 2010.

Lenin, Vladimir Ilyich. *Materialism and Empirio-Criticism.* Beijing: Foreign Languages Press, 1972.

Linebaugh, Peter. *The Magna Carta Manifesto: Liberties and Commons for All.* Berkeley: University of California Press, 2009.

Losurdo, Domenico. *Liberalism: A Counter-History.* Translated by Gregory Elliott. London: Verso, 2011.

Lovisek, Joan A., Leo Waisberg, and Tim Holzkamm. "'Deprived of Part of Their Living': Colonialism and Nineteenth-Century Flooding of Ojibwa Lands." In *Papers of the Twenty-Sixth Algonquian Conference,* edited by David H. Pentland, 226–339. Winnipeg: University of Manitoba, 1995.

Lowe, Lisa. *The Intimacies of Four Continents.* Durham: Duke University Press, 2015.

Lutz, John Sutton. *Makúk: A New History of Aboriginal-White Relations.* Vancouver: UBC Press, 2009.

Luxemburg, Rosa. *The Accumulation of Capital.* 2nd ed. London: Routledge, 2003.

Lytwyn, Victor P. *Muskekowuck Athinuwick: Original People of the Great Swampy Land.* Winnipeg: University of Manitoba Press, 2002.

Macdonell, Miles. "Extract of Letter from Miles Macdonell to Selkirk, May 31, 1812." In *The Canadian North-West, Its Early Development and Legislative Records: Minutes of the Councils of the Red River Colony and the Northern Department of Rupert's Land,* edited by Edmund Henry Oliver, vol. 1, 177. Ottawa: Government Printing Bureau, 1914.

Macdougall, Brenda. *One of the Family: Metis Culture in Nineteenth-Century Northwestern Saskatchewan.* Vancouver: UBC Press, 2010.

MacKay, Douglas. *The Honourable Company: A History of the Hudson's Bay Company.* Indianapolis: Bobbs-Merrill Company, 1936.

Mackenzie, Alexander. *Voyages from Montreal through the Continent of North America to the Frozen and Pacific Oceans in 1789 and 1793.* Vol. 1. New York: A.S. Barnes and Company, 1801.

Mackie, Richard S. *Trading beyond the Mountains: The British Fur Trade on the Pacific, 1793–1843.* Vancouver: UBC Press, 2011.

MacKinnon, Doris Jeanne. *The Identities of Marie Rose Delorme Smith: Portrait of a Metis Woman, 1861–1960.* Regina: University of Regina Press, 2012.

Mackintosh, W.A. "Economic Factors in Canadian History." *Canadian Historical Review* 4, no. 1 (1923): 12–25.

MacLeod, Margaret, and W.L. Morton. *Cuthbert Grant of Grantown.* Montreal and Kingston: McGill-Queen's University Press, 1963.

Mainville, Sara J. "Manidoo Mazina'igan: An Anishinaabe Perspective of Treaty 3." LLM, University of Toronto, 2007.

Malthus, T.R. (Thomas Robert). *An Essay on the Principle of Population, as It Affects the Future Improvement of Society.* London: J. Johnson, 1798.

Mamdani, Mahmood. *Citizen and Subject: Contemporary Africa and the Legacy of Late Colonialism.* Princeton, NJ: Princeton University Press, 1996.

Mancke, Elizabeth, and Rupert's Land Research Centre. *A Company of Businessmen: The Hudson's Bay Company and Long-Distance Trade, 1670–1730.* Winnipeg: Rupert's Land Research Centre, 1988.

Mandelbaum, David Goodman. *The Plains Cree: An Ethnographic, Historical, and Comparative Study.* Regina: Canadian Plains Research Center, 1979.

Mandelbaum, David Goodman, and Fine Day. "Fine Day Interview #2." August 8, 1934. http://ourspace.uregina.ca/handle/10294/1768.

Martin, Archer. *The Hudson's Bay Company's Land Tenures and the Occupation of Assiniboia by Lord Selkirk's Settlers.* London: William Clowes and Sons, 1898.

Martin, Chester. *Lord Selkirk's Work in Canada.* Vol. 7. Oxford Historical and Literary Studies. Oxford: Clarendon Press, 1916. http://archive.org/details/lordselkirkswork07martuoft.

Marx, Karl. *Capital.* Vol. 2. New York: Penguin Group US, 1993.

–. *Capital: A Critique of Political Economy.* Translated by Ben Fowkes. Vol. 1. New York: Vintage Books, 1977.

–. *Capital.* Vol. 3. Translated by David Fernbach. Vol. 3. London: Penguin Classics, 2006.

Marx, Karl, and Friedrich Engels. *Collected Works of Marx and Engels: 1844–45.* Vol. 4. New York: International Publishers, 1975.

–. *Collected Works of Marx and Engels: 1845–1848.* Vol. 6. New York: International Publishers, 1976.

–. *Collected Works of Marx and Engels: 1857–61.* Vol. 29. New York: International Publishers, 1987.

–. *Collected Works of Marx and Engels – Engels: Anti-Dühring; Dialectics of Nature.* Vol. 25. New York: International Publishers, 1987.

–. *Collected Works of Marx and Engels: General Works 1844–1895.* Vol. 26. New York: International Publishers, 1987.

McClintock, Anne. *Imperial Leather: Race, Gender and Sexuality in the Colonial Context.* London: Routledge, 1995.

McCormack, Patricia A. *Fort Chipewyan and the Shaping of Canadian History, 1788–1920s: "We Like to Be Free in This Country."* Vancouver: UBC Press, 2011.

McCrossan, Michael. "Contaminating and Collapsing Indigenous Space: Judicial Narratives of Canadian Territoriality." *Settler Colonial Studies* 5, no. 1 (2015): 20–39.

McCullough, A.B. *Money and Exchange in Canada to 1900.* Toronto: Dundurn, 1996.

McDermot, Andrew. "The Peguis Land Controversy." *Nor'Wester,* May 14, 1860, 1.

McGillivray, William. "Letter, 28 November 1815." In *Papers Relating to the Red River Settlement: 1815–1819,* 35–37. London: House of Commons, 1819.

McHugh, Paul. *Aboriginal Societies and the Common Law: A History of Sovereignty, Status, and Self-Determination.* Oxford: Oxford University Press, 2004.

McIntyre, John W.R., and C. Stuart Houston. "Smallpox and Its Control in Canada." *Canadian Medical Association Journal* 161 (1999): 1543–47.

McKenzie, Henry ("Mercator"). *The Communications of Mercator, upon the Contest between the Earl of Selkirk and the Hudson's Bay Company, on One Side, and the North West Company on the Other.* Montreal: W. Gray, 1817. http://peel.library.ualberta.ca/bibliography/105.html.

McLaren, John, A.R. Buck, and Nancy E. Wright. "Property Rights in the Colonial Imagination and Experience." In *Despotic Dominion: Property Rights in British Settler Societies,* edited by John McLaren, A.R. Buck, and Nancy E. Wright, 1–21. Vancouver: UBC Press, 2004.

McManus, Edgar J. *Law and Liberty in Early New England: Criminal Justice and Due Process, 1620–1692.* Amherst: University of Massachusetts Press, 2009.

Means, Russell. "The Same Old Song." In *Marxism and Native Americans,* edited by Ward Churchill, 19–34. Boston: South End Press, 1983.

Meyer, David, Terry Gibson, and Dale Russell. "The Quest for Pasquatinow: An Aboriginal Gathering Centre in the Saskatchewan River Valley." *Prairie Forum* 17, no. 2 (1992): 201–23.

Meyer, David, and Paul C. Thistle. "Saskatchewan River Rendezvous Centers and Trading Posts: Continuity in a Cree Social Geography." *Ethnohistory* 42, no. 3 (1995): 403–44.

M'Gillivray, Duncan. *The Journal of Duncan M'Gillivray of the North West Company at Fort George on the Saskatchewan, 1794–5.* Toronto: Macmillan, 1929.

Miller, Cary. "Gifts as Treaties: The Political Use of Received Gifts in Anishinaabeg Communities, 1820–1832." *American Indian Quarterly* 26, no. 2 (2002): 221–45.

Miller, James Rodger. *Compact, Contract, Covenant: Aboriginal Treaty-Making in Canada.* Toronto: University of Toronto Press, 2009.

–. "Compact, Contract, Covenant: The Evolution of Indian Treaty-Making." In *New Histories for Old: Changing Perspectives on Canada's Native Pasts,* edited by Theodore Binnema and Susan Neylan, 66–91. Vancouver: UBC Press, 2007.

Milloy, John. "'Our Country': The Significance of the Buffalo Resource for a Plains Cree Sense of Territory." In *Aboriginal Resource Use in Canada: Historical and Legal Aspects,* edited by Kerry Abel and Jean Friesen, vol. 6, 51–70. Manitoba Studies in Native History. Winnipeg: University of Manitoba Press, 1991.

–. *The Plains Cree: Trade, Diplomacy, and War, 1790 to 1870.* Winnipeg: University of Manitoba Press, 1988.

Mitchell, Ross. "Early Doctors of Red River and Manitoba." *Transactions* (Manitoba Historical Society), Series 348 (1947–1948). http://www.mhs.mb.ca/docs/transactions/3/earlydoctors.shtml.

Moodie, Wayne. "The Trading Post Settlement of the Canadian Northwest, 1774–1821." *Journal of Historical Geography* 13, no. 4 (1987): 360–74.

Morantz, Toby. "Economic and Social Accommodations of the James Bay Inlanders to the Fur Trade." In *The Subarctic Fur Trade: Native Social and Economic Adaptations,* edited by Shepard Krech III, 55–80. Vancouver: UBC Press, 1984.

–. "Foreword: Remembering the Algonquian Family Hunting Territory Debate." *Anthropologica* 60, no. 1 (2018): 10–20.

–. "'So Evil a Practice': A Look at the Debt System in the James Bay Fur Trade." In *Merchant Credit and Labour Strategies in Historical Perspective,* edited by Rosemary E. Ommer, 203–22. Fredericton: Acadiensis Press, 1990.

Moreman, Tim. "'Watch and Ward': The Army in India and the North-West Frontier, 1920–1939." In *Guardians of Empire: The Armed Forces of the Colonial Powers c. 1700–1964,* edited by David Killingray and David E. Omissi, 137–56. Manchester: Manchester University Press, 1999.

Moreton-Robinson, Aileen. *The White Possessive: Property, Power, and Indigenous Sovereignty*. Minneapolis: University of Minnesota Press, 2015.

Morrison, Jean. *Superior Rendezvous-Place: Fort William in the Canadian Fur Trade*. 2nd ed. Toronto: Natural Heritage, 2007.

Morton, W.L. "The North West Company: Pedlars Extraordinary." *Minnesota History* 40, no. 4 (1966): 157–65.

Murray, David. *Indian Giving: Economies of Power in Indian-White Exchanges*. Amherst: University of Massachusetts Press, 2000.

Napoleon, Val. "Living Together: Gitksan Legal Reasoning as a Foundation for Consent." In *Between Consenting Peoples: Political Community and the Meaning of Consent*, edited by Jeremy Webber and Colin M. Macleod, 45–76. Vancouver: UBC Press, 2010.

National Inquiry into Missing and Murdered Indigenous Women and Girls (Canada). *Reclaiming Power and Place: Final Report of the National Inquiry into Missing and Murdered Indigenous Women and Girls*. Ottawa: Privy Council Office, 2019. http://epe.lac-bac.gc.ca/100/201/301/weekly_acquisitions_list-ef/2019/19-23/publications.gc.ca/collections/collection_2019/bcp-pco/CP32-163-2-1-2019-eng.pdf.

Nichols, Robert. "Disaggregating Primitive Accumulation." *Radical Philosophy* 194 (2015): 18–28.

Nigol, Paul C. "Discipline and Discretion in the Mid-Eighteenth-Century Hudson's Bay Company Private Justice System." In *Laws and Societies in the Canadian Prairie West, 1670–1940*, edited by Louis A. Knafla and Jonathan Swainger, 150–82. Vancouver: UBC Press, 2005.

"Notice Published in the *Quebec Gazette*, Dec 12, 1811." In *The Canadian North-West, Its Early Development and Legislative Records: Minutes of the Councils of the Red River Colony and the Northern Department of Rupert's Land*, edited by Edmund Henry Oliver, vol. 1, 176–77. Ottawa: Government Printing Bureau, 1914.

Nugent, David. "Property Relations, Production Relations, and Inequality: Anthropology, Political Economy, and the Blackfeet." *American Ethnologist* 20, no. 2 (1993): 336–62.

Oliver, Edmund Henry. *The Canadian North-West, Its Early Development and Legislative Records: Minutes of the Councils of the Red River Colony and the Northern Department of Rupert's Land*. 2 vols. Ottawa: Government Printing Bureau, 1914.

Ommer, Rosemary E. "Introduction." In *Merchant Credit and Labour Strategies in Historical Perspective*, edited by Rosemary E. Ommer, 9–15. Fredericton: Acadiensis Press, 1990.

Ormsby, Margaret A. "Douglas, Sir James (1803–1877)." In *Dictionary of Canadian Biography*, vol. 10. Toronto: University of Toronto; Laval: Université Laval, 1972. http://www.biographi.ca/en/bio/douglas_james_10E.html.

Osgood, Herbert L. "The Proprietary Province as a Form of Colonial Government." *American Historical Review* 2, no. 4 (1897): 644–64.

–. "The Proprietary Province as a Form of Colonial Government, II." *American Historical Review* 3, no. 1 (1897): 31–55.

Pal, Maïa. *Jurisdictional Accumulation: An Early Modern History of Law, Empires, and Capital*. Cambridge: Cambridge University Press, 2020.

Parker, Leanna. "Labour Relations in the Rupertsland Fur Trade and the Formation of Métis Identity." In *Hidden in Plain Sight: Contributions of Aboriginal Peoples to Canadian Identity and Culture*, edited by Cora J. Voyageur, David Newhouse, and Dan Beavon, 86–102. Toronto: University of Toronto Press, 2011.

–. "Re-Conceptualizing the Traditional Economy: Indigenous Peoples' Participation in the Nineteenth Century Fur Trade in Canada and Whaling Industry in New Zealand." PhD diss., University of Alberta, 2011.

Pashukanis, Evgeny Bronislavovich. *General Theory of Law and Marxism.* Edited by Chris Arthur. Translated by Barbara Einhorn. 2nd ed. Piscataway, NJ: Transaction Publishers, 2007.

Peers, Laura L. *The Ojibwa of Western Canada, 1780 to 1870.* Winnipeg: University of Manitoba Press, 1984.

–. "The Ojibwa, Red River and the Forks, 1770–1870." In *The Forks and the Battle of Seven Oaks in Manitoba History,* edited by Robert Coutts and Richard Stuart. Winnipeg: Manitoba Historical Society, 1994. http://www.mhs.mb.ca/docs/forkssevenoaks/ojibwa.shtml.

–. "Rich Man, Poor Man, Beggarman, Chief: Saulteaux in the Red River Settlement." In *Papers of the Eighteenth Algonquian Conference,* edited by William Cowan, 261–70. Ottawa: Carleton University, 1987.

–. "Subsistence, Secondary Literature and Gender Bias: The Saulteaux." In *Women of the First Nations: Power, Wisdom, and Strength,* edited by Christine Miller and Patricia Marie Chuchryk, 39–50. Manitoba Studies in Native History 9. Winnipeg: University of Manitoba Press, 1996.

Peers, Laura, and Jennifer S.H. Brown. "'There Is No End to the Relationship among the Indians': Ojibwa Families and Kinship in Historical Perspective." *History of the Family* 4, no. 4 (2000): 529–55.

Peguis. "Important Statement of Pegowis, the Indian Chief." *Nor'Wester,* October 14, 1863, 3.

–. "Native Title to Indian Lands." *Nor'Wester,* February 14, 1860, 3.

–. "An Open Letter to the Queen's Representatives." In *Manitowapow: Aboriginal Writings from the Land of Water,* edited by Warren Cariou and Niigaanwewidam James Sinclair, 14–16. Winnipeg: Portage and Main Press, 2011.

–. "A Reply to the Selkirk Settlers' Call for Help." In *Manitowapow: Aboriginal Writings from the Land of Water,* edited by Warren Cariou and Niigaanwewidam James Sinclair, 13–14. Winnipeg: Portage and Main Press, 2011.

Pentland, H. Clare. *Labour and Capital in Canada 1650–1860.* Toronto: James Lorimer and Company, 1981.

Podruchny, Carolyn. "Baptizing Novices: Ritual Moments among French Canadian Voyageurs in the Montreal Fur Trade, 1780–1820." *Canadian Historical Review* 83, no. 2 (2002): 165–95.

–. *Making the Voyageur World: Travelers and Traders in the North American Fur Trade.* Lincoln: University of Nebraska Press, 2006.

–. "Trickster Lessons in Early Canadian Indigenous Communities." *Sibirica* 15, no. 1 (2016): 64–80.

–. "Unfair Masters and Rascally Servants? Labour Relations among Bourgeois, Clerks and Voyageurs in the Montréal Fur Trade, 1780–1821." *Labour/Le travail* 43 (1999): 43–70.

Podruchny, Carolyn, and Nicole St-Onge. "Scuttling along a Spider's Web: Mobility and Kinship in Metis Ethnogenesis." In *Contours of a People: Metis Family, Mobility, and History,* edited by Nicole St-Onge, Carolyn Podruchny, and Brenda Macdougall, 59–92. Norman: University of Oklahoma Press, 2012.

Poole, Thomas. *Reason of State: Law, Prerogative and Empire.* Cambridge: Cambridge University Press, 2015.

Prevost, George. "Instructions for the Good Government of the Indian Department, 1812." In *Collections and Researches Made by the Michigan Pioneer and Historical Society*, vol. 23, 86–94. Lansing, MI: Robert Smith and Company, 1895.

Pritchard, John, Pierre Chrysologue Pambrun, and Frederick Damien Heurter. *Narratives of John Pritchard, Pierre Chrysologue Pambrun, and Frederick Damien Heurter, Respecting the Aggressions of the North-West Company, against the Earl of Selkirk's Settlement upon Red River*. London: John Murray, 1819.

Pritchett, John Perry. *Red River Valley, 1811–1849*. New York: Russell and Russell, 1970.

Promislow, Janna. "'It Would Only Be Just': A Study of Territoriality and Trading Posts along the Mackenzie River 1800–27." In *Between Indigenous and Settler Governance*, edited by Lisa Ford and Tim Rowse, 35–47. London: Routledge, 2012.

–. "One Chief, Two Chiefs, Red Chiefs, Blue Chiefs: Newcomer Perspectives on Indigenous Leadership in Rupert's Land and the North-West Territories." In *The Grand Experiment: Law and Legal Culture in British Settler Societies*, edited by Hamar Foster, Benjamin L. Berger, and A.R. Buck, 55–76. Vancouver: UBC Press, 2008.

–. "'Thou Wilt Not Die of Hunger ... for I Bring Thee Merchandise': Consent, Intersocietal Normativity, and the Exchange of Food at York Factory, 1682–1763." In *Between Consenting Peoples: Political Community and the Meaning of Consent*, edited by Jeremy Webber and Colin M. Macleod, 77–114. Vancouver: UBC Press, 2010.

"Protest of Proprietors of the Hudson's Bay Company, against the Grant to Lord Selkirk." In *A Narrative of Occurrences in the Indian Countries of North America, since the Connexion of the Right Hon. the Earl of Selkirk with the Hudson's Bay Company, and His Attempt to Establish a Colony on the Red River: With a Detailed Account of His Lordship's Military Expedition to, and Subsequent Proceedings at Fort William, in Upper Canada*, edited by Samuel Hull Wilcocke, Simon McGillivray, and Edward Ellice, Appendix 1–4. Covent-Garden, UK: B. McMillan, 1817.

Ray, Arthur J. *Aboriginal Rights Claims and the Making and Remaking of History*. McGill-Queen's Native and Northern Series 87. Montreal and Kingston: McGill-Queen's University Press, 2016.

–. "The Decline of Paternalism in the Hudson's Bay Company Fur Trade, 1870–1945." In *Merchant Credit and Labour Strategies in Historical Perspective*, edited by Rosemary E. Ommer, 188–202. Fredericton: Acadiensis Press, 1990.

–. *Indians in the Fur Trade: Their Role as Trappers, Hunters, and Middlemen in the Lands Southwest of Hudson Bay, 1660–1870*. 2nd ed. ACLS Humanities E-Book. Toronto: University of Toronto Press, 1998.

–. "Periodic Shortages, Native Welfare, and the Hudson's Bay Company 1670–1930." In *The Subarctic Fur Trade: Native Social and Economic Adaptations*, edited by Shepard Krech III, 1–20. Vancouver: UBC Press, 1984.

Ray, Arthur J., and Donald B. Freeman. *"Give Us Good Measure": An Economic Analysis of Relations between the Indians and the Hudson's Bay Company before 1763*. Toronto: University of Toronto Press, 1978.

Ray, Arthur J., J.R. Miller, and Frank Tough. *Bounty and Benevolence: A History of Saskatchewan Treaties*. Montreal and Kingston: McGill-Queen's University Press, 2000.

Rediker, Marcus. *The Slave Ship: A Human History*. London: Penguin, 2007.

Reid, John Phillip. *Patterns of Vengeance: Crosscultural Homicide in the North American Fur Trade*. Pasadena, CA: Ninth Judicial Circuit Historical Society, 1999.

–. "Principles of Vengeance: Fur Trappers, Indians, and Retaliation for Homicide in the Transboundary North American West." *Western Historical Quarterly* 24, no. 1 (1993): 21–43.

Relland, Michael. "Saulteaux Indigenous Knowledge: Elder Danny Musqua." *Native Studies Review* 13, no. 2 (2000): 91–111.

Rich, E.E. "Trade Habits and Economic Motivation among the Indians of North America." *Canadian Journal of Economics and Political Science/Revue canadienne d'économique et de science politique* 26, no. 1 (1960): 35–53.

Richards, Eric. *Debating the Highland Clearances*. Debates and Documents in Scottish History. Edinburgh: Edinburgh University Press, 2007.

Rivera, Julio César. "The Scope and Structure of Civil Codes, Relations with Commercial Law, Family Law, Consumer Law and Private International Law, a Comparative Approach." In *The Scope and Structure of Civil Codes*, edited by Julio César Rivera, 3–42. Dordrecht: Springer, 2013.

Roberts, William Clare. *Marx's Inferno: The Political Theory of Capital*. Princeton: Princeton, NJ: Princeton University Press, 2016.

Rogers, Nicholas. "From Vernon to Wolfe: Empire and Identity in the British Atlantic World of the Mid-Eighteenth Century." In *The Culture of the Seven Years' War: Empire, Identity, and the Arts in the Eighteenth-Century Atlantic World*, edited by Frans De Bruyn and Shaun Regan, 25–52. Toronto: University of Toronto Press, 2014.

Ross, Alexander. *The Red River Settlement: Its Rise, Progress, and Present State: With Some Account of the Native ...* London: Smith, Elder and Company, 1856.

Russell, Dale R. *Eighteenth Century Western Cree and Their Neighbours*. Hull, QC: Canadian Museum of Civilization, 1991.

Selkirk, Thomas Douglas. "Letter from Selkirk to Miles MacDonell, 1811." In *The Canadian North-West, Its Early Development and Legislative Records: Minutes of the Councils of the Red River Colony and the Northern Department of Rupert's Land*, edited by Edmund Henry Oliver, vol. 1, 175. Ottawa: Government Printing Bureau, 1914.

–. "Letter from Selkirk to Miles Macdonell, June 12, 1813." In *The Canadian North-West, Its Early Development and Legislative Records: Minutes of the Councils of the Red River Colony and the Northern Department of Rupert's Land*, edited by Edmund Henry Oliver, vol. 1, 178–83. Ottawa: Government Printing Bureau, 1914.

–. "Lord Selkirk's Advertisement and Prospectus of the New Colony." In *A Narrative of Occurrences in the Indian Countries of North America since the Connexion of the Right Hon. the Earl of Selkirk with the Hudson's Bay Company, and His Attempt to Establish a Colony on the Red River*, edited by Samuel Hull Wilcocke, Simon McGillivray, and Edward Ellice. Covent-Garden, UK: B. McMillan, 1817.

–. "Observations on the Present State of the Highlands of Scotland, with a View of the Causes and Probable Consequences of Emigration." In *The Collected Writings of Lord Selkirk 1799–1809*, edited by J.M. Bumsted, 101–241. Winnipeg: Manitoba Record Society, 1984.

–. *A Sketch of the British Fur Trade in North America with Observations Relative to the North-West Company of Montreal*. London: Printed for James Ridgway, 1816.

Selkirk, Thomas Douglas (Fifth Earl of), and John Halkett. *A Letter to the Earl of Liverpool [Relating to the North-West Company's Attack upon the Red River Settlement]*. London: J. Brettell, 1819.

Simmons, Deidre. *Keepers of the Record: The History of the Hudson's Bay Company Archives*. Montreal and Kingston: McGill-Queen's University Press, 2007.

Simpson, Audra. *Mohawk Interruptus: Political Life across the Borders of Settler States*. Durham, NC: Duke University Press, 2014.

Simpson, Audra, and Andrea Smith. "Introduction." In *Theorizing Native Studies*, edited by Audra Simpson and Andrea Smith, 1–30. Durham, NC: Duke University Press, 2014.

Singh, Nikhil Pal. "On Race, Violence, and So-Called Primitive Accumulation." *Social Text* 34, no. 3 (2016): 27–50.

Skinner, Alanson. "Plains Ojibwa Tales." *Journal of American Folklore* 32, no. 124 (1919): 280–305.

Slattery, Brian. "Paper Empires: The Legal Dimensions of French and English Ventures in North America." In *Despotic Dominion: Property Rights in British Settler Societies*, edited by John McLaren, A.R. Buck, and Nancy E. Wright, 50–78. Vancouver: UBC Press, 2004.

–. "The Royal Proclamation of 1763 and the Aboriginal Constitution." In *Keeping Promises: The Royal Proclamation of 1763, Aboriginal Rights, and Treaties in Canada*, edited by Jim Aldridge and Terry Fenge, 14–32. McGill-Queen's Native and Northern Series 78. Montreal and Kingston: McGill-Queen's University Press, 2015.

Sleeper-Smith, Susan. "Introduction." *William and Mary Quarterly* 63, no. 1 (2006): 3–8.

Smail, John. "Credit, Risk, and Honor in Eighteenth-Century Commerce." *Journal of British Studies* 44, no. 3 (2005): 439–56.

Smandych, Russell. "Colonialism, Settler Colonialism, and Law: Settler Revolutions and the Dispossession of Indigenous Peoples through Law in the Long Nineteenth Century." *Settler Colonial Studies* 3, no. 1 (2013): 82–101.

Smith, James G.E. "The Western Woods Cree: Anthropological Myth and Historical Reality." *American Ethnologist* 14, no. 3 (1987): 434–48.

Smyth, David. "The Niitsitapi Trade: Euroamericans and the Blackfoot-Speaking Peoples, to the Mid-1830s." PhD diss., Carleton University, 2001.

Spraakman, Gary. *Management Accounting at the Hudson's Bay Company: From Quill Pen to Digitization*. Bingley, UK: Emerald Group Publishing, 2015.

Stark, Heidi Kiiwetinepinesiik. "Nenabozho's Smart Berries: Rethinking Tribal Sovereignty and Accountability." *Michigan State Law Review* 2 (2013): 339–54.

–. "Respect, Responsibility, and Renewal: The Foundations of Anishinaabe Treaty Making with the United States and Canada." *American Indian Culture and Research Journal* 34, no. 2 (2010): 145–64.

Stark, Heidi Kiiwetinepinesiik, and Gina Starblanket. "Towards a Relational Paradigm – Four Points for Consideration: Knowledge, Gender, Land, and Modernity." In *Resurgence and Reconciliation: Indigenous-Settler Relations and Earth Teachings*, edited by Michael I. Asch, John Borrows, and James Tully, 175–208. Toronto: University of Toronto Press, 2018.

Stasiulis, Daiva K., and Nira Yuval-Davis. "Introduction: Beyond Dichotomies – Gender, Race, Ethnicity and Class in Settler Societies." In *Unsettling Settler Societies: Articulations of Gender, Race, Ethnicity and Class*, edited by Daiva K. Stasiulis and Nira Yuval-Davis, 1–38. London: SAGE, 1995.

Stephen, Scott. "'Covenant Servants': Contract, Negotiation, and Accommodation in Hudson Bay, 1670–1782." *Manitoba History* 60 (2009): 14–27.

–. "The Fork in the Road: Red River, Retrenchment and the Struggle for the Future of the Hudson's Bay Company." *Manitoba History* 71 (2013): 39–47.

–. *Masters and Servants: The Hudson's Bay Company and Its North American Workforce, 1668–1786*. Edmonton: University of Alberta Press, 2019.

Stevens, Wayne E. "The Organization of the British Fur Trade, 1760–1800." *Mississippi Valley Historical Review* 3, no. 2 (1916): 172–202. https://doi.org/10.2307/1886434.

St-Onge, Nicole. "'He Was neither a Soldier nor a Slave: He Was under the Control of No Man': Kahnawake Mohawks in the Northwest Fur Trade, 1790–1850." *Canadian Journal of History* 51, no. 1 (2016): 1–32. https://doi.org/10.3138/cjh.ach.51.1.001.

–. "Uncertain Margins: Métis and Saulteaux Identities in St-Paul des Saulteaux, Red River 1821–1870." *Manitoba History* 53 (2006). http://www.mhs.mb.ca/docs/mb_history/53/uncertainmargins.shtml.

Sutherland, Donna. "Peguis, Woodpeckers, and Myths: What Do We Really Know?" *Manitoba History* 71 (2013): 48–54.

Sweeny, Robert C.H. "Understanding Work Historically: A Reflection Prompted by Two Recent Studies of the Fur Trade." *Labour/Le travail* 41 (1998): 243–52.

Sweezy, Paul M. "A Critique." In *The Transition from Feudalism to Capitalism*, 33–56. London: Verso, 1978.

Tamanaha, Brian Z. "The Folly of the 'Social Scientific' Concept of Legal Pluralism." *Journal of Law and Society* 20, no. 2 (1993): 192–217.

Taylor, Hannis. *The Origin and Growth of the English Constitution*. Vol. 2. Boston: Houghton, Mifflin and Company, 1900.

Taylor, Jeffery. "Capitalist Development, Forms of Labour, and Class Formation in Prairie Canada." In *The West and Beyond: New Perspectives on an Imagined Region*, edited by Sarah Carter, Alvin Finkel, and Peter Fortna, 159–80. Edmonton: Athabasca University Press, 2010.

Thompson, E.P. *The Making of the English Working Class*. New York: Vintage, 1966.

–. *Whigs and Hunters: The Origin of the Black Act*. London: Penguin Books, 1990.

Thompson, Neville. "Bathurst, Henry, Third Earl Bathurst (1762–1834)." In *The Oxford Dictionary of National Biography*, edited by H.C.G. Matthew and B. Harrison. Oxford: Oxford University Press, 2004. http://www.oxforddnb.com/view/article/1696.

Thwaits, William, Robert Whitehead, John Inglis, John Fish, Edward Ellice, and Alexander McKenzie. "Protest of Proprietors of the Hudson's Bay Company, against the Grant to Lord Selkirk." In *A Narrative of Occurrences in the Indian Countries of North America*, edited by Samuel Hull Wilcocke, Simon McGillivray, and Edward Ellice, Appendix I, 1–4. Covent-Garden, UK: B. McMillan, 1817.

Tobias, John L. "Protection, Civilization, Assimilation: An Outline History of Canada's Indian Policy." In *As Long as the Sun Shines and Water Flows: A Reader in Canadian Native Studies*, edited by Ian A.L. Getty and Antoine S. Lussier, 39–55. Nakoda Institute Occasional Paper 1. Vancouver: UBC Press, 1983.

Todd, Zoe. "An Indigenous Feminist's Take on the Ontological Turn: 'Ontology' Is Just Another Word for Colonialism." *Journal of Historical Sociology* 29, no. 1 (2016): 4–22.

Tomlins, Christopher. *Freedom Bound: Law, Labor, and Civic Identity in Colonizing English America, 1580–1865*. Cambridge: Cambridge University Press, 2010.

–. "The Legalities of English Colonizing: Discourses of European Intrusion upon the Americas, c. 1490–1830." In *Law and Politics in British Colonial Thought: Transpositions and Empire*, edited by Shaunnagh Dorsett and Ian Hunter, 51–70. New York: Springer, 2010.

Tough, Frank. "From the 'Original Affluent Society' to the 'Unjust Society': A Review Essay on Native Economic History in Canada." *Journal of Aboriginal Economic Development* 4, no. 2 (2005): 30–70.

Troian, Martha. "After Tina Fontaine: Exploitation in a Prairie City." APTN National News, August 22, 2018. https://aptnnews.ca/2018/08/22/after-tina-fontaine-exploitation-in-a-prairie-city/.

Trotsky, Leon. *History of the Russian Revolution*. Translated by Max Eastman. Chicago: Haymarket Books, 2008.

Tuhiwai Smith, Linda. *Decolonizing Methodologies: Research and Indigenous Peoples*. London: Zed Books, 2012.

Van Kirk, Sylvia. *Many Tender Ties: Women in Fur-Trade Society, 1670–1870.* Winnipeg: Watson and Dwyer, 1996.

–. "The Role of Native Women in the Fur Trade Society of Western Canada, 1670–1830." *Frontiers: A Journal of Women Studies* 7, no. 3 (1984): 9–13.

Veracini, Lorenzo. "Containment, Elimination, Settler Colonialism." *Arena Journal* 51–52 (2018): 18–39.

Vibert, Elizabeth. *Traders' Tales: Narratives of Cultural Encounters in the Columbia Plateau, 1807–1846.* Norman: University of Oklahoma Press, 1997. http://archive.org/details/traderstalesnarroooovibe_i7n8.

Voth, Daniel. "Her Majesty's Justice Be Done: Métis Legal Mobilization and the Pitfalls to Indigenous Political Movement Building." *Canadian Journal of Political Science/Revue canadienne de science politique* 49, no. 2 (2016): 243–66.

–. "The Race Question in Canada and the Politics of Racial Mixing." In *A People and a Nation: New Direction in Contemporary Métis Studies,* edited by Jennifer Adese and Chris Andersen, 67–91. Vancouver: UBC Press, 2021.

Waisberg, Leo, and Tim Holzkamm. "'We Have One Mind and One Mouth. It Is the Decision of All of Us': Traditional Anishinaabe Governance of Treaty #3." Grand Council Treaty #3 Draft Confidential Working Paper, October 2001.

Walters, Mark D. "'Looking for a Knot in the Bulrush': Reflections on Law, Sovereignty, and Aboriginal Rights." In *From Recognition to Reconciliation: Essays on the Constitutional Entrenchment of Aboriginal and Treaty Rights,* edited by Patrick Macklem and Douglas Sanderson, 36–62. Toronto: University of Toronto Press, 2015.

–. "'Your Sovereign and Our Father': The Imperial Crown and the Idea of Legal-Ethnohistory." In *Law and Politics in British Colonial Thought: Transpositions and Empire,* edited by Shaunnagh Dorsett and Ian Hunter, 91–108. New York: Springer, 2010.

Warren, William Whipple. *History of the Ojibway People.* Edited by Theresa Schenck. 2nd ed. St. Paul: Minnesota Historical Society, 2009.

Watts, Vanessa. "Indigenous Place-Thought and Agency amongst Humans and Non-Humans (First Woman and Sky Woman Go on a European World Tour!)." *Decolonization: Indigeneity, Education and Society* 2, no. 1 (2013): 20–34.

White, Richard. *The Middle Ground: Indians, Empires, and Republics in the Great Lakes Region, 1650–1815.* Cambridge: Cambridge University Press, 2011.

Wilcocke, Samuel Hull, Simon McGillivray, and Edward Ellice, eds. *A Narrative of Occurrences in the Indian Countries of North America, since the Connexion of the Right Hon. the Earl of Selkirk with the Hudson's Bay Company, and His Attempt to Establish a Colony on the Red River: With a Detailed Account of His Lordship's Military Expedition to, and Subsequent Proceedings at Fort William, in Upper Canada.* Appendix 1–4. Covent-Garden, UK: B. McMillan, 1817.

Williams, Glyndwr. "The Hudson's Bay Company and Its Critics in the Eighteenth Century." *Transactions of the Royal Historical Society* 20 (1970): 149–71.

Witgen, Michael. *An Infinity of Nations: How the Native New World Shaped Early North America.* Philadelphia: University of Pennsylvania Press, 2011.

Wolfe, Patrick. "Settler Colonialism and the Elimination of the Native." *Journal of Genocide Research* 8, no. 4 (2006): 387–409.

Wood, Ellen Meiksins. *The Origin of Capitalism: A Longer View.* Revised ed. London: Verso, 2002.

–. "The Separation of the Economic and the Political in Capitalism." *New Left Review* 127 (1981): 66–95.

Wood, Louis Aubrey. *The Red River Colony: A Chronicle of the Beginnings of Manitoba.* Glasgow: Brook, 1915.

Wood, Neal. "The Social History of Political Theory." *Political Theory* 6, no. 3 (1978): 345–67.

Yerbury, J. Colin. "Protohistoric Canadian Athapaskan Populations: An Ethnohistorical Reconstruction." *Arctic Anthropology* 17, no. 2 (1980): 17–33.

Zeleke, Elleni Centime. *Ethiopia in Theory: Revolution and Knowledge Production, 1964–2016*. Leiden: Brill, 2019.

Index

Note: "(i)" after a page number indicates an illustration or map; HBC stands for Hudson's Bay Company; NWC stands for North West Company.

Adams, Howard, 9, 189*n*10, 189*n*15
Ahenakew, Edward, 29
alliances/allegiances, Indigenous peoples', 29, 30–31, 43, 83, 152, 169; with Red River Colony, 119–21, 137, 142, 145, 148–49, 150–52, 162, 164, 169; treaties and, 57
American Fur Company, 73
American Revolution, 23, 58, 85–86, 90, 100–1, 127; aftermath of, 16, 56–57. *See also* United States; War of 1812
Anievas, Alexander, and Kerem Nişancıoğlu, 49, 204*n*150, 205*n*153
Anishinaabe, 21–23, 27, 150; and concept of land, 22–23, 176; and reciprocity, 22–23, 30–31; and use of "father," 118–19, 162. *See also* Ojibwe; Saulteaux
Assiniboia, Council of, 108–12, 126, 171, 176; first meeting of, 117; Semple and, 155, 170
Assiniboia, District of, 129, 147, 166, 169; as area of Selkirk grant, 95, 130, 133; Macdonell as governor of, 96; map of, 116(i); and Pemmican Proclamation, 130, 131–34, 144–45, 148–49, 150; thefts from HBC posts in, 146, 167. *See also* Macdonell, Miles
Assiniboine (people), 68, 134, 152, 153, 162, 169, 177; disease outbreaks among, 97, 179–80; and Iron Alliance, 29, 201*n*93; and Pemmican Proclamation, 144, 148–49
Assiniboine River, 59, 71, 172–73. *See also* Forks, The; Red River
Astor, John Jacob, 73
Atcheson, Nathaniel, 93, 216*n*106
Athabasca region: costs of moving into, 59, 60; HBC–NWC rivalry in, 76, 79–80, 94, 103, 132, 155, 157, 164; HBC's

move into, 142, 145, 147, 150, 183; plight of Denesuline in, 71
Auld, William, 113–14, 127, 128, 132–33, 144; as critic of Macdonell, 113, 114, 136–38
autonomy, of Indigenous peoples: as crux of HBC exploitation, 4–18, 19, 181–86; dispossession and, 4–5, 8–9, 11, 16, 19, 28–29, 33, 42, 49–52, 53–54, 66–72, 78, 82–83, 127–28, 130–31, 148–49, 178, 181, 185–86; fur trade rivalry and, 16–17, 54–72, 82, 168; labour compulsion and, 9–12, 26, 49–52, 107–8, 181, 183–84, 210*n*255; legal aspects of, 13–15, 17, 18; NWC's experience of, 61, 102; ongoing threat to, 185; Pemmican Proclamation and, 130–34, 145, 147, 148–49, 153–54, 157; as perplexing to capitalist mindset, 4; reciprocity and, 32, 104; relations of exchange and, 8–9, 10, 46, 49–51; settler colonialism and, 4–5, 10–13, 17, 58, 85–89, 127–28; Seven Oaks and, 159, 165, 166–67, 245*n*118; social differentiation and, 8–9, 11, 16, 50–51, 130–31, 148–49, 185–86; social relations of land and, 11–12, 13, 14, 25–27, 28, 33, 67–68, 81–83, 85, 102, 105–8, 151–52, 177–78, 181, 185, 187; societal transformations related to, 4–5, 8–16, 18, 19–52, 53, 87–89, 102, 130–31, 151–53, 184, 185–87; Treaty of 1817 and, 171–78; truck system and, 53, 66–71, 78–83, 87, 102
Awashish, Philip, 24, 199*n*49

Bannister, Jerry, 36
Bathurst, Henry, Third Earl Bathurst, 143–44, 156, 169–70
Batis (Métis man hired by HBC), 156
beaver, 24, 40, 199*n*47; decline of, 73, 120, 217*n*120; as not always hunted by

Indigenous peoples, 61, 70; sharing of, after hunt, 31; skin of, as unit of value, 48–49, 84

Benton, Lauren, 103; and Richard Ross, 14

Berens, Joseph, Jr., 140, 143, 170

Bird, Louis, 25, 41–42

Black Cat (Mandan leader), 61

Blackfoot (people), 29, 151, 152

Bonhomme (Métis leader), 152

Borrows, John, 29–30

Bostonais (Métis leader), 135, 247n182, 248n185; as captured by HBC, 146, 155; father of, 152

Bourgeault, Ron, 153

Brandon House (HBC post), 68, 71, 84, 161, 162, 251n27

Brenner, Robert, 11–12, 205n153

British North America: governor-in-chief of, 105, 144, 158; HBC's monopoly in, 36–41; and Passenger Vessels Act, 121; truck system in, 34–36. See also North America; War of 1812

Brock, Isaac, 139

Brown, Jennifer, 59, 87, 152

Bryce, George, 62, 64, 190n19, 232n112

buffalo: decline in, 26, 83; sacred roots of, 30; as source of pemmican, 66. See also entry below; pemmican

buffalo hunt, 23, 26, 95; Macdonell's proclamations and, 132–34, 137–38, 141; settlers and, 115, 124, 129, 137; vs trapping for fur, 66–67, 68, 70

Bumsted, J.M., 138, 164

Burley, Edith, 60, 80, 84, 124

Burn, Richard: The Justice of the Peace, and Parish Officer, 110–11, 132

Byrd, Jodi, 53, 100

Cadotte, Joseph, 251n27

Cameron, Duncan, 136; and desertion of servant-settlers, 139, 143, 147, 148, 150, 156; HBC's arrest of, 160–62

Cameron, J.D., 160

Canada: Confederation of, 180, 184, 186; HBC's sale of land to, 36–37, 184

Canada Jurisdiction Act (1803), 75, 81, 88, 99, 107

Canard Noir (Black Duck; Saulteaux leader), 117–18

capitalism: exploitation and, 6–7, 41, 48–51, 64–66, 69, 90, 185–87; free trade and, 120; as identified with order, 9–10, 12, 13, 178, 186–87; Indigenous peoples and, 4, 41, 46, 47–51, 59–60; legal context of, 99, 103; redundancy and, 90–91; as requiring expedited production, 104, 107–8; self-valorization of, 64–66; settler colonialism and, 120–21, 154, 171, 185–87; slave trade and, 104–5. See also entry below

capitalism, transition to: Marx on, 7–8, 33; stagist theory of, 9–10, 12, 13, 178, 186–87. See also extra-economic force, of pre-capitalist labour compulsion; pre-capitalism, and entry following

Carlos, Ann M., 45, 82; and Elizabeth Hoffman, 65; and Frank D. Lewis, 46, 47

Carlson, Hans, 25

"Cayach Cobion" (Anishinaabe leader), 150, 241n5

Charles II, 37

Chipewyan (people). See Denesuline

Colpitts, George, 132, 133, 134

Coltman, William Bachelor, and Seven Oaks commission, 170–71, 172, 184, 248n192, 249n210; report of, 180–81, 182

Colvile, Andrew. See Wedderburn (later Colvile), Andrew

Constitutional Act (UK, 1791), 57

Continental Blockade (1806), 73

Corrigal, William, 79, 80

Coulthard, Glen Sean, 102, 130–31, 203n131

courts: British, 76, 81, 110–11, 112, 114; of Lower/Upper Canada, 75, 81, 88, 99, 107, 110, 114, 131, 134, 154, 180, 181–82; Red River Colony and, 75, 84, 94–95, 109–11

Cowley-Head, Blanche, 23

Cree, 21, 43, 71; alliances/kinship ties of, 83, 169; "Elder Brother" figure of, 29–30; leverage exercised by, 68; and Ojibwe, 23, 202n108; peoples/territories of, 24–25, 197n18; and settler colony site, 127; and Treaty of 1817, 172, 249n207, 249n210. See also Eeyou; Maškekowak; Nēhiyawok

Cruise, William, 109–10

Cumberland House (HBC post), 24, 58, 62, 70, 97

276   *Index*

customary laws/practices, Indigenous peoples', 14–15, 20; reciprocity and, 16, 29–33, 42–43, 49–51; storytelling and, 29–30; truck system and, 16, 19, 36, 40–45. *See also* reciprocity, as customary practice, *and entry following*

Dane-zaa (Beaver Indians), 63, 71
Daschuk, James, 97
Davidson, Gordon, 61, 62, 79
debt-based obligations: as form of "decentralized administration," 36, 45, 69–70; Indigenous peoples and, 36, 40–45, 50–51, 67–71, 78–83, 85, 100, 102, 106, 151–52; as restricting Indigenous peoples' mobility, 81, 82, 135, 181; servants and, 39–40, 42, 84, 122, 154, 181; truck system and, 35–36, 39–45, 50–51, 66, 67–71, 78–83, 85, 100, 101–2, 106, 122, 135, 151–52, 154, 181
"decentralized administration," of HBC territory, 88; courts/justice and, 110–11; debt-based obligations and, 36, 45, 69–70; and Mamdani on concept of, 206*n*174, 210*n*255, 222*n*111
Delorme (or Enos/Hénault), François, 135
Dene (peoples), 63, 71
Denesuline (people), 63, 79; plight of, in Athabasca region, 71
dialectical materialism, 5–6, 7, 191*n*35; transformation resulting from, 87–88, 108
differentiation, social, of Indigenous peoples, 8–9, 19, 33, 42, 51, 69, 72, 82; as allies, 8, 18, 137–38, 146, 150–54, 157, 181; crime/punishment and, 107, 125–26; gender-based, 27–28; after HBC–NWC merger, 182–84; Indigenous peoples' autonomy and, 8–9, 11, 16, 50–51, 130–31, 148–49, 185–86; Métis alienation/exclusion and, 18, 134–38, 148–49, 151, 152–54, 156, 157, 159, 161, 162–63, 172, 177, 179; Pemmican Proclamation and, 131–38, 148–49, 153–54; relations of exchange and, 8–9, 19, 33, 42, 44–45, 47, 51, 69, 72, 82, 88–89, 121–29; vs servants, 9, 11, 51, 88–89, 121–29; as trade captains, 8, 19, 44–45, 47, 88; Treaty of 1817 and, 171–78

disease, outbreaks of, among Indigenous peoples, 25, 71, 72, 97–98, 179–80
displacement, of Indigenous peoples: disease/scarce resources and, 71, 72, 98, 117; in US, 61
dispossession, of Indigenous peoples, 4–18; distortion of reciprocity and, 16, 19–52, 78, 85–86, 101–2, 151, 158–59, 171–78, 181; exploitation and, 4–5, 14, 16, 19, 28–29, 33, 42, 69, 72, 78, 98, 178; as fragmented/non-linear process, 14, 16, 28, 37, 45, 68–69, 78, 178; Indigenous peoples' autonomy and, 4–5, 8–9, 11, 16, 19, 28–29, 33, 42, 49–52, 53–54, 66–72, 78, 82–83, 127–28, 130–31, 148–49, 178, 181, 185–86; labour compulsion and, 9–16, 33, 39–40, 45, 50, 60, 67, 70–71, 102, 103–8, 178, 180–81, 183–84, 186–87; Pemmican Proclamation and, 18, 130–31, 136, 140–41, 148–49, 166–67; settler colonialism and, 4, 6–7, 10–11, 12–13, 14, 15, 33, 73–74, 85–89, 95–98, 103–4; social relations and, 6–9; treaties and, 57; Treaty of 1817 and, 171–78; truck system and, 16, 17, 78, 88, 97–98; in US, 61; as whitewashed by "adventurers" narrative, 3–4, 12, 62–64, 82, 185–86
distortion, of reciprocity. *See* reciprocity, distortion of
Dobbs, Arthur, 86–87
Dodds, James, 40–41, 51
Doerfler, Jill, 22, 53
Dominion Lands Act (1872), 186
Dorchester, Guy Carleton, First Baron, 56
Drummond, Sir Gordon, 158, 160, 161–62
Dunbar-Ortiz, Roxanne, 51, 57

East India Company, 34, 36; and *Sandys* case, 109–10
Edwards, Abel, 139
Eeyou (people), 21, 24–25, 26, 68, 199*n*49
Eeyou Istchee (lands), 24, 40, 68
"Elder Brother" (Cree/Ojibwe cultural figure), 29–30
Elizabeth I, 34
Elizabeth II, 60
Engels, Friedrich: on dialectical materialism, 5–6; on Haudenosaunee, 191*n*37. *See also* Marx, Karl, and Friedrich Engels
Enos (or Hénault/Delorme), François, 135

Ens, Gerhard, 164, 165, 166, 237*n*53; and Joe Sawchuk, 137

exchange, relations of, between Indigenous peoples and HBC: and distortion of reciprocity, 8, 41, 48–51, 59, 63, 65–66, 85, 101–2, 145–46; exploitative nature of, 8–9, 10, 17, 19, 32–33, 40–45; and Indigenous peoples' autonomy, 8–9, 10, 46, 49–51; and labour compulsion, 9–12; and social differentiation, 8–9, 19, 33, 42, 44–45, 47, 51, 69, 72, 82, 88–89, 121–29; and truck system, 16, 19, 36, 40–45, 47–51, 53, 68, 78, 81–82, 85, 102, 108

exploitation: capitalism and, 6–7, 41, 48–51, 64–66, 69, 90, 185–87; dispossession and, 4–5, 14, 16, 19, 28–29, 33, 42, 69, 72, 78, 98, 178; Indigenous peoples' autonomy and, 4–18, 19, 181–86; of Indigenous peoples' labour, as enabling legacy of "free" settler/worker, 12, 122, 186; of Indigenous women/girls, as ongoing, 3, 184–85; of reciprocity, 8–9, 17, 19, 32–33, 40–45; truck system and, 16, 19, 36, 40–45, 47–51, 53, 65–66, 68, 78, 104, 106; as whitewashed by HBC's "adventurers" narrative, 3–4, 12, 62–64, 82, 185–86. *See also* differentiation, social, of Indigenous peoples; dispossession, of Indigenous peoples; reciprocity, distortion of

extra-economic force, of pre-capitalist labour compulsion, 9–12, 178, 186–87; assumed violence of, 9–12, 13, 33, 69–71, 101–2, 107–8, 131, 178, 181, 186; dispossession and, 9–16, 33, 39–40, 45, 50, 60, 67, 70–71, 102, 103–8, 178, 180–81, 183–84, 186–87; Indigenous peoples' autonomy and, 26–27, 46–47, 49–52, 107–8, 181, 210*n*255; legal context of, 13–14, 103–4, 107, 181; Marx on, 7–8; misleading assumptions about, 9–10, 12, 26–27, 33, 46–47; Pemmican Proclamation as instance of, 18, 130–34; vs "silent compulsion," 7–8, 9, 12, 33, 178, 186. *See also* labour compulsion, *and entry following*

factors (heads of HBC posts): as absent at Red River Colony, 128, 235*n*192; and exchanges with trade captains,

44–45, 48, 49–51, 88. *See also* trade captains

Falcon, Pierre, 245*n*118; Seven Oaks ballad by, 165–66

Fidler, Peter: as attacked/harassed by NWC men, 79–80; lament for Red River Colony by, 167; and negotiations with Métis, 152–54; and Pemmican Proclamation aftermath, 148, 151–54, 155, 161, 162, 167, 221*n*68; on Treaty of 1817, 248*n*185

Fitzpatrick, Peter, 14

Fletcher, John, 172

Fontaine, Nahanni, 3

Fontaine, Tina, 3

food: and HBC–NWC rivalry, 132–34; Indigenous peoples' precedence of hunting for, 66–67, 68, 70; Indigenous peoples' provision of, 83, 120, 157; Macdonell's procurement of, 112, 129; Macdonell's withholding of, 124–25; and reciprocity, 30–31; and Red River Colony's self-sufficiency, 17, 123, 128–29, 130, 141, 152–53; scarcity of, 90, 115, 129, 131–34, 155; and threat of starvation, 71, 120, 135, 144–45, 157, 160. *See also* buffalo, *and entry following*; pemmican

Ford, Lisa, 15

Forks, The (junction of Assiniboine and Red Rivers), 29; forts located at/near, 77, 160, 163; ice fishing on, 183(i); Métis and, 160–63; Red River Colony as located at, 95; and Treaty of 1817, 172–73. *See also* Red River Colony

Fort Chipewyan (NWC fort): Mackenzie's trek from Montreal to, 63(i)

Fort Daer (HBC fort near Pembina Post), 119, 173

Fort Douglas (HBC fort at The Forks), 163, 169, 173

Fort Gibraltar (NWC fort; later Fort Garry), 160, 161, 163, 232*n*106

Fort Michilimackinac (American fort): as captured by British, 139–40; trading post at, 54

Fort Rouge (NWC fort at The Forks), 77

Fort William (NWC fort, formerly Kaministiquia; now part of Thunder Bay), 56, 80, 136, 137(i), 150, 213*n*22, 245*n*118; Selkirk's capture of/arrest of NWC men at, 167–70, 180, 181–82

278 *Index*

Foster, Hamar, 81, 106
"free posts," of early fur trade, 54
freemen ("free Canadians"), 9, 115, 117, 139, 154, 216n106; and attack on Red River Colony, 151; as contract workers, 134–35; and Indigenous peoples, 71, 80, 135, 162; and NWC, 134, 140–41; peace overtures toward, 143, 156, 160
French Revolution, 90, 100, 128
fur trade: beginnings of, 20–21; early post types of, 54; map of key sites in, 55(i); servant class of, 39–40, 112–13; and slave trade, 104–5; and US border, 54, 56–58. *See also entry below*; labour compulsion, of fur trade
fur trade/settler colonialism, modified Marxist approach to, 5–16; and dispossession, 6–7, 10–11, 12–13, 14, 15; and geopolitical context of legal/economic transformations, 12–16; and Indigenous peoples' labour, 9–12; and social relations, 6–9; and social relations of land, 11–12, 13–15; and violent labour compulsion, 9–12, 13

George II, 87
Gordon, Robert, 252n51
Grand Portage (NWC post), 56, 60, 62, 75, 213n22
Grant, Cuthbert (Métis leader): and Macdonell, 145, 147, 148; and NWC, 152, 155, 159–61; and Seven Oaks, 163–64
Grant, Cuthbert (Sr.), 152
Greer, Allan, 188n9, 190n21, 214n67, 252n51
Gregory, C.A., 44
Grotius, Hugo, 101

Hackett, Paul, 106
Haiti, 127; slave revolution in, 100, 101
Haldane, John, 79
"halfbreeds," as term for Métis, 156, 160, 161, 164, 248n185, 237n53. *See also* Métis
Haudenosaunee, 22; Engels on, 191n37
HBC, 36–41; "adventurers" narrative of, 3–4, 12, 62–64, 82, 185–86; charter of, 33, 36–39, 41, 60, 101, 170; charter monopoly of, 19, 36–38, 182–83; and claim to Rupert's Land, 37, 40, 74, 75, 83, 86–88, 94; "decentralized

administration" by, 36, 45, 69–70, 88, 110–11; establishment of, 33, 37; and exploitation of Indigenous peoples' customary reciprocity, 8–9, 17, 19, 32–33, 40–45; and fallout from Treaty of 1817, 173, 175–78, 179; and feudal/paternalistic relationship with employees, 7–8, 37, 39, 40, 66, 84–85, 122, 124, 127, 141–42; forts of, 119, 163, 169, 173; grant of land by, to Selkirk, 17, 73–74, 88–102, 108, 130, 133; and legal claim to Red River Colony site, 108–12, 126, 143, 144–45, 151, 156–57, 159; and Maškekowak, 4, 25, 41–45, 70, 228n26; and Métis, 4, 134–38, 141, 142, 145, 146, 148–49, 151, 152–54, 156, 177, 162–67, 177, 183; and move into Athabasca region, 142, 145, 147, 150, 183; officers/servants of, 37; and Pemmican Proclamation/aftermath, 130–49, 150–71; and Red River Colony, 17, 73–74, 85–89, 103–29, 180; retrenchment plan of, 39, 83–86, 114, 130, 133, 142; sale of land by, to Canada, 36–37, 184; and Saulteaux, 4, 119–21, 137–39, 142, 145, 148–49, 150–52, 162, 164, 169, 175, 246n154; Seven Oaks casualties of, 18, 150, 163–64; and truck system, 16, 19, 36, 40–45. *See also entries below*
HBC charter, 33, 36–39, 41, 60, 101, 170; and legal claim to Red River Colony site, 108–12, 126, 143, 144–45, 151, 156–57, 159; legality of, 109, 159, 173, 180; monopoly granted by, 19, 36–38, 182–83; and Pemmican Proclamation, 130, 133; and settler colonial project, 17, 86–89
HBC History Foundation: vignettes produced by, 3–4, 62, 64, 82, 188n2
HBC monopoly: as granted by charter, 19, 36–38, 182–83; and legal claim to Red River Colony site, 108–12, 126, 143, 144–45, 151, 156–57, 159; NWC's challenges to, 16–17, 38–39, 53, 58–61, 75–78, 93–94, 99–100, 130, 135–36, 155, 156–57, 168; rescinding of, 60; and settler colonial project, 17, 86–89, 91, 92–93; and truck system, 40–41, 42, 67–68; US opposition to, 57–58
HBC–NWC rivalry: and access to pemmican, 18, 130, 132–34, 136, 138, 139,

140, 153; in Athabasca region, 76, 79–80, 94, 103, 132, 155, 157, 164; and contest over Indigenous peoples' labour/land, 16–17, 54–72, 82; legal aspects of, 74–78, 103, 130, 131–34, 136, 140, 143, 144–45, 147, 148, 150, 151, 156–57, 159, 161, 165, 167–68; and merger, 15, 18, 66, 166, 182–84; Selkirk on, 79–82; violent confrontations of, 78–83, 93. *See also* North West Company (NWC)

HBC servants: contracts of, 7–8, 9, 37, 39–40, 74, 84–85, 95, 96, 112–13; as differentiated from Indigenous peoples, 9, 11, 51, 88–89, 121–29; discipline/punishment of, 74, 84–85, 124–25; HBC's feudal/paternalistic relationship with, 7–8, 37, 39, 40, 66, 84–85, 122, 124, 127, 141–42; and HBC's later austerity measures, 141–42; as intended to become "free" workers/landowners, 122–23, 141–42, 143, 148, 154, 171; labour compulsion and, 39–40, 84–85; land allotments to, 85, 117–18, 121–22, 127–28, 143; proletarianization of, 50; as settlers, 17, 85, 95, 112–29; and truck system/debt-based obligations, 39–40, 42, 84, 154; as unwilling to defend land, 142–43, 146–47, 160. *See also* Red River Colony, servant-settlers of

HBC trading posts, 42, 43, 44, 62; avoidance of, due to disease, 25; NWC's thwarting of, 79–80; Red River Colony's appearance as, 96–97, 115, 120; thefts from, 146, 167. *See also* Brandon House; Cumberland House; factors; Henley House; Qu'Appelle River; York Factory

Hearne, Samuel, 58

Heney, Hugh, 117

Henley House (HBC post), 106, 228n26

Henry, Alexander (the Younger), 71

Henry, John, 93, 216n106

Hervieu, Mr. (fur trader), 75

Hilton, George, 35

Hobsbawm, Eric, 166

Holdsworth, George, 133, 138

Homme Noir, L' (The Black Man, or Kayajieskebinoa; Saulteaux leader), 142, 150, 172

Horn-Miller, Kahente, 8, 32

Howse, Joseph, 134

Hudson's Bay Company (HBC). *See* HBC, *and entries following*

Hunt, Alan, 15

Indian Act (1876), 88, 186, 252n52

Indigenous peoples: as allies and benefactors of settlers/HBC, 119–21, 137, 138, 139, 142, 145, 148–49, 150–52, 162, 164, 169, 175, 246n154; legal/economic standing of, 9, 107, 153; mobility of, 26, 51; and relations with settlers, 115, 117–21, 129, 134, 146, 151–52, 155–56; and United States, 22, 23, 53, 56–58, 61, 100–1, 158; and voyageurs, 22, 61. *See also specific groups and individuals; specific topics*

Indigenous peoples' labour, 4, 27, 120; debt-based obligations and, 36, 40–45, 50–51, 67–71, 78–83, 85, 100, 102, 106, 151–52, 181; exploitation of, as enabling legacy of "free" settler/worker, 12, 122, 186; gift-giving and, 16, 19, 32–33, 42–45, 49–51, 67, 68, 102, 105–6, 120–21, 151, 181; for HBC, on occasional basis, 27, 39–40; HBC–NWC contest over, 16–17, 54–72, 82; HBC profit and, 48–49; HBC retrenchment plan and, 83–86; as ignored in HBC histories, 62–64, 82; labour compulsion and, 9–16, 33, 39–40, 45, 50, 60, 67, 70–71, 102, 103–8, 178, 180–1, 183–84, 186–87; productivity/demand and, 45–48, 50–51; Red River Colony's dependence on, 17, 83–84, 85, 104, 128, 145, 154, 155–56, 157, 159, 171, 179; seasonal nature of, as determining placement of trading posts, 62; truck system and, 36, 40–45, 47–51, 67–71, 104, 106, 151–52

Innes, Robert Alexander, 29–30, 83, 169, 202n121

Irish: Selkirk on resettlement of, 91, 121, 123, 124; as settlers, 96, 113, 121, 123, 124, 148

Iron Alliance (Nehiyaw Pwat), 29, 201n93

Island Fort (Fort de l'Isle), 74

Jacobs, Norma, 185

James, C.L.R., 100

Jay, John, 57

280 *Index*

Jay Treaty, 57–58
Jefferson, Thomas, 100–1
Johnson, Sir John, 105
Johnston, Basil, 27

Kaamischii (Charlton Island, James Bay), 76
Kamiokisihkwew (Fine Day) (Nēhiyaw leader), 30
Kaye, Barry, 92
Keveny, Owen, 182
"king's posts," of early fur trade, 54

labour, of HBC servants. *See* HBC servants; Red River Colony, servant-settlers of
labour, Indigenous peoples'. *See* Indigenous peoples' labour
labour compulsion: capitalist, as "silent," 7–8, 9, 12, 33, 178, 186; pre-capitalist, as extra-economic, 9–12, 13, 33, 69–71, 101–2, 107–8, 131, 178, 181, 186. *See also entry below*; extra-economic force, of pre-capitalist labour compulsion
labour compulsion, of fur trade: dispossession and, 9–16, 33, 39–40, 45, 50, 60, 67, 70–71, 102, 103–8, 178, 180–81, 183–84, 186–87; HBC servants and, 39–40, 84–85; Indigenous peoples' autonomy and, 9–12, 26–27, 46–47, 49–52, 67, 105–6, 107–8, 181, 183–84, 210n255; legal context of, 13–14, 103–4, 107, 181; NWC servants and, 60; Pemmican Proclamation and, 18, 130–34; in relation to direct, violent coercion, 9–12, 13, 33, 69–71, 101–2, 107–8, 131, 178, 181, 186; settlers and, 115–17, 124–25, 143; truck system/debt-based obligations and, 39–45, 50–51, 69–71, 106, 154
Lagimodière, Jean-Baptiste, 134–35
Lamothe, Joseph Maurice, 74, 75
land, as covered by HBC charter/monopoly, 37, 40, 75, 83, 86–88, 94; "decentralized administration" of, 88; and grant to Selkirk, 17, 73–74, 88–102, 108, 130, 133; as sold to Canada, 36–37, 184. *See also* HBC, *and entries following*; Rupert's Land

land, Indigenous peoples': and concept of ownership, 22–23, 175–76; HBC–NWC contest over, 16–17, 54–72, 82; Selkirk's proposal of vaccine for, 97–98; and Treaty of 1817, 18, 171–78, 179, 186. *See also* social relations of land
land, as "private property," 9, 46, 186, 252n51; vs social relations of land, 11–12, 19–20, 23, 26–27, 28, 177–78; territorial claims and, 25; Treaty of 1817 and, 177–78
land, of Red River Colony site: and allotments to settlers, 85, 117–18, 121–22, 127–28, 143; ownership of, 22–23, 117, 151, 175–76; settlers' unwillingness to defend, 142–43, 146–47, 160. *See also entries above beginning with* land
LaRocque, Emma, 53
law and order, in Red River Colony: and issue of court system, 75, 84, 94–95, 109–11; Macdonell's role in, 99–102, 107, 110–17, 124–26, 131–34, 138, 140; and military support, 99, 143–44, 157, 159–60, 161–62, 167, 170, 171, 172, 181; and policing, 94–95, 100, 121, 134; Prevost on, 105–6; War of 1812 and, 99, 105, 121, 160. *See also* courts; policing
"leased" posts, of early fur trade, 54
Lewis, Meriwether, and William Clark, 61
Losurdo, Domenico, 100
Louisiana Purchase (1803), 61
Lowe, Lisa, 124
Lower Canada, government of: legal jurisdiction of, 74, 75, 81, 88, 99, 107, 110, 131, 134; and Macdonell's appointment as magistrate, 98; and NWC contracts, 60; and Selkirk's arrest warrant, 168, 181
Luxemburg, Rosa, 7, 13, 37, 104, 107, 171
Lytwyn, Victor, 25, 106

Macdonell, Alexander, 156, 232n106, 249n207, 251n27
Macdonell, Miles: as appointed governor of Assiniboia, 96; attitude of, to Indigenous peoples, 96, 118–21, 128, 147–48; background of, 226n203; bombastic nature of, 117, 140, 169; as civil magistrate, 98, 99; council of, 108–12, 117, 170, 171, 176; as factor, 128–29; as "Father," 118–19, 162,

232n125; and first group of settlers, 19, 113–17, 121–22, 124–29; inexperience/poor judgment of, 96, 114–15, 119, 131–32, 136–41, 146–47; and issue of land ownership/allotments, 117–18, 121–22, 127–28; and law/order in Red River Colony, 99–102, 107, 110–17, 124–26, 131–34, 138, 140; and Métis, 135–38, 141, 146, 153, 155, 237n51, 246n156; and NWC, 99–100, 115, 117, 128, 129, 131–42, 145, 147, 150–57, 169, 232n106; paternalism of, 112, 118–19, 121, 186; and Pemmican Proclamation/aftermath, 18, 130–57; and recapture of Fort Douglas, 169; and reciprocity, 118–21, 128; and Saulteaux, 117–21, 142, 150, 151, 162, 169; Selkirk's instructions to (1811), 96–98, 101, 102, 105, 120, 122–23, 146, 158, 173, 186, 247n177; and surrender to NWC/trial on felony charge, 151, 152–57; and Treaty of 1817, 172. *See also* Pemmican Proclamation, *and entry following*
MacDonnel, Aeneas, 80
Mackenzie, Alexander, 24, 182; explorations by, 62–63, 63(i), 64; nephew of, 63, 131; and Selkirk/HBC, 92–94; and XY Company, 59
Mackenzie River, 66, 76
"made beaver" (MB), as unit of value, 48–49, 84
Mainville, Sara, 23
Mainwaring, William, 93
Malthus, Thomas: as influence on Selkirk, 90–92, 127
Mamdani, Mahmood, 10, 32, 122, 206n174; on colonial governance, 88, 178; on customary practices, 49, 51–52; on "decentralized administration/despotism," 206n174, 210n255, 222n111
Mancke, Elizabeth, 65
Mandan (people), 61, 151
Mandelbaum, David G., 24, 30
Manitowabi, Barb, 185
Martin, Chester, 163–64
Marx, Karl: on commodity production, 50; on origins of/transition to capitalism, 7–8, 33; on population redundancy, 90; on "primitive accumulation," 7, 11, 69; on self-

valorization of capital, 64, 65. *See also entry below*; Engels, Friedrich; fur trade/settler colonialism, modified Marxist approach to
Marx, Karl, and Friedrich Engels: on truck system, 34, 35
Maškekowak (people), 21, 26; and HBC, 4, 25, 41–45, 70, 228n26; mourning rituals of, 106; sharing/cooperation among, 31, 42; territories of, 25; women's role among, 27
McClintock, Anne, 232n125
McCormack, Patricia, 33
McDermot, Andrew, 176
McDonald, Archibald, 148
McDonald, John, 76, 220n33
McGillivray, Duncan, 65, 75, 77, 93, 102, 216n106
McGillivray, Simon, 112
McGillivray, William, 131, 136, 158, 159
McHugh, Paul, 86
McKay, Donald, 68, 71
McKenzie, Alexander, 63, 131
McKenzie, Charles, 61
McKenzie, Daniel, 168
McKenzie, Hugh, 152
McKenzie, James, 79
McLeod, Archibald Norman, 75, 131, 139, 143, 146
McLeod, John, 235n192
McTavish, Simon, 59
Métis, 4, 16; agency of, 18, 26, 152–54, 156, 157, 158–63, 177; as associated with Red River area, 21, 26, 197n19, 199n63; autonomy of, 18, 148–49, 152–54, 166–67, 245n118; as excluded from Treaty of 1817, 172, 177, 179; as "halfbreeds," 156, 160, 161, 164, 248n185, 237n53; as ignored by Selkirk, 157, 159, 161, 162–63, 172, 177, 179; as Indigenous peoples, 26; and Iron Alliance, 29; and later land use changes, 248n203; and later status in HBC, 183; and Macdonell, 135–38, 141, 146, 153, 155, 237n51, 246n156; mobility of, 26, 134, 199n64; nationhood of, 149, 154–57, 161, 164–66; and NWC, 66, 83, 132, 135, 152, 154, 156, 160, 163, 164–66, 246n156; and Pemmican Proclamation, 134–38, 141, 142, 145, 146, 148–49, 151, 152–54, 156, 157, 158–63, 177; under

282 Index

Riel, 184, 237n49; and Seven Oaks, 18, 163–67, 180, 245n118
Meyer, David, 24
Miller, Cary, 43–44
Milloy, John, 24, 30, 83
missing and murdered Indigenous women and girls, 3, 184–85
mobility: of Indigenous peoples, 26, 51, 134, 199n64; restrictions on, 28, 81, 82, 135, 145, 181
Montour, Nicholas (father of Métis leader), 152
Moore, Rebecca, 185
Morantz, Toby, 40, 68, 199n49, 200n82
Moreton-Robinson, Aileen, 3, 27, 193n64
Morton, Arthur S., 75, 78, 216n106
Morton, W.L., 60, 64, 106
Mowat, John, 80–81
Musqua, Danny, 23, 202n108

Napoleon, Val, 14–15
Napoleonic Code, 127
Napoleonic Wars, 108, 130, 166; and Napoleon's defeat, 138, 140
National Inquiry into Missing and Murdered Indigenous Women and Girls, 3, 184–85
Nēhiyawok (people), 21, 24, 26, 134, 162; effects of disease on, 71, 179–80; and HBC, 4, 16, 70; and Iron Alliance, 29; and Macdonell, 147; and Métis, 83; mourning rituals of, 106; and Saulteaux, 23–24; and Treaty of 1817, 172–73, 175–76, 177; women's central role among, 27
Nehiyaw Pwat (Iron Alliance), 29, 201n93
Newfoundland fisheries, 35–36
Norris, Robert, 105
North America: Mackenzie's explorations through, 62–63, 63(i), 64; map of (1779), 2(i). See also British North America; War of 1812
North Saskatchewan River, 29, 74, 102. See also Saskatchewan River
North West Company (NWC), 58–61; beginnings of, 59; and challenges to HBC monopoly, 16–17, 38–39, 53, 58–61, 75–78, 93–94, 99–100, 130, 135–36, 155, 156–57, 168; cost-cutting by, 77–78; ethnic divisions within, 59–60, 66;

importance of pemmican to, 66–67; on Indigenous peoples, 102, 158; Indigenous peoples' labour for, 59; Macdonell and, 99–100, 115, 117, 128, 129, 131–42, 145, 147, 150, 169, 232n106; Macdonell's surrender to/ subsequent trial, 151, 152–57; Mackenzie's explorations and, 59, 62–63, 63(i); Métis and, 66, 83, 132, 135, 152, 154, 156, 160, 163, 164–66, 246n156; militarization of, 139–40, 146; and move northwest, 16–17, 59, 61–66; and opposition to Selkirk grant, 94–95, 112, 131; and Pemmican Proclamation/aftermath, 130–51; and Red River Colony, 93–96, 109, 112, 115, 120, 129, 130–54, 156, 160, 167; Saulteaux and, 71, 117, 118, 137, 150, 162, 163; Selkirk and, 155, 156–57, 160–61, 167–70, 180, 181–82; and Semple's death, 163, 182; servants of, 60, 61; southern trading routes of, 16, 61, 73, 77; and voyageurs, 59–60, 61, 78, 136, 139; XY Company and, 59, 61, 64–65, 75–76, 77, 83. See also HBC–NWC rivalry; XY Company
Northwest Passage, 38, 207n193
Nor'Wester (newspaper), 176, 177

Ogden, Peter Skene, 229n36
Ojibwe, 21, 57; and Cree, 23, 202n108; "Elder Brother" figure of, 29–30, 202n104; names of, 197n18. See also Anishinaabe; Saulteaux
Oliver, Edmund Henry, 111, 126
Ommer, Rosemary, 34
Omushkegowak (Maškekowak), 21, 25, 26, 41–42. See also Maškekowak
Oregon Trail, 61

Pangman, Bostonais. See Bostonais
Pangman, Peter (father of Bostonais), 152
Passenger Vessels Act (UK, 1803), 121
Peace River, 24; deaths from starvation at, 160
Peers, Laura, 23, 68, 83, 104, 106, 197n18; on Saulteaux hardships/resilience, 151–52; on Saulteaux relations with Red River Colony, 119–21, 142, 164
Peguis (Saulteaux leader), 21(i), 241n13; as ally and benefactor of settlers/ HBC, 120, 138, 139, 145, 151–52, 164, 169,

175, 246*n*154; on claims to Red River Colony lands, 22, 175–76; as mediator/ peacemaker, 151–52, 246*n*156; names of, 120, 233*n*136; and Treaty of 1817, 30, 172, 175–76, 177, 179. *See also* Saulteaux

Pelham, Thomas (Lord Pelham), 91

Pembina Post (HBC), 115, 144, 173; Macdonell and, 117, 118, 119

pemmican, 66–67; HBC–NWC battle over, 18, 130, 132–34, 136, 138, 139, 140, 153; Métis as suppliers of, 132, 134, 136, 166–67; Red River Colony's increased need for, 130, 131, 132

Pemmican Proclamation, 18, 130–49, 150, 160, 165, 186, 248*n*203; aftermath of, 150–71; and cycle of dispossession, 18, 130–31, 136, 140–41, 148–49, 166–67; as extra-economic force, 18, 130–34; factors resulting in issuance of, 130–32; as followed by buffalo hunt prohibition, 137–38; and Indigenous peoples' autonomy, 130–34, 145, 147, 148–49, 153–54, 157; and later militarization of NWC, 139–40, 146; Macdonell's crafting of, 132–33; and Macdonell's evictions of NWC men, 140, 145; Macdonell's justification for/breakdown over, 131–32, 138–40; Métis alienation over, 134–38, 141, 142, 145, 146, 148–49, 151; NWC's reactions to, 131–34, 136–38, 141; Selkirk's reactions to, 131–32, 141, 144–45; social differentiation and, 131–38, 148–49, 153–54; social relations of land and, 135, 145, 149. *See also entry below*

Pemmican Proclamation, events in aftermath of: destruction of Red River Colony, 150–51, 159; dispersal of settlers, 150–52, 154, 155, 159–60; HBC's capitulation to NWC/Métis, 152–54, 155; later arrival of new settlers, 155–56, 157; Macdonell's surrender to NWC/trial on felony charge, 151, 152–57; Métis' agency, 152–54, 156, 157, 158–63; Selkirk's legal/strategic activities, 156–57, 159–62, 167–68; violence at Seven Oaks, 130, 150, 159, 163–67. *See also* Seven Oaks, clash at

"Place-Thought," 6, 11

Podruchny, Carolyn, 23, 39, 60; and Nicole St-Onge, 26, 153

policing: on prairies, 184, 251*n*46; of Red River Colony, 94–95, 100, 121, 134

Pond, Peter, 74

posts, trading. *See* HBC trading posts; trading posts, early, *and entry following*

pre-capitalism, 7, 8; as identified with extra-economic force, 9–10, 12, 13, 178, 186–87; "primitive accumulation" and, 7, 69. *See also entry below*; capitalism, *and entry following*; extra-economic force, of pre-capitalist labour compulsion; labour compulsion

pre-capitalism, assumptions about violence regarding labour compulsion during, 9–12, 13, 178, 186–87; dispossession and, 9–16, 33, 39–40, 45, 50, 60, 67, 70–71, 102, 103–8, 178, 180–81, 183–84, 186–87; Indigenous peoples' autonomy and, 9–12, 26, 49–52, 107–8, 181, 183–84, 210*n*255; legal context of, 13–14, 103–4, 107, 181; Marx on, 7–8; misleading assumptions about, 9–10, 12, 26, 33, 46–47; Pemmican Proclamation and, 18, 130–34; as pertaining to Indigenous producers involved in fur trade, 9–12, 13, 33, 69–71, 101–2, 107–8, 131, 178, 181, 186

Premier, the (Ouckidot or Grandes Oreilles of the Bear Clan; Saulteaux leader), 172, 238*n*78; and Macdonell, 118–19, 128, 145, 146, 148; and NWC, 138, 162; on settlers, 117

Prevost, Sir George, 105, 136, 140, 158

Promislow, Janna, 31, 43, 44

Qu'Appelle River (HBC post), 161

Ray, Arthur J., 31, 40, 42–43, 51, 67, 68, 73; and Donald Freeman, 31–32, 43

reciprocity, as customary practice, 29–33; gift-giving and, 16, 30–31, 33, 42–43, 49–51; Macdonell and, 118–21, 128; as reflected in treaty negotiations, 22–23, 171–78; social obligations of, 29, 30–31, 33, 43. *See also entry below*

reciprocity, distortion of, 9, 19, 32–33, 65–70; debt-based obligations and, 36, 40–45, 50–51, 67–71, 78–83, 85, 100, 102, 106, 181; dispossession and, 16, 19–52, 78, 85–86, 101–2, 151, 158–59, 171–78,

181; exploitation and, 8–9, 17, 19, 32–33, 40–45; gift-giving and, 16, 19, 30–33, 42–45, 49–51, 67, 68, 97–98, 102, 105–6, 120–21, 151, 181; manipulation/negation of social obligations and, 8, 32, 33, 36, 67, 81, 102, 118–21, 128, 145, 150–54, 158–59, 173, 181; truck system and, 16, 19, 36, 40–45, 47–51, 53, 68, 78, 81–82, 85, 102, 108; unequal exchanges and, 8, 41, 48–51, 59, 63, 65–66, 85, 101–2, 145–46

Red River, 60, 66, 97, 115; Mackenzie's explorations along, 92. *See also* Forks, The

Red River Colony, 103–29; as case study in dispossession/exploitation of Indigenous peoples, 3–18; establishment of, 85–86, 88–89, 92–102; first settlers at, 17, 112–29; geopolitical context of, 100–1, 121, 127; HBC's legal claim to, 108–12, 126, 143, 144–45, 151, 156–57, 159; Indigenous peoples' labour enforcement issues at, 104–8, 126; Indigenous peoples–settler relations at, 115, 117–21, 129, 134, 146, 151–52, 155–56; intended self-sufficiency of, 17, 123, 128–29, 130, 141, 152–53; and issue of court system, 75, 84, 94–95, 109–11; land allotments/ownership in, 22–23, 85, 117–18, 121–22, 127–28, 143, 151, 175–76; later settlers at, 138, 155–56, 157, 169, 171; law and order in, 99–102, 107, 110–17, 124–27, 131–34, 138, 140; location of, 95; as nascent proprietary government, 126; NWC and, 93–96, 109, 112, 115, 120, 129, 130–54, 156, 160, 167; and Pemmican Proclamation, 130–49, 150–51; and Pemmican Proclamation aftermath, 150–63, 167, 169–71; policing of, 94–95, 100, 121, 134; Saulteaux as allies of, 119–21, 137, 142, 145, 148–49, 150–52, 162, 164, 169; Selkirk's approaches to, 121–29; Selkirk's visit to, 145–46, 150, 155, 170–76, 180–81; threat of starvation at, 120, 135, 144–45, 157; as "trading post," 96–97, 115, 120; and Treaty of 1817, 18, 171–78, 179, 186; truck system at, 154. *See also entries below*; land, of Red River Colony site; law and order, in Red River Colony; settler colonialism

Red River Colony, background to establishment of, 17, 73–102; competing jurisdictional claims, 74–78; disputes over Indigenous peoples' purported debts, 78–83; HBC's decision to shift to settler colonialism, 17, 73–74, 85–89; HBC's grant of land to Selkirk, 17, 73–74, 88–102, 108, 130, 133; HBC's retrenchment plan, 39, 83–86; NWC's dispute of HBC claims, 93–96; Selkirk's attitude to Indigenous peoples, 96–98; strategies of legal control, 88, 99–102

Red River Colony, servant-settlers of, 17, 112–29; contracts of, 95, 96, 112–13, 122, 123, 124, 125, 141–42, 143, 145, 148; desertion by/dispersal of, 125, 137, 146–47, 150–51, 152, 154, 155, 159–60, 167; as differentiated from Indigenous peoples, 9, 11, 51, 88–89, 121–29; disciplinary issues of, 113–16, 123–25, 138; exploitation of, 123–24; first arrival of, 112–15; hardships of, 115, 120, 124, 128–29, 131, 132, 135–36; insurrectionary tendencies of, 113–14, 123–24; Irish immigrants as, 96, 113, 121, 123, 124, 148; labour compulsion and, 115–17, 124–25, 143; as lacking requisite skills, 116–17, 128–29, 135; land allotments to, 85, 117–18, 121–22, 127–28, 143; later arrivals of, 138, 155–56, 157, 169, 171; legal/economic standing of, 9, 85, 112–13, 125–28, 154; potential relocation of, 121, 139, 142, 143; and relations with Indigenous peoples, 115, 117–21, 129, 134, 146, 151–52, 155–56; Scottish immigrants as, 96, 112, 113–14, 123, 142, 155; and truck system, 154; as unwilling to defend land, 142–43, 146–47, 160. *See also* HBC servants

Rediker, Marcus, 105

Reinhard, Charles de, 182

residential school system, 186, 252n52

"The Riders of the Plains" (poem), 184

Riel, Louis, 184, 237n49

Robe Noir, La (The Black Robe, Blue Robe, or Mechkaddewikonaie; Saulteaux leader), 169, 172

Robertson, Colin, 156–57, 159, 160–61; and arrest of Duncan Cameron, 160, 161; as previously at NWC, 147, 156; and return of deserting settlers, 147, 150, 155

Rogers, Nicholas, 87
Ross, Alexander, 179
Royal North West Mounted Police, 184, 251n46
Royal Proclamation (1763), 52, 85–86, 100
rum: as given to fur trade servants, 60, 208n213; as given to Indigenous peoples, 71, 105, 121, 150
Rupert, Prince (first HBC governor), 37
Rupert's Land, 91, 131, 138, 201n97; HBC's claim to, 37, 40, 74, 75, 83, 86–88, 94; HBC's Code of Penal Laws in, 127–28; name of, 37
Russell, Dale, 24

Sandys, Thomas, case of, 109–10
Saskatchewan River, 26, 29, 55(i), 66–67, 159; Cumberland House as located on, 24, 58, 62; north branch of, 29, 74, 102
Saulteaux (people), 4, 16, 21, 26; as allies and benefactors of settlers/HBC, 119–21, 137, 138, 139, 142, 145, 148–49, 150–52, 162, 164, 169, 175, 246n154; and debt-based obligations/increased competition of fur trade, 68, 71, 81, 181; effects of disease on, 71, 179–80; and Iron Alliance, 29; and Macdonell, 117–21, 142, 150, 151, 162, 169; mourning rituals of, 106; name of, 21–22; and Nēhiyawok, 23–24; vs Sioux, 29, 118, 119, 134, 142, 150, 151, 152; and Treaty of 1817, 172–78, 179; women's central role among, 27–28. See also Peguis
Scotland: Highland clearances in, 89–91, 123; Jacobite Rebellion in, 85, 89–90; Orkney Islands of, as home to many HBC servants, 37, 39, 142; servant-settlers from, 96, 112, 113–14, 123, 142, 155
Selkirk, Dunbar Douglas, Fourth Earl of, 89, 90
Selkirk, Thomas Douglas, Fifth Earl of, 83, 89(i), 89–93; attitude of, to Indigenous peoples, 96–98; attitude of, to Métis, 135, 157, 161, 172, 177, 179; death of, 182; and early ideas about resettlement, 90–92; and establishment of Red River Colony, 85–86, 89, 92–102; on HBC and NWC, 79–82; HBC's grant of land to, 17, 73–74, 88–102, 108, 130, 133; and instructions to Macdonell (1811), 96–98, 101, 102, 105, 120, 122–23,

146, 158, 173, 186, 247n177; Malthus's influence on, 90–92, 127; on proposal of vaccine for land, 97–98; and Seven Oaks, 167–71, 181–82; and Sioux, 172; *Sketch of the British Fur Trade*, 79–81; and Treaty of 1817, 18, 171–78, 179, 186. *See also* Treaty of 1817
Semple, Robert, 161–64, 170; as appointed Assiniboia governor-in-chief, 147, 155; arrival of, at Red River Colony, 157, 159, 160, 162; as killed at Seven Oaks, 163–64, 166, 182
servants, HBC. *See* HBC servants
servant-settlers. *See* Red River Colony, servant-settlers of
settler colonialism: capitalism and, 120–21, 154, 171, 185–87; dispossession and, 4, 6–7, 10–11, 12–13, 14, 15, 33, 73–74, 85–89, 95–98, 103–4; HBC's decision to shift to, 73–84, 85–89; Indigenous peoples' autonomy and, 4–5, 10–13, 17, 58, 85–89, 127–28. *See also* fur trade/settler colonialism, modified Marxist approach to; Red River Colony, *and entries following*
Seven Oaks, clash at, 66, 107, 130, 159, 163–67, 221n68; ballad commemorating, 165–66; Coltman's commission of inquiry into, 170–71, 172, 180–82, 184, 248n192, 249n210; HBC men killed in, 18, 150, 163–64; scholarship on/views of, 164–67; Selkirk's reactions to/arrest following, 167–71, 181–82
Shaw, Angus (father of Métis leader), 152
Sherbrooke, Sir John, 170, 172
Siegl, Audrey, 187
Simpson, Audra, 53
Simpson, George, 183–84
Sioux: vs Saulteaux, 29, 118, 119, 134, 142, 150, 151, 152; Selkirk's attempted peace negotiations with, 172
Sixties Scoop, 286, 252n53
slavery/slave trade and economy, 39, 100–1, 124; fur trade and, 104–5, 205n153; in Haiti, 100, 101; Inuit and, 193n58; Selkirk on, 123
smallpox: outbreaks of, 25, 71; and Selkirk's proposal of vaccine for land, 97–98
Smandych, Russell, 87
Smith, Adam, 89

Smith, James, 24
Smith, Linda Tuhiwai, 5, 188n9
Smyth, David, 71
Smyth, Mrs. (Macdonell's cook), 125
social differentiation. *See* differentiation, social, of Indigenous peoples
social relations of land, 11–12, 13–15, 19–29; expansion of fur trade and, 63–64, 66–70; Indigenous peoples' autonomy and, 11–12, 13, 14, 25–27, 28, 33, 67–68, 81–83, 85, 102, 105–8, 151–52, 177–78, 181, 185, 187; Métis and, 153; Pemmican Proclamation and, 135, 145, 149; vs "private property," 11–12, 19–20, 23, 26–27, 28, 177–78; reciprocity and, 16, 29–33, 42–43, 49–51, 67, 102, 105–6, 181; settler colonialism and, 104; Treaty of 1817 and, 176–78; truck system and, 41–43, 47, 49–51, 53, 63–64, 66–67, 69, 81
Sonnant, Le (Mache Wheseab or Senna of the Wapucwayanak; Nehiyaw leader), 172, 175–76, 177
Spencer, John, 111, 133, 138, 139, 140, 157
Stark, Heidi Kiiwetinepinesiik, 22
St. Clair, Arthur, 57
Steinbruck, John, 76
Stephen, Scott P., 194n84, 208n206, 208n214
Stevens, Wayne, 54
Sutherland, James, 155
Sutherland, Joseph, 148, 155, 161
Swain, James, 25, 80

Thomas, Thomas, 141, 208n213
Thompson, David, 24
Thompson, E.P., 47, 123
trade captains (Indigenous middlemen): appointment of, 8, 19, 44, 209n241; HBC factors and, 44–45, 48, 49–51, 88; HBC's gifts to, as inducement to produce more furs, 45, 49–50; later decline in reliance on, 58–59, 70–71, 218n143; as redistributors of gifts, 44, 47
trading posts, early, 54. *See also entry below*; HBC trading posts
trading posts, NWC, 62, 133. *See also* Grand Portage
Tranchemontagne (Métis supplier of provisions), 135

treaties, numbered, 184, 201n97
Treaty of 1817, 18, 171–78, 186, 247n177; exclusion of Métis from, 172, 177, 179; as incomplete when originally signed, 249n207; Indigenous peoples and, 172–78, 179; map from, 174(i); Peguis and, 30, 172, 175–76, 177, 179; text from, 175(i)
Treaty of Ghent (1814), 144
Treaty of Paris (1783), 56, 57
Troian, Martha, 3
Truck Act (UK, 1831), 35
truck system, 34–36; as adopted by HBC, 16, 19, 36, 40–45; debt-based obligations and, 35–36, 39–45, 50–51, 66, 67–71, 78–83, 85, 100, 101–2, 106, 122, 135, 151–52, 154, 181; dispossession and, 16, 17, 78, 88, 97–98; exploitation and, 16, 19, 36, 40–45, 47–51, 53, 65–66, 68, 78, 104, 106; Marx and Engels on, 34, 35; at Newfoundland fisheries, 35–36; reciprocity and, 16, 19, 36, 40–45, 47–51, 53, 68, 78, 81–82, 85, 102, 108; Red River Colony's use of, 154; servants and, 39–40, 42, 84, 122, 154, 181; social relations of land and, 41–43, 47, 49–51, 53, 63–64, 66–67, 69, 81; as sumptuary control, 35, 36, 71, 218n155

United States: border of, 54, 56–58, 144, 162; fur trade in, 16, 53, 54, 56, 59, 61, 73, 77, 95, 120; importance of liberty in, 100, 125; Indigenous peoples and, 22, 23, 53, 56–58, 61, 100–1, 158; opposition to HBC monopoly in, 57–58; Red River Colony's importation of wheat seed from, 182; Revolutionary War of, 16, 23, 56–57, 58, 85–86, 90, 100–1, 127; Selkirk's rejection of settlers from, 91–92. *See also* War of 1812
Upper Canada: dispossession of Indigenous peoples in, 57; and government's legal jurisdiction, 74, 75, 81, 88, 99, 107, 110; relocation of settlers to, 139; Selkirk's inquiries in, following settler dispersal, 160; and Selkirk's legal proceedings, 180, 181–82; Selkirk's settlement proposals in, 91, 92, 224n155; and War of 1812, 138, 139

vaccine, smallpox, 97–98
Van Kirk, Sylvia, 28
voyageurs (French-Canadian fur traders), 54, 82–83, 126, 197n22; Indigenous peoples and, 22, 61; NWC and, 59–60, 61, 78, 136, 139

Walters, Mark D., 119
War of 1812, 103, 108, 130; end of, 144; and law/order in Red River Colony, 99, 105, 121, 160; and NWC, 136, 138–40; and relations with Indigenous peoples, 105–6, 120–21
Washington, George, 57, 100
Watts, Vanessa, 6, 22, 196n6. *See also* "Place-Thought"
Wedderburn (later Colvile), Andrew, 83, 147, 183–84
White, James, 148

White, Richard, 49, 211n290
women, Indigenous: gift-giving by, 30; impact of commercial fur trade on, 27–28; intermarriages of, 27–28, 135; later HBC attitude toward, 183; missing and murdered, as legacy of exploitation, 3, 184–85; trafficking of, 71, 79; turn to agriculture by, 151
Wood, Ellen Meiksins, 187

XY Company, 59, 74, 76, 79; and merger with NWC, 59, 61, 64–65, 75–76, 77, 83

York Factory (HBC post), 25, 114, 155; Macdonell's ill-advised visit to, 138–39, 140; Maškekowak at, 44–45; as servant-settlers' first stop, 113; trading at, 40, 42–45, 46, 48–49; value of commodities at, 48–49

Printed and bound in Canada by Friesens
Set in Helvetica Condensed and Minion by Apex CoVantage, LLC
Copy editor: Dallas Harrison
Proofreader: Judith Earnshaw
Indexer: Cheryl Lemmens
Cartographer: Eric Leinberger
Cover designer: Will Brown